Indirect Perpetrators

Indirect Perpetrators

The Prosecution of Informers in Germany, 1945–1965

Andrew Szanajda

LEXINGTON BOOKS

A division of

ROWMAN & LITTLEFIELD PUBLISHERS, INC.
Lanham • Boulder • New York • Toronto • Plymouth, UK

Published by Lexington Books
A division of Rowman & Littlefield Publishers, Inc.
A wholly owned subsidiary of The Rowman & Littlefield Publishing Group, Inc.
4501 Forbes Boulevard, Suite 200, Lanham, Maryland 20706
http://www.lexingtonbooks.com

Estover Road, Plymouth PL6 7PY, United Kingdom

British Library Cataloguing in Publication Information Available

Library of Congress Cataloging-in-Publication Data

Szanajda, Andrew, 1967-
Indirect perpetrators : the prosecution of informers in Germany, 1945-1965 / Andrew Szanajda.
p. cm.
Includes bibliographical references and index.
ISBN 978-0-7391-4283-7 (cloth : alk. paper) — ISBN 978-0-7391-4285-1 (electronic)
1. Malicious accusation—Germany—History. 2. Denunciation (Criminal law)—Germany—History. 3. Informers—Legal status, laws, etc.—Germany—History. 4. Germany (Territory under Allied occupation, 1945-1955). Control Council. 5. Evidence, Hearsay—Germany—History. 6. Justice, Administration of—Germany—History. 7. Crimes against humanity—Germany—History. 8. National socialism—Germany. I. Title.
KK9491.S93 2010
345.43'05042—dc22 2009036004

™ The paper used in this publication meets the minimum requirements of American National Standard for Information Sciences—Permanence of Paper for Printed Library Materials, ANSI/NISO Z39.48-1992.

Printed in the United States of America

In memory of Professor Detlef Mühlberger

Contents

Acknowledgments

I owe a great deal of gratitude to John Pope, whose editorial hand helped make this work possible, and who offered constructive advice in addition to posing questions to be addressed. This work was also made possible by the National Science Council of Taiwan through their generous research funding. I also would like to thank Wolfgang Fritzsche, Thomas Reinshagen, and Sanne Veltuis for having contributed to procuring research materials.

I must also thank Christian Schafferer for reviving my thoughts about investigating the contents that will follow, as well as offering helpful encouragement. My underlying inspiration in completing this work arose from keeping my pledge to the late Professor Detlef Mühlberger to undertaking new research in the field of German history. This book is thereby respectfully dedicated to him.

My great gratitude is also extended to the professional and helpful staffs at the Bundesarchiv in Koblenz, the Archives de L'Occupation Française en Allemagne et en Autriche in Colmar, the Hessisches Hauptstaatsarchiv in Wiesbaden, the Staatsarchiv in Darmstadt, the Institut für Zeitgeschichte in Munich, and the Landesarchiv Nordrhein-Westfalen in Detmold. Their conscientious efforts at procuring the necessary archival materials will always be remembered.

Introduction

Bringing perpetrators and supporters of National Socialist crimes to justice by calling them to account for their actions was one of the aspects of dealing with the past in postwar Germany. The problem lay in discovering who had acted in the interests of the regime, and determining the extent to which their actions had served this purpose. Those who were directly responsible for the crimes that had been committed during the National Socialist regime were judged according to the crimes they had committed. The Allied occupation powers opened the way for the retroactive prosecution of crimes against humanity and peace, and war crimes and crimes against peace in Germany through the enactment of Allied Control Council Law No. 10 of 20 December 1945. This law enabled the prosecution of acts against German criminal law that had not been adjudicated during the National Socialist regime, as well as retroactively prosecuting inhumane acts that were not defined by law that hitherto had not been enacted for this purpose, and were intolerable from the viewpoint of legal consciousness. This included prosecution for the inhumane consequences that were incurred by alleged internal enemies of the National Socialist regime, which were disproportionate to their acts that were considered unlawful at the time, such as making disparaging remarks about the regime. Those who had reported others for having committed these acts were thus to be prosecuted, having acted intentionally against others while being conscious of the unlawful and immoral persecution that would ensue, and also being aware of how the consequences that would ensue would violate the rule of law.[1]

Proceedings for the indictment of prosecution of the leading perpetrators of the National Socialist regime were held at the International Military Tribunal in Nuremberg where crimes against humanity were adjudicated for the first time on the basis of Control Council Law No. 10. Separate proceedings against lesser offenders were held in the four military occupation zones. The prosecution of those who had been guilty of contributing to crimes against humanity by denouncing others to the authorities of the National Socialist regime was considered an example of such a crime. Whether or not they had intended to support the National Socialist regime or serve personal interests, their conscious intentions to set the machinery of political persecution into motion while having been conscious of the potential gravity of the consequences of their actions made them subject to prosecution for crimes against humanity at a time when the rule of law was suspended.

These types of cases were dealt with following separate legislation in the four occupation zones, which were initially subject to the sanctions of the respective occupation powers, and later by the sanctions of the government of the Federal Republic of Germany. Crimes that had been committed during the National Socialist regime that had not been illegal at the time would consequently be addressed by legislation dealing with the injustices that had been perpetrated. This entailed the problem of how to deal with unlawful actions that had been committed under the regime retroactively and bringing the perpetrators to justice. Confidence in the justice system could only be restored if the principles of the rule of law could be restored, which would necessarily involve prosecuting the perpetrators of crimes committed under the National Socialist regime.[2]

In principle, an action is subject to prosecution according to the laws currently in force. That principle was set in Article8 of Military Government Law No. 1 and Art. 116 of the Weimar constitution, but was overridden by Control Council Law No. 10 of 20 December 1945 on "Punishment of Persons Guilty of War Crimes."[3] The provisions of Control Council Law No. 10 called for four types of crimes to be adjudicated by the International Military Tribunal: (1) crimes against peace; (2) war crimes; (3) crimes against humanity; and (4) membership in or association with an organization that the International Military Tribunal declared to be criminal.[4] Cases dealing with crimes committed by Germans against Germans or against displaced persons were, if so authorized by the respective occupation power, to be transferred to a German court.[5]

The International Military Tribunal at Nuremberg declared that Control Council Law No. 10 represented the prevailing principles of international law that superseded the law at the national level.[6] Its application was theoretically to complement German criminal law by allowing for the imposition of sanctions against violations committed against the precepts of humanity and human rights[7] that had previously been committed. Although it was argued that administering justice retroactively was a violation of the rule of law, court proceedings for crimes against humanity demonstrated that the prohibition against the retroactive application of criminal law retroactively was not a necessary requirement of justice, and that it was justifiable with regard to securing the law in special circumstances. It could instead contribute to achieving the higher goal of administering justice, especially with regard to judging those who had acted according to criminal laws that violated the laws of humanity[8] and were directed against individuals who were not afforded the protection of the rule of law. Applying the law retroactively would thus serve the purposes of bringing the perpetrators of crimes against humanity to account for their actions, and would also uphold the interests of the victims retroactively.[9]

It followed that crimes of persecution perpetrated during the National Socialist regime could be prosecuted under the authority of Control Council Law No. 10, even though they could not be tried at the time. This also related to the actions committed by third parties who had turned to the authorities to initiate actions against another, while being conscious of the consequences that could be incurred by the denounced individuals. Being aware of the National Socialist regime's methods of suppressing political dissent meant they could be accused of acting on political grounds, even when the motives were completely personal,[10] since their actions were seen as contravening the commonly accepted universal laws of humanity. Since German law did not include provisions for the newly instituted and widely defined crimes against humanity, the law was applied retroactively in individual cases to prosecute the hitherto unprecedented injustices. It was in fact necessary to prosecute those who had acted in supporting a state that had abolished the rights of humanity and arbitrarily exploited the force of the law against its citizens, rather than for the benefit of their security by maintaining the principles of the rule of law and justice, and who had abolished the rights of humanity. Hence, it was necessary to call to account those who had contributed to upholding a criminal regime through inhumane actions, since it would serve to restore the principles and practice of legal security and consciousness.[11]

The prevailing view of the wide public and some jurists was that the prosecution of those who had persecuted others on political grounds was understood to be the prosecution of those who had denounced others to the political authorities of the time, and consequently consciously caused injury to those they had denounced—rather than the actual act of persecution itself, which was undertaken against them, that affected their life and liberty. The act of initiating an act of inhumane persecution was therefore seen as constituting the act of persecution itself, which would be considered inhumane from the universal viewpoint of modern civilization, regardless of the individual acts that were perpetrated.[12] Control Council Law No. 10 opened the way for the possibility of prosecution through applying the law retroactively until it was possible to prosecute all types of crimes against humanity under German law, such as denunciation cases,[13] although this law did not specifically mention this type of crime. Calling both those who were accused of being indirect as well as direct perpetrators of inhumane acts of persecution to account for their actions when this became possible would make the law to be seen to work, as it was meant to be seen to work in a constitutional state governed by the rule of law.

In practice, the implementation of Control Council Law No. 10 proved to be very problematic with regard to the existing German law, due to its especially unclear legal status, the nature of its provisions and jurisdiction, and its retroactive application.[14] There were serious reservations among jurists about administering the law retroactively,[15] even if it meant serving the cause of justice due to their previous conceptions on how the law was to be administered. They were in favor of prosecuting National Socialist crimes according to the standards of German criminal law.[16] German legal thought made it imperative that formal and material illegality had to be proven to be separate. Judges administered the law based on the precepts of legal positivism, which meant that the actions of the defendant in a crime remained in the sphere of material illegality since they had willingly taken actions that were in violation of the human rights of freedom, dignity, life, and well-being.[17] When it was evident that denunciation cases were concrete material acts that were directed at and led to unjustified death or imprisonment of individuals, and that these acts were also deliberately undertaken and intentionally carried out either as an indirect action or as an accessory to the crime, they could only be prosecuted as crimes committed under the provisions of Control Council Law No. 10 or German law.[18] The problem was that these specific crimes were not crimes in the formal sense as there were not any articles in the German criminal code that allowed for the prosecution of individuals making truthful denunciations, regardless of the consequences suffered by those denounced.

However, the German jurists' disapproval of retroactive legislation thus had to be overcome while they functioned independently, while applying both German and occupation law in the exercise of their functions. German courts operating under the supervision of the occupation powers began the task of redressing injustices from the past in their respective areas of jurisdiction while subject to separate ordinances that were enacted in those areas. In addition to the lack of uniformity in the administration of Control Council Law No. 10 in the four occupation zones, the legal situation was further complicated by the conflict between the application of occupation law and the irrevocable principle of *nulla poene sine lege*,[19] which has formed a vital part of the foundation of the rule of law in any democratic society in modern history.

These theoretical considerations thus became a stumbling block among jurists in the British and French occupation zones who were hesitant with regard to fulfilling the expectations of the occupation powers in bringing perpetrators of crimes against humanity to account for their actions. Meanwhile, the U.S. occupation authorities were determined to circumvent potential complications in the application of Control Council Law No. 10 by not granting jurisdiction over such cases to the judicial organizations in their zone for the duration of the military occupation. This law was in conflict with the administration of German criminal law, but its political character was justified on the grounds that it was needed for the purpose of prosecuting the criminal actions and thus carried a justifiable political character, demanding that criminal actions that led to the political persecution under the National Socialist regime. It was also argued that the willingness to prosecute both the direct perpetrators of crimes against humanity and the indirect perpetrators who had contributed to the perpetration of these crimes would serve the cause of justice.

Those who had denounced others had contributed to making crimes against humanity possible in the political environment of the National Socialist regime by reporting others to the authorities of the time, which in turn then put into motion the persecution apparatus of the regime into motion.[20] It was the responsibility of the courts to ascertain how a perpetrator had consciously acted to cause another to face unjust and severe consequences at the hands of the powers of tyranny.[21] Perpetrators who were indirectly responsible for crimes against humanity were called to account for the criminal consequences of these actions that had cruel consequences for those who had been denounced, after the collapse of the regime made it possible to prosecute such cases through the restored postwar German judicial organizations by applying the law retroactively. The collapse of the National Socialist regime and the application of retroactive legislation through the restored postwar German judicial organizations made it possible to prosecute these individuals who through their denunciations were to be called to account for the consequences of these actions, which had led to cruel consequences for those who had been denounced.

Chapter 1

Theoretical Considerations

The enactment of Control Council Law No. 10 opened the way for the prosecution of informers who had denounced others to the National Socialist authorities through the making of truthful reports about remarks or other acts that violated the political laws of the National Socialist regime, but this process was especially marked by legal difficulties. This law would make informers liable for criminal sanction in accordance with the doctrine of "indirect perpetration" for crimes that had been committed by other perpetrators. This meant that the defendant was subject to prosecution for having caused the commission of a criminal act while not actually committing the act themselves.[1] These truthful denunciations usually led to severe consequences for the person denounced, which made the informers indirect perpetrators of crimes against humanity because the act of denunciation was the initiating cause for the commission of such crimes.

In order to make their prosecution possible, the enactment and then the application of this retroactive legislation needed to be considered a justifiable and legitimate act. While this unprecedented law laid out the framework for the prosecution of crimes against humanity committed by the perpetrators of indirect crimes, it also laid the groundwork for a debate among jurists and other interested parties about how this law would actually work in practice, as it was in conflict with the provisions of the German criminal code and the underlying principles of German law. There were also concerns about the actual status of this law with German law, and which law was to take precedence over the other in the prosecution of these cases. There were also concerns about the appropriate interpretation of this law as well as questions about how the guilt of direct and indirect perpetrators of crimes against humanity could be properly ascertained and then punished with an appropriate sentence.

German law was predicated upon the principles of legal positivism, and this approach to the law was seen as a major hurdle in the prosecution of denunciation cases as crimes against humanity. According to legal positivism, the law is a manifestation of state authority that is recorded in codes and statutes and interpreted by the judiciary in separate cases in contrast to a system of law based on a system of precedents, as found in common law.[2] A law is therefore interpreted solely according to how it is recorded, without questioning the validity of its intrinsic justice or consciously assessing it within the context and values of democracy or morality.[3] It was believed that legal positivism had made the German judiciary defenseless against laws that contained arbitrary or illegal contents, because judges considered themselves bound by the principle that "the law is the law," just as the principle that "orders are orders" bound soldiers to their duty regardless of their own personal beliefs and ideas. In practice, that meant that the judges tended to emphasize and value the upholding of the law of the state without necessarily upholding the principles of justice or concerning themselves with any possible discrepancies between the positive law promulgated by the legislature of the state and the principles of natural law and justice that were not included in the definitive provisions contained in these laws.[4]

Helmut Coing argued that although judges are bound by the laws enacted by the executive authority of the state, their obedience to the law could not be compared to soldiers subject to military orders. In his opinion, a judge was obliged to decide what is just, and the correct decision is to be made within the context of the standards of the law and justice. A judge who applied laws that contravened the principles of justice also contravened the responsibilities of the judicial office and instead merely turned it into an extension of the executive authority.[5] This raised the question about the extent to which the law could be applied before it could be questioned as being contrary to the principles of justice. It would be the task of the jurists to differentiate between the purposes of the law as the instrument for the administration of justice in view of the circumstances in which the offenses against the law were perpetrated while upholding the principles of both the law and justice in these cases.

Professor Gustav Radbruch, a renowned lawyer, maintained that with regard to the issue of cases of denunciation there was no legal obligation to denounce others in the German criminal code, whether out of a political or any other conviction, and he held that this was still true during the National Socialist regime.[6] He argued that what was of decisive importance was whether an informer served the interests of the administration of justice, as defined by its lawfulness, its striving for justice, and its promotion of legal security, which were all the requirements of justice. He noted that these preconditions were absent in the politicized criminal justice system of the National Socialist regime, when it was expected that those who were denounced could only expect arbitrary rather than lawful court proceedings with legal guarantees for the ascertainment of the truth along with fair-minded judgment.[7] In his opinion, these acts of denunciation could not be considered legally defensible, since they did not serve the cause of justice even though those who denounced others had actually reported actions that were considered illegal at the time.

He argued that those who had denounced others in politically criminal cases had served the purpose of upholding the regime rather than the cause of justice, and consequently, they were guilty of being indirect perpetrators of the crimes committed by the state against those who were prosecuted in these cases. Whoever had contributed to causing an unlawful death sentence against another was guilty of intending to commit murder according to Article 211 of the German criminal code. The perpetrators of these actions had exploited the judicial organization in a way that had not been foreseen—which had made it possible for a criminal to use a German court to commit an offense.[8] He also noted that the individuals could not be held accountable for these actions at the time when the rule of law had been suspended to secure the interests of the National Socialist regime while the rights of the defendant were not maintained, until the enactment of Control Council Law No. 10 opened the way for the prosecution of these indirect crimes that were perpetrated under the pretext of protecting the interests of the regime.

In Radbruch's opinion, the tradition of legal positivism had severely handicapped the German judiciary with respect to the appropriate interpretation of the arbitrary and criminal contents of the law in the National Socialist regime, which meant that legal positivism could not by itself be used to justify the legitimacy of the authority of the law or serve as the sole basis of maintaining the minimal standards of legal security. He further argued that maintaining the concept of legal security was in itself insufficient as a decisive factor in fulfilling the purposes of maintaining the law for the common good, which had to be supplemented with practicability and fairness. While the tradition of legal positivism had made the German legal system incapable of dealing with the prosecution of denunciation cases, the problem remained as to how equitable judgments could be achieved in practice through the application of this new legislation to redress the injustices of the past while upholding the rule of law.[9]

This concern with the bringing to justice of those who had informed upon others in the National Socialist regime was not just confined to German legal circles. The general state prosecutor in Gera had expressed his contempt for informers by describing them as "the most evil and basest emergence of the Nazi state" and that National Socialism had bred "these creatures with its trained system of spies."[10] He also noted that many people had also demanded that the informers be called to account for their actions and be prosecuted for the horrible events that they had caused. He added that taking these decisive measures to prosecute these indirect perpetrators of criminal actions would contribute to re-establishing justice.[11]

Among those who had incurred and indeed suffered the consequences of denunciations was the Association of the Persecuted of the National Socialist Regime. They published a pamphlet in which they argued that not prosecuting anyone who had been directly or indirectly responsible for the political death sentences of those who opposed the National Socialist regime through its administration of justice would contravene every form of justice, as they were to be considered responsible for the National Socialist terror that was directed against its enemies. They argued that the prosecution of denunciation was possible under Article 162 of the German criminal code which addressed the issue of those who had made a false accusation against another, either against their better conscience or due to carelessness, and that they could accordingly receive a sentence ranging from a month to five years' imprisonment.[12]

However, there was a problem with this approach because this particular article did not take *political* denunciations into consideration, which were denunciations that possibly consisted of a truthful accusation that led to severe consequences for those who were denounced. It was therefore necessary to find a way of prosecuting everyone who had made a political denunciation during the National Socialist regime, whether it was truthful or false, as they had contributed to the upholding of the regime and its measures of terror against its opponents within the population.

Among the other issues confronting the potential prosecution of those who had denounced others was how the crimes were to be assessed and how the perpetrators were to punished by the courts. They noted that following the letter of the law entailed taking the cause for prosecution into consideration, but this did not entail evaluating the consequences of the act of denunciation on the basis of the political laws which violated the spirit of justice. They argued that the punishment for those who were guilty of political denunciations was to be imprisonment with sentences commensurate with the severity of the consequences that they had brought about, or intended to bring about, for those they had denounced. If an informer's report against another had led to a death sentence for those they had denounced, they were to be indicted on the charge of murder or aiding and abetting murder. If their report resulted in another being imprisoned for over a week, the informer ought to be sentenced for causing unlawful imprisonment. If someone who was denounced incurred mistreatment by officials, the informer was to be judged as if they had taken part in this offense as having caused or contributed to it, and thereby receive the appropriate prison sentence. Sentencing was also to apply in cases in which the denounced had evaded the consequences, since the criminal code also cited penalties for attempts to perpetrate offenses.[13] These cases in their opinion could be adjudicated under the appropriate provisions of German law, such as those dealing with manslaughter and unlawful imprisonment and therefore prosecuted as such. These laws had been codified before these actions took place so the questions and problems concerning the retroactive application of Control Council law No. 10, a law that came into force after these crimes were committed, would no longer come into consideration when dealing with these cases.

The Association of the Persecuted of the National Socialist Regime also stated that there was in their opinion no justification for any decent and upright individual to denounce another while being aware of the consequences that were or would be sustained by those they had denounced, such as the deprivation of freedom, mistreatment by the authorities, or even death.[14] They noted that those who had denounced others could have defended their actions by arguing that they had been compelled to report others for having violated the existing law. They could also have argued that they were obliged to do so under the existing law, especially Article 139 of the criminal code, which stated that neglecting to report actions that were considered treasonable or acts that caused damage through the use of weapons or were life threatening would make them subject to a prison sentence. However, they noted that this law also stated that no penalties would be imposed on any individuals if no such actions were actually committed. It would thus follow that those who had resisted the application of National Socialist laws of terror would have been considered to have acted legally, in contrast to those who had acted in supporting the immoral actions of the ruling authorities of the time.[15] The question of whether actions in the past were morally and legally justifiable would in their opinion be addressed through the enactment of post war legislation.

The questions remained as to whether the guidelines outlined in Control Council Law No. 10 clearly defined what were to be considered crimes against humanity and whether it could address cases that were not hitherto included in German law, and whether this law could be administered through German courts when the facts of these types of cases could also be dealt with using existing German law. It was determined that the technical prescriptions of this law were not identical to the prescriptions found in the German criminal code, especially the provisions concerning what constituted murder, unlawful imprisonment, or violent acts. They were completely different with regard to the definition of what constituted persecution on political, religious, or racial grounds. Cases regarding crimes against humanity were therefore to be adjudicated according to a different and independent standard.[16] German jurists were therefore to consider the underlying tacit subjective political character of Control Council Law No. 10, a consideration that was not found in German criminal law, in addition to the criminal nature of the offenses that could have been defined as having been perpetrated on the basis of political, religious, and racial motives in serving the interests of the National Socialist regime.

The questions as to whether the application of this law was justifiable and compatible with German law in view of the general prohibition against retroactive legislation were deemed irrelevant with regard to the political expediency of this law's application and the special circumstances of the time. This type of extraordinary legislation was seen as the only means possible to redress the crimes committed during the National Socialist regime, and this requirement outweighed any potential threat that this legislation posed to the historical developments of the law during the eighteenth and nineteenth centuries which had focused on limiting the authority of the state and protecting the rights of individuals against the potential arbitrariness of laws enacted by the state.[17] A retroactive application of the law was therefore justifiable for the purpose of redressing past injustices when the rule of law had been suspended. This meant that the German judges were to recognize that while occupation law was in itself incompatible with the principles of German law, they were to uphold the principles of international law which as a matter of necessity were to take the precedent over German law because this was the only way to restore the rule of law. In addition to this, they were also expected to apply the German laws that they had sworn to uphold.

It could not be denied that the National Socialist regime had destroyed the rule of law through subjugating the state and its administration of justice, especially the administration of criminal justice, to serve its political purposes. It was therefore necessary to restore the principle of legality in the minds of the judiciary and a societal trust in the administration of criminal justice through the restoration of the principles of the rule of law, a process would have to involve prosecuting crimes that were committed during the National Socialist regime, which was seen the most important way to achieve this purpose.[18]

Hodo von Hodenberg, the President of the Celle regional court, published a paper in which he outlined and discussed the problems confronting the German courts which were given the task of contributing to the restoration of the rule of law through the application of occupation legislation and German law, and the difficulties that could be encountered in reconciling these two different sources of law with regard to the adjudication of crimes against humanity. Von Hodenberg argued that the differences between German law and occupation law were predicated upon a clash between what he called conventional law which consisted of German law and what he termed extraordinary law, the law that was enacted by the occupation authorities. In his opinion, the vast majority of the defendants could be found guilty of a crime or offense according to German law and be judged accordingly, as German law would suffice for calling them to account for their actions in view of the types of crimes that were committed, without the necessity of defining and classifying them as crimes against humanity. He also argued that crimes defined under Control Council Law No. 10 ought to have been left within the jurisdiction of the courts of the occupation powers that could deal with cases in which the facts of the cases were not limited by the provisions of German law. He also added that the retroactive application of Control Council Law No. 10 also raised the question of whether this was a violation of German law with respect to the principle of *nullum crimen sine lege*. He also noted that there could be difficulties in determining whether these were actions that were not subject to prosecution under German law, but conversely could be prosecuted under Control Council Law No. 10. The provisions cited in this law were also very general and indefinite, and this, in his opinion, would inevitably lead to reservations about how they could be interpreted, in contrast to conventional German law with its clearly defined list of crimes and offenses. The only problem was that these crimes could not be subject to prosecution under German law, as the retroactive application of the law was contrary to German legal thought.[19]

There was also the problem of the potential hazards emanating from the political motives of those who had suffered from political prosecution during the National Socialist regime. There was the possibility that these people would demand the imposition of draconian sentences, without a sufficiently objective consideration of the facts of the cases. The range of the possible sentences therefore had to be clearly set out and maintained in practice to prevent this possibility,[20] and the sentences would have to be drawn from both the recommended range of sentencing options set out in Control Council Law No. 10, as well as the appropriate sentences for actions defined as criminal offenses in German law.

Another problem with occupation law being administered through German courts concerned the specific subject of denunciation cases. Adjudicating these types of cases would create a considerable crisis of conscience among judges, since they had been severely reproached for having been too compliant in applying laws that were contradictory to the principles of the rule of law during the National Socialist regime. Hodenberg argued that it was important for the judiciary to be independent of political or other pressures, with each judge acting according to his own conscience with regard to the conflict between the obligations of legal positivism in applying formal laws that were in conflict with the concepts of natural law. In his opinion, it was this conflict that would make it difficult for judges to reconcile themselves with the idea of applying the law retroactively.[21]

There was also the danger of German courts adjudicating denunciation cases being exposed to political incitement emanating from the public and especially the press. Judges acting on their conscience with regard to the application of the law could potentially face criticism as a result of handing down unpopular verdicts in a time when the administration of justice was already treated with mistrust. The expectation that judges would apply the law retroactively would only exacerbate the situation with them being forced to act against their conscience in applying the principles of German criminal law. These cases would also need to be adjudicated while there was no German law that could be applied to them,[22] and this was another problem for the German jurists who would be responsible for applying the law in these types of cases that lay outside the body of German criminal law.

The application of occupation law could lead to difficulties regarding the appropriate interpretation of what constituted crimes against humanity and when it was to be applied. It remained for the German jurists to accept the application of occupation law and administer it in the same manner as German law in the exercise of their duties in the interest of serving the cause of justice. However, theoretical reservations would be difficult to overcome in practice in view of the unprecedented nature of the legal circumstances of the time, as well as their unmitigated tradition of legal positivism, which outweighed any notions that they could consider themselves to be "trustees of an abstract humanitarian ideal or of justice per se."[23] There remained the underlying necessity to adhere to the letter and spirit of occupation law that was necessarily to be applied retroactively, since there was no other alternative for serving the cause of redressing past injustices. This was to take precedence over matters of conscience and theoretical jurisprudence, and thereby contribute to restoring the rule of law which was to be the decisive factor overriding other concerns with this law.

The necessity of imposing penalties for crimes against humanity in keeping with the letter of Control Council Law No. 10 involved questions concerning the roots of law and morality that affected justice and legal security.[24] This included the question of how to deal with denunciation cases on the basis of the retroactive application of this law. Those who were to be prosecuted in such cases could be described as those who had made truthful reports about others following actual or presumed legal or special responsibility for doing so. It was this presumed duty or special responsibility to report another person that was to be evaluated in these cases based on an examination of the motives of the defendant in these cases.[25]

Those who were subject to prosecution for making truthful reports against others were those who were not under any legal obligation to report another to the authorities, and did so out of personal and other negative reasons while seeking personal advantages at the expense of the denounced. These cases would be examined and prosecuted in view of the consequences that had been incurred by the denounced at the hands of the Gestapo. Other cases that were to be examined and prosecuted included denunciations on the basis of false accusations, denunciations on the basis of unjustifiable truthful reports according to the legal or customary obligations at the time, and other acts that could not be prosecuted retroactively, or a combination thereof while taking the prevailing recognizable motives into consideration. Prosecuting such cases would open the way to serving the demands of legal security and justice.[26]

There remained the problems ensuing from how the retroactive application of the law could be justified in view of the reservations expressed by the German jurists and reconciling their views with the imposition of occupation law as a matter of necessity due to the exceptional circumstances of the time. Different jurists put forward their arguments in favor of this retroactive legislation in spite of the principle of *nulla poene sine lege* due to the extraordinary circumstances of the time that served as a justification for the introduction of this legislation. The legal division of the British military government also encouraged the publication of works that supported the application of Control Council Law No. 10, and went so far as requesting that an article written by Georg Strucksberg be published as widely as possible.[27]

Strucksberg argued that the German courts in the British and French occupation zones had a responsibility to adjudicate crimes against humanity based on Control Council Law No. 10, and that the reservations concerning the interpretation of this law and its application though German courts were unfounded. He argued that the body of German law did not sufficiently address the problem of prosecuting crimes against humanity, which had to be addressed on a case by case basis, and acknowledged that the retroactive application of this law was necessary in such cases.[28] The German judiciary was to adjudicate these cases in keeping with the precedent set by the International Military Tribunal at Nuremberg, regardless of the theoretical differences between German law and international law, since these issues were concerned with the underlying theoretical principles of justice rather than with differences between German and international law. He argued that the application of Control Council Law No. 10 through the German courts would further reinforce the precedent set at Nuremberg, and that there should not be any limitations placed on international law[29] even though the German jurists perceived it to be contrary to their conscience in comparison to the accepted prescriptions of the letter of codified German law.

He also noted that the public demanded the prosecution of denunciation cases, which lay outside the range of the letter of existing German law, as it did not provide the legal framework for prosecuting crimes against humanity in the context of upholding the inalienable universal rights of humanity. Dealing with the exceptional circumstances of the National Socialist regime could only be achieved by the instituting of this exceptional legislation. This meant that it was necessary for the German jurists to overcome their reservations about administering it in practice.[30] Therefore, the application of occupation law was necessary as it compensated for the unforeseen shortcomings of codified German law[31] which was inadequate for the unprecedented post war task of prosecuting the unlawful acts committed during the National Socialist regime.

In addressing the problem of prosecuting informers as having contributed to the perpetration of crimes against humanity, Professor Richard Lange at the University of Jena put forward the argument that informers could not argue that they were compelled to act against another individual, and in doing so they had committed an act that could be seen as constituting political persecution. He also argued that they could not have been unaware of the cruel consequences that would befall the victims of political denunciations. This meant that that these informers could be seen as having contributed to political persecution, and therefore had thus indirectly taken part in a crime against humanity, regardless of whether their motives arose from racial, or political, or religious motives as cited in Control Council Law No. 10, or from personal motives that were most often the case.[32] While acts of denunciation were encouraged by the regime of the time, such cases were typically characterized by self-serving opportunism. In his opinion, those whoever could foresee and approved of their victims being delivered into inhumane persecution deserved a severe reproach through prosecution, whether they had felt justified in doing so by acting out of political fanaticism or personal interests. He further argued that the prosecution of these individuals would set a precedent for such injustices in the future.[33]

The director of the Constance regional court, A. Henneka, argued that the crimes that had been committed during the National Socialist regime could not have been prosecuted prior to its collapse, which meant that they could only be prosecuted through a retroactive administering of the law. The crimes that had been committed contravened the principles of law and justice, but they were not subject to prosecution before a change in the legal situation was effected. While the retroactive application of the law violated the universally accepted principle of international law, that one could only be called to account for actions that contravened the codified law at the time it was committed, this view was not at all compatible with criminal law. This principle was meant to prevent the arbitrary use and abuse of the law, rather than serving the higher purpose of justice. Henneka argued that this higher purpose superseded the existing standards of criminal law, and opened up the question of the possibility of judging the legal order of the state in which the crimes were committed. Control Council Law No. 10 was specifically directed at enabling the adjudication of crimes that were committed at a time when human dignity and rights were disregarded during the National Socialist tyranny. The fact that this law was specifically drawn up to deal with certain types of cases in general and was based on international law was immaterial as it could be applied objectively for the sole purpose that it was meant to serve, dealing with the circumstances found in Germany at the time.[34]

He added that the act of making a truthful report about another could constitute a crime against humanity during this time. The motives for taking this action contributed to the reinforcing of the interests of an illegal regime that was not limited by the principles of the rule of law, which resulted in the illegal persecution of those who were denounced, regardless of the motives of those who denounced them, if the alleged offenses contravened the rule of law while legal security was abolished.[35] In his opinion, what constituted justice and the principles of the rights of humanity did not cease to exist while the codified German law that maintained these principles was temporarily suspended during the National Socialist regime. In view of these circumstances, whoever had made an unlawful report about another that led to the inhumane treatment of those denounced was guilty of initiating the process of prosecution. The perpetrator's consciousness of the potential inhumane treatment that would be incurred as a result of their action of denouncing another as well as the unlawfulness of the act itself further attested to their guilt. This prior knowledge of the contradiction between the precepts of the law and the so-called National Socialist world view was in his opinion a typical attribute of a crime against humanity.[36]

The chief prosecutor at the Constance regional court, Max Güde, noted that there were distinct inhibitions in the German administration of justice about applying Control Council Law No. 10 as a distinctive criminal law, as it lacked clear prescriptions for the facts of the cases that came under its jurisdiction, in contrast to the standard practices of German criminal law. In addition to the lack of clarity of the law's contents, the obligation to act against the principle of *nulla poene sine lege* also proved to be another obstacle that jurists were reluctant to face. It therefore remained for German jurists to recognize that this "skeleton law" was to be applied in the German courts as if it were German criminal law following the example set out by the International Military Tribunal in Nuremberg, regardless of the lack of additional regulatory statutes and its possible conflict with codified German law.[37]

He argued that Control Council Law No. 10 represented the universally recognized principles in criminal law recognized by all of civilized humanity and states, out of which emanated the source of natural criminal law before it was codified by the state.[38] This interpretation of what constituted a crime against humanity was necessarily to take precedence over the application of codified law to serve the purpose of administering justice. It was to be applied by independent jurists interpreting occupation law in the exercise of their functions, in spite of there being a lack of clearly defined definitions of the types of crimes and what codified law had actually prescribed for the imposition of penalties. The jurists' interpretations of what constituted crimes against humanity were thus to overcome the limitations of the vague definitions found in occupation law.

While denunciation cases were not specifically cited as a crime against humanity in Control Council Law No. 10, they were, as Güde argued, to be judged as actions that were politically and morally deplorable in view of the facts of these cases. They were to be considered as having been indicative of an individual's indirect participation in the political abuse of authority, whenever the act of denunciation led to the human rights of the defendant victims being violated. The informers who had been part of the process of such political persecution were thus to be prosecuted accordingly, regardless of the specific motive for this crime. The participation in a crime against the human rights of another in conjunction with denunciation was to be considered substantially illegal, and morally reprehensible,[39] given the consequences of the ensuing political persecution that violated the principles of justice and legal security This type of crime superseded what had been codified in German law, and it was only the imposition of occupation law that opened the way for such crimes to be prosecuted.

The prosecution of these and other types of crimes against humanity could only be achieved by the retroactive application of the law. The promotion of justice required that these types of crimes be prosecuted by a different standard that was not hitherto found in existing codified criminal law to suit the exceptional circumstances of the recent past. Doing this would safeguard the compelling precept of justice by prosecuting the violations of the most elementary human rights that occurred as a result of the abuses of political power during the National Socialist era. Such abuses were to be judged in accordance with the provisions set out in Control Council No. 10, as well as those found in German law insofar as it was practicable, which would help restore the principles of universal criminal law in the German administration of justice.[40]

The renown lawyer Gustav Radbruch argued that in contrast to the legal positivist interpretation and views of the law, an assessment of the truthful reporting of incidents that were unlawful at the time could not be separated from a consideration of the consequences of denouncing others to the authorities, as well as a consideration of whether or not the subject of the reports were given a fair trial in a judicial system that had become corrupted with regard to the hearing of offenses of a political nature. Radbruch argued that a law that was to be applied retroactively could only be enacted when the content of this law reflected the universal law that existed at the time to which it was meant to correspond.[41] Hence, persecutions on political, racial, or religious grounds during the National Socialist regime, including those ensuing from denunciations, were unlawful at that time just as at any other time since the institution of the fundamental rights of humanity.[42]

The Nuremberg statute and Control Council Law No. 10, were to be understood as a new form of international law that superseded law at the national level which would make the prosecution of crimes against humanity possible through this new and independent level of jurisdiction. The enacting of this law meant that these crimes could now be adjudicated due to this new interpretation of the facts of these cases that until then could not be dealt with using the codified German criminal code as it did not contain any definition of what could or could not be considered atrocities. Radbruch did concede that what constituted crimes against humanity needed to be clarified as a basic principle of justice[43] through the continuous application of occupation legislation in the courts hearing these cases. Judgments in such hitherto unprecedented cases would amount to the practice of judge-made case law as found in English common law that would lead to the defining of how crimes against humanity could be interpreted as such and likewise redress past injustices. The achieving of this would unavoidably entail a retroactive application of the law.[44]

He also argued that the prohibition on retroactive legislation was meant to benefit a society that was founded on the ethical principles of the rule of law, while the National Socialist regime did not consider itself to be bound by any ethical principles. Hence, it was justifiable to make an exception to the breaching of the principle of *nulla poene sine lege* to compensate for the grave unlawfulness that had been perpetrated under National Socialist rule. It was also argued by others that prosecuting crimes against humanity through Control Council Law No. 10 did not violate the prohibition against retroactive legislation by any means, since the actions perpetrated according to extraordinary law had been unlawful at the time that they had taken place. Another argument was that this law followed the Anglo-Saxon principle of judge-made law, which deviated from the principles of natural law, and this meant that judges needed to accommodate their decision making accordingly[45] and overcome their reservations about violating the principle of *nulla poene sine lege* in such cases for the unprecedented purpose of adjudicating crimes that could not have been prosecuted at the time they were prosecuted.

August Wimmer, the President of the Highest Appeal Court of the British Occupation Zone, put forward the view that the rule of law required an ethically established, fully developed, and planned criminal law to protect the community that it served from unethical actions, and that these requirements took greater precedence than theoretical concerns about the legal basis of its principles in the interest of preserving the legal security. This included the ethical obligation of breaching legal principles to make certain crimes subject to prosecution retroactively, even if it entailed modifying the constitution through new legislation, when it proved necessary to punish serious crimes as an obligation to uphold the compelling demands of the rule of law, and when the applicable criminal law was inadequate in upholding its interests in certain cases, due to hitherto unknown and unforeseen developments in criminality. Objections to the enactment of this law due to judicial unease based on the tradition of legal positivism were therefore, in his opinion, rendered inadmissible in these exceptional cases.[46]

Wimmer argued that ethical considerations should take precedence over the shortcomings of the codified criminal law as it was the undisputable ethical duty of the state to prosecute all crimes against humanity as a means of atonement for the actions of the perpetrators of the past and their victims, so as to prevent such actions occurring in the future. Since German law did not sufficiently address these types of offenses, the creating of a new and exceptional retroactive legislation to allow for prosecuting these crimes against humanity was an ethical necessity, insofar as this was deemed practical to outweigh the underlying principle of *nulla poene sine lege*. He also argued that this type of exceptional law would not infringe upon an individual's fundamental rights in the present or the future and that it would permit the prosecution of crimes against humanity which would serve to completely restore the certainty of the law, including the fundamental rights of an individual, in the eyes of the German jurists and all of civilized humanity.[47]

The practical application of Control Council Law No. 10 created widespread concern and raised many questions, which required elaboration on its theoretical underpinnings. Wilhelm Kiesselbach argued that reservations among the judiciary concerning the principle of *nulla poene sine lege* contravened how the application of Control Council Law No. 10 was intended to open the way for the prosecution of crimes that could not have been adjudicated under German law at the time that they were perpetrated, and that German jurists were responsible for its application, just as they were responsible for upholding German law. It remained for German jurists to adjudicate cases of crimes against humanity in accordance with occupation law that was specifically enacted for this purpose.[48]

Professor Richard Lange argued in favor of the application of Control Council Law No. 10. He stated that the legal basis of this law was predicated upon the existing principles of international law, as it was laid out by the International Military Tribunal in Nuremberg, as well as the principles of criminal law, which opened the way for the imposition of criminal sanctions for offenses committed against the principles of humanity and human rights. He further argued that although the principle of the retroactive application of the law was contrary to existing legal norms, the conscious intention of committing a crime at the time it was perpetrated was separate from what could be considered a crime. He likewise argued that the prohibition against the retroactive application of criminal was not a requirement for justice, but simply a requirement for legal security[49] to protect the rights of the defendant against unjust accusations. Exceptions to this rule could be justified when the promotion of justice as a higher goal of the legal system made it unavoidable. Prosecuting crimes committed against the rights of individuals[50] was such an exception and therefore it could not be constrained by formal codified law, which was superseded by Control Council Law No. 10 that provided the justification for justice to be served in the sphere of material law. It followed that when the intended purpose of a denunciation resulted in the wrongful death or imprisonment of a victim or was an attempt to cause such consequences, the informer was to be judged in accordance with their indirect involvement or as a participant in this crime, under either Control Council Law No. 10 or German law.[51]

Kiesselbach, Güde, Radbruch, and Wimmer all came to the same conclusions in their examinations and interpretation of the culpability of crimes against humanity. They all agreed that all the National Socialist laws that had contravened the rights of humanity were illegal since they were unethical, and contradicted rational law. They also agreed that the unalienable principle of *nulla poene sine lege* needed to be rescinded since it did not constitute an unalterable fundamental right and that this was necessary for prosecuting crimes against humanity. Retroactive prosecution would be justifiable in any exceptional case in which it was determined that a grave violation of an individual's human rights had been committed which would warrant a deviation from this principle of material justice and legal security. The absolute demand that punishment must follow a crime became more compelling when the gravity of the crime had been evident to the perpetrator in the context of natural law.[52]

Another jurist agreed with Radbruch that these crimes could be dealt with in the manner of English judge-made case law, by which statutory provisions could be created as precedents that would then be re-evaluated in similar cases thereafter and which would then validate the original judgment. This could serve as a means to providing a definition, but he noted that this was not the intention of the occupation powers, which was to lay out the groundwork for a consistent principle of criminal law for the prosecution of these crimes that was not subject to modifications.[53] He also noted that there remained a considerable number of difficulties in the practical application of Control Council Law No. 10. The legally protected interests of the defendant were to be defined in individual cases while developing the significance and extent of the cited or circumscribed legal norms in cases of offenses that were not defined by German criminal law. In his opinion occupation law was to compensate for these potential shortcomings by forming the legal basis for crimes against humanity that hitherto had not been anticipated, and therefore necessitated a contravention of the principle of *nulla poene sine lege* that needed to be evaluated in every individual case. Each case was to be treated separately to determine which legally protected interests were to be maintained, and to determine whether each case represented the blatant violation of natural law, which then justified the rescinding of legal security for the purpose of serving justice.[54]

The question of dealing with cases of denunciation was particularly significant in connection with the violation of human rights through the excesses perpetrated by the political authorities in the National Socialist era. Those who had made truthful reports about alleged "political, racial, or religious enemies" of the state did not themselves actually carry out an abuse of political authority, but their actions led to this result. Güde put forward the argument that they ought to be subject to prosecution for having caused a crime involving a violation of human rights, while both foreseeing and approving the consequences for the denounced. These consequences were not to be considered less substantial than the motives for their actions, whether they were perpetrated out of political conviction or base motives such as vindictiveness or greed, since criminal court judges were responsible for punishing these immoral and unlawful acts. Therefore while the perpetrators in such cases did not necessarily act on political, racial, or religious motives, they were nevertheless to be prosecuted for the inhumane consequences that they had caused while having been aware of the nature of those consequences.[55] On the other hand, he noted that an evaluation of the personal motives of the perpetrator could be considered incompatible with the definition of persecution as set forth in Control Council Law No. 10.[56]

The general nature of the provisions of this law meant that it could be interpreted in many different ways as it did not provide clear and accurate provisions on how to interpret the extent to which an indirect perpetrator had approved of a crime against humanity being committed, even though they encouraged a third party to act against another. It also lacked clarity as to whether indirect perpetrators could be accused of attempts to cause crimes against humanity, as an attempt to commit a crime was defined under German criminal law, and whether these attempts could justifiably be prosecuted in the appropriate manner.[57]

In contrast to the jurists who were in favor of the retroactive application of occupation law as a matter of necessity for redressing crimes against humanity, Hans-Georg Meister wrote an article on "The Non-conflicting Character of The Legal System" that was opposed to the application Control Council Law No. 10. He argued that laws pertaining to a legal system could not provide legal liabilities for acts that were in conflict with each other. Hence, if an individual did not have any choice but to infringe upon the letter of two different laws in certain circumstances, they were not be subject to prosecution if they infringed upon a law that was meant to protect a less important interest in the event it was possible to avoid an offense against a law that protected an important interest.[58] This general legal principle was to be applied to cases in which an individual could not avoid committing a crime against humanity, as defined by Control Council Law No. 10, in order to avoid risking criminal prosecution for disobeying the orders of a superior.[59]

While admitting that respecting the rules of humanity served a higher purpose than obeying superior orders, he concluded that since the crimes against humanity were not punishable under German law at the time they were committed, this meant that the perpetrators could not be punished for them in the present since they had been unable to defend themselves in a trial for disobedience in the National Socialist regime by citing the laws of humanity.[60] Meister therefore argued that these types of offenders ought to be potentially exempt from prosecution for committing a crime against humanity, even if the risk of criminal punishment for disobedience would have been very lenient,[61] since this would be a necessary consequence of the principle of the non-conflicting character of the legal system. According to this theory, exemption from punishment would even be granted in cases in which the requirements of urgent necessity as cited in Article 54 of the German Criminal code were not met, which he considered to be inapplicable to crimes against humanity, even if the offender did not risk an imminent danger of punishment.[62]

This argument was tantamount to an out and out repudiation and rejection of the application of Control Council Law No. 10 before it came into force, a position that was considered as completely untenable by the London-based British Special Research Unit. They considered that it was absurd to regard the National Socialist legal system and Control Council Law No. 10 as belonging to the same legal order that could not be allowed to come into conflict with each other, since Control Council Law No. 10 was not yet in force in the time of the National Socialist regime. This theory essentially claimed that National Socialist law took precedence over occupation law since an individual could not be punished for such a crime under occupation law if they faced punishment under National Socialist law.[63] They rejected his argument that the application of Control Council Law No. 10 would be unfavorable to the offenders, since it denied them the possibility of using the defense that they could have been charged with a crime for disobeying an order to perpetrate an act that was later considered to be a crime against humanity.

The British military government took exception to Meister's conclusions on the grounds that they were considered tactless and unwise as well as unconvincing. While disavowing censorship of non-official publications in the interest of maintaining the freedom of the press as an elementary democratic principle, this article was considered by the British Military Government as being intolerably detrimental to the interests of the occupation powers at a time when there were already enough difficulties with the application of Control Council Law No. 10. The decision was made that the Central Judicial Office of the British occupation zone would be hostile toward any steps taken by German lawyers that would undermine the interpretation of Control Council Law No. 10 by the German courts, or the trials of members of criminal organizations, and that the editor of the *Monatsschrift für deutsches Recht* would be asked not to publish articles of a similar nature.[64] This article was an exception in contrast to the numerous articles supporting the application of Control Council Law No. 10, and its unconvincing argument could not serve as an effective rebuttal to the purposes of the spirit of this law. The greatest difficulties encountered with its application remained within the judicial organization while several other judicial experts lent their support by writing more objective and convincing jurisprudential treatises on the subject of its interpretation.

Professor R. H. Graveson of the University of London commented on the series of articles written by German jurists on the subject of whether the application of Control Council Law No. 10 actually contradicted the principle of *nulla poene sine lege*. Graveson proffered the argument that this principle had evolved over time to encompass different but related meanings. The most important of them that remained was the idea that a criminal law could not be applied if it did not directly pertain to the legal facts of the case, which led to the prohibition of prosecution by analogy. Another important one was the idea that criminal law could also not be applied to actions that were committed before it was published, which was the basis of the prohibition against retroactive legislation.[65] It was these precepts that had prompted von Hodenberg to argue that the retroactive nature of Control

Council Law No. 10 represented a violation against a compelling principle of German criminal law. Graveson accepted this, but noted that occupation law superseded German law since it emanated from the supreme authority of the Allied forces in Germany.[66]

Apart from the obligation to administer occupation law along with German law, it was unnecessary in the opinion of Graveson to attach undue importance to the retroactive effect of the law insofar as it concerned the application of what serving justice prescribed.[67] Graveson argued that this consideration necessarily outweighed the uncompromising intellectual considerations concerning precepts that were codified, as proceeding otherwise would mean disregarding the ethical considerations on which legal principles were established and which would undermine their inherent justification. The principle of *nulla poena sine lege* was meant to serve the ideals of legal security and justice during normal circumstances, which the National Socialist regime had destroyed, and culminated in the crimes that were cited in Control Council Law No. 10. It was therefore their duty to apply this law, regardless of their personal beliefs.[68]

It therefore followed that German jurists were to exercise greater flexibility in the independent exercise of their functions in upholding the law while facing the pragmatic realities of the present circumstances. They were to apply Control Council Law No. 10 to redress the extraordinary injustices, regardless of any qualms that they had about the law itself or concerns about its theoretical limitations. They were to be guided by practical considerations, since considerations concerning the application of any law were not to be made independently of whether its provisions corresponded to universal law. It was to be recognized that a strict adherence to the principle of *nulla poena sine lege* would altogether nullify the meaning of Control Council Law No. 10 and the purposes for which it was enacted .[69] Richard Lange likewise noted that arguments based on legal positivism could not sustain the claim that the prohibition on retroactive legislation was based on natural law and justice, rather than just being an empirical rule for the purpose of serving legal security in a consistent manner and the functions of criminal law. German jurists were therefore to accept that the justified purpose of the occupation law was to uphold justice outside the conventional application of criminal law by prosecuting crimes against humanity, which lay outside the scope of conventional German law, however inconsistent it appeared to be with the hitherto commonly accepted principles of German law.[70]

He argued that occupation law was likewise to be justifiably applied in denunciation cases for the purpose of upholding justice. It was to be acknowledged that there was no justification for reporting another about their alleged criminal activity in upholding the prevailing laws of the time, especially those concerning political legislation that were inherently unlawful, considering that these laws were not oriented toward the purpose of serving justice. Such cases would have to be examined on an individual basis to determine how the unlawfulness had been perpetrated and the motives of the perpetrator for committing the injustices that were inflicted on others.[71] They were to be prosecuted according to the consequences that they had intentionally but indirectly caused or contributed to bringing about, in the event that it could be established that these consequences constituted inhumane persecution on the basis of political, religious, or racial motives resulting from the act of denunciation.[72]

Theodor Klefisch, a distinguished jurist, noted that truthful reports had never been considered as or prosecuted as criminal offenses, or defined as crimes against humanity. Since the prosecution of denunciation cases had hitherto been unprecedented, the adjudication of these types of cases could only necessarily be instituted within the context of Control Council Law No. 10 and its retroactive application in cases that it classified in certain specific circumstances to be crimes against humanity. The justification for their prosecution was formulated through court judgments that took these circumstances into consideration while evaluating them as crimes against humanity through their interpretations of the broadly defined provisions of this law.[73] Judgments in these types of cases and the putting forward of jurisprudential theory concerning the justification of why these denunciation cases were to be prosecuted in practice would follow from the earlier precedents, following the underlying principles of the necessity for prosecuting denunciation cases, and would thereby call to account those who were responsible for willingly contributing to inflicting unjust and inhumane consequences on others during the National Socialist regime.

It remained for the German jurists to recognize that these considerations that traditionally lay outside the conventional principles of German criminal law were to be used in adjudicating crimes against humanity for the purpose of serving justice and restoring the rule of law. Whereas the principle of *nulla crimen sine lege* was to serve as a guarantee for legal security in a state governed by the rule of law, the new law had to be applied retroactively in what were considered to be exceptional cases that had not previously been envisaged. Occupation law was to be administered through the German courts when they were granted the jurisdiction to adjudicate on the broadly defined term of crimes against humanity, which required the German judiciary to take subjective considerations of occupation law into consideration while judging both direct and indirect perpetrators of these crimes, in addition to applying the material provisions of German law and maintaining its principles. Occupation law was necessarily to take precedence over German law whenever its shortcomings made the prosecution of crimes against humanity impossible, although there also remained a number of open questions about how such crimes could be adjudicated in view of the broadly defined terms of Control Council Law No. 10 that was to be administered at the jurists' independent discretion.

These contradictions, in view of the extraordinary circumstances following the collapse of the National Socialist regime, raised concern among the western occupation powers about whether these types of cases could be tried with appropriate objectivity, as there remained reservations among the German judiciary regarding the retroactive application of the law. There were still many unanswered question related to Control Council Law No. 10. There were doubts as to whether article II section 1c of Control Council Law No. 10 concerning crimes against humanity specifically cited or envisaged the prosecution of denunciation cases. There were also theoretical doubts about the claim that this law emanated in whole or in part from either international law or German law or a combination of both. There were also doubts about the claim that the necessity to adjudicate these types of cases was to take the precedent over these theoretical criticisms.[74]

These debates could have at least served to encourage those who were involved in the legal processes in restoring the principles of the rule of law, after the characteristically arbitrary methods of administering justice in the National Socialist regime had eliminated these principles. The practical application of Control Council Law No. 10 was a measure to restore the rule of law through the adjudication of these individual cases after the German courts were conferred with the authority to adjudicate the types of cases that were cited in this law. However, there was often a conflict between the occupation powers and the German jurists regarding what German law prescribed, and debates over what was defined as a crime against humanity with a sufficient amount of objectivity in view of the consequences, and how justice could be served in view of the shortcomings of German law in prosecuting these types of cases. This matter would be resolved through the practical application and the lessons that would be drawn from various precedent-setting judgments amid controversies between what Control Council Law No. 10 prescribed and the German jurists' adverse reactions to the retroactive application of this law.

Control Council Law No. 10 enabled the German courts to adjudicate all forms of crimes against humanity wherever they were granted this jurisdiction, without specifying whether such crimes were directly or indirectly perpetrated. Denunciation was not specifically mentioned in this law, but this type of case was encompassed in Article II section 1c. The application of this law with regard to denunciation was administered differently in the four occupation zones due to different legislation governing their jurisdiction.[75] German courts in the British, French, and Soviet zones were empowered with adjudicating denunciation cases according to the terms of their respective military government ordinances, and courts in Berlin were empowered to hear such cases under the terms of Control Council Law No. 10 and German law. Although such cases could not be prosecuted in the US occupation zone, they could be tried upon special application in exceptional cases if they also constituted a violation of German law. They were otherwise evaluated in the denazification proceedings[76] as part of the society-wide vetting process to help determine the extent of an individual's political guilt for having allegedly supported the National Socialist regime.

Chapter 2

The American Occupation Zone: Theory and Compromise

The constraints in occupation policy and German criminal law regarding denunciation cases as a crime against humanity prevented the prosecution of these types of cases in German courts in the American occupation zone. In spite of all of the requests by the German judicial authorities for them to be granted jurisdiction over all forms of crimes against humanity, the American military government was reluctant to allow the German courts in the American zone the authority to apply Control Council Law No. 10. This reluctance was due to the inherent problems associated with a retroactive application of this law,[1] and the expected difficulties they would face in persuading the German judiciary to uphold its provisions in practice. Jurisdiction over cases of crimes against humanity was later conferred on the German courts through *Land* government legislation. However, the adjudication of these cases was conducted solely according to German law,[2] while denunciation cases were mainly adjudicated by the denazification tribunals rather than through the judicial organization. Hence the sanctions that were normally imposed were based on political considerations rather than criminal legislation.

The US military government argued that those types of cases could not be adjudicated by German courts, since there was no German law covering such cases—which meant that individuals who had denounced others could not be charged with such an offense. Any law enacted by German authorities to make such actions open to prosecution would be retroactive and therefore would not be looked upon favorably.[3] Since existing law did not allow for the criminal prosecution of indirect responsibility for the commitment of a crime, the ministers of justice in the US occupation zone drafted a law to prosecute those who had carried out the denunciations to help facilitate the denazification process by prosecuting those who had willingly collaborated with the National Socialist regime at any level of society. Although the sanction of such a law would contradict the principle that criminal laws should not possess retroactive power, there was public demand for the prosecution of informers[4] whose actions were considered criminal matters in the other occupation zones and were adjudicated accordingly as crimes against humanity.

Several representatives of the administration of justice did not approve of the prosecution of denunciation cases due to the prohibition against a retroactive application of the law, and there was opposition among jurists against applying Control Council Law No. 10 since the truthful reporting of incidents had always been admissible and had never been prosecuted as being unlawful.[5] They did not want to relinquish lawful reports of truthful occurrences as a means of criminal prosecution. Hence, although the motives for denunciations were universally considered to be morally reprehensible, they were not subject to prosecution and they were therefore irrelevant in criminal proceedings from a judicial rather than moral viewpoint.[6]

The prosecution of informers was not authorized by the American military government, which was concerned that either the volume of evidence on those informers would bring a proliferation of litigation, or that cases of "minor" criminals would be considered low priority in view of "more important" work faced by the understaffed courts, on the principle that such cases could be disregarded instead of prosecuting the more significant war criminal cases.[7] Therefore, practical reasons for using the scarce judicial resources tended to outweigh all other considerations in favor of prosecuting informers as having committed crimes against humanity. As a result, efforts at administering crimes against humanity as defined in the provisions of Control Council Law No. 10 in the American occupation zone dealt with other types of crimes against humanity, while those that involved denunciations remained outside the scope of cases that would be prosecuted as crimes against humanity in the criminal courts.

There were several proceedings initiated in Hesse concerning acts of political persecution through denunciation, but the outcomes were unsatisfactory because of the remarks that the victims had made, such as comments about the hopeless military situation and crimes perpetrated by the National Socialist regime, and that so-called defeatist or treasonous comments could not be proven to be false. It therefore proved impossible to impose a conviction in these denunciation cases,[8] since the informers reported remarks to the authorities that were allegedly true, and this meant that there was no legal basis for prosecuting them under existing German law. However, the informers in such cases could conceivably have been indicted on a charge of being an accomplice to murder or deprivation of freedom.[9] It remained that German criminal law could not be applied to the same extent that occupation law opened the way for prosecution of indirect acts of political persecution. The perpetration of malicious denunciations specifically included "persecutions on political, racial, or religious grounds" in Article2(c) of Control Council Law No. 10, but the question remained how the term "persecution" should be construed in such cases. Article 104 of the German Criminal Code stated that denunciations were not open to prosecution if the denunciations were true.[10] Article 164 of the Criminal code only allowed for prosecution for *false* denunciation, while those based on fact, such as when the denounced individual had listened to forbidden foreign radio broadcasts, were not unlawful; therefore, the offenders were not indictable.[11]

Cases of denunciations that involved political persecution could only be prosecuted in the event that German criminal law could be applied to the cases of truthful denunciations. In one such example, a defendant hereafter cited as H. had initiated Special Court investigation proceedings against his tenant, hereafter cited as G. on the basis of unfounded claims of political offenses. H. had told the state prosecutor that G. was an enemy of the state who had to be destroyed. H. thus prompted another, hereafter cited as S. to file a report against G. with the Gestapo so that H. could himself appear as a leading witness for the prosecution. In the report it was alleged that G. had said he was not stupid enough to let himself get shot like the "stupid swine" at the front, in addition to H.'s claims that he often listened to foreign radio broadcasts; there were claims that he had his own transmitter in his home; had known about Mussolini's abdication before his overthrow; had persistently criticized the measures of the NSDAP and its personalities; and that he had often had short conversations with enemies of the state in Berlin from his home. G. was arrested by the Gestapo on 1 December 1943 on the grounds of these accusations, which H. maintained as a witness for the prosecution. However, these incidents were proven to be false and the prosecution proceedings were stayed on 30 December 1943, and G. was released from custody. Despite this, G. was re-arrested by the Gestapo and was going to be sent to a concentration camp, but his employer succeeded in countermanding this order, arguing that he was involved in work that was valuable for the war effort, and he was eventually released on 7 January 1944 with the condition of having to make a "voluntary contribution" of 2000 RM to the NSV (*Nationalsozialistische Volkswohlfahrt*).[12]

The criminal court at the Frankfurt-am-Main regional court convicted H. on 22 November 1946 on the charges of false accusation in connection with slander and causing severe unlawful imprisonment. The court argued that H. had envied the younger G.'s income and professional standing, and had therefore intentionally made these false accusations against him in order to bring grave disadvantages to him in view of the circumstances of the time, while being aware of the unlawful consequences of his actions. He was thus sentenced to two years' imprisonment, after taking into consideration as mitigating factors the fact that he was seventy years old at this time and that his moral values had potentially been undermined by National Socialist propaganda.[13]

The supreme regional court in Frankfurt-am-Main later quashed this verdict on 2 April 1947 upon an appeal by the state prosecutor to reject the merely inferred indictment of attempted murder, since this court had not proven whether H. had acted with the direct intent to achieve this purpose. The proceedings were therefore to be re-opened to examine the possibility of whether he could also be indicted on the grounds of this additional charge,[14] in view of how he could have expected and approved of the possibility of G. being killed.[15] However, new proceedings were stayed due to H.'s sustained period of illness that made him unable to stand trial until his death in 1963.[16]

In another case, proceedings that were initiated could not be upheld in the trial. Denunciations by a worker at a machine factory in Frankfurt-am-Main in 1941 led to the arrests of several of his workmates by the Gestapo, and their prosecution at the supreme regional court in Kassel for preparing to commit high treason and listening to foreign broadcasts. Some of these victims were later executed or died while they were imprisoned, while others were released or were later liberated by Allied troops.[17] The widow of one of the executed victims initiated legal proceedings.[18] However, whether the state prosecutor in Frankfurt-am-Main could maintain the investigation proceedings depended on the approval of the American military government to authorize the German courts to try cases of crimes against humanity on the basis of Control Council Law No. 10,[19] which was not forthcoming. The adjudication of the crime against humanity in this case was therefore to be dealt with by the denazification tribunal in Gießen instead.[20] He was later called to account for his actions in the Soviet occupation zone where he had been detained in a prisoner-of-war camp. He was held in judicial custody from 15 July 1950, and was prosecuted by the Magdeburg regional court on 12 February 1952 for crimes against humanity under Control Council Law No. 10 and Control Council Directive No. 38, part II, article 2, section 9 on the prosecution of denunciation, and was sentenced to ten years' imprisonment along with other sanctions.[21]

The same legal circumstances in the American occupation zone prevented a conviction from being imposed in a different case. A resident of Bonsweiher, hereafter cited as J. G., had been interrogated by the Gestapo in Bensheim in 1944 for having allegedly made remarks in a local tavern that were hostile to the state,[22] having said that there would soon come a time when they, two of the accused in this case, hereafter cited as A. W. and A. M., would also have something to say in the event of the regime's collapse when the Communists would take their revenge.[23] A. W. forwarded the details of J. K.'s remarks to the mayor of Bonsweiher, hereafter cited as A. M., so that this incident would be forwarded to the local *Ortsgruppenleiter,* L. v. M., and also reported the incident to a local police official, hereafter cited as L. S., who reported it to L. v. M. Two weeks later, A. W., A. M. and L. S. sent a written report about the incident to L. v. M.[24] A. W.'s denunciation thus initiated J. K.'s persecution by the Gestapo that led to his death.[25] J. K. was initially released from Gestapo custody after their interrogation,[26] but about two weeks before the advance of American troops, L. S., ordered him to go to the Gestapo office in Bensheim, where he was killed with a gunshot to the neck on 13 March 1945.[27]

W., A. M. and L. S. were later charged on 14 November 1946 with aiding and abetting murder, in connection with Article III. 1c of Control Council Law No. 10. The state prosecutor argued that these three defendants had delivered J. G. into the hands of the Gestapo and that they were fully conscious that this would lead to his death. They were therefore to be charged with aiding and abetting murder while having acted out of base motives as well as violating the laws of humanity.[28]

Rather than these proceedings being initiated at the Darmstadt regional court, the defendants were to be judged by the local denazification tribunal.[29] These charges had to be withdrawn since it could not be proven that the defendants could have expected the victim to be killed during the last days of the war. Moreover, an accusation on the basis of Control Council Law No. 10 was not possible due to the military government's refusal to extend the jurisdiction of this law to the German courts. In addition, since the remarks were truthful, a conviction could not be sustained on the grounds of making a false accusation.[30] Since it appeared that German criminal law could not be applied to the facts of this case, sanctions would have to be imposed under the Law for Liberation from National Socialism and Militarism of 5 March 1946 which would make it a political rather than a criminal matter. This absolved the judiciary in the American zone from having to become reconciled with dealing with cases of a political nature, which would require them taking greater subjective interpretations of the facts of the cases into consideration.

The purpose of the existing German criminal law against making false denunciations was intended to protect individuals from those who would use the law against them,[31] but its originators could not have foreseen how truthful denunciations would be exploited to serve to uphold the interests of the regime, rather than protecting the interests of individuals under the guise of protection by the state. Truthful denunciations that were made to uphold the interests of the regime rather than the interests of individuals led to an institutionalized perversion of justice that led to inhumane consequences, which necessitated the formulation of new legislation to bring the perpetrators to account for their actions, a solution which remained separate from trying to modify the existing law. Many jurists argued that imposing legal sanctions against crimes against humanity could only be achieved if a new law was enacted to define the circumstances under which such actions would be made subject to prosecution, considering that these actions were not unlawful in the National Socialist regime. Since the prosecution of crimes against humanity as defined by Control Council Law No. 10 could only be undertaken retroactively, this would necessarily constitute a contravention of the principle of *nulla poene sine lege*. This would have inevitably led to a crisis of conscience among the German jurists whose training and oath of office bound them to the principles of the rule of law, which could potentially be undermined by them being expected to comply with military government legislation.[32]

There was some degree of risk for the occupation powers in empowering the German judges with the authority to apply a law that contravened the fundamental principles of the rule of law. The arguments and judicial reasoning against contravening the prohibition on retroactive legislation made it appear that maintenance of this prohibition was ultimately more significant for the judges than the unlawfulness that had been perpetrated in the National Socialist regime. This debate indicated to the occupation authorities the reservations among the postwar jurists toward prosecuting crimes that had been committed during that time,[33] as well as their inability to make the narrow differentiations between jurisprudential theory and how it was to be administered as justice in practice. Moreover, the experience of the National Socialist regime had greatly shaken the authority of the German administration of justice, and as a result, those who spoke for the judiciary had the reasonable intention of not wanting doubt to be cast on it again[34] by being expected to apply the law more subjectively than as objectively as legal positivism had presumably made possible, especially in cases of a political nature. Meanwhile, it could not be denied that the consequences of denunciations had led to grave disadvantages having had been inflicted on the denounced, and therefore redressing these crimes and rehabilitating the victims essentially required that a new law had to be enacted to define the new and extraordinary legal circumstances of the postwar period. Legislation to be implemented through the judiciary would make this possible, provided that there was the willingness to face the exigencies of the postwar situation with the appropriate approach toward political crimes perpetrated in the past.

While jurisdiction for administering Control Council Law No. 10 was not forthcoming in the US occupation zone, the Ministers of Justice of Baden-Württemberg, Hesse, and Bavaria sponsored their own legislation[35] to prosecute crimes against humanity that reinforced the possibility of prosecuting offenses against German law committed by Germans against German victims. They created The Law for the Prosecution of National Socialist Crimes[36] that substantially restated the provisions of Article II, sections 1(c), 4, and 5 of Control Council Law No. 10, insofar as the offenses were subject to prosecution under the provisions of the German criminal code.[37] Nevertheless, interpretations of German law could not be extended to the retroactive prosecution of informers during the National Socialist regime, so new legislation would be needed to remove the obstacles to adjudicating cases that involved what could be interpreted as indirect involvement.

During a conference in Stuttgart on 17 April 1946, the Ministers of Justice deliberated whether the existing law or the new legislation under consideration could be applied to the retroactive prosecution of denunciation cases. They concluded that it was necessary to enact a special criminal law for that purpose of prosecuting informers, since imposing sanctions against indirect perpetration of criminal actions was not possible under existing law. Although such sanctions countered the principle of the prohibition of retroactive legislation, the general public strongly considered the punishment of informers to be necessary. Moreover, the provisions of the Law for the Liberation from National Socialism and Militarism of 5 March 1946 were inadequate for imposing sanctions in most denunciation cases, especially since this law did not prescribe sanctions in such cases.[38] Moreover, this law served the purpose of setting the norms for the implementation of the denazification program in the American occupation zone, and could not be considered to be a criminal law.[39] If there was evidence to sustain grounds for prosecution on the basis of the evidence of the conduct of an accused who had indirectly contributed to a crime against humanity, they would be called to account for their actions by being judged by the lay jurors.

The Ministers of Justice agreed that the provisions of this law would be encompassed in a draft of the Law for the Prosecution of National Socialist Crimes that was under discussion at this time, and would supplement the terms of the earlier Liberation Law by granting German courts jurisdiction over such cases. They proposed that whoever had directly or indirectly subjected another individual to political persecution as a result of a denunciation, whether deliberately or through negligence, which had caused severe consequences, particularly imprisonment in a concentration camp or death, would be sentenced to prison. Perpetrators who had acted out of self-interest, vengeance, or other reprehensible motives would be sentenced to imprisonment in a penitentiary and be deprived of their civil rights.[40]

Those provisions were not introduced into any new German legislation in the American occupation zone. German legislation had to be approved by the military government, and the military government opposed the prosecution of denunciation cases since it was assumed that it could have potentially opened a floodgate of litigation. Such cases could still have been prosecuted under Article2(c) of Law No. 10, which specifically provided that prosecution of actions was possible "whether or not in violation of the democratic laws of the country where perpetrated." Prosecution was also technically possible under Article3(d) of Law No. 10, provided that the tribunal that could be charged with prosecution of a case could be a German court, in cases of crimes committed by Germans against other Germans, or—if prior authorization for the prosecution had been granted by the military government—to a German court holding the appropriate jurisdiction.[41]

The US military government and the reconstituted German political authorities thus arrived at a compromise solution. Upon special application, exceptional cases of denunciation could be prosecuted subject to the provisions of German law. Individuals guilty of such actions were otherwise subject to denazification sanctions under the Law for the Liberation of National Socialism and Militarism of 5 March 1946.[42] Article 7, paragraph II, section 8 of this law specifically cited them as a major offender by having been an activist if they had acted as a provocateur, agent, or informer who had brought about or tried to bring about the institution of proceedings to the disadvantage of another because of their race, religion, political opposition against National Socialism, or contraventions against National Socialist regulations.[43]

These provisions were reproduced in Control Council Directive No. 38 of 12 October 1946 in Part II, Article II, section 9, which defined a major offender as someone who had actively cooperated with the Gestapo, the SD, the SS, or a similar organization by denouncing an enemy of the National Socialist regime, or who had contributed to their persecution out of self interest or profit seeking. Article III, paragraph II, section 8 added the definition of an activist by reproducing the terms found in Article 7, paragraph II, section 8 of the Liberation Law.[44] Legislation in the US occupation zone thus did not grant the German courts jurisdiction in denunciation cases, but informers could face legal sanction in certain cases by being judged by the denazification tribunals that were staffed by laypeople, rather than being heard in criminal law courts that were subject to the jurisdiction of the laws of the Allied Council, the American military government, and the German Criminal Code.

Since the German courts in the American occupation zone were not granted the jurisdiction to apply Control Council Law No. 10, the adjudication of denunciation cases could only follow the provisions Law for Liberation from National Socialism and Militarism that was enacted in each *Land*.[45] However, sanctions that could be imposed according to its provisions could not be considered or defined as criminal sentences in comparison to those that could be passed by a criminal court, as this was not a criminal law.[46] It merely provided a means for imposing sanctions in denunciation cases that at least spared the ordinary courts from being concerned with what could be considered a political matter.[47] There was still the general demand that denunciation cases should be dealt with as criminal actions in view of the consequences that had been brought about for the denounced, and the Minister of Justice of Hesse continued to express interest in drafting a law to prosecute informers, citing the shortcomings of this law for serving this purpose. The problem was that it was not possible to use German criminal law to adjudicate cases of true denunciations that had worked in favor of the National Socialist regime which consequently led to unjustifiable imprisonment, assault, or death. Therefore, this gap needed to be redressed with a new criminal law to serve this purpose of prosecuting indirect perpetrators,[48] and therefore dealing with crimes that had not been previously foreseen by legislators in the past who could not have foreseen the unconventional circumstances in which the denunciation of others would become known as crimes against humanity.

It necessarily followed that such a law would have a retroactive nature. Since the German courts in the French, British, and Soviet occupation zones had been granted authorization to administer Control Council Law No. 10, the US military government was again asked to likewise consider granting the ordinary German courts in the American occupation zone the power to prosecute informers according to the provisions of this law in the interest of legal uniformity. Although Article 5, section 9 and Article 7, part II, section 8 of the Law for Liberation offered the possibility of classifying informers as major offenders or offenders thereby allowing the imposition of the appropriate sentences on them, the measures that could be taken against them as could be derived from Article 22 of the this law, which merely stated that criminal proceedings could be instituted against them without there being a legal base for that purpose.[49] The requirement for imposing the appropriate sentences could thus be subject to a wide interpretation at the discretion of the denazification tribunals staffed by lay jurors without sufficiently accurate guidelines for suitably redressing such crimes.

The differences between administering retribution against activities supporting the National Socialist regime and prosecuting crimes against humanity came to the fore in a trial of three notorious local Gestapo informers at the Frankfurt-am-Main regional court. The Hesse *Spruchkammer* had sentenced them to ten years' imprisonment with hard labor for having inflicted bodily harm to innumerable victims who had been investigated by the Gestapo and persecuted for their so-called crimes. The German authorities used this decision to once again put forward their case for the German courts being authorized to adjudicate these cases under the provisions of Control

Council Law No. 10, while expressing their dissatisfaction with not yet being empowered with the ability to prosecute informers when their denunciations did not consist of false statements and therefore did not constitute criminal offenses under German law. The German authorities deplored the fact that they could not comply with requests from the British, French, and Soviet zones to prosecute informers, while being concerned about the appearance that they lacked ardor in redressing National Socialist crimes. The German population also could not understand why authorization had not been granted for prosecuting informers.[50]

The Legal Division of the Office of Military Government for Hesse was in favor of the local German courts being granted this authorization while the policy of the Legal Division for the Office of Military Government for Germany was for the denazification tribunals to deal with such cases. They argued that these tribunals were not instruments of criminal justice, which meant that they could not fulfill the same functions of ordinary law courts. The population also did not consider these tribunals to be adequate for the administering of criminal justice, and they were not satisfied with the sentences passed by a *Spruchkammer* on individuals they had considered to be "obedient and willing tools of Nazi terrorism."[51] The Legal Division of the local military government remained obliged to withhold any authorization from the courts in Hesse to adjudicate cases under the provisions of Control Council Law No. 10 in keeping with military government policy, but they continued to recommend that such cases be prosecuted in the manner that been put forward by the Minister of Justice for Hesse, and which was put into practice through Ordinance No. 47 in the British occupation zone.[52] The widest possible extent of criminal sanctions was thus called for in such cases with them being considered criminal rather than political offenses. The local occupation authorities, the German jurists, and the local population considered the assessment and punishment of these offenses based on the extent of political subservience to the National Socialist regime as defined by an administrative authority composed of lay jurors operating in the political context of the denazification program to be less significant than them being subject to a formal judicial process that would evaluate the criminal nature of such offenses.

The American military government had stated that cases involving informer denunciations could be tried by German courts if the case revealed *prima facie* malicious intent by the informer, and if the person against whom it was directed incurred "grave disadvantages.[53] In practice, the military government authorities disapproved of overburdening the courts with minor cases that did not involve principles of public interest or injustice. It therefore ruled that the German courts would not be authorized to deal with denunciation cases under any circumstances until appropriate legislation had been enacted, since the individual courts would otherwise have to handle such a wide array of different cases that justice itself could have been jeopardized.[54]

Another denunciation case as a crime against humanity was judged by a local denazification tribunal in Hesse in the summer of 1947,[55] although the public prosecutor at the Limburg-an-der-Lahn regional court had considered it to be a case of greater significance which should have been tried as a crime against humanity[56] as it was a violation of Control Council Law No. 10. The defendant, hereafter cited as J.G., had worked as a masseuse in Wetlar for years. She had gained the trust of several families, and had exploited this advantage to spy for the Gestapo. At the end of 1943, she denounced a municipal civil servant, hereafter cited as H., for making defeatist remarks about the National Socialist regime.[57] While having coffee in someone's home, H. remarked that the NSDAP itself knew that the war was being lost. He was subsequently arrested by the Gestapo and investigations were instituted by the Frankfurt Special Court. The proceedings were only closed due to lack of evidence after he had been imprisoned for six months.[58] Among other claims and facts that led to his arrest was the defeatist remark that he had made in her presence, her claim that he had influenced others in his role in the Catholic resistance movement, and that he had taken measures to protect five under-aged Jewish children. Although H. sought to offer possible mitigating circumstances in J. G.'s favor, he also described her as remaining incorrigibly and unscrupulously bent on exacting revenge against her alleged enemies, stating that she characterized a textbook example of someone who would denounce another for malicious purposes.[59]

In another example of her behavior, it was revealed that she had contacted the Gestapo about a Jewish woman, hereafter cited as P., who planned to escape to Switzerland in 1943 to flee from National Socialist persecution. She and her husband had entrusted her with keeping this attempt secret, but they were arrested thereafter and imprisoned for a month. Following being in custody while she was under investigation, P. was later taken to Ravensbrück concentration camp and was never heard from again. Before she was arrested, P. had entrusted to J.G. a rhinestone necklace, a Leica camera, and 1000 RM for her to take to her husband, but instead she kept these goods and cash for herself, claiming that P. had given them to her. Witnesses refuted this claim.[60]

At the same time, the defendant also denounced the local criminal secretary who knew about this escape attempt and hoped and prayed that it would be successful. Driven to despair about being unable to endure the exertions and suffering in Gestapo custody, he chose to shoot himself instead. During the same time, she denounced the chief supervisor of the Gestapo prison in

Frankfurt, hereafter cited as B., to the Gestapo for taking a letter from P. to her husband in Wetzlar. B. was imprisoned as a result of J. G.'s complicity.[61] In another case, she had remarked that she had also denounced another individual who had been arrested by the Gestapo. J.G. had told the Gestapo about how this woman had sent a lice comb to a former fellow inmate from a fake address after she had been released. This matter was then subjected to a Gestapo investigation.

Although the public prosecutor had recognized the criminal significance of the defendant's actions as constituting crimes against humanity, the German courts could only judge crimes against humanity with the expressed prior authorization of the zonal military government,[62] and this case was otherwise only subject to prosecution to the extent that codified German criminal law would make this possible. The Ministry of Justice stated that it was not possible for this case to be judged within the jurisdiction of a criminal court, since the local office of the US military government had hitherto not issued their approval for the German courts to judge crimes against humanity on the basis of Control Council Law No. 10. Therefore, any potential bill of indictment to work toward a conviction could only cite the provisions stipulated in the Criminal Code.[63] Barring this possibility, and the unlikely possibility at this time that the local military government would grant their authorization to allow a German court to administer Control Council Law No. 10, proceedings would have to be suspended.[64]

This case was heard at the Wetzlar county court on 24 November 1947 as a crime against humanity as perpetrated by a false accusation and misappropriation of goods, and resulted in an acquittal.[65] The defendant cited Article 164 of the criminal code in her defense, saying that H. had in fact made a defeatist remark and that she was justified in denouncing him to the Gestapo. Although it was determined J. G. had denounced H., she could not be prosecuted according to this law since it was also determined that what was said was truthful, and she had not acted against her conscience as expressly cited in this law. She was also acquitted of the second charge due to insufficient evidence.[66] The public prosecutor's attempt to bring this judgment to the appeal court was likewise rejected[67] in favor of the earlier judgment. Unlike in the other occupation zones, such denunciations that resulted in grave disadvantages for the victims could not be prosecuted, as the German courts had not been empowered to do so by the US military government. The provisions contained in the Criminal code that could have been used as a basis of prosecution in these cases were in themselves insufficient with regard to properly dealing with them.

A case in which judgment was pronounced at the Limburg regional court on 2 December 1947 demonstrated how a German court in the American zone attempted to prosecute a war crime that encompassed a case of denunciation, and also how the scope of its jurisdiction did not allow it to prosecute this type of case as a war crime in spite of the evidence that was presented. Two days before the capitulation of Wetzlar to American troops on 29 March 1945, one of the defendants, hereafter cited as K., was a noncommissioned officer in a flak battery there, who apprehended a local elderly civilian, hereafter cited as Sa., who had affixed a piece of cardboard on the door of his house with the words: "Protect my home. We are not Nazis. We welcome the liberators"[68] and brought him and this sign to the NSDAP *Kreisleiter*, hereafter cited as H.[69]

A witness hereafter cited as Da., who spoke to K. as he was taking Sa. and the cardboard sign to the local command post, tried to dissuade him from taking him to the military authorities, admonishing K. to let Sa. go free, telling him to give him a kick in the backside and spare an older man from being hanged or shot. K. refused to listen, saying that he was a soldier who had stuck his neck out for six years and had to bring a traitor to the local commanding general. The commanders of the military authorities were not interested in dealing with a political matter, and told K. to take Sa. to H., the local *Kreisleiter*. He was not able to find him since he had earlier left Wetzlar, so he then took him to the police officials back at the command post and told them: "We have stuck our necks out for such bastards for six years!"[70]

Sa. stood with the police officials outside the command post while. K. went to find the leading police officer and gave him the sign that Sa. had written, and demanded that he be arrested. This police officer, hereafter cited as So., declined to make the arrest for what he considered to be an inconsequential matter, since the enemy was at the city gates and Sa. had obviously acted out of fear. Besides, the police prison was subject to bombardment. He therefore declined to take further action. K. then went out to look for the *Kreisleiter* again and found him at a "Brown House," where he took Sa. and told H. about the incident, whereupon H. thanked him for doing so and asked him to bring in other "such elements."[71] H. was also the *Kreisvolkssturmführer* in Wetzlar and called the *Gauleitung* in Romrod/Oberhessen, which conveyed the order of the summary court for Hessen-Nassau for six members of the local *Volkssturm* to execute Sa. He was publicly hanged as a traitor from a tree in the city marketplace with the sign around his neck to set an example of deterrence[72] against further such "defeatism" amid the local population. H. was tried for murder, while K. and seven other defendants who hanged Sa. were tried for aiding and abetting manslaughter.[73]

K. had hitherto been classified as a major offender by a denazification *Spruchkammer* in Wetzlar on 11 August 1947 and was sentenced to six years in a labor camp. He had appealed this decision, which remained undecided at this time. The present jury court proceedings heard the case as a criminal matter regarding Sa.'s murder. Rather than letting Sa. go following an admonition by a bystander to do so and a police officer's unwillingness to taking action in the matter, K. willingly took him to H. as the local political authority at the time and thus expected and approved of H. having Sa. killed. He therefore stood accused of aiding and abetting manslaughter for having made this possible by reporting Sa. and bringing him to the local military commander, and then to H. rather than choosing to let him go. In all probability, the consequences for Sa. would have been different had K. done so.[74] The facts of the case showed how he stubbornly refused to do so until it appeared certain to him that Sa. would summarily be dealt with, while the other authorities would not take responsibility for taking political action when it appeared that the war and the regime was nearly over for them.

K. stated in his defense that he had intended that Sa. be punished for being a traitor, which, from his point of view, was justifiable since he had risked his life in the fighting for six years. He considered himself obliged to report him to the authorities since he was ordered to do so by a superior officer, and therefore claimed that he had to do this as he was acting under orders. In the view of the court, whether two superior officers or K. himself had arrested Sa., as was testified by a witness in the earlier *Spruchkammer* proceedings, was irrelevant. The fact remained that he had intended to have Sa. punished, while being fully aware of, and having approved of the possibility of this leading to an indiscriminate killing.[75]

He had long known from his experience in the German Labor Service (RAD), then in the navy, and later in the army how traitors and defeatists were threatened with severe punishments. He therefore knew that the sign that Sa. had written would be considered an example of treason and undermining the war effort, and was further expressly reminded of the consequences by Da., further to him calling Sa. a traitor that he had to report. Moreover, everyone in Wetzlar knew that H. was capable of doing this as he was a radical National Socialist. K. therefore could expect that H. would treat Sa. in an arbitrary way, without any court proceedings, and have him killed.[76]

It was argued that it had been unnecessary for him in fulfilling his duty as a soldier to apprehend an older civilian, and it also noted that he would not have suffered any adverse consequences had he not done so, especially in contrast to his prior knowledge of what would happen to Sa. In spite of the evidence that indicated his motive for having Sa. killed, the jury court did not have the authority to scrutinize his conduct as a crime against humanity according to Article II section 1c of Control Council Law No. 10. German courts in the American occupation zone were not granted the jurisdiction in judging such crimes as defined in Article III, section 1, part 2 of this law, and as a result K. was acquitted. Since a moral and political appraisal of the facts of this case could not be carried out by a criminal court, this matter remained for a *Spruchkammer* to take into consideration[77] as it was the only way for the German authorities to impose retribution for an indirect perpetration of a crime against humanity.

This decision conformed to the policy of the American military government during this time, which required that the denazification tribunals rather than the German administration of justice was to deal with these types of offenses[78] since they had not been authorized to apply Control Council Law No. 10. H. was convicted of manslaughter on the basis of Article 212 of the German criminal code, while the other remaining defendants were acquitted.[79] Whereas the legal restrictions imposed by the American occupation authorities thus prevented cases of denunciation to be tried, the possibility of imposing justice in this case fell to the denazification tribunals that were governed by separate legislation that made sanctions possible in such cases.

Another similar case took place a few months later. A director of the *Reichsbahn* (national railway), hereafter cited as Z., had said in August 1943 that the *Führer,* Göring, and Goebbels ought to be chopped into pieces for having brought disaster on the country, and that he would help to do it himself. Two informers, hereafter cited as E. M. and E. L., forwarded these remarks to the Gestapo in Frankfurt-am-Main, with the expectation that he would at least face the consequence of being imprisoned in a concentration camp. He was consequently tried by the People's Court for undermining the war effort and sentenced to death on 5 January 1944 and was later executed on 6 March 1944.[80]

His widow later instituted proceedings in early 1946, but they were stayed since the defendants could not be charged with making a false accusation, or charged under criminal law for their acts. This matter was therefore to be judged by a denazification tribunal in accordance with the terms of the Law for Liberation from National Socialism and Militarism.[81] The denazification tribunal in Frankfurt-am-Main classified both defendants as major offenders in its judgment on 10 March 1947 for having denounced an opponent of National Socialism, and for causing his arrest and subsequent death. Their actions were classified as a crime against humanity as they had been conscious of the consequences of their actions during that time, when it was common knowledge that such truthful denunciations would result in imprisonment in a concentration camp or a death sentence. E. M. was thereby sentenced to six years' and E. L. to four years' imprisonment in a labor camp.[82] While these sanctions were imposed for the crime of indirectly perpetrating manslaughter, it had remained for the lay jurors to make this decision due to the shortcomings in criminal law for prosecuting such crimes of a political nature.

Although cases of denunciations conveying accurate information did not violate any specific provision of the Criminal code and Control Council Law No. 10, the regional court in Hesse set a precedent for such cases to be tried under civil law. That court ruled that an individual who had denounced another for a political offense during the National Socialist regime had to have known about the possibility that the matter would be heard in an arbitrary manner by an ordinary law court, or possibly by the Gestapo. Therefore, a denunciation to a public authority containing only accurate information which could not have been considered contrary to good morals under the conditions that had been prevalent under the National Socialist regime, could be considered as such under a government of law. The regional court in Hesse therefore awarded damages to the plaintiff on the basis of paragraph 826 of the civil code, concerning "Intentional Damage Contrary to Public Policy"; which stated that a person who, in a manner contrary to public policy, intentionally inflicts damage on another person is liable to the other person and has to make compensation for the damage. The *Land* military government's legal division agreed that the action of such informers could be seen as constituting tort, even if they were not criminal offenses.[83]

The US military government had removed restrictions on the jurisdiction of German courts to adjudicate alleged crimes against humanity on 15 October 1946, insofar as it was an offense against German law and had been committed by Germans against Germans or individuals who were not United Nations nationals. However, these alleged crimes against humanity were also necessarily required to be offenses against codified German law which could not be applied to certain types of persecution or denunciation cases. As a result, the German ordinary courts were not authorized to adjudicate such cases since American military government policy remained for the denazification tribunals to deal with these types of offenses.[84] Further deliberations on extending the jurisdiction of the German courts in the US zone to adjudicate cases under Control Council Law No. 10 continued.

The failure to grant the German courts the jurisdiction over cases of crimes against humanity in accordance with Control Council Law No. 10 meant that these types of cases could only be adjudicated under the provisions of German criminal law, which meant that there was therefore a justifiable reason to assume that a large number of individuals would evade prosecution, while the military government war crimes tribunals and the quasi-judicial denazification tribunals were insufficient for the adjudication of cases of crimes against humanity. The Justice Ministers of the US occupation zone at the request of their respective *Land* governments met on 13 February 1948 to further deliberate on the question of German courts applying Control Council Law No. 10. In contrast to their earlier requests, it was decided that, in principle, a general and unlimited assumption of this law would not be advocated because of the experiences in its application in the other zones. The reason for this recommendation was not only the difficult and precarious legal and political principles that were involved in the application of this law, but also the contravention against the democratic principle of *nulla poene, nulla crimen sine lege*. In the example of cases of denunciations, this law was only to be applied in cases that resulted in death as a consequence of the denunciation. If the *Land* governments agreed to recommend to the military government that German courts should be granted the authority to apply this law with certain limitations, it would be recommended that the Justice Minister would have to decide which individual cases would be brought to trial.[85]

In view of the anticipated economic and administrative fusion of the American and British occupation zones, it was seen as necessary to resolve the differences in the two zones regarding the application of Control Council Law No. 10. Otherwise, the judges in the German courts in the British zone would fall into a very precarious and most unenviable situation in comparison with their colleagues in the American zone, because the British military government remained committed to maintaining the principles set forth in Control Council Law No. 10 and Ordinance No. 47. Hence, the British military government legal division recommended urging the American military government to assume the guidelines that had been set forth in Ordinance No. 47 in their zone, regardless of the Justice Ministers' views, by having it enacted as bizonal legislation with the hope that most types of crimes against humanity could be prosecuted under German law. However, there was still the problem that German law was not as extensive as Control Council Law No. 10,[86] and therefore there remained the same shortcomings therein concerning how the prosecution of denunciation cases could be brought about.

During a meeting of the *Länderrat* in April 1948, the *Land* governments of Bavaria and Württemberg-Baden, Hesse, and Bremen continued to express interest in the idea that the German courts in the US occupation should be granted the authority to apply Control Council Law No. 10, and representatives of the OMGUS Administration of Justice Branch agreed that this course of action would be advantageous before the American war crimes tribunals and the Office of the Chief Counsel for War Crimes (OCCWC) in Nuremberg would be dissolved. The British military government legal branch thus expected that the US military government could be persuaded to apply the principles of the British military government Ordinance No. 47.[87]

Considerations about whether to grant the German courts in the American occupation zone the power to adjudicate all forms of cases as defined by Control Council Law No. 10 continued into late 1948, when discussions took place between the British and the American occupation authorities concerning the coordination of legislation in the two zones. The British emphasized in April 1948 that they did not have any intention to rescind Ordinance No. 47 that authorized the German courts in their zone to apply Control Council Law No. 10, and wanted the American occupation authorities to empower the German courts in the American zone to do the same. If unable to do the same, they wanted them to at least find a compromise solution, in order to overcome the prevailing contrasting legal situation in the two zones. The American occupation authorities continued to argue against following the British example, citing the uncertainty among German jurists as to whether Control Council Law No. 10 violated the *ex post facto* principle.[88] As a result, the American occupation authorities chose not to risk the potential difficulties that could be encountered in the German courts in spite of the jurisprudential arguments and official support in favor of adjudicating such cases, and the successful experiences of the German courts prosecuting denunciation cases in the British, French, and Soviet occupation zones.

The US military government authorities also argued that empowering the German courts in the US zone with the authority to apply Control Council Law No. 10 was unnecessary as well as impractical. The US military government legal division also argued that that most criminal offenses that qualified as crimes against humanity under Control Council Law No. 10 were also punishable offenses under the German criminal code, and were thus being adjudicated by German courts in the US zone that would otherwise have been tried under occupation law. On the other hand, there were certain offenses that could be adjudicated under Control Council Law No. 10, but not under German law. This gap between German and occupation law was especially prevalent in denunciation cases. In such cases, the German courts had convicted the defendants after a denunciation had taken place, but often found it impossible to justify the conviction in accordance with the provisions of the German Criminal Code. While being aware of these serious shortcomings present in codified German law, especially with regard to denunciation cases, it was believed that justifiable and sufficient retribution could be accomplished through the denazification procedures.[89]

Experts in jurisprudence had put forward arguments in legal journals that were in favor of prosecuting informers as having committed crimes against humanity, and therefore had to be addressed in the law courts in spite of the uncertainties among German jurists and the shortcomings of codified German law. There were also many successful experiences in the other zones in prosecuting such cases, such as the landmark judgment against Helene Schwärzel that contributed to lifting doubts about Control Council 10 violating the *ex post facto* principle in practice.[90] A private individual in Bavaria, whose sister had been killed shortly following a denunciation and who had doubts that the local denazification tribunal would be sufficiently severe in its sentencing, appealed to the American military government to allow the German courts to administer Control Council Law No. 10, stating that there had been numerous similar such cases that needed to be addressed.[91] Nevertheless, jurisdiction over denunciation cases remained withheld from the German law courts in the US zone for the duration of the military occupation for what they considered practical reasons. Sentencing was thus left to be done by lay jurors in the denazification tribunals. Those who expected to see justice served could hope that the perpetrators would be judged adequately, as would have been the case if such cases were tried by ordinary law courts. Nevertheless, the task that was assigned to these tribunals by the occupation authorities was to administer the immediate postwar task of political cleansing, and the sentences they were empowered to impose on the convicted did not have the same status of judgments that could have been passed by the courts of the conventional administration of justice.

The jurisdiction for prosecuting crimes against humanity in the US zone was limited to the extent that the US occupation authorities allowed the reconstituted German courts to administer the law in such cases as in the other occupation zones, but they were not granted the jurisdiction to adjudicate these denunciation cases as crimes against humanity since the legislation that had been drafted for this purpose was overruled by the American occupation authorities. They were also not granted the jurisdiction to do so in accordance with the provisions of Control Council Law No. 10, since it was deemed impractical for such cases to be adjudicated by German courts. They argued that the potential problem of jurists' reactions to a retroactive application of the law could have increased the problem of supervision and control of the courts by the American military government. Meanwhile, these additional types of cases could have added to the overburdening of the understaffed courts whose work was already delayed by the shortage of judicial personnel.[92] The American occupation authorities therefore disavowed the underlying principle that indirect perpetration of crimes against humanity should be prosecuted in the law courts, deciding not to risk entrusting jurists with this task. It was expected that the denazification tribunals could judge these cases more effectively and impose punishments without being hindered by any jurisprudential hairsplitting regarding the legitimacy of retroactive legislation.

Cases of indirect perpetration of crimes resulting from truthful denunciation that related to aiding and abetting murder, manslaughter, or unlawful imprisonment as defined in German law could be prosecuted accordingly, when it could be established that the conduct of the defendant had demonstrated hostile intentions by filing a report against another. In one such case reviewed at the

Bamberg supreme regional court, a woman who had turned to other men while her husband was serving in the army since 1940, and who harbored the intention of becoming separated from him, filed a report against him in October 1944 with the local *Ortsgruppenleiter*, stating that he had made disparaging remarks about Hitler and other NSDAP leaders, and that he had expressed his regret that they had not "gone to the devil on 20 July 1944."[93] She stated in this report that in her opinion someone who could say such things is no longer worthy of being among other people. This report later led to military court proceedings, in which she appeared as the leading witness for the prosecution. The death sentence was passed against him, but this was not executed since he was returned to the front after a week's imprisonment.

This court passed judgment on 27 July 1949 and it stated that in view of the circumstances, the defendant's intention was to cause the unlawful imprisonment of her husband, which was irreconcilable with the rule of law.[94] She had indirectly fulfilled the first condition for the arrest and imprisonment of her husband, and had initiated his prosecution on the basis of National Socialist legislation that was obviously contrary to natural law, and threatened him with the possibility of receiving an excessively harsh sentence. She was also not under any obligation to file a report against him, while having intentionally acted against him with the prior knowledge of the consequences that he would face. Her actions were therefore interpreted as having caused unlawful imprisonment in accordance with § 239 of the German criminal code.[95] This case was later reviewed at the Bamberg supreme regional court after the regional court rejected the public prosecutor's justification for her being charged with unlawful imprisonment, and she was acquitted.[96]

The courts in the American zone had been forbidden from adjudicating denunciation cases, which had been left to the denazification tribunals operating under the Law for Liberation, without specific directives on how denunciation cases were to be adjudicated. While jurisdiction over denunciation cases was not established in the American occupation zone, which prevented such cases from being adjudicated, the Bamberg supreme regional court's interpretation of the facts of this case set a new precedent in which German criminal law could be applied in such cases hereafter. These cases involved criminal intentions and actions, and could be judged accordingly when the facts of these cases were not considered to be solely political offenses.

There were twenty cases of denunciations in Hesse alone that led to the death of the victims, of which nine individuals were judged and sentenced to death by the People's Court or military courts, and seven died in concentration camps, with three others being killed by the Gestapo and one being killed in a "euthanasia institution." Out of nine suspected denunciation cases, only one was sentenced for a denunciation that led to the execution of the victims.

This case was only adjudicated after the end of the military occupation. Only two convictions were imposed, while five other cases resulted in acquittals, and one of the proceedings ended due to the defendant's death. Most of the fifty-nine proceedings initiated by state prosecutors in Hesse involving a hundred and thirteen accused had to be stayed due to legal reasons. Eight suspects died before proceedings could be initiated, and in two cases, proceedings were stayed as a result of the amnesty. Although informers who had denounced others were not convicted in law courts, many were sentenced to imprisonment in labor camps as retribution for their actions on the basis of the Law for the Liberation from National Socialism and Militarism,[97] which served as a compromise solution in averting the potential legal difficulties with extending the jurisdiction of Control Council Law No. 10 to the German judicial organization in the American occupation zone. Denazification tribunals thus served as an alternative to the conventional administration of justice that not only classified individuals' political conduct during the National Socialist regime and imposed sanctions for this purpose, but also imposed criminal sanctions outside the penal system for politically motivated crimes that could not be adjudicated by the ordinary law courts that were not granted jurisdiction over such cases.

Informers who were guilty of having committed crimes against humanity could be called to account for their actions insofar as it could be proven that they could have foreseen the consequences of their actions. However, the legal situation in the American occupation zone prevented their prosecution, which would be mostly delayed until after the end of the military occupation when denunciation cases could be uniformly tried under German law in accordance with the provisions of the German criminal code throughout the Federal Republic of Germany. In comparison to the French and British occupation zones, those who had committed this type of crime against humanity in the American zone were not subject to prosecution in criminal courts, but they could face retribution for the consequences they had brought about from the denazification tribunals. The question of whether lay jurors or jurists were better suited to hear such cases remained open, subject to the errors in judgment, the availability of existing evidence, and the problems concerning how legislation could be implemented under German criminal law. The earlier limitation on legal jurisdiction was lifted along with the military occupation regime, and denunciation cases became subject to prosecution throughout the newly-established Federal Republic of Germany. Hence, the courts in Baden-Württemberg, Hesse, Bavaria, and Bremen could begin adjudicating such cases after the end of the military occupation and when the application of legislation concerning the prosecution of crimes against humanity later became uniform in the Federal Republic of Germany.

Chapter 3

The French Occupation Zone: Legislation and Practice

Discussions concerning the application of Control Council Law No. 10 by the German courts in the French occupation zone took place soon after this law was enacted. The German authorities took an interest in the application of this law while debating how it could be administered in conformity with the already existing German law. In early 1946, the French military government in Germany expressed interest in publicizing the important and unprecedented judgments of German courts concerning National Socialist crimes[1] that had not been hitherto subject to prosecution due to the political conditions of the time, and which were thereafter to be considered criminal actions under the provisions of the German criminal code. The reconstituted German administration of justice also emphasized the need for such cases to be brought to trial as a matter of priority.[2] The military government soon resolved thereafter to authorize the German courts in the French occupation zone to prosecute crimes perpetrated during the National Socialist regime.[3] It was decreed that any form of crime cited in Article II, section 5 of Control Council Law No. 10 perpetrated between 30 January 1933 and 1 July 1945 would not be subject to any statute of limitations or any measures for immunity from prosecution, or any reprieve or amnesty enacted under the National Socialist regime.[4] The German courts were formally empowered with administering the provisions of Control Council Law No. 10 under the official authorization of a French military government directive issued on 2 May 1946. They were authorized to adjudicate cases that involved acts perpetrated against other German nationals or stateless persons[5] and there were no other restrictions placed on the extent of the German courts' jurisdiction. This left the application of this law open to interpretation, with violations of German law serving as a basis for determining how such cases could be prosecuted until further instructions from the military government or actual practice could provide the courts with a clearer interpretation of this law.

The military government's investing of the German courts with the jurisdiction and the legal and moral authority to deal with crimes against humanity committed by Germans against other Germans was part of the process by which they were to take responsibility for beginning to deal with the past, through the use of the retroactive legislation that would make this possible. The application of this law encompassed cases of denunciations that led to inhumane consequences for those who were denounced by the informers, which were to be adjudicated under the broad definition of crimes against humanity. Although there proved to be a widespread reluctance to prosecute crimes of a political nature, the German jurists in the French occupation zone thereafter formulated arguments that put Control Council Law No. 10 into practice in prosecuting cases of denunciations, on the basis that these cases were to be considered crimes against humanity.

The French military government was forced to issue clarification about these particular types of cases when they were informed that their prosecution could potentially come into conflict with certain provisions of German law. Articles 164 and 165 of the German criminal code stated that only false denunciations were subject to prosecution, so the military government decreed that the denunciations that resulted in harmful consequences for the victims were also to be prosecuted, using Article 239 of the German criminal code on false imprisonment. The military government then gave its approval for public prosecutors to bring such cases to trial.[6] The prosecution of such cases as crimes against humanity as broadly defined in Control Council Law No. 10 was approved in view of the consequences that acts of denunciations had caused during the National Socialist regime. This meant that the German courts would hereby prosecute cases of denunciations ensuing from the National Socialist regime whenever the denounced parties had themselves incurred punishments[7] for their actions that had been reported to the authorities of the time.

Political informers would be subject to prosecution in accordance with the consequences of their actions as instigators, co-perpetrators, or accomplices in such crimes and would be called to account for their actions accordingly, as they could be defined by the provisions of German criminal law. When a political report had caused another's death, informers would be subject to prosecution on the charge of aiding and abetting murder. In cases resulting in imprisonment, those accused of making political reports would be subject to prosecution for having caused unlawful imprisonment. In cases that resulted in the denounced being assaulted by the Gestapo, they would be accused of causing bodily injury. In cases in which the denounced had been forced to make financial contributions to the NSV, the informers would be accused of coercion. Whether the proceedings would be considered irrelevant in view of the consequences that were incurred, such as death, false imprisonment, dismissal from office, or bodily injury, these consequences would be taken into consideration in the judgments to be passed on the informers.[8]

The local government of Hessen-Pflaz announced its intentions to prosecute political denunciations in a press release on 21 May 1946. It was reported that the adjudication of such cases had been temporarily problematic due to the absence of a legal basis that would make this possible. A solution was provided through the enactment of Control Council Law No. 10, which opened the way for the adjudication of actions that were not subject to prosecution during the National Socialist regime, although they indisputably violated the principles of humanity and justice. At this time, there were 120 such cases being processed, with five approved and two completed. The general prosecutor for Hessen-Pflalz pledged that all such cases would be prosecuted, depending on the reports that would be instituted and evidence then presented to the public prosecutors, so that these instigators, co-perpetrators, or accomplices of principal offenders in injustices perpetrated through National Socialist injustice would be dealt with and punished.[9] The prosecution of these cases could be initiated either by the prosecutor receiving evidence of such a crime and then instituting a bill of indictment to the respective occupation authority for their approval, or the prosecutor could forward the case directly to the occupation power for prosecution.[10] The decision to prosecute these cases would depend on the prosecutor being able to locate the necessary documents that would provide evidence for the case, but they would also act on reports that were forwarded to them anonymously. This evidence would then be assessed to see if judgments made in these cases had been made on racial or religious grounds, and then forwarded to the courts for prosecution as criminal cases; it would also be determined who had denounced another in such cases. This would include cases involving remarks about the end of the war or listening to foreign broadcasts that resulted in heavy sentences, such as imprisonment in a prison or in a concentration camp, or brutality at the hands of the Gestapo, or a death sentence. Informers would have to have had prior knowledge of the severe consequences of their denunciations, thus undoubtedly demonstrating that their malevolent conduct could be considered as constituting a crime against humanity in view of the severe consequences that they had brought about.[11]

The views expressed by the general prosecutor of Hessen-Pfalz confirmed that an interpretation of the provisions of Control Council Law No. 10 made denunciation cases subject to prosecution in the French occupation zone, as was the case in the British and Soviet zones. A very large number of denunciations could definitely be considered crimes against humanity, and Article II, section 1d of Control Council Law No. 10 made German courts responsible for prosecuting crimes perpetrated by Germans against other Germans. The wide range of sentencing cited in Article II, section 3 also allowed the possibility for the appropriate punishments to be imposed in each individual case.[12] The French military government confirmed its approval for the prosecution of political denunciation cases based on the provisions of the German criminal code. In addition, it was also confirmed that the more general provisions of Control Council Law No. 10 could also form the judicial basis in the prosecution of such cases, as in any types of crimes against humanity that emanated from political, racial, or religious grounds.[13] This jurisdiction was extended to the German courts involving only the types of cases as defined by Article III, section 1d, line 2 of Control Council Law No. 10, involving crimes against humanity perpetrated by Germans or stateless persons against Germans and stateless persons, unless the courts of the military government expressed their intentions to prosecute particular cases.[14]

One of the first trials of a case of denunciation as a crime against humanity in the French occupation zone took place soon after the passing of the French military government directive. The case was heard in the Offenburg regional court, which pronounced its sentence on 4 June 1946. The defendant had been held in the custody of the French authorities while under suspicion for crimes against humanity since 20 November 1945, and then later under the custody of Baden-Baden county court from 29 March 1946 while awaiting trial. Another individual had been in French custody from 18 November 1945, and was also later in the custody of the Baden-Baden county court from 29 March 1946. The two accused had been in a pub in January 1944 and heard a rather drunk soldier on furlough make several disparaging remarks about the National Socialist regime while they were talking about the war. They heard him say that the war was going to be lost and that the German troops in the east were constantly in retreat after the regime had boasted that the Russian army had been shattered. He also mentioned that Göring had bellowed that no foreign aircraft would cross Germany's borders, but that the present situation was different; he also commented how Goebbels used to have a big mouth, but was not to be heard from anymore. Several weeks later, the first of the defendants, who had been a member of the NSDAP, said at a party meeting that he had heard the soldier say "stupid things" that could have cost him his head.[15] This indiscretion on the part of the first accused would prove to have dire consequences.

A few weeks later, a police officer and a member of the Gestapo aggressively pressed the defendants for details about what the patron had said.

After they hesitated to do so, claiming that it had been a long time ago, the two civil servants threatened them with arrest and even with execution. The first of the two accused simply said he had heard the soldier make defeatist remarks about the eastern front while knowing that making such statements could cost him his head. The second accused confirmed these statements, while it was assumed by the court that the first had given additional testimony against him. The soldier was arrested for the crime of subverting the army on the basis of the statements that the two accused relayed to the authorities. He was thereafter brought before the central military court in Berlin on 7 July 1944 that passed the death sentence on him, and he was then executed on 21 August 1944.[16]

The first accused was charged with crimes against humanity in accordance with Article2, section 1c of Allied Control Council Law No. 10 of 20 December 1945 on persecution on the basis of political beliefs. The court ruled that the so-called defeatist remarks that the soldier had made were made within a small circle of people. However, they were later repeated within a larger group of NSDAP members, and therefore it was to be assumed that these remarks would be viewed in a harsher light by the authorities of the regime, who were responsible for dealing with such disparaging remarks. It was therefore decided that the first accused had tacitly approved of the idea that the soldier should be called to account for what he had said, and had therefore caused the military court proceedings to be initiated against him. On the other hand, a light sentence was passed on the grounds that the first accused individual had never been prosecuted, was in good standing in his community, and did not intentionally file a denunciation report.[17] He was therefore sentenced to nine months' imprisonment, counting the six months and two weeks that had already been served. The second accused was acquitted. She had spoken the truth under duress as a witness to the soldier's remarks, without having taken the initiative to forward the soldier's remarks that would have led to grievous consequences. Hence, she was considered not guilty of any intentional act of denunciation.[18]

A landmark legal precedent was set by the Berlin regional court that had sentenced Helene Schwärzel, who had denounced Dr. Karl Gördeler, the former mayor of Leipzig and a leading member of the German resistance to National Socialism, who would have been appointed the president of Germany had the 20 July 1944 conspiracy succeeded in killing Hitler and instituting a regime change. She had received a one million Reichsmark reward for having identified him on 12 August 1944 while he was in her workplace at the Elbing air base and then notifying the local military authority, who in turn had him immediately placed under arrest. He was sentenced to death for high treason by the People's Court and was subsequently executed on 2 February

1945.[19] This case became one of the highlights of the postwar German administration of justice, not only because of the significance of the victim, but also as a landmark precedent for other cases of denunciations that had inhumane consequences for those who had been denounced.

She was initially brought before the jury at the Berlin regional court on the charge of having committed a crime against humanity through her indirect involvement in murder. On 14 November 1946, this jury court sentenced her to fifteen years' imprisonment for committing a crime against humanity on the grounds of political persecution. Although she did not intend to have a part in his killing, her actions resulted in her being indirectly responsible for his murder.[20]

On 17 May 1947, the Berlin *Kammergericht* (supreme appeal court of the second instance) reviewed its verdict after a further examination of the facts of the case. Control Council Law No. 10 had made crimes against humanity subject to prosecution if they were committed on the basis of political, racial, or religious principles. The facts of such cases and how they were to be prosecuted had hitherto not been established under German law, which meant that these cases were to be seen as constituting a new sphere of criminal law that needed to be clarified. This court maintained its decision that Law No. 10 concerned facts that could not be interpreted and subject to prosecution within the scope of hitherto established German law. This meant that these new types of cases that could be subject to prosecution were to be adjudicated to a much wider extent on a case by case basis, whether or not these actions could be prosecuted in accordance with German criminal law or were committed before Law No. 10 was enacted.[21]

The terms of this Control Council law were to take precedence over hitherto existing German law, and it was necessary for German jurists to overcome their reservations about applying this law and administering justice retroactively, which appeared to contravene the principle of *nullum crimen sine lege*. This was not the case, since Control Council Law No. 10 followed the establishment of the statute of the International Military Tribunal in Nuremberg that had jurisdiction over the major cases of crimes against humanity, war crimes, and crimes against peace. Lesser cases came under the jurisdiction of Law No. 10.[22] Retroactively administered justice would thus be applied solely in these types of cases with a view toward dealing with the past when the rule of law was put back into practice.

The purpose of prohibiting retroactively applied administration of justice is to protect citizens from the arbitrary application of the law by the state, and thereby afford them the protection of the law as a principle of justice by serving the cause of legal security. In the view of this court, the meaning of this principle would be completely misjudged if those who had assisted a criminal regime that had rescinded legal security and had trampled on the rights of humanity were not held responsible for their inhumane actions by citing the rights of humanity in their defense against taking responsibility for their actions after this regime had collapsed. Calling them to account for their actions would serve to restore legal security and consciousness of the law that had been shattered, rather than endanger legal security.[23]

Acts of political persecution committed during the National Socialist regime as described by Law No. 10 were to be punished, even though prosecution of such cases was not admissible under existing German criminal law. The act of denunciation that led to some form of harm to whomever was denounced if they were persecuted by a third party because of their political or religious beliefs or race was to be interpreted as a crime against humanity. For these reasons, the defendant was to be called to account for her actions in bringing about inhumane consequences for Görderler.[24] As in other denunciation cases, the act of delivering another into the hands of indiscriminate and inhumane authority of the National Socialist regime while being aware of its methods, particularly those of the Gestapo, sufficed in itself to be considered a form of political persecution. The consequences of the action outweighed personal or purely political motives, considering that those who served the interests of the regime in this form of action were aware that the consequences of their actions would be inhumane, regardless of whether they were or were not aware that they would be contributing to injustice.[25]

The nature of the action of the defendant in this case constituted a crime in the spirit of Law No. 10 that had been enacted to restore the protection of the law that had been abrogated during the rule of the National Socialist regime. Neither the existing provisions of German law nor the contradiction of the principle of retroactive justice were relevant to the extent that either of them could override the facts of this case as a crime against humanity. The purpose of this law was to call such individuals to account for their actions at a time when their actions would have been determined to be crimes, as if it had been possible to prosecute them at the time of their actions when such actions were not subject to the rule of law.

This verdict was abolished since the jury court did not deal with the question of whether the defendant had acted on political motives in view of the political circumstances of the time. Since it had been commonly known that not conforming to the regime through so-called political reliability along with non-conformity was ruthlessly suppressed, the reporting of another to the authorities of the time for any form of hostility to the regime while being aware of its ruthless and inhumane methods of suppression constituted acting against them on political grounds, regardless of whether the perpetrator had been politically active in any way. Denunciations were especially considered an example of the concept of persecution on political grounds, even if the perpetrator's motives were personal, since they had intended to bring about inhumane consequences as a result of their conscious decisions to act against another[26] by setting the apparatus of political suppression into motion against them.

The case was once again tried by a jury court to clarify whether the defendant's motives could be considered to have been political. On 1 November 1947, the jury court at the Berlin regional court ruled in agreement with the state prosecutor that it was unnecessary to apply Article 211 of the criminal code in this case, since the defendant had not intended to take indirect action in the murder of Gördeler. However, the facts of the case constituted a crime against humanity according to an interpretation of Control Council Law No. 10. These facts precluded the time that this law had come into force, which encompassed crimes that hitherto had not been prosecuted and did not contradict the principle of *nulla peona sine lege*.[27] The purpose of this law was to objectively evaluate actions that would be considered illegal as well as inhumane under normal circumstances in the rule of law, and therefore the jurisdiction of German criminal law would not serve the cause of justice in adjudicating crimes that had taken place during the National Socialist regime.

The objective facts of the case demonstrated that she was responsible for Dr. Gördeler's death by having persecuted him out of political motives as a third party devoted to the authorities of the time. She had known that many of the co-conspirators of the 20 July 1944 bomb plot had hitherto been convicted and executed, and thus was aware of what would happen if he was apprehended. Her intervention in the matter had led to inhumane consequences for the persecuted and this meant that she was subject to prosecution according to Control Council Law No. 10.[28]

Her actions were also considered inhumane in a subjective sense, in addition to her being fully aware of the consequences of her actions. The court also assessed her personality defects as part of the circumstances of the case, in the context of what could be construed to be her motives, and they noted that she was very opinionated and suffered from a craving for admiration. The court found that it was these factors, rather than any political fanaticism or personal hatred, that motivated her to denounced Dr. Gördeler. Even though she did not possess any ideological convictions, her actions were nevertheless subject to prosecution for the resulting inhumane persecution due to political reasons. She had persistently chosen to act by identifying Dr. Gördeler and telling the local military authority not to let him get away. This took place while he was being sought by the authorities, which were known for their violent and repressive methods, during a time of high political tension after the failed assassination attempt on Hitler on 20 July 1944. While she acted on psychological rather than political motives, her actions resulted in serving solely political purposes.[29]

In evaluating the facts of the case, the court did not concede that her craving for admiration and her being opinionated undermined her soundness of mind to any considerable extent, nor did she face the dilemma of having to act under the duress of being in an extreme situation in which she was in personal danger. It was especially unnecessary for her to be so persistent in identifying him and not allowing Dr. Gördeler sufficient time to avoid being arrested after she had identified him. She could have chosen to be quiet about him without putting herself into any real danger. She had thus made it clear that her intention was for him to be arrested.[30]

Further to the psychological evaluation of the motives of the defendant, the court took her personality defects into account. Two experts agreed that she was emotionally unbalanced, slightly immature, and prone to hysteria, and lacked talent and ambition in addition to possessing certain tendencies toward stubbornness and vanity. She was not pleased about the financial reward she had received, she was bitterly sad about Dr. Gördeler's arrest, and she suffered from a fever caused by her emotional problems. Moreover, she had given a complete confession about her actions. Given the facts of the case, the extenuating circumstances in her favor, and the significance of the victim, this court sentenced her to six years' imprisonment and a loss of civil rights for six years, along with the confiscation of all of her property in accordance with Article II, section 3b of Law No. 10.[31]

This verdict came under further examination at the Berlin *Kammergericht* that quashed this verdict concerning the reduced sentence in its judgment on 30 June 1948. This court reprimanded the jury court of the regional court for having violated provisions of the law on court procedures. The jurors were not drawn from a valid list of sufficiently objective jurors, since they had been recommended by political parties. Moreover, a leading judge was excluded without a valid reason.[32]

In addition to the various procedural errors, the verdict was also determined to be flawed in view of the facts of the case that had been established in the verdict pronounced on 17 May 1947. The regional court jury court did not take the matter of inhumane persecution on political grounds into sufficient consideration in the spirit of Control Council Law No. 10. It was to be maintained that the defendant knew why Gördeler was sought by the National Socialist authorities, and that she was aware of its violent and oppressive methods. These facts meant that her lack of interest in politics and not being a member of the NSDAP or any of its affiliated organizations did not undermine the interpretation of her action of delivering a politically persecuted individual over to the authorities as a political action.[33] The fact that she had done so was to be considered as a crime against humanity, and was to be prosecuted as such.

The court maintained that the defendant had acted in an inhumane manner both objectively and subjectively. In an objective sense, it was to be concluded from the manner in which criminal court proceedings against those who were politically persecuted were commonly carried out, especially the proceedings initiated against Gördeler, contravened the principles of humanity. The jury court was in agreement with the earlier judgment of the *Kammergericht* that the defendants in such proceedings were not afforded the protection of the law, and that by being exposed to indiscriminate and inhumane treatment, they were brought to the hangman rather than before a judge.[34]

Moreover, the subjective interpretation of the inhumanity of the actions of the defendant was not dealt with to a sufficient extent. The jury placed too much emphasis on the personal factors of the defendant as additional detail, which should not have distracted them from the facts of the case and the gravity of the crime. They acknowledged the experts' opinions on her feelings of inferiority as a motive for her actions, but argued that this emphasis had the adverse effect of undermining the significance of how those who had taken part in the 20 July assassination attempt had been inhumanely annihilated; this consequence had been common knowledge at the time, and was known to the defendant. She had intentionally acted inhumanely with prior knowledge of the consequences that would surely follow for Görderler. This fact in itself sufficed without further argument that there were no extenuating circumstances that made it necessary to reduce the original sentence.[35] The revised sentence that had been pronounced by the jury court on 1 November 1947 was therefore quashed,[36] thus leaving this infamous defendant to serve the original sentence of fifteen years' imprisonment that had been pronounced earlier.

This landmark case opened the way for the prosecution of informers and calling them to account for their actions. Cases of denunciations were hereafter considered a specific type of case that could be adjudicated retroactively as crimes against humanity, when the intention of their actions could demonstrate that they had prior knowledge of the potentially grave consequences of their actions as defined in Control Council Law No. 10. The enactment of Control Council Law No. 10 was based on moral considerations in view of the crimes that had been committed in the National Socialist regime, which overrode the judicial principle in the rule of law that justice must not be administered retroactively. Those individuals who had taken action in denouncing others to the authorities who would in turn take cruel actions against them were therefore subject to prosecution as indirect perpetrators of crimes against humanity. Subsequent experiences and judgments in the German criminal courts clarified how these cases could be adjudicated, while ultimately remaining subject to the supervision of the French military government authorities.

Although there had been an element of risk in charging the German judicial organization with the task of adjudicating political cases, the French military government had nevertheless considered it to be sufficiently stable following the early implementation of its denazification policies. Supervision of the German administration of justice indicated that that German judges executed their duties conscientiously and effectively.[37] They gradually became proud of their regained independence while appreciating the spirit of justice that the military government expected them to apply[38] in administering German law efficiently without being disposed toward National Socialist ideology,[39] and without any considerations for political, racial, or religious grounds.[40] The French military government noted the German judiciary's sincere efforts to resolve the numerous new jurisprudential problems in a democratic spirit, but there remained the tendency to administer the law according to a strict application of legal positivism in contrast to the so-called dynamic interpretation of the law during the National Socialist regime. This was reinforced by their anxiety over making unpopular judgments in cases of a political nature, which resulted in unquestionably lenient sentences. It was therefore strongly recommended that the independence of judges and public prosecutors was to be reinforced to afford them protection from the polemics of immoderate press reporting.[41] There could have been psychological reasons for the lenient sentencing that ensued from the judiciary's experiences during the National Socialist regime, when sentencing had been excessive and even cruel. Although the reconstituted courts deviated from those earlier practices in reaction to the past, the excessive leniency practically reached crisis proportions, as the sentences were not commensurate to the offenses that were tried.[42] Apart from working with sufficient promptness and imposing judgments that were considered too lenient, the military government recognized that the functioning of the German administration of justice was overall considered satisfactory.[43] However, judicial independence appeared to have been undermined in political cases, in which jurists seemed to give priority to reconciling judgments with public opinion, which in general had a negative influence on the discharge of their duties.[44]

This confidence in the German administration of justice was severely shaken by the judgment rendered on 21 November 1946 at the Offenburg regional court in the case against Heinrich Tillesen for his part in the murder of the former finance minister Matthias Erzberger. This case ended in an acquittal, upholding the amnesty for this crime that had been enacted on 21 March 1933 by contending that he had acted out of "excessive patriotism." This was the first German court verdict that the French military government abrogated. This case was later reviewed at the French military court in Rastatt on 6 January 1947, and then shifted to new proceedings at the Constance regional court where on 28 February 1947, Tillesen was sentenced to fifteen years' imprisonment.[45]

This incident highlighted the extent to which German jurists failed to recognize the spirit of Control Council Law No. 10, and it provoked suspicion in the French military government as to whether the reconstituted German administration of justice was capable of applying the law in cases of a political nature. Their behavior in this case was also seen as a test of the extent of democratic maturity of German jurists. In the view of the French military government, the judiciary remained "prisoners of an outrageous judicial formalism"[46] that demonstrated that the German jurists still remained subject to the concept of legal positivism and were thus "unable to elevate themselves to a vibrant and realistic concept of the law or to serve the ideals of democracy."[47] It was perceived that the German jurists who had administered the law in the spirit of National Socialism using the principles of analogy and so-called healthy popular emotions continued to withdraw behind ingrained textual formalism. This had likewise had the harmful effect of them falling victim to moral and ethical weakness and the passing of lenient sentences against political opponents during the Weimar republic.[48] This attitude of jurists entrenching themselves behind texts and superior jurisdictions was interpreted as them deliberately avoiding taking responsibility and lacking civic courage.[49]

The French military government assumed that the Tillesen case demonstrated a psychological representation of the German judiciary which had lost its sense of responsibility and its appreciation of the value of the rights of humanity after many years of National Socialist oppression. Independent thought was further hindered by their tendency to put faith in the literal interpretation of texts following the notion of formal legal positivism, which had earlier served to overcome their scruples of conscience during the National Socialist regime, while being expected to apply cruel and iniquitous legislation. Judges hereafter dealt with cases of a political nature with a degree of apprehension,[50] but in view of subsequent cases that involved political motives, it appeared that this case proved to be an exceptional anomaly among the notoriously conservative jurists.

There were several problems associated with Control Council Law No. 10 that made it very difficult for the German courts to use it for adjudicating cases concerning crimes against humanity. It lacked a sufficiently precise definition for what constituted crimes against humanity, as it was a very brief and concise document that only provided a minimal framework that required greater legislative explanation to complement its application.[51] Nevertheless, subsequent experiences in the adjudication of denunciation cases as crimes against humanity proved to be so successful that there was no justification for criticisms or interventions by the French military authorities. Denunciation cases continued to be prosecuted at different courts. The general prosecutor in Landau reported that ninety-three proceedings with a political background had been heard by 28 January 1947, with forty-three of them emanating from the events of 10 November 1938, and that most of the remaining cases were denunciation cases.[52]

The restoration of confidence in the German judicial organization in dealing with such cases in a fair and objective manner began with the proceedings, judgment, and the appeals process that followed a denunciation case heard at the Landshut regional court on 2 September 1947.[53] The defendant had been a convinced National Socialist in 1933, and had been a member of the NSDAP since 1937 as well as the DAF (*Deutscher Arbeitsfront*), NSV, and WHW (*Winterhilfswerk des Deutschen Volkes*). He had served as a *Blockleiter* in the building he resided in during 1939 and 1940, where one of his neighbors, hereafter cited as Gei., was known to listen to foreign radio broadcasts during the war and spread the news that he heard, in spite of repeated warnings from the neighbors that it was illegal.[54] He would later suffer the consequences for his openly non-conformist disposition.

Gei. had been quite open to his neighbors with regard to how he listened to foreign broadcasts, but the defendant had initially not taken action against him until his indiscretions became excessive. In one incident at the end of October 1939 when the son of a neighbor told his mother, Geol.'s neighbor hereafter cited as K., that he was home early from school because Hitler was going to give a speech. Gee. made insulting comments about Hitler in front of her child, saying that he was an idiot rather than a leader. He then spat on her and told her that she had bred one of Hitler's subjects. K. wanted to complain about Geol.'s behavior to the defendant, who had come to her home where she was told about this incident as well as that Gee. had listened to foreign broadcasts.[55]

The defendant then reported Gee. to his *Ortsgruppenleiter* and *Kreisleiter,* hereafter cited as W., who knew Gee. and disliked him. He then forwarded the report to the Gestapo, and Gee. was arrested a few days later. He was later tried at the Mannheim Special Court on 30 March 1940 for spreading adverse news and listening to foreign radio broadcasts, and was sentenced to four years' imprisonment with a deprivation of civil rights for the same amount of time. After serving this sentence, he was taken to Sachsenhausen and then Belsen concentration camps, where he presumably perished in February 1945, as there was no more news from him after this time.[56]

The defendant claimed in his defense that he was obliged to report Geol.'s conduct to his superiors, and had assumed that the *Ortsgruppenleiter* would give Gei. a warning. He also claimed that had not expected that that a report would be filed against him, and that had he known that court proceedings would be initiated against him, he would have simply filed a report against him at the Gestapo office himself. Nevertheless, the court determined that he could have expected that his report would be forwarded to other authorities, and that this would have ended in court proceedings being instituted against Gee. If he had intended to avoid these consequences, he could have gone to Gee. and personally given him a very stern warning, rather than having given a report that was so detailed that a witness said no further enquiries were necessary.[57]

The defendant also disputed the claim that he had acted out of political convictions. He claimed that as a *Blockleiter,* he was responsible for reporting Geol.'s misconduct and was concerned about being judged by his superior if he did not take any action. However, the court dismissed this claim, maintaining that Gee. had been persecuted and sentenced on political grounds, while the defendant had filed the report since he wanted to avoid appearing to be politically unreliable. He was therefore to be sentenced for crimes against humanity, as defined under Article II, paragraph 1c of Control Council Law No. 10.[58]

The defendant's report resulted in Geol.'s imprisonment in both a prison and a concentration camp where he was presumed to have later perished, and the defendant was partly responsible for this, and therefore he was to be called to account for his actions. In a discussion of any possible mitigating circumstances, the court took into consideration that the defendant did not have any prior convictions and enjoyed a good reputation. They also noted that it could be argued that he had to report Gee., who was commonly known to have listened to foreign broadcasts, as even children on the street had spoken about it, and they noted that he had been repeatedly warned against doing so. This made it likely that the defendant could have faced serious repercussions if he had not reported the matter to the higher authorities to whom he was responsible, and that Gee. himself was to a certain extent also responsible for the consequences of his own actions. Moreover, the defendant did not forward the report to the Gestapo directly. In view of these circumstances, he was sentenced to six months' imprisonment.[59]

This conviction was sustained at the Freiburg-im-Breisgau regional court on 11 December 1947, with the additional order for the case to be reopened at the Waldshut regional court for further deliberation about the sentencing. The public prosecutor argued that the defendant had not filed a report and did not want to do so. He had merely given a message to the *Ortsgruppenleiter* that Geiser had listened to foreign broadcasts, but did not have any intention of initiating court proceedings against him. The prosecutor therefore questioned the validity of the charge of political persecution. This claim was rejected, considering the argument that reporting another to a third party rather than to an authority could constitute political persecution when this form of intervention would lead to some form of injury for the persecuted party. The defendant had reason to expect that his message to the *Ortsgruppenleiter* would in turn lead to the initiation of court proceedings, and he had therefore approved of this consequence.[60]

This appeal court also dismissed the public prosecutor's claim that the defendant's message constituted political persecution, since this was part of exercising his duties as a *Blockleiter,* and not an action done to persecute Gee. because he was a Communist and an anti-fascist. However, the motive for fulfilling this obligation was of a political nature, since the defendant reported a matter that concerned activity that was hostile to the state at the time, when it was commonly known that political convictions other than those of the state were not tolerated and were ruthlessly suppressed. The Waldshut regional court had also justifiably argued that the defendant had made the report to the *Ortsgruppenleiter* to avoid facing unpleasant consequences by appearing to be "politically unreliable." Moreover, he was not under any legal obligation to make the report, and Article II, paragraph 4b of Control Council Law No. 10 expressly stated that he could not be absolved from assuming responsibility for his actions that had inhumane consequences if he had been aware of these consequences at the time. He therefore could not justifiably claim that Gee. would have been merely warned about his conduct. In view of the evidence and the consequences that had been incurred, the conviction and sentencing was considered to be justifiable. However, this court disputed the claim that the defendant was partly rather than fully responsible for the consequences that had been brought about, and therefore raised the question about the extent of the sentencing, which should have been greater than six months. The case was thereby sent back to the Waldshut regional court for this sentenced to be revised.[61]

New proceedings were opened at the Waldshut regional court on 8 October 1948. While not denying or downplaying the severe consequences that the defendant had brought about, several mitigating factors were put forward in his favor. The indictment at Geol.'s trial at the Mannheim Special Court had included other incriminating actions other than his having listened to foreign broadcasts, which were not ascribed to the defendant's report against him. A medical expert witness also testified in the present proceedings that Gee. had been in poor health at the time he was convicted, and therefore the possibility of death from natural causes could not be discounted. Another mitigating factor was that while the defendant had acted out of his own volition, he had also taken action at the instigation of Geol.'s neighbor whom he had often insulted and complained about her children. It was also maintained that while he was guilty of making a report as a third party, he had faced the risk of adverse consequences if his political superiors had become aware of about Geol.'s misconduct. He had been cautious about this whole case as he was aware of the open hostility between Gee. and the Z. household, and he had been told by *Ortsgruppenleiter* W. that he expected him to give Gee. a warning. In addition, he could not have anticipated the severity of the sentence that could have been imposed by the Special Court so soon after the enactment of the law against listening to foreign radio broadcasts. He also could not have anticipated that Geol.'s conduct could have led to persecution by the Gestapo, and that he would be taken to a concentration camp after serving the prison sentence because he had been a Communist. In view of these circumstances, this court passed a sentence of ten months' imprisonment.[62]

Another denunciation case that was heard during the same time was at the regional court in Freiburg-im-Breisgau, where sentence was passed on 12 September 1947.[63] An individual who had been a *Reichstag* representative of the German Social Democratic Party (SPD) for Baden until June 1933, and who had then been imprisoned from 17 March 1933 until 9 March 1934 for being a leading member of this party,[64] later spoke his mind about his convictions, at a time when free speech was illegal, to someone who acted on the basis of their personal animosity against him. On 17 June 1941, four days before Germany's attack on the Soviet Union and while German troops were massing on the eastern border, a tobacconist, hereafter cited as M., had made several antiwar statements, such as how Hitler wanted to swallow up all states. Austria had wanted nothing to do with Germany; and that Hitler had said he wanted nothing from Czechoslovakia, and then had hauled away all of its gold in armored vehicles; that the attack on England had come to nothing; that the attack on the Balkans turned out to be nonsense; and that the generals were all against Hitler—in addition to describing Hitler as an absolutely bloodthirsty Genghis Khan.[65]

The other of the two accused in this case, another business owner to whom he had made these remarks, hereafter cited as H., was extremely agitated about what she had heard and repeated them on the following day to the second accused, hereafter cited as E., a police officer. She also took this opportunity to express her bitter envy at how M.'s tobacco business was running better than her own garage business, which she deemed was more important to the war effort, and she was very unhappy that she only had limited use of her own vehicle. Moreover, she commented on the alleged danger that he would spread such remarks while driving around the country in his truck to make deliveries for his tobacco business.[66]

E. had reservations about doing anything about her report, but knew that intentionally neglecting to do anything would lead to his imprisonment, and was aware of the possibility that H. would press the issue if he did not act on it. He suspected that H.'s motive for her report was envy, but E. reported the issue to his superior at the police station who likewise sought to be cautious in following it up. After the report was made at the police station, H. repeated M.'s remarks to the Gestapo in unmitigated detail two weeks later on 4 July 1941, without any regard to the potential consequences her words would have. It was commonly known in Germany at this time in the summer of 1941 that remarks about Hitler's personality and personal views against the war would lead to at least a lengthy sentence in a prison or a concentration camp, if not immediate death.[67] She later also served as the leading witness at his trial at the Special Court in Freiburg-im-Breisgau that began on 21 October 1941.[68]

As a result of his statements, M. was found guilty of violating Article 5 No.1 of the special wartime criminal ordinance of 17 August 1938 on undermining the war effort. He was sentenced to three years' imprisonment with three years' loss of citizenship rights, with the remaining time of his sentence to be served at Mauthausen concentration camp, where he allegedly died from heart failure on 19 September 1944. Considering that he had not had any history of heart trouble, it was to be assumed that he died either as a result of being driven to death by exhaustion, or that he was killed toward the end of his sentence.[69]

The defendants were indicted with the crime of persecution on political grounds as a crime against humanity in accordance with Control Council Law No. 10, Art.2 1c. Although there was no provision that was applicable for charging them for their actions under German law at this time or at the time of the action, this court was called on to pass judgment on them in conformity with the directive of the Baden military government of 2 May 1946.[70] This directive granted German courts the jurisdiction of applying Control Council Law No. 10 in cases of offenses committed by Germans against Germans. Rather than administering what could be applied under existing German law and its prohibitions against retroactive legislation, the court would form its judgment according to what was overwhelmingly acknowledged to be justifiable in the current legal thought. This judgment was made in view of the present circumstances when the concept of crimes against humanity in the form of persecution on political, religious, or racial principles was beginning to be defined through German courts passing judgments citing Control Council Law No. 10 in individual cases when German law could not be applied.[71] Crimes against humanity were not clearly defined in a codified system, but like international law, such crimes belonged in the sphere of case law and were to be prosecuted to put the law in such cases into practice.[72]

While the rule of law prohibited the principle of *nulla crimen sine lege* and *nulla poene sine lege* in a state governed by the rule of law, justice was to be administered retroactively in order to prosecute injustices that hitherto could not have been prosecuted during a state of state-sanctioned lawlessness. Since the security provided by the law and consciousness thereof had been shattered by the lawless arbitrariness of the National Socialist regime, it was ethically justifiable and necessary for the restoration of the law to administer justice retroactively by applying Control Council Law No. 10 in special cases, such as in the precedent set by the sentencing against Helene Schwärzel.[73] Moreover, German courts and judges were responsible for administering the law enacted by the Allied Control Council as the highest authority in occupied Germany, and to interpret the Nuremberg Military Tribunal judgments of 30 September and 1 October 1946 and their corresponding basis in international law, rather than relying solely on German law that did not follow precedents when passing judgments.[74] The defendants in this case were thus to be called to account for the inhumane consequences of their actions in view of what has been considered justice in a civilized constitutional state, when individuals and their rights are under the protection of the law from arbitrary actions by the state, rather than by what the law had been at the time of their actions during the National Socialist regime.

The court determined that H., like every other average citizen in Germany in 1941, was aware of the potentially cruel consequences of her actions, in terms of knowing what M.'s fate would be at the hands of the National Socialist administration of justice, and therefore did not act in an ethically responsible manner. Being conscious of acting on what was objectively known to contradict the law in itself constituted an offense, and ignorance of the law was not grounds for innocence.[75] Awareness of perpetrating unlawfulness did not require prior knowledge of culpability of the action, since the perpetrator needed only to know that they committed an offense against a definite criminal norm of which they did not necessarily need to be aware.[76] Persecution on political grounds was also subject to prosecution when it represented a crime against humanity that had cruel and inhumane consequences in which universal human rights were violated through the abuse of power by the political and state authorities.[77]

These actions were presumed to have been motivated by envy of the fact that another business owner enjoyed the advantage of being able to drive his vehicle while she could not drive her own. This envy had led her to report what he had said in order to lead him to his demise at the hands of the National Socialist state, maintaining that M. was a politically unreliable enemy of the state.[78] The court therefore ruled that the defendant had committed a crime against humanity and was sentenced to three years' imprisonment in view of the fact that the defendant had not wanted M. to die in a concentration camp.[79]

It was found that E. did not have had any subjective motive in being involved in this case other than fulfilling his duty at the time, since there were no political influences on him within the police force. While he could have taken action to resist what was unjust, an examination of the underlying circumstances did not indicate that his conduct in the exercise of his duties contravened the law. Moreover, he had taken a risk by not reporting H.'s report about M. immediately, and only did so after H. had asked about the matter a second time, which could have led him to presuppose that he could have put himself in the position of being accused of criminal negligence by not officially filing the matter when H. had insisted on pursuing it further. He had been further endangered since she had repeated what M. had said to other parties, and therefore the matter could not have been easily quashed at his discretion without the possibility of him facing some very serious consequences. He was therefore granted the defense of justifiable mitigating circumstances and was therefore acquitted.[80]

The decisions were later upheld by the regional court in Freiburg-im-Breisgau on 15 December 1947. This court maintained that H. was not compelled to make the report that constituted political persecution according to an accurate interpretation of Control Council Law No. 10, Article II, section 1c., and that E. himself was obliged to file the report against M. Any objections to the judgment were thereby dismissed.[81]

Judgment was pronounced in another denunciation case that was heard at the Saarbrücken regional court on 15 December 1947. On 26 January 1937, one of the defendants, hereafter cited as Se. spoke with a drunken worker in a pub, hereafter cited as S., who made several disparaging political remarks. He maintained that children in Germany were starving while there was enough to eat, that the Saar vote two years previously had been rigged, and that if there was another referendum about becoming a part of Germany, 80% of voters would choose to maintain the previous status quo. He added that workers at the time had to work for a low wage while working as if they were living in Siberia. The primary accused, hereafter cited as W., took offense at these remarks and called the Gestapo who immediately came to arrest S. He was thereafter prosecuted at the Saarbrücken Special Court, which sentenced him on 15 May 1937 to eight months' imprisonment for violating the "Law of 20 December 1934 on Insidious Attacks on the State and Party and for the Protection of the Party Uniform" (*Heimtückegesetz*).[82]

W. testified in his defense that he had repeatedly told Sc. not to speak about political matters, but to no avail. On the day Sc. was arrested, another patron at the pub had told him that he had to call the Gestapo or else he would face the consequences. This patron accompanied him to the phone to ensure that he would make the call, and this led him to claim in court that he had acted under duress. These claims could neither be confirmed nor refuted, but this did not alter the nature of the offense as a crime against humanity. The purpose of the law of 20 December 1934 was meant to prevent any criticism of the institutions and measures of the NSDAP and its leaders, and therefore served to suppress the freedom of opinion. This law therefore encroached upon the right of individuals to express themselves in responsible ways, which meant that it was also a violation of the universal idea of dignity and freedom as an inalienable right. Repression on the grounds of this law represented an attack on this right, and therefore constituted a crime against humanity as defined by Article II, section 1c of Control Council Law No. 10. It followed that anyone who unnecessarily delivered another who did not perpetrate an immoral act into the hands of National Socialist tyranny, such as by making a report against them that led to court proceedings, was guilty of a crime against humanity.[83]

The court found that W. was conscious of the consequences of his actions, having been aware of the political conditions of the time from everyday experiences and publications. He had known that criticisms of the National Socialist regime were forbidden by the notorious law of 20 December 1934, and that they would be severely punished after he called the Gestapo. His making this call was a sign that he supported the regime's violence against political nonconformists and that he was acting out of political motives. What was all the more reprehensible is that he had known that S. was under the influence of alcohol at the time, and was therefore liable to make rash and careless remarks that should not have been taken seriously. It would have sufficed for Sc. to have been reproached by being removed from the pub and told that such political remarks would not be tolerated, but he chose to act otherwise. W. had also known that in early 1937, no obvious disadvantages would be sustained by him for not reporting political remarks, and therefore he could not claim to have acted under any duress at the incitement of another to report S.'s remarks to the local political authorities. Moreover, he had also further incriminated S. while he was questioned by the police and served as a witness in the Special Court proceedings, adding further that Sc. had often made politically suspect remarks. He was therefore found guilty of acting inhumanely as a result of political motives.[84]

In determining if there were any mitigating circumstances, the court ruled that it could not be refuted that W. had acted under the influence of a patron who told him that it had been his duty to call the political authorities. He also could not have expected that Sc. would be subject to the boundless arbitrariness and cruelty of the criminal authorities at that particular time, before this sort of reaction became the norm. Although W. should have considered Sc.'s state of mind at the time, the fact that Sc. had spoken carelessly about politics was also taken into account. In view of all of these circumstances, W. was sentenced to three months' imprisonment.[85]

Se. was also found guilty as a result of his confession about having encouraged that the report be made about Sc., but it could not be determined whether he had acted out of political motives. He was therefore sentenced to a monetary fine of 3000 francs, or one day in jail for each 200 francs that could not be collected.[86]

Another denunciation case was later heard at the same court, where judgment was passed on 22 December 1947. In 1942, the defendant, hereafter cited as K., lived as a lodger in the home belonging to the landlady hereafter cited as J. K., who often heard J. listen to illegal foreign radio broadcasts, threatened to report her to the authorities because of a dispute between them, because J. had accused her of having relationships with different men while her husband was serving in the military. She in fact reported the matter to a police official in Homburg, hereafter cited as R., who went to J.'s home on the evening of 27 June 1942 and arrested her after determining that her radio was tuned into a short wave broadcast. J. was thereafter sentenced by the Saarbrücken Special Court on 25 August 1942 to two years' imprisonment.[87]

K. testified in her defense that R. had approached her about reporting J. after he allegedly overheard her argument with K. while he was visiting her, and had heard the radio broadcast while he was there. The evidence drawn from R.'s report of 28 June 1942 essentially disproved this testimony, as it could be shown that K. had in fact taken the initiative in instituting proceedings against J. The report stated that K. had already reported J. on 23 June 1942, and also noted that she considered herself to be obligated to do so while citing political considerations and requesting that the report ought to be handled with the utmost confidentiality.[88]

The court found that K's conduct constituted a crime against humanity. The National Socialist authorities had forbidden the population from listening to foreign broadcasts in order to prevent them learning the truth about the war, especially the criminal means by which the war was started and was being fought. The National Socialist regime suppressed every possible freedom regarding the formation of opinion and knowledge about reality in order to hide the true nature of the regime, and they employed extremely harsh and cruel punishments to do this. The ordinance forbidding the listening to foreign broadcasts had the appearance of being a law, but it was in fact nothing more than a means to suppress political non-conformists. J. had not done anything immoral or repugnant by listening to foreign broadcasts, but she became an innocent victim of inhumane repression in the spirit of Control Council Law

No. 10. K. had been aware of the consequences of her actions, having known from the press about the heavy penalties that would be imposed for this offense, and must have been able to reason that these penalties were not commensurate with the gravity of the action. The punishments in such cases were clearly nothing more than political repression. Although the direct cause for her having denounced J. was not motivated by any political beliefs, the fact remained that the defendant had exploited the regime's system of repression against someone who had annoyed her. Hence, the objective and subjective facts of the case were seen as constituting a political motive.[89]

In assessing the extent of the sentencing, the court considered the base character of the defendant who used reprehensible means to alleviate her personal differences with another person, while taking into consideration the possibility that J. may not have survived a long period of imprisonment due to her advanced age. In a consideration of any possible mitigating circumstances, they noted that the defendant had been young and had never experienced life under a democracy. She may also have been provoked by J.'s talk of her suspicions about K. having had relations with other men. The fact that K. had four children was also taken into consideration, since they would be affected by her imprisonment, so she was therefore sentenced to ten months' imprisonment.[90]

The number of judgments in cases concerning crimes against humanity appeared to decrease by late 1947, when certain courts, especially those in Constance, demonstrated a marked reluctance in applying Control Council Law No. 10.[91] The press and the population reproached the administration of justice for passing judgments that were considered to be excessively lenient. The French military government continued to criticize the sentencing in significant political cases on the grounds that they were not sufficiently severe, which required them to spend more time intervening in the court's decisions to demand harsher sentences. The German courts also continued to demonstrate a hesitation in judging cases of crimes against humanity, which meant that they remained under constant supervision.[92]

This hesitation in judging cases involving crimes against humanity continued into early 1948, and the extent of the sentencing imposed on the convicted was also slightly less severe than before, which continually prompted the military government to demand the revision of verdicts in several such cases.[93] The German jurists had by this time been influenced by some arguments put forward by some of their colleagues who argued for a more restrictive application of Control Council Law No. 10. The prosecutor at the Constance regional court, Dr. Güde, argued for a very limited application of this law, which he considered to be too vague in its present form. As a result, several witnesses who came forward to file cases of crimes against humanity at this court were left unheard. He had also argued at a conference of public prosecutors in Freiburg-im-Breisgau in April 1948 that they should only take action in accusations of crimes against humanity when it was absolutely necessary.[94] In cases involving denunciations, the chances of such cases being brought to trial were also reduced when they were not considered to properly constitute crimes against humanity.[95] Crimes against humanity were beginning to be adjudicated at the discretion of the public prosecutor at a time when judgments in such cases had already became increasingly lenient. Since neither the French military government nor the local government had issued any further legislation to clarify what was to be considered a crime against humanity, it was therefore left for the public prosecutors to evaluate the available evidence that came from reliable witnesses.

A later denunciation case was heard at the Freiburg-im-Breisgau regional court, where judgment was passed on 12 August 1948. The defendant, hereafter cited as H., was convicted for committing a crime against humanity and was sentenced to six months' imprisonment.[96] In this case, the motive for actions of the defendant did not entail either political inclination or personal animosity. Rather, he acted under the duress of blackmail and to protect his bride as well as himself from facing what he considered to be potentially dire consequences. In fact, he had done too much to curry favor with the authorities that had put pressure on him.

The defendant had been active in the Catholic youth movement where he had met his wife. In April 1942, she had been later been sent to work in a work camp, where she continued the same activity for the Catholic church. There she had attracted the attention of the camp leader who had monitored her correspondence with the defendant, and it was found to contain disparaging remarks about the camp. The camp leadership denounced her to the Gestapo and she was arrested in September 1942 for undermining the war effort. Proceedings were also initiated against the defendant since he had agreed with her remarks in his correspondence to her, and because he had sent her prayer books, the arrival of which had sparked strong disapproval with the camp leadership. He was summoned to the Gestapo office in Karlsruhe on 2 November 1942, where he underwent an examination by the criminal commissar for church affairs who threatened him with arrest and prosecution, as had been the case with his fiancée who faced a long period of imprisonment. However, the proceedings against both of them could be dismissed if he agreed to be an informer for the Gestapo and report on illegal activities in the church. After some hesitation, he agreed to do so to get himself and his wife out of a very difficult situation.[97]

The defendant thereafter did not make any useful reports to the Gestapo, and on 27 November 1942 he was severely reproached for not doing so and was again threatened with the initiation of criminal proceedings against him and his fiancée. Faced with this threat to bring results, he was presented with the chance to do so shortly thereafter when he attended a wedding reception in Freiburg to which he had been invited by a friend. The couple completely trusted him, even though they knew that the defendant's fiancée had been imprisoned, and he had told them that the Gestapo had approached him about working for them. Later that day or on the next day, the newlywed couple and their guests listened to a Swiss radio broadcast in his presence after his friend's wife had tuned into it. He also found out at this time that the bride was not of completely "Aryan" descent, being either Jewish or half Jewish.[98]

The defendant was again summoned by the Gestapo in December 1942 and again in January or February 1943. On 2 April 1943, the Gestapo arrested the three aforementioned individuals. The defendant friend's wife gave up the names of the others who had heard the foreign radio broadcast, who were in turn arrested. One of them, a curate, was released after three months' imprisonment, while the four others were brought before the local Special Court and were sentenced to imprisonment for a year and a half for intentionally listening to "subversive news" from a foreign radio broadcast and then spreading the news. The bride who was allegedly of not completely "Aryan descent," was sentenced to ten months' imprisonment for listening to the same broadcasts. Two other people who listened to the same broadcast were likewise sentenced to prison. The first individual who had tuned into the broadcast, was sentenced to a year and the other was sentenced to eight months imprisonment. In keeping with the agreement that the Gestapo authorities had made with the defendant, his fiancée, who had remained imprisoned during this time was freed on 20 April 1943, while he thereafter continued to be an informer for them.[99]

The married couple were both to be interned in a concentration camp after the end of their prison sentences. The husband was sent to Dachau, where he died a premature death in January 1945. His wife was sent to Ravensbrück, where she remained until 28 April 1945 when the survivors of this camp were taken to the Malchov extermination camp where she would have died a violent death if she had not escaped during the confusion caused by a heavy Russian aerial bombardment.[100]

The court judged the defendant's denunciation to be a crime against humanity in accordance with Art. II, section 1c of Control Council No. 10. Although the act of denunciation in itself was not persecution, the defendant had brought about the effect of the persecution of three people on political grounds by the National Socialist authorities through his report, which led to the aforementioned brutal consequences. According to Article II, section 2 of Control Council Law No. 10, any form of involvement in the crime against humanity, whether it was direct or indirect, through either instigation or acting as an accessory, made the defendants subject to be called to account for their actions. Therefore, the defendant in this case could not use the defense that his report was not illegal according to the law of the National Socialist regime.[101]

The court held that the prohibition on listening to foreign radio broadcasts was an abuse of state authority for the purpose of maintaining the tyranny of the National Socialist regime by maintaining its one-sided propaganda in reporting world events. Even when considered from the point of view of wartime exigencies, this did not pertain to a justifiable limitation of personal freedoms that are defined by natural law. Being forcibly deprived of the freedom of hearing the news was a violation against the basic principles of generally recognized human rights and dignity that had been in existence since the creation of modern western civilization. Courts that were no longer independent were forced to impose inhumanely harsh and cruel sentences for these alleged offenses, and it had become increasingly standard practice from year to year for the Gestapo to take individuals convicted on radio broadcast offenses to a concentration camp after they served their sentences.[102]

The defendant had known about these circumstances, and had accepted the possibility that the National Socialist authorities would take all of these stern measures against such political offenses. Namely, he knew that his report would lead to persecution on political grounds, which in turn would bring about a heavy sentence with the possibility of the victims of his action being imprisoned in a concentration camp, just as he and his fiancée had experienced. He was also aware that his report was an offense against the rights and dignity of humanity, which are protected by legal standards that could not be simply legislated out of existence, even by a violent regime. In addition, he knew that his denunciation would deliver someone into the hands of National Socialist terror apparatus, which was not only contemptuous, but also contravened legal consciousness and was an injustice. Denunciation on the grounds of political principles was first made a criminal offense under Control Council Law No. 10. Although such cases were to be prosecuted retroactively, the defendant could not plead ignorance of the law as a defense, especially since this law imposed sanctions on offenses against the laws and rights of humanity. Although he could have been considered an opponent of National Socialism by being an active Catholic, who did not therefore seek to uphold the regime, this in itself did not in any way negate that what he had done was an act of political persecution.[103]

In his defense, it could be argued that he had acted under duress, being himself in serious danger if he did not cooperate with the Gestapo. However, the court was not himself and his fiancée out of danger was to denounce the other three people, since the consequences of his actions outweighed the danger that he and his fiancée had faced. The penalties for breaking the law by listening to foreign radio broadcasts were far more severe than were those for religious activity. Moreover, the extent of the defendant's functions as a Gestapo informer before this event was limited to reporting on any mention of political news in the church, such as making reports on sermons containing political allusions. In the opinion of the court, this would have sufficed for the Gestapo to be satisfied with his cooperation, and these actions would not have caused serious consequences for anyone. Instead, however, he had chosen to sacrifice others for his own advantage.[104]

With regard to any possible mitigating circumstances in his favor, in spite of his loathsome conduct, the court held that they could not underestimate the fact that the defendant had been in a dilemma in which he sought to save himself and his fiancée. Moreover, he had been suffering from serious stomach and intestinal enteritis from his early childhood, which he had feared could have made imprisonment fatal.[105] He otherwise did not sufficiently foresee the complete extent of the terrible consequences of his actions. After duly considering all of the circumstances, the court sentenced the defendant to six months' imprisonment.[106]

This case came under appeal at the Freiburg-im-Breisgau appeal court on 9 December 1948, where the jury court's judgment was sustained.[107] The court maintained that the defendant was not in an emergency situation, and the way he acted while allegedly under duress was not the only way he could have averted the danger threatening him and his fiancée, especially as he was aware of the consequences of his actions.[108] This court had also earlier decided on 21 November 1947 that denunciation in cooperation with terroristic measures by the state or political power constituted a crime against humanity, and therefore the defendant was to be judged accordingly. The earlier judgment made by the Freiburg *Schwurgericht* was thus maintained.[109]

Another denunciation case was heard at the Offenburg regional court at about the same time, and this court pronounced its judgment on two defendants, hereafter cited as S. and G., on 25 October 1948.[110] On the late evening of 10 August 1943, a passenger on a crowded train traveling from Altenheim to Lahr-im-Schwarzwald, hereafter cited as U., made disparaging remarks about the National Socialist government and the conditions in Germany at the time. The details of exactly what he had said could no longer be determined with complete certainty, since the files of the Freiburg Special Court could not be acquired. The witnesses to this occurrence were likewise unable to say exactly what had been said in detail, which led to proceedings being initiated against U. for allegedly preparing to commit high treason and undermining the war effort, which led to a sentence of two years' imprisonment in jail and later detention in a concentration camp.[111]

According to the evidence made available to the court by one of the witnesses who was on the same train, G. had heard the derisive remarks U. had made, while praising Stalin.[112] While making small talk on the street during the next day, G. told S., the local leader of the National Socialist Women's Association (*Blockfrau der NS-Frauenschaft*) about what had happened on the train on the previous night. Later that day, S. reported the matter to the office of the local administration while naming two potential witnesses, G. and another hereafter cited as K.[113]

They were summoned to the office shortly thereafter. G. declined to make a statement at that time, since she did not have time to do so before taking a train. A Gestapo agent appeared at her door a few days later and wanted to know who U. was, and showed her a picture of U. The Gestapo agent accused her of not providing the appropriate information, and he threatened her with a prison sentence if she did not tell him everything she knew, adding that K. had already done so. Having been frightened in this manner, G. thereafter told everything she knew. Meanwhile, S. had known that "something could happen" to U. when making the report about him to the local authorities, and admitted to knowing that what he had said to G. in Germany at the time could lead to imprisonment in jail, prison, or a concentration camp. Nevertheless, that did not prevent her from making the report.[114]

On 24 August 1943, U. was placed into custody. He was later brought before the criminal court of the Stuttgart regional court on 22 February 1944, where G. gave her testimony as a witness at these court proceedings. He was sentenced to two years' imprisonment for preparing to commit high treason and undermining the war effort. This verdict was later revised through a so-called extraordinary objection by the state prosecutor of the People's Court on 11 August 1944, in order to impose a heavier sentence. After an initial period of imprisonment in prison in Ensisheim and then Berlin-Moabit, he was taken to Dreibergen concentration camp.[115]

He survived his time in internment and was liberated by Russian troops on 4 May 1945, and was able to return home on 16 November 1945. However, he died soon afterward on 15 December 1945 as a consequence of lung tuberculosis. He had already incurred heart and lung trouble as an infantry soldier during the First World War, which had spared him from being eligible for military service thereafter. The jury court was convinced that this lung condition was aggravated by his imprisonment. The court charged the two accused with persecuting U. on political grounds, and therefore with a crime against humanity according to Article2, Sections 1c and 2b of Control Council Law No. 10.[116]

S. did not have any personal interest in seeing U. prosecuted, considering that she did not know him. She had been a member of the *NS-Frauenschaft* from 1933, and had been inculcated with the necessity for immediately reporting any insults to the NSDAP, the government, and Hitler. She claimed that she had done so with great reluctance. She was also afraid of any considerable unpleasantness that could result if she did not notify the authorities about the occurrence, and therefore would not risk not doing so, and therefore she made the report on G.'s behalf.[117]

The court determined that the motivations for the involvement of the two accused in this case differed in the composition of their personalities. G. had acted out of fear of the Gestapo authorities who had previously intimidated her and her husband in 1942, and she did not imagine that her idle chatter with her neighbor S. could lead to difficulties for anyone. Moreover, she had not known S. to be interested in talking to others about politics.[118] S.'s motivation for her involvement in this matter was altogether different. She had made the report because she had thought it had been her duty to do so, but this was also part of her inhumane and merciless duty as an NSDAP official. This duty was misguided rather than humane, since her motivation was apparently to curry favor with the local NSDAP authorities, as she otherwise had nothing to fear from G., who was not a member of any NSDAP organization, and whose husband was likewise not a member of the NSDAP.[119] Hence, she could not justifiably claim that she had acted under any duress. Her motivation for making the report was thus made for her personal gain.

The court determined that S. had indeed committed a crime against humanity according to the interpretation of this term, in the sense that it constituted an attack on the well-being, health, and freedom or honor of a person according to the generally accepted and inviolable, indivisible principles of criminal law among all civilized nations. Thus, it constituted an offense that was subject to prosecution under current law. She had not known U., but made the report against him out of political motives and thus participated in the persecution of U. in the interest of so-called party discipline while seeking personal advantage for herself at the expense of someone she did not know at all. Hence, she callously delivered him into the hands of the terroristic apparatus of the ruling party and the state without any misgivings while being aware of the consequences of doing so. It was thus maintained that denunciation was a leading example of a crime against humanity, and was to be prosecuted according to Article II, section 1c of Control Council No. 10. Meanwhile, G. had not intended to commit the act of denunciation, and was only guilty of making stupid gossip, which was not a crime against humanity, so she was therefore acquitted.[120]

In determining the severity of the sentence for S., the court reasoned that she was rather narrow-minded and was heavily influenced by the *NS-Frauenschaft* into thinking that she was obliged to report disparaging remarks against the National Socialist regime. It was assumed that due to her personality weakness, she may have overlooked the full scope of the consequences of her actions. Moreover, she was fifty-eight years old, and had never been prosecuted. Taking these matters into consideration in her favor, the court sentenced her to four months' imprisonment.[121]

A later case of denunciation in Germany under French jurisdiction[122] was heard at a jury court at the Berlin regional court on 4 November 1948. The defendant was found guilty on two separate counts of crimes against humanity in accordance with Article II, sections 1c, 2, and 3 of Control Council Law No. 10, and was thereby sentenced to fifteen years' imprisonment with a ten years' deprivation of civil rights.[123]

The defendant, Salomea Maag, was born of Polish parents in Poland, and had married a Jewish builder in 1916 who died in 1928. She then later remarried a German police chief in 1938, and this marriage ended in divorce in 1940. She had joined the NSDAP in 1933, claiming that her second husband, who himself had never joined the party, told her to do so to cover up her Polish origins and the fact that she had been married to a Jew. This claim was later refuted by her ex-husband. She supported herself by subleasing accommodation in her large seven and a half room apartment in Charlottenburg. Among the lodgers there were some high-level party leaders. Witnesses testified to her two-faced nature, saying that while she appeared hospitable and helpful on one hand, she was also fanatically devoted to National Socialism and they all feared the possibility of her denouncing them. She had even warned new lodgers of this possibility when they moved in. The facts later showed that she denounced one of her neighbors who had lived on the same floor of the building, the former Interior Minister of Hesse and Social Democratic union leader, Leuschner, to the Gestapo, which subsequently led to his arrest and hanging[124] after the 20 July assassination attempt.

Leuschner had been dismissed from his position in Hesse after the National Socialist takeover and then lived with his family in Berlin. Maag's relationship with his wife was not especially good due to some gossip. Tension between these neighbors increased after a local National Socialist district leader from Hesse (*Gauamtsleiter*) called Becker moved in as a new tenant on 9 May 1942. He was charged with spying on Leuschner. It was the opinion of the court that her claim that she did not know Leuschner was a lie, since all of the lodgers who were questioned were well aware of who he was. She was also aware of Becker's job, which was something she also denied, but this was refuted by the testimony of someone who had been a lodger in the apartment who stated that she frequently had conversations with Becker, from which it could be inferred that he was spying on Leuschner. Another witness who was also a lodger in the same apartment testified that she knew what Becker was doing from as early as the autumn of 1937, because she said to her that the National Socialist state should not allow someone who had spent a year in a concentration camp to have a six room apartment.[125]

Following the assassination attempt on Hitler on 20 July 1944, Leuschner's wife was arrested for not telling the authorities about her husband's whereabouts. Leuschner occasionally went to their apartment before and after her arrest, and to avoid arrest he used the back entrance to avoid being seen. The defendant found this out, and according to the landlady of the building who testified as a witness, she told the Gestapo about it. The defendant had also known that he often stayed with a cleaning lady who lived on a nearby street, and she had also told the Gestapo about this. This acquaintance could later testify that the Gestapo waited for him at her apartment, where he was arrested.[126] The facts of the case thus made the defendant guilty of crimes against humanity as defined by Article II, sections 1c, 2, and 3 of Control Council Law No. 10, whereby a perpetrator against this law could be prosecuted for reasons other than political, racial, or religious persecution. Her actions had led to the arrest and execution of Leuschner, and she was thereby subject to prosecution for the causal connection of these events that she had intentionally initiated, especially having spied on Leuschner and informed the Gestapo about where he could be found, which led to his arrest and later to his hanging.[127]

The court also put forward the view that the defendant had acted on political motives, citing how she had precisely known about the cruel and inhumane methods and practices of the National Socialist regime and the Gestapo before she betrayed his whereabouts and delivered him into the hands of the hangman. She had even said that mourning for him after he was killed should be reported to the police. This, in the opinion of the court, was an example of the highest form of inhumanity[128] that was in itself a testament to her political fanaticism as well as her willingness to denounce others without the slightest provocation.

She was also accused of reporting Leuschner's wife to the police many times before his arrest, including twice about making hostile statements about the state. However, she was not found guilty of making these reports, since the available evidence suggested that these were mere suspicions that could not be entered into evidence, or that perhaps she had also denounced the witness who could have testified against her. The seven witnesses who were examined in this case also could not provide any further evidence. Mrs. Leuschner could only testify that she was questioned by the Gestapo sometime in 1942 about having made political remarks in front of the defendant. Having denied doing so, she was dismissed thereafter without suffering any further consequences, other than the Gestapo confiscating a large amount of fruit that the Leuschners had intended to give to a hospital, after the defendant had given the Gestapo advance notice about it. There was no evidence in this matter to indicate that there was a political basis for her persecution of Mrs. Leuschner for the alleged disparaging remarks she had made about the state, which were ultimately undetermined. This charge was therefore dismissed for lack of evidence.[129]

In a third case, she was accused of reporting her former husband Arthur Maag to the police for aiding and abetting Jews. After they had known each other for ten years and lived together happily, their marriage had come to an end in 1940 due to her having been unfaithful to her husband by having a relationship with another woman. His handling of this matter by suing her for a divorce angered her, and her desire for revenge led to her reporting him and one of his colleagues to the police on 8 August 1940. She claimed that they had associated with and accepted gifts from a Jewish-owned business in Charlottenburg for eighteen months. As a result, Mr. Maag was sentenced to six months' imprisonment on 16 May 1941.[130]

There was a lack of clear evidence with regard to her motives for reporting her former husband to the authorities. While she claimed that her intention was to clear charges of passive bribery, it was not clear whether the report stated that he helped Jews secure illegal departure travel permits. Nevertheless, he was prosecuted for passive bribery as a consequence of her report against him. The jury court deduced that there was no political character to the report, considering that the extent of the sentence was only six months in jail, rather than him being delivered to the Gestapo, or to the police, and then being detailed in a penitentiary. However, she exploited political means to have her former husband persecuted by the authorities as a result her desire for personal revenge. This charge therefore did not merit being considered an example of inhumane treatment in the spirit of Control Council Law No. 10, since it did not result in his persecution at the inhumane hands of the National Socialist regime. The defendant was therefore also acquitted of this charge due to lack of evidence.[131]

She was found guilty in a fourth charge of denunciation. One of her lodgers, Wilhelm Krügel, was initially in good standing with her since he declared his intention to marry her, but their friendship was later embittered by a laborious civil process that he leveled against her. During a chance conversation, Krügel said something to the effect about Hitler being a "house-painter" who did not know what he wanted, and commented on the death of a Hitler Youth leader by saying: "Thank God one of the bloodhounds is now gone. Hopefully the others will be gone soon too. I myself will help eliminate the bricklayers."[132] Witnesses testified that the defendant made a note of these remarks in a notebook before she filed a report about them. Criminal proceedings were then instituted against Krügel who was sentenced to two years' imprisonment.[133]

The jury court found the defendant guilty of Article II, sections 1c, 2, and 3 of Control Council Law No. 10. She had undoubtedly made the report because of feelings of personal revenge since she was angered about Krügel not marrying her, and because of the possibility of having to return a large sum of money to him. However, this did not preclude that she was guilty of a crime against humanity, considering that she was aware of the consequences of her actions, which would lead to the persecuted being subject to the indiscriminate and inhumane violence of the National Socialist regime. Such denunciations made on the basis of purely personal considerations, such as feelings of personal revenge against or a disagreement with the persecuted individual, could therefore be interpreted as persecution on political grounds. She had again used political means against Krügel by denouncing him for making hostile statements against the state. She knew that the courts would exact a heavy punishment on someone for making such defamatory remarks about Hitler, which would often result in death in a concentration camp. The defendant had therefore contravened the most basic law of humanity, knowing that the consequences of her actions would lead to his inhumane treatment at the hands of the Gestapo. It was thus the view of the court that she had intended for Krügel to be killed.[134]

In considering the severity of the sentencing, the jury court took into consideration the fact that not only had she been found guilty in two cases of acting inhumanely in the spirit of Control Council Law No. 10, but that she had a completely inhumane and immoral character as had been indicated by her remark that someone should be denounced for mourning Leuschner's violent death. It was decided that such an individual who could be so brutal, even if she was a woman, did not deserve any leniency. The same inhumane attitude was often revealed by one of her favorite phrases: "I cause one or another to blow up."[135] At another time, she gladly hinted that she would have to report any remark that was unacceptable to the National Socialist regime to Becker, knowing that he was a spy, thus demonstrating her willingness to denounce anyone under the guise of political principles. She expressed the same attitude to Leuschner's son Wilhelm in an air raid shelter after his father was convicted, cynically saying, "One of our Vice-Chancellors will probably be missing today."[136]

The jury court had deliberated whether the defendant should receive the death penalty or a lifelong sentence, but in a consideration of her advanced age of nearly sixty-three, it was decided to impose a sentence of fifteen years imprisonment for the Leuschner case. She received an additional two years' imprisonment for the Krügel case, and the court ruled that the earliest possibility of release would only be after fifteen years. She was also to be deprived of her civil rights for ten years.[137]

This case was brought to the appeal court where judgment was again pronounced on 1 June 1949. They dismissed the possibility of revising the verdict of the jury court as there were no grounds for a revision. It was determined that the jury court had objectively judged the defendant on the basis of the provisions of Control Council Law No. 10, by taking into consideration how these sorts of cases were distinguished by injustices in the National Socialist regime, and how the defendant had contributed to perpetuating such injustices. She had also undoubtedly been aware of the consequences of her actions while willingly using her knowledge of Leuschner's whereabouts to deliver him into the hands of the arbitrary violence of the National Socialist regime. The appeal court also maintained the verdict regarding the Krügel case, likewise maintaining that the call for revision was without merit, maintaining that the defendant had used political means to perpetuate a crime against humanity. Hence, she was to be held responsible for being conscious of the consequences of her actions. Although the sentences in these two cases were severe, they were not inappropriate or cruel in view of the harsh consequences that the conduct of the defendant had caused. Hence, they were justified by what was prescribed by existing German criminal law in Article 74 of the criminal code.[138] As is other such cases, she was therefore called to account for her actions, and was to take responsibility for having been aware of the inhumane consequences of exploiting the circumstances of the time, in which one could indirectly bring such consequences to bear on others under the guise of legality or even wartime exigencies.

By the end of 1948, the German courts throughout the French occupation zone continued to demonstrate an unwillingness to adjudicate denunciation cases of a political nature. This conservative tendency was buttressed by the argument that most of these denunciations were justified, and thus they would only take responsibility for adjudicating cases that resulted in ill-treatment or inhumane consequences for the victims, while the more minor cases were to be dismissed by the public prosecutors. In one example during this time, a public prosecutor dismissed a charge against a notorious National Socialist who denounced another for having had contact with a Russian prisoner-of-war. The denounced individual was sentenced to six months' imprisonment, but the charge against the informer was dropped on the grounds that the denunciation had been in conformity with existing regulations at the time. German courts at this time continued to apply Control Council Law No. 10 with a diminishing frequency while the justifications for any new indictments were based on previous judgments.[139] Although the conservative tendency in not bringing crimes against humanity to justice remained evident, cases that resulted in grave consequences for the victims continued to be heard, as the extent of those consequences could not be easily dismissed as having been standard at the time.

A later denunciation case also entailed politically conformist considerations on the part of the defendant, where judgment was pronounced at the Offenburg regional court on 16 February 1949. The defendant, hereafter cited as E., had been a member of the NSDAP from 1 May 1937 and held the position of *Blockleiter* in Kittersburg from late 1938 until he was drafted to serve as a mechanic in the *Waffen* SS on 15 April 1943.[140] Upon a chance meeting with a former schoolmate, hereafter cited as G., on 21 March 1943 in Kittersburg, he told him that he was about to be drafted into the military. This remark gave cause for G. to comment on the political situation of the time, telling E. to avoid military service it were at all possible, since things would inevitably turn out badly. He believed that Germany would collapse by May of that year, and that no other state would deal with a state that would only deal with other states with violence. Upon E.'s objection that Germany had to win the war under any circumstances to prevent its destruction, G. continued that Germany deserved to perish since it was solely responsible for starting the war. After E. tried to protest that the *Führer* would set things right, G. continued that Hitler was not worth talking about since he was a sick, broken man who would soon be in a lunatic asylum. Meanwhile, one could not believe the falsehoods reported in the newspapers. Hitler remained a murderer, and Göring no longer had much to say. Hitler had called on Brauchitsch to return, but he should have responded that he was not willing to pull the corporal out of a mess again, rather than returning to the eastern front to save soldiers and prevent the collapse. The NSDAP was a brown pestilence and the atmosphere in Munich was miserable. Students there had written: "Down with Hitler, the murderer" on walls at night time in agreement with the police.[141]

E. had later first told his since deceased father-in-law in the apartment that they shared about what he had heard on that day; both of them were rendered speechless over how someone could make such unbelievable remarks. Three days after this conversation had taken place, he repeated what he had heard at the time to the *Ortsgruppenleiter* in Kehl, hereafter cited as P., whose office was in the same building as the DAF office with which E. had matters to discuss. Since there was no personal or professional relationship between these two political acquaintances,[142] E. acted on his own initiative in doing so. P. in turn passed on these statements to the *Kreisleiter* Schall in Strasburg. About three or four days after E.'s conversation with P., the Gestapo in Kittersburg questioned E. and his father-in-law, who both told them the details of the conversation that E. had had with G. G. was later arrested in Munich on

18 May 1943 and placed into custody. Knowing that he had been denounced by E., G. was brought before the People's Court where E. and his father-in-law testified as the only witnesses at the proceedings, and he was convicted and sentenced to death on 23 August 1943 for undermining the war effort. He was later executed on 11 October 1943.[143]

When this case of denunciation came to trial, E. confessed to all of these events, saying he intended to report the statements to P. to determine whether G.'s remarks were true. He also claimed that he had been unaware that they would be forwarded to the Gestapo thereafter and would result in proceedings being initiated against G., as G. had made the same remarks in public in an inn, but was only shown the door for having done so.[144] This court addressed these objections that he made in his defense in view of the objective administration of the law as it had hitherto been done in all of such cases.

The view of this court was that E. had committed a crime against humanity on the basis of persecution other than on political principles, as defined in Article II, section 1c of Control Council Law No. 10. The events in this case were interpreted as had been done previously in such cases—as cruel and inhumane actions taken against the universally recognized inviolable and inalienable rights of every individual, which thereby attacked the notions of human dignity and value, and consequently expressing contempt for these rights of humanity. Most importantly, these included the rights of life, well being, personal freedom, and freedom of beliefs. Although these rights may be subject to restrictions in wartime, limitations on these rights constituted an offense against the universal principles of all civilized nations and moral law. While it was assumed that defeatist remarks in the Second World War were considered subject to prosecution in all belligerent nations, someone being prosecuted in Germany for being a defeatist was not in itself a contravention against human rights. However, acting on vengeance against such remarks in the National Socialist regime was distinguished by such contraventions, in view of the widespread disrespect for the principles of regulated criminal proceedings, the abuse of legal rights, the penalties that were out of proportion to the offenses, and the contradiction of every sense of justice.[145]

The way in which the defendant forwarded G.'s remarks to the *Kreisleiter* represented an example of how someone made another mercilessly subject to persecution by the Gestapo and to unrestrained arbitrary proceedings that disregarded the most primitive principles of universally recognized human rights. Given the political circumstances of the time, there was no justifiable cause for the defendant to pass on G.'s remarks that he had made in a private conversation, since they did not affect him personally and he would not have faced any trouble if he had chosen to not say anything.[146] Hence, he had willingly acted to support the regime and its indiscriminate, hostile actions against those who opposed it in any way. As had been determined previously by the regional court in Freiburg-im-Breisgau, whoever had given cause for another to have been subject to the arbitrariness of the Gestapo had thereby taken part in the inhumane actions of the National Socialist authorities, and therefore, from an objective viewpoint, had also conducted themselves in an inhumane manner.[147]

The defendant was thus held responsible for making the report to the *Kreisleiter* and for supporting this report to the People's Court. A witness in the present case refuted the claim he had made about G. making such statements at a tavern in Kittersburg, while other witnesses testified that only E. could have made the report about G. This excluded the possibility of his father-in-law having made the report, as was indicated by a note that G. had smuggled out of prison to his daughter stating that his former schoolmate had made the accusation against him. This therefore provided further evidence that E. had begun the persecution against G.[148]

A crime against humanity presupposes even a limited intentional action when the perpetrators were at least aware that their actions that were motivated by political, racial, or religious persuasion would lead to measures taken against another with considerably detrimental consequences. They ought also to have been aware of the circumstances in which proceedings of an inhumane nature would be initiated, and therefore they must have approved of the foreseen potential consequences. Regardless of the claim made by the defendant that he did not intend for criminal proceedings to be initiated against G., the act of forwarding evidence of a defeatist statement sufficed to constitute political persecution in view of the historical record of how such events turned out. This depended on to whom the remark was forwarded, in which circumstances it had been made, and how the receiver of the information would handle it.[149]

The defendant had forwarded G.'s remarks to the *Kreisleiter* who occupied a position of responsibility in the regime. Someone in this position was a convinced National Socialist who was responsible for upholding the regime's ideology in the population, and for suppressing all opposing political views. More specifically, it was his duty to oppose anyone making defeatist statements that could restrict or undermine the willingness of the population to maintain the war effort, and call any propagators of such statements into account for what they had said.[150]

This task was seen as vital for the regime's survival after the serious defeat at Stalingrad and the driving of the German military out of North Africa, which led to loud voices everywhere being heard to say that continuing the hopeless struggle would a crime against the German people. It was also well known how the newspapers reported the severe and draconian measures that would be taken against defeatists and how such "elements" would be ruthlessly eradicated. This was also made obvious at meetings of NSDAP officials in which these events were discussed, and every official was charged with the duty of taking action against defeatists. The defendant could not have failed to notice this, given his intelligence and political experience as a *Blockleiter* that gave him a greater insight into the NSDAP apparatus than most of the population. He was also undoubtedly aware of the methods the regime would employ to dispose of those who were other than its sworn enemies—those who dared voice disparaging criticisms or even cast doubts about the possibility of final victory, which by 1943 was evidently known to the entire German population. He was therefore well aware that the NSDAP leadership had made the *Kreisleiter* responsible for forwarding any "subversive" criticisms to the Gestapo or to superior departments so that the necessary measures would be taken against any offending parties. In doing so, he was also undoubtedly aware of the severe consequences that G. would have to face. Hence, it could be hardly explained that the defendant's motives were anything other than political, and that he approved subjecting G. to inhumane treatment as a political opponent of the regime, and that he had willingly taken part in its methods of suppressing such forms of opposition.[151]

The defendant's conduct thus contravened that of every decent and upright person, whether they were a member of the NSDAP or not at the time, or anyone else thereafter who would not only disapprove of, but also abhor exposing another to persecution by the regime of the time for making political remarks against the regime. Tolerance for political views and the personal freedom to express them belong to the universal law of every nation, and since the defendant offended against these fundamental laws in the most serious way possible, his actions could only be described as cruel and inhumane. He was thereby subject to prosecution as a perpetrator of crime against humanity as defined under Article II, section 1c of Control Council Law No. 10.[152]

In considering any possible mitigating circumstances in favor of the defendant, it was noted that he had only previously been found guilty of an insignificant misdemeanor that was punished with a fine. He otherwise enjoyed a good reputation in his home community as an industrious, skillful, and conscientious worker who looked after his family well, and was not known to be a hateful and dangerous party fanatic. Moreover, no witness could confirm that he was especially devoted to the goals of the NSDAP or that he had been intolerant toward its political opponents. On the other hand, his conduct was inexcusable, considering that G.'s remarks did not affect him personally, he did not have any reason to report him to the authorities, and they did not have any personal differences between them. In view of these circumstances and the fact that he was aware of and approved of the severe consequences he had caused for G., the court sentenced him to a year's imprisonment.[153]

The Waldshut regional court pronounced judgment on another denunciation case on 16 February 1949 that was motivated by political considerations. The defendant, hereafter cited as W., had been active in the NSDAP from 1930 before becoming a member of the party on 1 February 1931. He had been a SA leader in Waldshut and had risen to the rank of *Standartenführer,* and was later an *Ortgruppenleiter* of the NSDAP. He later left these positions in Waldshut upon becoming a *Kreisleiter* in Constance on 1 December 1939, and continued to serve in this position until its dissolution, and then he joined the *Volkssturm.*[154]

The defendant had taken notice of how a neighbor, hereafter cited as Gee., formerly a member of the German Communist Party from 1917 to 1922, had made no secret of his opposition to the National Socialist regime. He had considered himself obliged to warn Geol.'s wife about the dangers of her husband making derisive about the regime, and that he should therefore tone them down. It could be surmised that perhaps he had not taken action against him at this time since he had been sentenced to three years' imprisonment in 1924 for attempted high treason against the Weimar Republic.[155] Gee. was an incorrigibly nonconformist individual in spite of this warning. After the enacting of an ordinance in September 1939 forbidding the population from listening to foreign radio broadcasts, Gee. installed a powerful receiver and spread the news he heard on the radio. Further to his recklessness, one of his neighbors who lived in the apartment above his and who had long endured his irritable nature, hereafter cited as Z., told the local *Blockleiter* T. in late October 1939 about hearing about foreign broadcasts from Gee. Z. also told him that in other circumstances, he would spit on her, and shouted at her that she had bred a "subject of Hitler," and in the past he had called out to her children saying that Hitler was an idiot rather than a leader.[156]

T. considered himself obliged to report these facts to his political superior in his capacity as a *Blockleiter*. In a chance meeting on the street with W., who he recognized from sight as the local *Ortsgruppenleiter,* T. told him how Gee. listened to foreign broadcasts and had called Hitler an idiot. W. thereupon brought T. to his office where he had him repeat what he had heard. W. then called the Gestapo to inform them that T. wanted to tell them about important remarks that Gee. had made, and sent T. to them, who in turn questioned him thoroughly about what he had heard.[157]

Gee. was then arrested by the Gestapo on 2 November 1939, and was then convicted by the Special Court in Mannheim on 30 March 1940 for reporting atrocities and listening to foreign broadcasts. This court sentenced him to four years' imprisonment with four years' deprivation of civil rights. After serving this sentence at the penitentiary in Bruchsal, he was taken to the Sachsenhausen concentration camp on 5 April 1944, and then to the Belsen concentration camp. His wife had last heard from him at the beginning of February 1945. He never returned, and his final whereabouts thereafter remained unknown.[158] In the expert opinion of Dr. G., Gee. was already seriously ill in 1940. He had suffered from a fairly serious hardening of the arteries and extreme nervous sensitivity at the time that the criminal proceedings were initiated against him, which caused a considerable mental breakdown of his intellectual capacity. The criminal proceedings and incarceration thus considerably worsened his condition, and it could not be ruled out that these conditions led to his death. It therefore remained open to question whether his death in 1945 came from violent or natural causes, regardless of the aggravating conditions.[159]

An examination of the witnesses proved that W. was responsible for making the report against Gee. through passing on the information he received from T. to the Gestapo, which caused Geol.'s imprisonment in a prison and then his eventual death at Belsen concentration camp. Although W. believed it was his duty to report statements and actions that were hostile to the state to the appropriate authorities, he was not required to cooperate in matters concerning criminal law, and thus was not in fact responsible for taking action in this matter. Nor could he cite the directives from his superiors in the NSDAP as justification for reporting Geol.'s statements, since he was not absolved from taking responsibility for his actions due to orders from superiors, as defined in Article II, section 4b of Control Council Law No. 10. W. also could not cite acting on necessity, admitting that he would not have sustained any personal disadvantages if he had suppressed the report. Hence, he willingly chose to lead Gee. into incurring the severe consequences that were completely out of proportion to his offense. This constituted an inhumane abuse of state power for political reasons, which as his actions indicated, he had accepted.[160]

He had been aware of Geol.'s previous conduct and his hostile attitude to National Socialism. He therefore knew that not only would Geol.'s misdemeanors that T. had initially reported to him be called into question, but also his personal past. The arbitrary and excessive sentences in political cases that were always published as a means of deterrence had made the general public aware of them, especially the ways in which state power had been used against Röhm and the SA leadership in 1934. After the beginning of the Second World War, aggression against alleged internal enemies of the regime worsened under the guise of strengthening the home front, and propaganda had made it known that deliberately listening to foreign broadcasts and spreading news from them, which would allegedly weaken the nation's will to resist its enemies, was punishable by death. This was known to W. who chose to set his career path at a higher priority than the harsh and cruel consequences that would surely follow for Gee. for perpetrating political offenses against the regime, which would be out of proportion to his actions, regardless of whether he could expect that Gee. would later be taken to a concentration camp after the end of his prison sentence. The court therefore determined that his conduct constituted a violation of Article 1c of Control Council Law No. 10, since he acted in an inhumane manner to persecute another on the basis of political principles. He had at least the potential intention to see that Gee. was subjected to arbitrary persecution while also being conscious of the unlawfulness of the proceedings that would be instituted against Gee.—proceedings that contravened universally accepted law.[161]

In considering mitigating circumstances while determining the sentencing for the severe consequences of the report, it was noted that he was not entirely responsible for Geol.'s death in view of the possibility that he could have died of natural causes. Moreover, W. had not acted on personal motives of revenge, hatred, or especial ill will, and considered himself bound by his duty to his political superiors on the basis of written directives. He also could not have necessarily anticipated that Gee. would be sent to a concentration camp. In addition, he did not have any prior convictions. While he was *Kreisleiter* in Constance, he had effectively intervened to assist politically afflicted parties, and was considered a good and helpful superior. Lastly, the fact that he had warned Gee. many times not to make himself conspicuous to the Gestapo was taken into consideration. This jury court therefore sentenced W. to a year and three months' imprisonment.[162] T. had testified before the Waldshut regional court as one of the witnesses. Considering his role in taking part in forwarding the report about Gee., he was later sentenced to ten months' imprisonment on 9 March 1948 for his cooperation in making the report that constituted a crime against humanity.[163]

Another denunciation case was later heard at the Berlin regional court, where judgment was pronounced on 31 May 1949. The accusation concerned whether the defendant, hereafter cited as B., had betrayed some young men and women who had fled to Grünewald in early 1945 where they were shot by the SS. However, the evidence entered in these proceedings was very limited. It was merely argued that the defendant, who had lived in an empty garage apartment in Grunewald, saw that there were some young people who had apparently deserted from the Köpernick *Volkssturm*, who were taking shelter in an empty neighboring villa with a substantial amount of foodstuffs.[164]

Neighbors saw from a distance of about 150 meters that the defendant had entered the house with an army captain, ostensibly to get the youngsters out of the basement. He was then observed looking for something in the foliage of the garden, but it could not be determined whether he was looking for buried uniforms, as Soviet troops had occupied the neighborhood two hours before. The youngsters left in a truck that was loaded with Italian prisoners of war under the command of German army officers, rather than in an SS unit that was supposedly the case, but no shots were heard after the truck left the villa.[165]

The facts of this case were insufficient to consider a prosecution on the basis of Control Council No. 10. It could not be established whether the defendant had called an unknown SS "raiding squad" (*Rollkommando*) or the commander overseeing Italian prisoners of war who were quartered at a nearby school. It also could not be determined whether the truck was used for the purpose of helping the youngsters from the Berlin borough of Köpenick. There was also no evidence about the whereabouts of the captain, or evidence that an execution had taken place, or any other events that taken place before the arrival of the Soviet troops.[166]

This court was inclined to believe that the defendant had aroused suspicion as a result of taking an interest in the foodstuffs in the youngsters' possession. According to witnesses' testimonies, the defendant had been unpopular in this community since he had already been previously convicted of twenty-two property crimes. It was therefore ruled that there was insufficient concrete evidence presented in this case, and these proceedings were thus closed.[167] This case also indicated how malicious intentions that had been given practically free rein in the National Socialist regime could be blocked by a court evaluating the available evidence fairly and objectively.

A later denunciation case was heard at the Offenburg regional court, where judgment was pronounced on 24 June 1949. The defendant had joined the NSDAP in 1937 after having been known to be an opponent of the National Socialist regime, but later he became a convinced National Socialist with radical tendencies. He supported the party by initially doing paperwork for the *Ortsgruppenleiter* in Offenburg in his frequent absences, and eventually becoming the driving and decisive force in the *Ortsgruppe* in Windschläg due to his high level of intelligence that made him indispensable to this authority. He was later appointed the local *Ortsgruppenleiter* at the beginning of the war, and later led a *Volkssturm* battalion at the time of the capitulation. After being interned until 27 February 1948,[168] he stood accused of denouncing another for what was interpreted to have been an allegedly hostile remark against the regime.

In late 1939, a railway attendant who had belonged to a local singing association, hereafter cited as Matthias S., was called on to join in providing musical accompaniment on the occasion of the conferring of mother's crosses. He refused to do so at the order of the defendant as the local *Ortsgruppenleiter,* saying to his fellow singers in the choral society that he would not sing for the "whore's cross." While the head of the choral society, hereafter cited as Sch., and another member hereafter cited as H., talked about this sometime later, the defendant unexpectedly came upon this conversation in the local office of the Labor Front as well as having received an anonymous tip about what had been said. He thereby told them to report everything they knew. After rebuking Sch. as the choral society leader for not having reported the matter earlier, he ordered him to go to the city hall on that day for questioning, where the remark he had heard was recorded in writing. At the end of the questioning, the defendant said that he would forward the matter to the *Kreisleitung* to deal with so that "the swine would be taken away immediately."[169]

The defendant had known before forwarding the matter onto the higher authorities that Si. had already been arrested for making a political remark, telling soldiers on exercises in Oberkirch that they should stop since it did not serve any purpose. The defendant had also known that Si. was known as a chatterbox through the entire village, and that nobody took him seriously or took offense about the things he said. Nevertheless, he willingly aggravated the situation by reporting the earlier offense. His report led to Si.'s arrest and three year sentence at Dachau concentration camp, and he later died in 1942 after his release due to a no-longer-determinable cause of death.[170]

The defendant denied reporting Si., instead claiming that he was ordered by a higher authority, probably the *Kreisleitung,* to examine four or five cited witnesses. On the other hand, the court disputed this assertion in view of the evidence. The leading witness, Si.'s widow, testified against him saying that he had told her that he had not made any secret of having reported her husband, since he had to do so. Moreover, he also maintained there was nothing that he could do to help her or her husband.[171] Her credible sworn testimony was hereby entered into evidence, while the defendant's profession of innocence was disputed given the fact that he could not name any more than one alleged witness that he was charged with questioning. Moreover, this person had not been called in for questioning. In addition, there were no witnesses who could confirm that there had been other witnesses who had been questioned in this small community of Windschläg, which made his claim even more unlikely. The two witnesses that had heard Si.'s comment about the mother's cross also testified that the defendant had not mentioned anything about the matter before they had told him about it, and therefore undermined the defendant's claim that he had had prior knowledge about what had been said and was instructed to investigate the matter.[172]

It was also established by examining several events that the defendant had been known to be a staunch supporter of the National Socialist regime with radical tendencies, and therefore would have been disposed toward hostile conduct against the regime's alleged opponents. In addition to a fellow party member who could maintain this claim, it was also shown that he had denounced others. These events testified to the defendant's conduct and personality at the time of the actions, which confirmed that he had reported Si. with a great sense of urgency.[173]

In 1943, a witness in the present proceedings, hereafter cited as S., had warned him that he ought to consider that his power would be gone soon, and that needed to think about what would come, while making a cutting gesture over her throat. He thereupon reported her for an offense against the state, and she was brought before the Freiburg Special Court. However, this court found that she was politically harmless, and her threat was the result of strained personal relations rather political motivations. She was therefore fined 50 RM for attempted coercion.[174]

The defendant also flatly denied that he had reported her at the time. However, a witness who had been employed by the police testified to the authenticity of the files concerning this written report while he had handled this matter. This case was also indicative of his disposition, as it was revealed how he had sought to expose her alleged "true disposition," as well as the extent of his own political convictions. The files showed how he had been ruthless and cruel in attaching political significance to her remarks, thus showing that he was capable of acting inhumanely against an older lady. It was also noted that both the *Kreisleitung* and the Gestapo had conceded she was politically harmless when they were involved in this case, which negated the consequences that the defendant had strived to bring about for her and her family as well.[175]

In a different case, he had threatened three other witnesses with imprisonment in a concentration camp as a result of their expressing differences in political opinions during conversations in a pub. The defendant was only ready to admit that he was unsatisfied with the amount of contributions that one of these witnesses' families had contributed to fund raising. While denying that he said at an *Ortgruppenstab* conference that this family should be excluded from the people's community, he admitted to ordering that they should be excluded from any associations. The court ruled that at the time, this practically meant an exclusion from the people's community.[176]

The defendant was also suspected of having reported a cabinetmaker in Windschläg, hereafter cited as W., to the Gestapo in 1943, who was kept in their custody from August 1943 to January 1944. He also denied making this denunciation, admitting only having made a report about him that included complaints about W. that had been forwarded to him. He claimed to have had misgivings about conveying this report, and had allegedly approached W. and spoken to him about it. Having been impressed by his explanations, he claimed to have destroyed this report after their conversation. A witness could only confirm that after W.'s arrest, the defendant had regretted not having the "previous papers" about W. The evidence proffered from other witnesses otherwise suggested that W. was reported for having broken his employment contract, which led to his arrest by the Gestapo. This charge against him was dropped,[177] but his reaction to W.'s arrest nevertheless indicated his hostile attitude toward another in cooperating with the authorities of the time, as was proven to be the case with Si.

The defendant was found guilty of crimes against humanity in accordance with Article II, section 1c of Control Council Law No. 10, for having persecuted Si. on political grounds. As in other cases before this time, the facts of this case demonstrated how cruel and inhumane actions were perpetrated in violating the universally accepted rights of humanity and the dignity and value of the individual. This was done at a time when these rights were treated with contempt in dealing with political opponents of the violent and arbitrary National Socialist regime. As a result of this action of having reported him to the authorities of the time, the defendant had caused Si. to spend three years in a concentration camp, which possibly contributed to his death thereafter. The inhumanity of the defendant's actions were demonstrated in the fact that Si. was not afforded the benefit of a fair trial as a result of the defendant's report, and was subjected to the injustice of the arbitrariness of the Gestapo that was indicative of National Socialist violence and tyranny. This exposing of him to the arbitrariness of the regime demonstrated a violation of humanity as the bearer and protector of the ideals of the values and rights of humanity, including life, liberty, and the right to the freedom of beliefs and expression. The harsh consequences that Si. suffered were not commensurate to any degree with his wisecrack about the mother's cross medal. Meanwhile, the defendant was responsible for those consequences, since the high courts in Germany thoroughly recognized how the jurisdiction of Control Council Law No. 10 extended to subjecting individuals to prosecution for making reports that brought about unduly severe penalties. It was also to be noted that the defendant was to have expected the consequences that would follow for Si. as a result of his report.[178]

It was also noted that the defendant had acted out of political motives, having forwarded his report to the *Kreisleitung*, rather than to a court or the state prosecutor, since he had considered Si.'s disparaging remark to be political in nature, especially since he was a party functionary who was anxious to demonstrate his loyalty to the party. Meanwhile, he had also been aware of the violent methods of suppression that the National Socialist regime had used against those possessing opposing political viewpoints, and thus consciously contributed to this political repression. The fact that he had threatened others with concentration camp imprisonment due to their difference in political opinions dispelled any doubts as to whether he was unaware of the regime's methods in suppressing political dissention. Whether or not the defendant foresaw and approved all possible consequences of his actions, the National Socialist regime was known to be a tyranny that was not constricted by the principles of the rule of law. This common knowledge of the regime's arbitrariness constituted the defendant's intentions in making his report to deliver a victim to these powers of tyranny and terror.[179]

The defendant was an intelligent individual who had already possessed knowledge of the methods the regime used against political opposition, especially since he had experience in actively serving the NSDAP, including as an acting *Ortsgruppenleiter*. Being a convinced follower of National Socialist ideology and an experienced party functionary, he had therefore undoubtedly known what kinds of indiscriminate measures would be initiated against Si. when he conveyed his report to the *Kreisleitung*. After the outbreak of the war, the worst types of consequences would follow reports of disparaging political remarks, and drastic measures were mercilessly taken against those dissenting from the ideal of political unanimity. He had undoubtedly intended for Si. to be taken to a concentration camp, but it could not be ascertained with complete certainty whether he could expect him to be killed.

The defendant was found guilty of committing a crime against humanity. It was also noted that the defendant had acted in an exceptionally rough manner, such as ignoring Si.'s wife pleas and considering it unnecessary to compensate for his injustice. He had also hardly expressed any remorse about the severity of the consequences he had perpetrated. The court therefore ascertained that in view of his intelligence and trust in the practices of the National Socialist regime, he did not recognize the complete extent of his actions. On the other hand, the fact that he had hitherto not had any prior convictions was also taken into consideration. In view of these considerations, he was sentenced to a year's imprisonment.

A later denunciation case was heard at the Offenburg regional court, where judgment was pronounced on 4 July 1949. The defendant, hereafter cited as E., had been a long-standing member of the NSDAP, having joined the party on 1 November 1931, and then serving as a *Blockleiter* from 1933, and later a *Zellenleiter* at the outbreak of the Second World War. He had been exempted from military service due to his diabetic condition until early 1943, after which he fought on the eastern and southeastern fronts as a tank driver until he was interned as a prisoner-of-war in May 1945 and then released later that month.[180]

While he was on leave and visiting his family in Stuttgart in March 1944, he and his wife went to visit the parents of a friend on 14 March, where they met their daughter, hereafter cited as T. and their son hereafter cited as A. In the course of the conversation at their apartment, the discussion turned to the always increasing intensity of bombing raid, after which A. spoke about his pessimism about how he expected the present situation to worsen. He then spoke about the overall situation of the war, and how things appeared especially bleak in the east, as it appeared that Rumania would fall and have to depend on Germany's support. He then also added that Hitler had started the war, as he had foretold in *Mein Kampf.* E. argued that if National Socialism had not been instituted in 1933, the communists would have come to power. A. refused to accept this, saying that there was no such danger in Germany. Their conversation became increasingly more agitated and louder thereafter. E. said that since he had seen Russia, it sufficed for him to stand for what he believed was true, but A. argued that Bolshevism had taken over a completely wrecked state that was still being restored, while Hitler had taken over an unencumbered and well-ordered state and there were now more communists in Stuttgart than one believed. E. then broke off the conversation and left the apartment saying he knew who was before him.[181]

His friend's parents and T. were alarmed at his leaving so suddenly, and feared that he would go make a report to the Gestapo. T. tried to reason with him outside her parents' home, saying A. did not mean what he had said and that there had been a misunderstanding, but E. refused to listen as he left determined to make a report about the incident. He added the veiled threat that A. should get a departure ticket since he would put his head on the block. A. also went after him to plead with him to listen, but E. merely roughly shoved him away. During the fifteen minute walk to the police station, his wife also pleaded with him to refrain from making a report and foolishly making such a fuss, but he still stubbornly refused. When he reached the local criminal police, he was referred to the Gestapo, which had jurisdiction in such matters. Upon reaching their office and reporting what he had heard, the agent there told him that this was an outright example of undermining the war effort that could cost someone their head.[182]

The Gestapo arrested A. on 20 March 1944, and proceedings were initiated against him at the People's Court for undermining the war effort through his remarks. On 26 January 1945, E. gave his testimony as a witness at the main proceedings, where he confirmed what he had previously told the Gestapo over ten months beforehand. A. was thereafter sentenced to three years' imprisonment, and died on 4 April 1945 in the Coswig (Anhalt) concentration camp. His widow was later notified in early 1946 that the cause of death was cardiac insufficiency and circulatory disorders.[183]

E. claimed in his defense that he had not intended for formal criminal proceedings to be brought about, and only expected that A. would be removed from the "people's community" for the duration of the war so that his "prattle" would not cause further trouble. He also considered himself to be responsible for making a report in the interest of supporting fellow soldiers at the front, citing the often repeated instruction to soldiers on leave to take action against "defeatists" and backbiters in the homeland. These explanations were taken into consideration as part of the subjective facts of the case[184] while other facts and circumstances were examined.

The court determined that the facts regarding the conduct of the defendant objectively constituted a crime against humanity on the basis of political principles, as defined under Article II, section 1c of Control Council Law No. 10. It was maintained that everyone was entitled to the inviolable fundamental rights of humanity that protected them from cruel and inhumane treatment in order to uphold the dignity and value of human life, which included the rights of life, well-being, freedom, and the right to free expression and freedom of expression. Although these rights could be subjected to certain limitations in wartime, there had to be a minimal guarantee to uphold them, as doing otherwise would constitute a violation of the generally accepted principles of all civilized nations and moral law. It could be implied that defeatist statements were subject to prosecution in all of the belligerent nations during the war. However, the prosecution for such remarks in National Socialist Germany broadly disregarded the principles of orderly criminal proceedings by abusing legal guarantees, and the punishments that were imposed were completely out of proportion to the level of guilt, and thus contradicted every sense of justice.[185]

The action that the defendant had taken in reporting A.'s defeatist remarks to the Gestapo did not justify the cruel and arbitrary persecution that resulted, which disregarded the principles of universally accepted rights of humanity. Moreover, there was no justifiable cause for the defendant to make a report, even in view of the political conditions of the time, since the remarks did not affect him personally, and there would have been no trouble for him if he had chosen to maintain his silence about what had been said in a private setting. It was therefore ruled that since he had unjustly delivered A. into the hands of the Gestapo and inevitably the People's Court thereafter, he had contributed to perpetrating an inhumane offense of the National Socialist regime, and therefore had himself acted inhumanely by causing A.'s persecution by having reported him[186] to the authorities of the time.

A crime against humanity required a demonstration of unconditional malicious intent, and the perpetrators therefore necessarily had to have prior knowledge that their politically motivated actions against another could result in considerable disadvantages for the victim of their actions. They therefore would have to have been conscious of the circumstances in which the inhuman consequences would follow, and possibly have approved of what could occur. The defendant's testimony was found to be completely irrelevant, since he was considered sufficiently intelligent and politically astute to recognize the effect that his report would have on the measures that would be taken against an alleged opponent of the regime. Moreover, his political experience as a long-standing member of the NSDAP, having occupied positions in the party, gave him a better insight into the working of the party apparatus that most of the population. He also did not deny having knowledge of the methods that the regime had used against its outspoken opponents, such as those who made disparaging criticisms or dared to speak about doubting the final victory. This was common knowledge at the time of his actions, although perhaps he lacked an insight into the political conditions on the home front after having been at the front for six months during serious military setbacks in Stalingrad and North Africa. However, the daily newspapers included increasingly frequent references to the types of serious and draconian measures "defeatists" could expect, and that such elements had to be ruthlessly eradicated. The defendant had acknowledged in these proceedings that these messages had not escaped his attention, and that he was not unaware of the consequences that would follow for A. in view of the remarks he had made when he was stubbornly on his way to report him to the authorities. It was therefore determined that he had expressly intended to expose an opponent of the regime to its inhumane methods of suppression.[187]

The defendant could not claim to have been unaware of the unlawfulness of his actions, and thus could not cite ignorance of the law in his defense. Besides, one could not use this pretext in opposing the existence of the universally accepted moral law. Nor could he be absolved of guilt for having considered himself obligated to act on his political ideals or out of his duty as a soldier. The NSDAP had attempted to institute political indoctrination through National Socialist political officers in the army toward the end of the war, who instructed soldiers on leave not to listen to "defeatists" and "backbiters" in order to prevent the undermining of their fighting spirit. In his own admission however, they were not specifically ordered to report defeatist remarks. Hence, he not could cite in his defense that he was following orders, which in any case was inadmissible according to Article II, section 4b of Control Council Law No. 10. Moreover, the court remained convinced that he was in fact conscious of the injustice of his actions in exposing another to inhumane consequences. It was therefore found that he had acted out of a reproachful disposition, and was found guilty of violating Article II, section 1c of Control Council Law No. 10.[188]

In evaluating any mitigating circumstances in determining the sentencing, it was noted that the defendant had not had any prior convictions and that there was nothing adverse about his reputation. There was also no evidence to indicate that he had been a spiteful or dangerous party fanatic. Moreover, he had admitted to his guilt and had expressed remorse at this time. It was also conceded that he had been influenced by National Socialist propaganda, and had thus acted out of a false sense of national feeling. On the other hand, it had been completely unreasonable to have ignored the objections and pleas of T. and his wife, and he had had a time to reconsider refraining from reporting A. on the way to the Gestapo office, rather than determining to act on outrageous stubbornness. He was therefore sentenced to two years' imprisonment, including the time that had already been served after having had already been interned since 15 March 1946.[189]

The experience of prosecuting cases of political denunciation in French occupied Germany was marked by the spectacular case against Helene Schwärzel and other such cases that followed this precedent-setting case. The adjudication of these cases demonstrated the feasibility of bringing indirect perpetrators of crimes against humanity to account for their actions. There were significant weaknesses in the inconclusive denazification program in the administration of justice that had led to insufficiently severe sanctions against former members of the NSDAP,[190] as well as insignificant sanctions imposed on most others. In the example of Württemberg, 63.6 percent of judges out of a total of the 69 percent who had formerly been members of the NSDAP incurred only very light sentences, while 57.6 percent of lawyers out of the 70.4 percent who had been NSDAP members only sustained monetary sanctions ranging up to 500 DM.[191] However, the reconstituted German courts in the French occupation zone executed their functions with satisfactory results in ordinary criminal and civil cases. Apart from the intervention by the French occupation authorities in the Tillesen case and demands for revisions in other cases, supervision by the regional court presidents and French military government authorities, which took special interest in cases of crimes against humanity,[192] revealed few setbacks. However, they noted that there was a diminishing interest in prosecuting such cases toward the end of the military occupation.

It was apparent by April 1949 that the concept of crimes against humanity as defined by Control Council Law No. 10 was ill received at all levels of the German administration of justice, and according to information revealed by public prosecutors, it was a legal concept that had lost practically all of its significance by this time. This was especially true with regard to its use in cases of political denunciations. These were now only prosecuted if the denounced had suffered severe consequences, such as those cases resulting in incarceration in a concentration camp and subsequent death. The original spirit of Control Council Law No. 10 had also become supplanted by the principles of common law that had been in practice since 1947. This mostly led to judges following the precedents set by previous types of cases, such as the prosecution of violent anti-Semitic excesses. The prosecution of cases of a political nature therefore tended to follow the basis of German law and the earlier precedents without taking the heaviest possible sentencing into account. The number of such cases coming before the courts decreased, and there was a tendency for the severity of the sentencing to become reduced, and for prison sentences to be replaced by the imposing of monetary penalties, which was a trend that was further entrenched by the institution of jury courts.[193] Public prosecutors appeared to continue to lose interest in bringing crimes against humanity to trial, while the local government did not oppose this trend. It appeared that too much time had already passed for these cases to rouse any passions about such cases, especially those concerning little-known individuals without any significant political connections,[194] which culminated in public expressions of disapproval in prosecuting such cases. Broadcasts of addresses over the radio at this time tended to contain disapproving opinions of court judgments regarding crimes against humanity.

In August 1949, a legal affairs correspondent on Radio Stuttgart expressed what the French military government considered an extremely tendentious analysis of a case of crimes against humanity at the beginning of the court proceedings before the judgment was passed. He distinctly favored the position of the defendants, and appeared to try to influence the verdict by demanding their acquittal while emphasizing that proceedings in such cases ought to be abandoned. This address echoed and aggravated the existing public opinion that was already hostile to the continuation of proceedings concerning crimes against humanity. It aroused heated comments in the press in both French and American occupied Wurttemberg, which pressed a number of political personalities to take a stand in this matter before the case would be heard at the regional court in Tübingen.[195]

Another such indignant address in Koblenz on 8 September 1949 concerned two defendants accused of crimes against humanity at the Mainz regional court. The commentator criticized this court's excessive tolerance on the grounds that it aroused mistrust in the postwar administration of justice. The defendants were provisionally released before they were re-arrested about twelve days before the end of the proceedings. The correspondent criticized the court's decision[196] in a discourse about why there was still a prevailing mistrust about the administration of justice, and why they still needed to be vigilant with regard to jurists who were acting against the interests of society. This commentator noted that the judicial authorities had settled back into its work exceptionally quickly after the collapse of the National Socialist regime. This raised suspicions that the administration of justice had been brought back into operation so quickly and smoothly that the process of renewal resulted in merely a rearranging of its external appearance without the judiciary changing its ideas about its role as part of the new beginning.

This could have been partly attributed to the fact that 95 percent of judges, public prosecutors, and lawyers had been members of the NSDAP. Most of them had been reinstated in their former positions as a result of the exceptionally lenient denazification of the legal profession, and preferential treatment extended to the judiciary. However, the administration of justice had repeatedly squandered its trust and reputation during the National Socialist regime and the Weimar republic. Although it had to be admitted that the judges were subject to making errors and miscarriages of justice, these could be revised through a number of safeguards in the new administration of justice. However, the sorts of political judgments that had been made in the recent past had provoked further criticisms as to whether a spirit of a democratic sense of justice was lacking among the judiciary while judges cautiously followed earlier precedents in reaching their verdicts. While individual errors in individual cases could be corrected, there remained the suspicion that individual jurists systematically and intentionally adjudicated crimes against humanity with undue leniency, which made them unapologetic supporters of injustice. It thus appeared that the judiciary was consciously following a course that involved the greatest possible political, moral, and judicial dangers. Judges who were vested with the responsibility and privilege of judicial independence appeared to be passing insufficiently severe sentences or acquittals in political trials. This set a bad example for the further adjudication of such cases in which the defendants could conduct themselves at such proceedings with an attitude of insolence and cynicism, while some jurists appeared to be exploiting their judicial independence to impede the administration of justice with arbitrary decisions.[197]

A case of crimes against humanity that had just been heard at the criminal court in Mainz was cited as an example of what appeared to be the judicial deficiencies in such cases. When a former Jewish resident in von Alzey demanded an additional 4800 RM from the city administration for the sale of a house, the former National Socialist mayor wrote a letter to the Gestapo to get rid of this inconvenient creditor, telling them to take this "audacious Jew S. B. F." to a concentration camp in the east. She was taken away soon thereafter and never came back. The defendant claimed during the proceedings that he had signed this letter, but had neither dictated nor read it, and had only had time to glance at his outgoing correspondence due to his heavy workload while his subordinates functioned in a rather independent manner. The court accepted this defense and he was acquitted since he could not be prosecuted for negligence. The public prosecutor thereafter forwarded this verdict to the appeal court.[198]

While the astonishment and anger over this acquittal had not yet subsided, another case of a crime against humanity likewise led to another dubious verdict. The Mainz regional court had convicted a former NSDAP *Stabsleiter,* hereafter cited as J. K., and a former major, hereafter cited as O. K., for crimes against humanity in June 1947. Although J. K. had been sentenced to life imprisonment and O. K. to eight years' imprisonment for murder and aiding and abetting manslaughter, they were later released on 29 July 1949. J. K. had been the mayor of Heidesheim near Mainz in early 1945, and the *Abschnittsführer* of the *Volkssturm* in the *Kreis* of Bingen. O. K. was posted at the military commander's office in Mainz when he was sent to Ingelheim on reconnaissance in the early days of 1945, where he established his absolute power as the military commander who was not subject to any superior authority. He had the *Volkssturm* leader there, hereafter cited as B., arrested on March 1945 for having intended to spare Ingelheim from destruction in view of the desperate military situation. B. was taken to the local party authorities, and after a farcical trial, was then taken to the marketplace where he was hanged from a tree. An application for appeal was instituted after the initial verdict was pronounced due to the extent of the sentence, and renewed court proceedings took place at the Mainz regional court two years later, when the acquittals were pronounced after brief deliberations in spite of the evidence of the grave incriminations. The same criminal court rejected an appeal from an individual who appealed a court decision that was imposed during the National Socialist regime, whereby he had been sentenced to eight years' imprisonment for allegedly undermining the military. It also undertook to begin redressing this judgment after being forced to do so following an appeal to the court of a higher instance.[199]

The attitude of resignation toward prosecuting crimes against humanity continued until the end of the military occupation and thereafter. Many cases of crimes against humanity continued to be resolved during October and November 1949, but the public remained increasingly disinterested in these proceedings. Meanwhile, the courts generally became increasingly lenient in their sentencing.[200] The continued prosecution of crimes against humanity that came before the courts required the cooperation of the public prosecutors and the judiciary to adjudicate such cases, as well as the appropriate legislation to define them, and the political willingness for the perpetrators to be brought to trial. However, this remained subject to the prevailing conditions of the time among the public, and the extent to which the judiciary could exercise its independence in determining what had to be done in spite of the unpopularity of such cases among the public. It also remained for the higher instance appeal courts to rectify any judgments that could not be justifiably upheld in view of the available evidence while serving the interests of justice.

The defendants in these denunciation cases were considered accomplices in the crimes that were committed, and were brought to justice accordingly on the basis of the underlying argument that those who had denounced others to the National Socialist authorities and made them subject to the inhumane consequences were considered at least partly responsible for those consequences. In spite of the decreasing numbers of such cases being brought to trial, the German courts would later maintain jurisdiction over such cases after the end of the Allied military occupation regime under new German legislation that superseded Control Council Law No. 10. Checks on judicial authority remained in place outside the judiciary in the form of responsible members of juries, as well as a free press that could also exercise its influence on court judgments, and was also representative of public opinion that was not necessarily justifiable in light of the evidence of the crimes that had been perpetrated.

Chapter 4

The British Occupation Zone: Legislation and Practice

The British military government empowered the courts in their occupation zone with jurisdiction over cases of crimes against humanity under the provisions of Control Council Law No. 10, and this jurisdiction was extended to specifically encompass the adjudication of cases of political denunciations. Since political denunciation was not specifically mentioned in Law No. 10 in its provisions for crimes against humanity, this type of case was included through a broader interpretation of the concept of political persecution.[1] Having been empowered to adjudicate these types of cases, it remained for the judiciary to administer justice retroactively in accordance with the spirit of Control Council Law No. 10 in spite of their reluctance about the necessity of administering justice through the use of retroactive legislation.

The German courts in the British occupation zone were granted jurisdiction over adjudicating crimes against humanity, as defined by Article II, paragraph 1(c) of Control Council Law No. 10, through Military Government Ordinance No. 47, issued on 30 August 1946.[2] This ordinance granted them specific jurisdiction over these cases that were committed by Germans against other Germans or stateless persons. After roughly one and a half years of political screening through the denazification program, and toward the end of the proceedings at the International Military tribunal in Nuremberg, the British military government considered the personnel and institutional reorganization of German judicial organization in its zone to have achieved a certain degree of stability. It therefore considered that the German judicial organization could thereafter be entrusted with jurisdiction over the prosecution of National Socialist crimes.[3] Certain cases would be tried by the military government courts in order for the sentences to serve as a precedent for the German courts to follow. A British military government decree on

10 September 1946 empowered the German courts to apply this law and to impose the penalties cited in Article II, section 3 when the charges were not applicable under German law. They could also apply Control Council Law No. 10 to prosecute offenses against German law, provided that the appropriate charges could be laid, and they could also use the provisions set out in Article II, section 5. However, the extent of sentencing was not to be limited by what was prescribed under German law for particular offenses. German courts could impose sentences in accordance with Article II, section 3 of Control Council Law No. 10 whenever the penalties cited in German law were considered inadequate to fulfill the requirements of justice.[4] This would particularly apply to the prosecution of criminal actions that were committed on political grounds during the National Socialist regime.[5] Extending the jurisdiction to German courts to adjudicate denunciation cases could also serve to placate public demand that had been expressed in the press for such cases to be prosecuted,[6] while the German administration of justice had been reproached by both the public and the political parties for its reservations about prosecuting cases of a political nature.[7]

The wide-reaching jurisdiction of Control Council Law No. 10, and Ordinance No. 47 was further clarified through new legislation. Further to the previous deliberations concerning the implementation of Ordinance No. 47, the British military government legal division determined that jurisdiction over these types of cases would be conferred upon German courts, and the sentences that they would impose would set precedents for such cases in the future. Guidance in adjudicating these types of cases could hereafter be drawn from Allied legislation and practice. This included Control Council Directive No. 38, Article II, paragraph 9, which decreed that "major offenders" ought to be sentenced to up to ten years' imprisonment for having actively collaborated with the Gestapo, SD, SS or similar organizations by denouncing or otherwise assisting in the prosecution of enemies of the National Socialist regime. The German courts could also follow the example of the precedent set by the conviction of Helene Schwärzel who had been sentenced to ten years' imprisonment, ten years' loss of her civil rights, and the confiscation of all of her property.[8]

German jurists had expressed their view to the legal division about the difficulties that could be encountered with obtaining convictions in certain cases of informers in which the facts of the case were not offenses against German law, and could be considered to be in conflict with the concept of *nulla poene sine lege*. Nevertheless, in spite of the potential difficulties in obtaining convictions under German law and overcoming the problem of applying the law retroactively,[9] the legal division remained undeterred from granting the German courts jurisdiction over these cases. The legal division preferred this option, rather than having these cases be dealt with in military government courts or special German tribunals that would be set up to deal with members of organizations convicted by the International Military Tribunal at Nuremberg. Any difficulties were to be referred to either the Central Judicial Office for the British zone in Hamburg that had been established on 1 October 1946 as the uniform legislative authority for the *Länder* of the British zone with the power to exercise the functions of the former national Ministry of Justice,[10] or the British military government legal division. Special German Tribunals would be set up to deal with members of organizations convicted by the International Military Tribunal at Nuremberg, and if necessary, also to deal with certain cases of prosecuting informers whenever it would be impossible to obtain convictions under German law due to possible transgressions of the principle of *nulla poene sine lege*. Since the trying of cases of members of criminal organizations was to receive priority, cases of informers were to be adjudicated by German courts whenever possible.[11]

The underlying basis of prosecuting crimes against humanity under German law was predicated on the definition of certain actions done in the past as criminal offenses, such as murder and manslaughter, which were defined as such in the time before they were perpetrated. However inadmissible this was in normal circumstances, this superseding of the principle of *nulla poene sine lege* was necessary, since the defendant could not be called to account for their actions when these violations of German criminal law were perpetrated due to the circumstances[12] of the time. It was therefore possible to reconcile the provisions of the German Criminal code with those of Control Council Law No. 10. Control Council Law No. 10 had been enacted to permit the prosecution of crimes against humanity and to safeguard the principles of law and justice in view of crimes that had been committed *before* the defendant could be brought to trial.

Most of the crimes against humanity, as defined by Control Council Law No. 10, were punishable under German law; however, crimes committed by informers were the exception that also probably aroused the most popular interest. The German courts were under the obligation to apply the law retroactively in these and other crimes against humanity. However, since administering retrospective law was contrary to the tradition and philosophy of German law, further instructions were necessary to alleviate the difficulties that were expected with German judges being ordered to act against their consciences in adjudicating crimes against humanity that were not subject to prosecution under German law.[13]

Although some jurists in the British occupation zone officially supported the military government's legislation on crimes against humanity and recognized that it necessarily had to be applied retroactively,[14] the military government expected enormous difficulties with the particular problem of adjudicating denunciation cases. As Professor Gustav Radbruch had argued in his article on lawful injustice and justice under the law, the prosecuting of informers under the provisions of German law would also entail prosecuting the judges who had passed the sentences in these cases as accessories to the same crimes. In spite of the difficulties, there remained the necessity of prosecuting these types of cases due to the amount of interest in them. If informers were to be left unpunished, the confidence of the German population in the administration of justice would be undermined. A British military government legal representative at this time envisaged that informers could otherwise be prosecuted by special denazification tribunals that would be established for the purpose of implementing the provisions of Control Council Directive No. 38, through which informers would be classified as major offenders.[15] While this denazification directive specifically cited how informers were to be subject to prosecution, there remained the problem of defining whether the jurisdiction over these types of cases was to be assumed by denazification tribunals or law courts.

The German judicial authorities requested further clarification on the implementation of Ordinance No. 47 to further define the extent of the German courts' jurisdiction in adjudicating the different types of crimes against humanity. Thus it could be determined what types of cases could be prosecuted under German law and those in which the authority for adjudication was granted by the British military government. There was also the problem of the German press criticizing the German administration of justice for its reluctance in adjudicating such cases[16] at a time when the population and various political parties demanded that these crimes be prosecuted to the widest possible extent. Meanwhile, the administration of justice also maintained reservations about prosecuting these cases while being under attack from the public for their insufficient political cleansing.[17] Support from the military government was therefore necessary to allay suspicions about the shortcomings of the functions of the administration of justice while it operated under its supervision. This first required the cooperation of the German judiciary in contributing to achieving the political aims of the military occupation.

The British military government also criticized the German jurists for their reluctance to adjudicate cases of crimes against humanity. It was the opinion of the legal branch that they were spending too much time and energy in academic discussions about the difficulties regarding bringing Germans to account for their actions, or debating which types of crimes could be seen as crimes against humanity, or whether cases in which other Germans had denounced others for activities that were considered hostile to the regime were crimes at all. The British military government stated that foremost task was for the German jurists to act on concrete recommendations and actions, rather than to write extensive treatises on criminal law and jurisprudential concepts. In spite of the difficulties concerning the judicial investigation of informers, Special Court judges and other persons who could be accused of crimes and prosecuted with the retroactive application of the law, it was maintained that the cases hitherto cited could not go unpunished. Hence, the German courts were responsible for prosecuting denunciation cases, and other such crimes were to be dealt as they arose, especially those concerned with other individual members of organizations that had been declared to be criminal by the International Military Tribunal in Nuremberg. The ordinary German courts would remain responsible for dealing with these cases until it was ordered that some of these cases could be prosecuted by special tribunals when there could be difficulties in obtaining a conviction as a result of contravening the principle of the retroactive application of the law.[18]

The British military government specifically addressed the matter of adjudicating cases of informers on 21 November 1946 when it decided that the ordinary German courts would adjudicate such cases when the facts of such cases could be considered as falling under the jurisdiction of Control Council Law No. 10 and Ordinance No. 47, such as in the precedent set by the trial of Helene Schwärzel. Sanctions were to be imposed on informers as cited in Control Council Directive No. 38 on denazification measures, by which they would be considered "major offenders" who were subject to penalties of up to ten years' imprisonment.[19] This decree circumvented the shortcomings in the German criminal code for prosecuting cases in which truthful denunciations resulted in grave consequences for those who were denounced.[20] The major shortcoming in the German criminal code was that it only contained regulations and sanctions for false accusations in Articles 164 and 165. Codified German law did not serve the purpose of prosecuting the types of crimes against humanity envisaged in Control Council Law No. 10—that is, those that were brought about by truthful accusations.[21] Hence, this military government decree could only serve the purpose of supplementing German law. However, the jurists could nevertheless evaluate the consequences of those accusations, especially those that had resulted in violations of the criminal law that would have occurred in ordinary circumstances. German jurists were therefore charged with applying both German and occupation law to obtain convictions in keeping with the letter and spirit of both possibilities to serve justice.

The military government also hoped to allay criticism of the administration of justice through extending the German courts' jurisdiction with regard to crimes against humanity. There had hitherto been noticeable discomfort among the public about the delay in the criminal prosecution of crimes against humanity by the German courts while their jurisdiction had been curtailed by the military government until certain proceedings of fundamental importance were first concluded in military government courts. The press was therefore authorized to announce that Ordinance No. 47 empowered the German courts to adjudicate crimes defined under Control Council Law No. 10 and that additional instructions in some categories of cases, such as denunciation cases, were going to be issued thereafter.[22] It remained to be seen how the administration of justice would perform in the exercise of its responsibilities while adjudicating such cases under its own jurisdiction.

Control Council Law No. 10 became part of German substantive law, but it remained necessary for the judiciary to overcome its reservations about its application. The British military government supported the German judiciary in cases in which it was called upon to adjudicate crimes against humanity under this law and in accordance with existing German law. This support was further emphasized after the judiciary became alarmed by the news that the French military government had dismissed and imprisoned a judge in Freiburg for having acquitted Tillesen. The military government also recognized that the applying of the law retroactively could be marred by the problem of the enduring reluctance among the German judiciary to put it into practice, even though it remained their responsibility to ensure that the interests of justice were served.[23]

These theoretical considerations about jurisprudence and concerns about the necessity of applying Control Council Law No. 10 continued to cause delays in prosecuting crimes against humanity. While the application of this law had been justified in legal journals, it remained for the administration of justice to overcome its reservations by upholding the spirit of this law and its purpose of adjudicating past injustices that had been perpetrated with impunity. The German administration of justice was to resolve all of these issues in practice while functioning under the supervision of the military government, even though there remained a hesitation to adjudicate cases of crimes against humanity among certain jurists. There were acute differences of opinion between some judges and public prosecutors, since the sentences imposed in the courts were far more lenient than those that the prosecutors recommended. Although certain judges were averse to applying Control Council Law No. 10, the public prosecutors began dealing with such cases emphatically and conscientiously. The prosecution of denunciation cases proceeded when evidence could be brought forward that informers had taken their own initiative to act against another with base motives.[24]

There were also indications that there could be doubts about how the application of Control Council Law No. 10 would work, as it was in conflict with corresponding provisions in German law. These doubts were aggravated by jurists who were very reluctant to apply Control Council Law No.

10 since it involved administering the law retroactively, and would favor adjudicating crimes against humanity under German law as a matter of expediency. In some cases, Control Council Law No. 10 was not cited in indictments against the defendant who were subject to prosecution under both this law and German criminal law. These cases which should have been prosecuted as crimes against humanity instead resulted in acquittals. It was decided that criminal procedure would have to be modified to clarify criminal procedure in these cases.[25]

The uncertainty over whether the German courts had jurisdiction over cases arising from Control Council Law No. 10 continued into early 1947. The directive of 21 November 1946 had not provided sufficient clarity about precisely which cases would not be adjudicated by the special tribunals, rather than what cases would specifically be adjudicated by the German courts, due to the underlying problem of resistance to applying the law retroactively. The general inspector of the Central Judicial Office therefore drafted arguments in favor of the courts assuming sole jurisdiction in these types of cases. The special tribunals that were patterned after the earlier jury courts at the lowest levels of jurisdiction differed from the ordinary courts with regard to the special tasks that were assigned to them. In the meantime, both the special tribunals and the ordinary courts were subject to the same principles of the rule of law, without the special tribunals composing a special form of legal jurisdiction. Both court organizations were equally responsible for applying Control Council Law No. 10 and to administer justice retroactively in crimes against humanity, in contrast to other types of cases, for the purpose of assisting in the implementing of military occupation policymaking.[26]

In practice, many judges were deterred from undertaking the responsibility for these special political criminal cases while holding the view that they could be assigned to the special tribunals instead, without realizing the fact that applying retroactive legislation in these cases did not represent an arbitrary abrogation of a principle of the rule of law. The judiciary had reservations about accepting the responsibility of assisting the state in applying the law to prosecute injustices of the past, citing the prohibition of applying retroactive legislation as a pretext for their reluctance without duly giving sufficient consideration to the injustices that had been perpetrated. If the frequency of the indecisiveness in judging these cases became too great, it appeared that the political authorities would have to decide whether such cases would have to be prosecuted outside of the German administration of justice, as had been the case in the American occupation zone, where they were adjudicated under the Law for the Liberation from National Socialism and Militarism. Meanwhile, it remained for the judiciary to take responsibility for applying Control Council Law No. 10, regardless of any reservations emanating from their conscience concerning passing judgments on the basis of a law they considered unconventional.[27]

The British military government had considered copying the practice adopted in the American zone of using special German courts (*Spruchgerichte*) that lay outside the conventional administration of justice to overcome the potential difficulties with the adjudication of denunciation cases. While the underlying problems of the retroactive application of the law led the judiciary to avoid these difficulties by trying to avoid the adjudication of crimes against humanity, the British military government attempted to clarify the legal situation with a new directive concerning denunciation cases and again reaffirmed that the judiciary would be held responsible for judging them.

The military government resolved on 23 May 1947 that denunciation cases would remain outside the jurisdiction of the *Spruchgerichte* that were established under Military Government Ordinance No. 69 on the "Trial of members of Criminal Organizations." The responsibility for judging these cases would hereafter remain within the jurisdiction of the ordinary German courts in accordance with Ordinance No. 47 on the implementation of Control Council Law No. 10.[28] There had been uncertainty about the jurisdiction over denunciation cases due to corresponding instructions in Ordinance No. 47 and the subsequent directive of 21 November 1946 that called for the prosecution of informers by German courts, while sanctions were also to be imposed on informers through denazification tribunals as cited in Control Council Directive No. 38. This raised uncertainty about whether jurisdiction over such cases was to be assumed by the ordinary law courts administering Control Council Law No. 10 or the denazification tribunals administering denazification regulations.[29] In fact, the provisions in Directive No. 38 concerning the prosecution of informers merely provided guidelines for the imposition of sentences in these cases by ordinary German courts.[30] This directive was not supposed to influence the extent of sentences imposed in denunciation cases, which were to be determined in accordance with the code of criminal procedure[31] while judging these cases as criminal actions. Moreover, many German judicial authorities, especially in Schleswig-Holstein, avoided dealing with these cases by referring them to the Central Judicial Office rather than giving a decision themselves. Ordinary German courts were henceforth solely made responsible for the adjudication of these types of cases.[32]

The German judiciary would therefore have to overcome its reservations in prosecuting cases of crimes against humanity in the exercise of their duties in all types of cases. Criminal legislation was to be applied as usual as in normal circumstances. However, the post-war situation placed new demands on the judiciary in that it required them to administer the law to a higher degree of justice based on the general concept of humanity. Extraordinary legislation that necessarily had to be applied retroactively would serve the provisional purpose of administering justice during the exceptional circumstances of the post war period, and would be outside the limitations prescribed in codified law, just as the Nuremberg trials had been based on the concept that the application of the law did not require the law to be formally codified to judge violations against the intrinsic universal laws of humanity.[33]

The initial progress in dealing with cases of crimes against humanity through the administration of justice continued to be extremely slow, which gave cause for concern. The highest appeal courts regularly found errors in the judgments of the lower courts, while the accumulation of such cases on the court dockets remained a serious problem throughout the British occupation zone. The delays in hearing such cases were partly due to the fact that many of the accused the witnesses were either in custody in civilian internment camps, or their whereabouts were unknown.[34] These delays also aroused suspicion in the legal division of the military government about whether it was a deliberate policy of delaying the hearing of these cases or just a willful neglect of duty by the German administration of justice in dealing with such cases.[35]

Special attention was given to denunciation cases in discussions between representatives of the military government and the Central Justice Office that led to some clarification on this matter.[36] This followed criticism in the press concerning the prosecution of denunciation cases in the British occupation zone. An article in the *Telegraf* in Berlin cited the general public prosecutor's view that the ordinary German courts were not responsible for adjudicating these types of cases, in keeping with the principle that one could not be prosecuted for perpetrating a crime that did not contravene the existing law at the time that it was perpetrated. The prosecution of these cases, in his opinion, therefore came under the jurisdiction of the denazification *Spruchkammer*, since informers were designated as active National Socialists in the spirit of the Nuremberg judgments and Control Council Law No. 10.[37]

This article aroused renewed concern in the Central Judicial Office regarding the need to redress the lack of clarity about the prosecution denunciation cases as crimes against humanity. The prosecution of these cases had hitherto been relinquished due to the extensively acknowledged misunderstanding of the military government's ordinance of 21 November 1946 concerning the necessity of applying the law retroactively in such cases as had been put forward in legal journal publications. While the German courts remained responsible for the adjudication of denunciation cases on the basis of Control Council Law No. 10, the negative press reports on this issue were a matter of underlying concern to legal authorities in the British occupation zone[38] because they were seen as a check on the independence of the administration of justice that was also under the constant supervision of the military government, and subject to criticism from both.

The German courts still displayed reluctance in dealing with cases of crimes against humanity, which led to the military government later criticizing the German courts in the *Land* of North Rhine-Westphalia for not dealing with offenses defined under this law with the necessary amount of energy and swiftness. Apart from delays attributed to difficulties reaching some of the accused and witnesses who were being held in custody in civil internment camps or witnesses who were residing in the other occupation zones, the Legal Branch of the military government interpreted this hesitation as mainly due to reservations in the German administration of justice, especially at the offices of the public prosecutors in Düsseldorf and Cologne, to handle cases that violated the principle of *nulla poene sine lege*.[39]

One of the early cases of denunciation was heard at the Siegen regional court, where judgment was pronounced on 9 September 1947.[40] The defendant, who the court determined to have mental inhibitions and an inferiority complex, acted on personal motives after having felt insulted by teasing from his workmate who had a sense of humor. This caused a falling out between him and his co-worker that led him to losing his job. Suspecting that his co-worker had caused his dismissal, the defendant denounced him for telling so-called political jokes, without regard for what the consequences would be for his former co-worker.[41] This led to his imprisonment and later a trial at the People's Court on 10 March 1944, where the defendant testified against him as one of the witnesses. This court sentenced him to death for undermining the war effort by having made defeatist propaganda statements and attacking the person of the *Führer*.[42]

While prosecuting the defendant, the terms of Control Council Law No. 10 conflicted with the principle of *nulla poena sine lege*, which states that the defendant could not be prosecuted under German law at the time of his actions that had led to his former co-worker's death. The court maintained that it was necessary to apply Control Council Law No. 10 for administering retroactive criminal justice when pronouncing judgments in cases in which convictions were justifiable on ethical principles in the interest of serving the cause of justice. It was decided that the defendant had evidently made the denunciation out of a desire for revenge. This reprehensible action led to a trial before the People's Court and a death sentence that was carried out for political reasons, and thus it constituted an offense under the terms of Control Council Law No. 10, Art II, section 1c citing persecution on political principles. This was confirmed by an interpretation of denunciation following the abrogated judgment made by a jury court against Helene Schwärzel and an earlier decision made by the Hamm regional court on 26 June 1947 that it was to be considered an inhumane action made against the civilian population.[43]

The defendant had initiated the inhumane persecution against another by making his report against him. He was aware that his actions would lead to inhumane consequences. Namely, it would lead to the imprisonment of his former co-worker at the hands of the Gestapo, and it was commonly known that this would be for an indefinite period of time. Hence, he had intentionally committed a crime against humanity while seeking to satisfy personal feelings of revenge against another individual.[44] While consideration was given to the facts that he was a psychopath with an inferiority complex, and that he had not been convicted of any prior offenses, and that he was in poor physical health, he was convicted of a crime against humanity under the provisions of Control Council Law No. 10, Article 2, section 1c, and was sentenced to five years' imprisonment with a suspension of his civil rights for five years.[45]

This judgment was later upheld by the regional court in Hamm on 2 February 1948.[46] This court confirmed that the criminal court had correctly ascertained that the defendant's conduct constituted a crime against humanity in the form of political prosecution, having known that his actions could result in the pronouncement of the death sentence against his former co-worker, regardless of whether or not he had foreseen or wanted this outcome. He had also known that reporting his former co-worker's harmless jokes and remarks would result in him being handed over to the Gestapo and that he would be placed under arrest for an indefinite period of time. This was done solely out of personal motive of revenge,[47] which constituted a crime against humanity in view of a broad definition of the term according to the court's interpretation of Control Council Law No. 10 Article 2, section 1c. The defendant was considered guilty of inhumane conduct causing considerable suffering and harm, without sufficient justification for making the denunciation that would lead to then known inhumane consequences at the hands of the Gestapo and the People's Court, such as forced confessions, imprisonment, torture, internment in a concentration camp, lengthy prison sentences, and death. It could therefore not be denied that the report of the defendant had led to the death of his co-worker who he had known would be subject to the uncertain terroristic arbitrariness of the state.[48]

While precedents were set in the initial judgments in cases of crimes against humanity, there remained judicial hairsplitting among certain jurists about how Control Council Law No. 10 was to be applied. They had problems reconciling the inherently abstract concept of what constituted a crime against humanity with the actual types of cases in which it was to be applied. There remained differences of opinion at the Braunschweig regional appeal court in October 1947 between the criminal court judges and the state prosecutor concerning the compatibility between the application of occupation law and the provisions of the German code of criminal procedure in such cases. It remained unclear whether the German courts were to apply occupation law independently of German law, or whether the facts of the case were to apply under both and thereby allow for the provisions of German law to be applied retroactively when indictments were submitted as crimes against humanity.[49]

An analysis of thirty-three cases that were stayed in the Detmold public prosecutor's jurisdiction demonstrated that there were two types of cases. In eighteen cases, numerous files, especially those concerning the Special Courts, had been destroyed, and therefore the necessary amount evidence needed to institute proceedings was lacking. In the remaining fifteen cases, the court did not consider the evidence to qualify prosecution as a crime against humanity on the basis of Control Council Law No. 10. It was argued in six of these cases that denunciation could only be prosecuted if it had been undertaken for personal gain or advantage in cooperation with the Gestapo or a similar organization.[50]

The public prosecutor argued that a denunciation case could be prosecuted as a crime against humanity if a report had been made with a reproachable and malicious disposition emanating either from hatred or revenge. Two proceedings against denunciation cases were stayed on this justification due to insufficient certainty about these preconditions. In one of these cases, someone was denounced by a business partner for criticizing the regime after having threatened to report them for fraud. The Hannover Special Court sentenced them to four years' imprisonment in 1941 as a result of this denunciation. In the other case, a *Kreis* inspector reported a subordinate in 1942 for making disparaging remarks about the regime in 1942, and he was consequently sentenced by the same Special Court to a year and three months' imprisonment. He claimed in his defense that his intention was to have his subordinate transferred to another department, rather than denounce him because of his way of thinking.[51]

Other investigation and proceedings in Detmold were stayed since it was the view of the court that an accused could only be prosecuted according to Control Council Law No. 10 for perpetrating a crime against humanity through the reporting of another. However, the public prosecutor also stayed proceedings in such cases when it was concluded that they could only be tried as crimes against humanity if those who were denounced were treated inhumanely. Hence, those who reported them could not be prosecuted for causing consequences for others that were not especially severe. In one such case, a so-called half-Jew was reported for having a relationship with an "Aryan," and was forced to end this relationship or else face arrest and imprisonment in a concentration camp. In another case, the Gestapo had confiscated a radio and had forbidden its owner to listen to any broadcasts.[52] Hence, not all proceedings that were stayed were done so for unreasonable causes. Such minor cases also could have been the cause for concern about the possibility of a floodgate of litigation regarding denunciation cases. It remained the responsibility of regional state prosecutors and the courts to establish justifiable reasons for putting legislation into practice with the purpose of serving justice as well as the law when it could be reasoned that perpetrators had inflicted severe disadvantages onto others.

In contrast to the general state prosecutor, the judiciary questioned the idea that occupation law was to take independent precedence over German law in cases in which German law did not take the facts of these cases into account, even though the underlying facts were common to both. Cases involving murder or manslaughter were also to be considered a crime against humanity when the facts of these cases included violations of the respect for the dignity of human life, although these subjective concepts were not expressly stated in German law. This raised the particular problem of prosecuting denunciation cases as indirect perpetrations of crimes against humanity, since the consequences of informers' actions could not be considered violations of German law. Some judges also expressed reservations about adjudicating certain types of cases, including denunciation cases, as crimes against humanity committed against single rather than groups of individuals, in contrast to the military government's stipulation that these cases were to follow the precedent set by the Helene Schwärzel case.[53] It therefore remained for the Central Judicial Office to begin to offer clarification on how occupation law could be interpreted on the basis of discourses on the subject and military government directives. The fact that the judiciary had decided that denunciation cases were not to be subject to prosecution was a total surprise. Further checks on misinterpretations and judicial errors could later be assessed through the Highest Appeal Court of the British Zone in Cologne and the jury courts that would be established in early 1948.[54] It therefore remained for the public prosecutor to indict those who could be accused under occupation law in view of earlier precedents, while passing judgments remained the responsibility of the judiciary.

It appeared that the judiciary avoided making any decisions involving the subjective elements of the principles of humanity when evaluating the facts of cases that arose from political circumstances, and instead primarily focused on the objective provisions expressly stated in German law. Further court proceedings would help resolve these shortcomings in making sufficiently precise judgments, given the difficulties in evaluating the unprecedented nature of the law that was to be applied in crimes against humanity. Whether these crimes could be considered violations of occupation or German law was clarified through the setting of further precedents that were reviewed by the military government and the higher courts of the appellate jurisdiction whenever necessary.

By the end of January 1948, about 3000 cases of crimes against humanity had been investigated by public prosecutors, of which 251 cases involving 318 individuals had been adjudicated by German courts as required under Ordinance No. 47. The progress in prosecuting these types of cases was considered relatively good in spite of many legal and administrative difficulties. It was hoped that the continued adjudication of cases of crimes against humanity through jury courts and the Highest Appeal Court of the British Zone[55] would bring about the necessary clarity and uniformity in the administration of justice, which would result in further and more satisfactory progress. The British military government remained committed to the implementation of the Control Council Law No. 10 without deviating from its principles, but it was also deemed important that most crimes against humanity, including denunciation cases, were to be successfully prosecuted through German law, although it was not as far-reaching as Control Council Law No. 10.[56]

Court judgments remained subject to review by the military government authorities, who rarely found reason to intervene in the German judicial organization, to uphold the law or individual interests in view of judicial errors. The military government intervened in two cases of crimes against humanity due to what they perceived to be the German courts' misinterpretation of extenuating circumstances. These cases were ordered to be submitted for a retrial as check against potential errors or abuses in the administration of justice.

On 21 March 1947, the Essen regional court sentenced a member of the Sauerland *Volkssturm* to five years' imprisonment for manslaughter. The defendant had killed another with two gunshots to the back in early April 1945, because he had suspected him of being a traitor who was allegedly intending to betray industrial secrets to the advancing Allied troops. The court imposed the minimum sentence of five years' imprisonment for this type of crime in view of what the judges perceived to have been mitigating circumstances concerning the defendant's character and the extraordinary influences of the wartime environment.[57] The Legal Division of the British military government examined this judgment and determined that the verdict should have been interpreted as a crime against humanity, and that it should have been reported to the military government as such. The court had also not obtained the potentially relevant evidence from high-ranking National Socialist officials. In view of the circumstances, it was decided that the five-year sentence was too lenient, and that an alternative charge should have been set forth under Control Council Law No. 10, Article II, section 1(c), rather than the provisions of German law found in Articles 211 and 212 of the German criminal code. The verdict was therefore quashed and the case was redirected to another court.[58]

The British military government was disinclined to interfere in the exercise of German jurisdiction, but military government policy maintained under Ordinance No. 47 Article II that charges had to be brought under Control Council Law No. 10 whenever the circumstances warranted it, while alternative charges *could* be brought under German law[59] when the perpetrators' actions were not specifically defined as crimes against humanity. These lapses in the proceedings resulted from the judges failing to acknowledge the circumstances in which an action could be defined as a crime against humanity, in addition to judging what constituted a crime under German law in view of the available evidence and reasoning that the application of German law was sufficient for the case. The German courts remained subject to supervision and control by the military government, while the judiciary continued its functions independently with the expectation that the motives for crimes against humanity would be recognized in view of the spirit of Control Council Law No. 10, in addition to the fact that the provisions of German criminal law were not to take precedence over how occupation law governed specific types of cases.

The British military government also intervened after the Hannover regional court pronounced its judgment in a denunciation case on 6 April 1948. The defendant had worked at an armaments factory during the war where the workers had often discussed the worsening military situation and criticized the national government. On one occasion, one of the workers hereafter cited as K., who had worked at the factory since 1936, had called Goebbels a liar, and said that one could not believe anything he said over the radio or in the press. In the course of the same discussion, he suggested that Hitler ought to be hauled out and put on display. A co-worker, hereafter cited as W., took offense at these remarks and immediately told the shop steward, hereafter cited as S. who also took serious offense at what had been said. On another occasion, in October 1943, K. infuriated the defendant by saying that the factory workers ought to thank Hitler for the bombing of Hannover. Whereas S. and the factory owner agreed to let the matter rest, the defendant reported what he had said to the local *Ortsgruppenleiter*. S. thereafter spoke about the incident to the factory owner again. In order to avoid personal disadvantages from the NSDAP, S. and the factory owner forwarded a report to the DAF authorities in Hannover on 18 November 1943 stating that K. had made remarks hostile to the state for a long time. K. was thereafter arrested and interrogated by the Gestapo on 1 December 1943. He was later tried by the Hannover Special Court on 18 February 1944 for making spiteful and virulent political remarks. He was sentenced to two and a half years' imprisonment, which he served until freed by advancing Allied troops.[60]

The defendant disputed the charge of persecuting another on political grounds by urging another witness to make a report against K. While conceding that he took offense at K.'s remarks at the time, he claimed that did not intend to take any action against him, and had only asked his *Ortsgruppenleiter* for advice on the right course of action as a member of the NSDAP at W.'s insistence. He also had not mentioned K.'s name at this time. He had only then taken the initiative to report the incident to S. as he had been advised to do, and otherwise claimed he did not intend for K. to face criminal charges, expecting him to face disciplinary measures within the enterprise, such as being ordered to pay a fine to the NSV.[61] The court determined that this defense could not be refuted, as there was no evidence as to whether he had acted against K. and, given W.'s questionable credibility since parts of his testimony could not be substantiated, it therefore could not be considered to be a decisive factor in this case.[62]

The *Ortsgruppenleiter* had not taken action after being made aware of the incident with K., and proceedings against him were instituted as a consequence of S.'s report to the DAF. The court therefore reasoned that the defendant could only be held responsible for the proceedings that were instituted against K. if he had willingly induced S. to make the report about K., whereas S. testified that he made the report upon hearing that the defendant had brought the incident to the attention of an NSDAP authority in order to avoid being subject to criminal prosecution. While it could not be ascertained whether the defendant intended to pressure S. into reporting K., the court questioned whether S. intended to place responsibility for doing so on the defendant in the present proceedings. Hence, the credibility of S.'s testimony was diminished in comparison with that of the defendant. The fact also remained that the defendant had not personally reported K. to the police or political authorities after the incident.[63] In addition to the mitigating factors, including the defendant having shown a friendly disposition toward K. when they were co-workers, and what was perceived to be S.'s hostile attitude toward the defendant during the proceedings, perhaps to absolve himself of guilt in the matter, the court determined that the evidence against the defendant was insufficient. He was therefore acquitted.[64]

The British military government later abrogated this judgment on 27 May 1948.[65] They noted that it had not been necessary for K. to take the initiative in reporting any incidents regarding K.'s remarks, but that he had considered himself bound by his political duty to bring them to the attention of the political authorities of the time. His having done so led to the shop steward proceeding as the political authorities would expect, or else face the possibility of incurring disadvantages for doing otherwise. Although the defendant had not pressed S. to report K. to the authorities, S. had acted under indirect pressure to take this action in view of these circumstances. Whether S. had made the report due to his belief that he was fulfilling his duty out of political motives or in the interest of avoiding personal difficulties with the political authorities remained an open question, since the evidence to support either position was not presented in this case. The defendant otherwise could not make the claim that he had acted under duress, and K. had long made such remarks in the presence of other witnesses who did not proceed to report him. His knowledge of the political conditions at the time would also have made him aware of the severe consequences for anyone who had repeatedly made disparaging remarks about the regime during wartime.

Intervention by the British military government in cases of crimes against humanity was only warranted in those two cases, but renewed proceedings due to errors in previous judgments were ordered by the higher appeal courts. In some cases, the higher courts could also exercise an influence on judgments of the lower courts within their jurisdiction based on their assessments,[66] or could confirm the precedents set by earlier judgments. In one such example, the appeal court ruled that a denunciation case did not contain the precondition of inflicting inhumane consequences on the person who had been denounced to the authorities. On 19 October 1944, the defendant in this case, a nineteen-year old soldier hereafter cited as E., went to visit his former schoolmate at his home in Bielefeld when he was hospitalized there. He had a conversation with his mother during this visit, hereafter cited as N., who expressed sharp opinions over Hitler's military capabilities and his choices over who had been appointed to the general staff, citing names such as Fritzsch, Udet, Paulus, von Kluge, and others. She also commented on what she thought were useless sacrifices in Stalingrad and St. Malo while also making disparaging remarks about the prosecution of the war and the outlook for success for the war that Hitler wanted, adding that she was saying what many others were thinking at the time but did not dare say. The defendant did not immediately react to these comments at this time[67] before contemplating what he thought he needed to do as a matter of his conscience.

The defendant claimed that he was not prepared for what he described as her speaking fanatically about these matters, which she insisted on continuing to talk about even though he tried to change the subject about matters he had hitherto never heard about, and did not completely grasp the significance of her remarks. After thinking about things for two days, he assumed that she was trying to incite him to mutiny and desertion, which he also thought was outrageous since she was an officer's wife. He therefore made the assumption that the things that she had talked about she must have heard from her husband, who he assumed was implicated in the 20 July 1944 conspiracy. Moreover, he still believed that Germany could win the war and he had the ambition of becoming an officer. He thus considered N.'s conduct to be treasonous and felt duty bound to take action against her. Not having anyone to talk to about this matter, since his father was recently deceased, he turned to a military superior, the National Socialist political officer at the military hospital, for advice[68] about what he had heard.

This political officer told the defendant that a verbal report would not be sufficient in reporting a case of treasonous conduct, and that he needed to put everything into writing, without mentioning the potential consequences for N. E. then wrote a report about N. on 22 October 1944 that was addressed to this military superior, without clearly knowing the consequences that could ensue. He had known that the leaders of the 20 July conspiracy had been executed, and that not all of the implicated officers had suffered this fate. He therefore did not expect N. to face a death sentence. He was unaware of how the People's Court had imposed death sentences for defeatist remarks and did not have any experience with the Gestapo's methods, and thus expected only for her to face proceedings in an ordinary court. He otherwise did not hear anything about what had happened to N. after he denounced her.[69]

N. was later arrested and interrogated by the Gestapo on 23 December 1944, and then taken to the local prison in Bielefeld on 27 December. The files concerning her were passed on to the state prosecutor at the People's Court, while she remained in prison in Bielefeld. The anticipated death sentence did not happen, as she was freed by American troops on 5 April 1945. The Bielefeld regional court found that apart from the mental strain of fearing for her life, this period of imprisonment and the Gestapo interrogation did not constitute especially harsh experiences, as was determined from her own testimony. The established facts of the case meant that this case could not be adjudicated under German criminal law and could only be adjudicated as a crime against humanity on the grounds of persecution on political grounds, as cited in Article II, section 1c of Control Council Law No. 10. The problem was that on the one hand, the facts of the case fulfilled the *objective* considerations of this law, but on the other hand they did fulfill them from a *subjective* viewpoint since it was not possible to find him guilty of having caused her to have suffered inhumane treatment.[70] Although the victim of this political persecution had potentially faced life-threatening consequences as a result of being denounced to the National Socialist authorities, the course of events that had transpired spared her from those possible circumstances.

In a discussion of any possible mitigating circumstances in favor of the defendant, it was noted that the defendant had been only eight years old in 1933, and like other German youth of the time, had become exposed to strong propaganda, ideas, and influences in school and in the youth organizations during the time when his critical thinking abilities were very limited. His life experiences were likewise politicized under the regime when he worked in the *Reich* labor service, and he was then enlisted in the army. The earlier propaganda in which he had become inculcated became further imbued with the propaganda notion that the 20 July 1944 conspirators were traitors, which was followed by him taking part in the tough fighting in northern France, Belgium, and Aachen and being wounded before returning to his home. Meanwhile, although his trust of the political and military leadership had been shaken, his upbringing meant that he continued to believe in the possibility of victory and never doubted any of the propaganda. N.'s careless remarks in her conversation with him after these events could only have caused a crisis of conscience for him due to his impressionable idealistic disposition. He did not report N. as a result of base motives, such as seeking revenge, or hatred, or trying to acquire personal advantages, nor was he acting out of any specific political grounds or with a willingness to cause inhumane consequences. Rather he was acting out of a soldierly perception that was also influenced by his lack of maturity, and did not know how to conduct himself otherwise. This court therefore acquitted the defendant in its judgment passed on 27 October 1947[71] for this suspected crime against humanity.

This verdict was later upheld at Hamm regional court on 12 February 1948.[72] This court confirmed the earlier judgment, supporting the ruling that he and his fellow soldiers had been instructed by their superiors after the 20 July 1944 assassination attempt that not reporting cases of treason made them subject to prosecution. The defendant therefore acted on this consideration without possessing the cognitive faculty at the time to have been aware of having acted inhumanely, and did not act out of any self-serving interests. Rather, he merely thought that he was fulfilling his duty as a soldier and was unable to act otherwise. Hence, the court confirmed that this case did not fulfill the subjective preconditions that were needed for a prosecution under Control Council Law No. 10.[73]

The court also found that the facts of the case did not represent what could be objectively construed as inhumane actions perpetrated on the basis of political, racial, or religious persecution, as defined under this law. The action that the defendant had taken by reporting N. to the political authorities led to consequences that could constitute evident damage to human dignity and the rights of humanity. E.'s act of denunciation against N. and the consequences that she had incurred as a result of this action could not justifiably be considered a crime against humanity, since the emotional trauma and insecurity she felt about the future, however enormous it was for a married woman with two children awaiting an expected death sentence while constantly being exposed to intensive air raids while in custody, could not be equated to physical suffering or pain.[74]

The court ruled that misguided individuals were not be to judged for their mistaken beliefs and if their action of denouncing another did not lead to fatal consequences, as had often happened or could have happened in other denunciation cases when informers had consciously sanctioned others about bringing such grave consequences about. This did not describe E.'s motivations for reporting N., as he acted out of misguided idealism and blind obedience resulting from indoctrination at school, the Hitler Youth, the *Reich* labor service, and the army. His actions were also motivated by the influence of National Socialist propaganda that caused him to fear the repercussions of not reporting alleged cases of treason after the events of 20 July 1944.[75] However, it remained for the prosecution to demonstrate that the alleged perpetrators had in fact consciously taken the initiative to denounce another to the authorities due to personal or political motives, while having been aware that their actions would result in inhumane consequences.[76] Their intended actions would thereby constitute political persecution as defined by Control Council Law No. 10 in view of the evidence that would demonstrate how the victim had incurred what could be interpreted as grave disadvantages that violated the rights of humanity.

There remained differences of viewpoints in this case in spite of these arguments. The general state prosecutor raised the objection of this court not applying Control Council Law No. 10, and demanded that this case be referred to the Highest Appeal Court of the British Zone[77] for further consideration. The general state prosecutor argued that the circumstances under which N. had undergone emotional distress following intervention by the Gestapo as a result of E.'s denunciation, and expecting a death sentence for months pending a forthcoming trial before the People's Court was undoubtedly a crime against humanity as defined in Article II, section 1c of Control Council Law No. 10. It was thus argued that E. ought to be prosecuted on the grounds of the objective considerations of this law,[78] which ought to have taken precedence over the subjective considerations as mitigating factors that led to the acquittal judgment.

There was evidence of malicious intent in view of how E. had envisaged the consequences of his actions, which would damage the interests of humanity. The general public prosecutor found it conspicuous that E. expected N. to be subject only to court proceedings, while claiming to not having expected any intervention by the Gestapo or having no knowledge of the fact that the People's Court imposed death sentences for defeatist remarks. This was especially suspect following his claim that according to his knowledge only the leaders and not all of the officers implicated in the

20 July conspiracy was sentenced to death and therefore likewise he did not expect N. to face the death sentence. It was suspected that E., as a battle-experienced soldier, did in fact have knowledge of the potential danger to which he had exposed N., especially following the events of 20 July 1944, and had decided to report N. after considering the matter for two days. It could thus be inferred that this that his action could be characterized as being inhumane, as he expected her to face a harsh fate after she had entrusted him with her thoughts in a friendly manner.[79]

His blind assumption that she had tried to persuade him to desert could not be substantiated. His claiming to have doubts about her opinions about the course of the war, especially after the events of 20 July, was also considered to be dubious. It was therefore difficult to accept that E. had acted without a prior knowledge of having acted inhumanely in view of his underlying disposition, regardless of the earlier verdicts that accepted the view that he did not act out of any base selfish motives. They ruled that rather than choosing to act in defense of humanity, he had chosen to act in favor of supporting the interests of the National Socialist dictatorship, and to make things worse he had had two days to consider all of the possibilities for the potential consequences of his actions. Rather than turning to a political authority to clear his conscience concerning the matter, he could have warned N. either verbally or in writing, as this would have sufficed. Instead, he decided to take the worst possible course of action that put N.'s life in jeopardy and endangered her family as well, for the purpose of contributing to the upholding of the regime under the guise of "soldierly" conduct. Since he had chosen to act against her, he should not have been exonerated for having made this choice, regardless of any considerations concerning the consequences of his upbringing, the effects of his environment, and his character that had influenced his unjustifiable way of thinking that made his actions subject to prosecution under Control Council Law No. 10.[80] Given the fact that he had committed a crime against humanity against another person and the refutation of the extenuating circumstances, he was therefore to be called to account for his actions.

This case came under further revision at the Highest Appeal Court of the British Zone on 22 June 1948. This court found that E.'s acquittal was unjustifiable, and referred the case to the Münster regional court for a new judgment. The criminal court judgment and its conclusions were deemed correct in terms of the external facts of the case as a crime against humanity. However, the conclusions did not comply with the preconditions of persecution on political, racial, or religious grounds in the application of state or political instruments of power, or an evident injury to human dignity or rights, when the denunciation did not result in the denounced suffering some atrocity. It thus followed that the court had decided that crimes against humanity could be divided into two types—cases involving atrocities and other inhumane actions having been committed, or cases involving persecution on political, racial, or religious grounds. The objective facts of such cases of crimes against humanity as interpreted under the broadly outlined provisions in Control Council Law No. 10 could not be excluded, and had to be taken into consideration in every instance as an offense against the ideals of the human rights of the victim. It thus followed from an objective viewpoint that the defendant's action of reporting remarks considered to be "hostile to the state" constituted an attack against the victim of this action, and injury was inflicted in the context of the violence and tyranny of the National Socialist dictatorship.[81]

While the previous judgments correctly concluded that the objective preconditions of the defendant's actions constituted a crime against humanity, the subjective considerations were considered untenable, since the objective considerations did not exculpate his national socialistic disposition. Meanwhile, N. had recognized the mortal danger that she had been in and underwent great emotional hardship as a result of having expressed her political opinions, which remained an inviolable right of humanity.[82] Although N. was spared the worst possible consequences and did not necessarily endure excessively harsh circumstances, E.'s having taken action against her, regardless of his background and reasoning, remained indefensible in view of respect for the rights of humanity as well as the common knowledge of the political conditions of the time. It therefore could not be denied that he was conscious of the cruel and arbitrary persecution that would ensue as a result of his reporting N., who recognized the danger that she would be sentenced to death.[83]

In view of the potential mitigating circumstances in favor of the defendant, it was granted that he had been thoroughly inculcated with National Socialist propaganda during most of his life experiences as a youngster, and then in the labor service and the military. As a result, it was understood that he had denounced N. as a matter of conscience, considering himself honor- and duty-bound as a soldier to report what he thought had been a case of treason, without being conscious of having acted inhumanely, and without acting out of any base motives or on specific political grounds. However, Control Council Law No. 10 withheld recourse to inculcation to National Socialist ideology as an objective defense against the charge of inhumane conduct.[84]

The sense and purpose of this law could not allow for acquittals for those who had acted on National Socialist doctrines out of misplaced idealism, misguided upbringing, obstinate ideology, or National Socialist convictions, or simply acted inhumanely or attacked another and thereby initiated an act of inhumanity without remorse or reservations. The earlier judgment therefore was incomplete in making allowances for the defendant's upbringing and National Socialist convictions. He could not be justifiably absolved of having acted out of these convictions that prompted him to expose N. to considerable danger, regardless of him having experienced a crisis of conscience about whether to take action against her.[85] Hence, the earlier acquittal verdicts had placed too much emphasis on the precedent of the mitigating circumstances concerning the defendant's misguided thinking that he was fulfilling his sense of duty, without giving sufficient consideration to the spirit of Control Council Law No. 10 as it was to be applied unvaryingly in all such cases. The defendant was therefore to be found guilty of crimes against humanity in accordance with an appropriate application of this law, and this case was hereby referred to a different court for a revised verdict.[86]

This case was heard again at the Münster regional court where judgment was pronounced on 30 August 1948, sentencing the defendant to nine months' imprisonment, following the revision of the judgment passed by the Highest Appeal Court of the British Zone and the provisions cited in Control Council Law No. 10, Article II, sections 3 and 4. No further elaboration was necessary with regard to the application of this law in this case and the earlier judgment that had been rendered at the highest appeal court. This court confirmed that the defendant was found to have buried his common humanity in his unswerving loyalty to the National Socialist state, and that he had as a consequence insidiously and remorselessly betrayed the trust of an older lady who had confided in him and then spent over four months imprisonment while awaiting and fearing an expected a death sentence.[87]

The Münster regional court rejected the previous judgment, ruling instead that the use of state or political instruments of power and denunciation for the purpose of persecution on political, racial, or religious grounds and evident injury to human dignity or rights did not necessitate an evaluation of the precondition of the absence of an atrocity actually having been perpetrated. Crimes against humanity could not be separated into cases involving atrocities and other forms of inhumane actions on one hand and persecution on political, racial, or religious grounds on the other.[88] The facts of the case were thus to be evaluated on the basis of the motive for the offense as well as the actions of the perpetrator and its consequences within the context in which the offense was committed. This case was to be judged as a case of political persecution, regardless of the defendant's limited abilities to reason whether his actions could be considered unjustifiable in the view of common knowledge of what would be considered just.

The facts in this case demonstrated how the defendant had committed actions that were to be evaluated objectively as an offense defined under Article II, section 10 of Control Council Law No. 10. E. had attacked another by exposing N. to the violence and tyranny of the National Socialist machinery of persecution by reporting the political remarks that she had told him in confidence. Rather than confront her about what she had said, he chose to take action against her that would lead to political persecution, which made his claim of alleged soldierly conduct untenable.[89] His having taken action against a defenseless older lady that led to the degrading circumstances of her imprisonment while awaiting a death sentence would be better described as cowardly, acting under the inexcusable motive of a political mindset and under the guise of following political orders, rather than choosing to stand for common humanity. The fact that he had attacked N. with knowledge and intent sufficed to justify a conviction for a crime against humanity on the basis of the objective facts of the case alone,[90] without allowing undue consideration for the background circumstances of his political convictions as possible mitigating circumstances from a subjective viewpoint.

In another early denunciation case as a crime against humanity, the Wuppertal regional court imposed a sentence of six months' imprisonment and a 5000 RM fine on 11 June 1947. The Düsseldorf regional court ordered this court on 14 November 1947 to revise this sentence to an acquittal, since the victim of the denunciation did not incur cruel treatment, therefore the objective facts of the case did not in their ruling sufficiently constitute a crime against humanity as defined by Control Council Law No. 10,[91] having ruled that the treatment of the victim of denunciation necessarily had to be clearly and obviously inhumane. While the victim in this case had been subject to distress, this did not in their opinion necessarily constitute inhumane treatment and therefore did not represent the consequences that the informer had intended to bring about.[92] As was determined in a later case at the Berlin *Kammergericht,* inconsequential intentions could not be subject to prosecution when they could not have been considered to have constituted political persecution.[93]

In a similar verdict, the Duisburg regional court pronounced a verdict on 2 March 1948 in which the defendant had reported a housemate for making disparaging remarks against the government and its policies in May 1940. The subject of the report had not suffered any disadvantages other than being interrogated. The defendant thus could not be subject to prosecution for persecuting another with the expectation that unlawful violent measures would follow for the denounced.[94] It would remain the responsibility of the public prosecutors and the judiciary to lodge cases in which Control Council Law No. 10 was to be administered according to suitable interpretations in view of the consequences that the victims sustained.

A later denunciation case was heard at the Flensburg regional court, where the sentence was pronounced on 30 March 1948. The defendant, hereafter cited as G. S., had initially had a good and friendly relationship with her landlord, hereafter cited as J., and his wife, until their relationship increasingly worsened during 1943. She eventually filed an unsolicited report against J.

on 15 November 1943 with a local official in Satrup, hereafter cited as H. She maintained that J. had horribly insulted Hitler, the nation, and the government, and that she wanted to persuade people that Germans were being made to look stupid and that the present situation was a repetition of the First World War all over again. When talking about the movie "The Liberation of the Duce," he said that it was made behind the front and only served to show how stupid Germans were supposed to be. When speaking about the Badoglio government, he said that the country will awaken and her husband would return within twenty-four hours without wearing his SS uniform. She retorted by telling him to leave her alone if her husband believed Germany would win the war, he struck himself in the head repeatedly as if Germans were crazy. At another time, he had said that although he had voted for Hitler, he would have liked to have voted for the best bricklayer or fitter rather than for a house painter. At the same time, she also reported how J. had cheated on his electricity bill and withheld reporting the amount of his livestock and farm produce, and had withheld giving to state charities, and how she had told others about how she would file a report against him, naming other potential witnesses who could testify against J.[95]

H. had known J. to be a good, hardworking, and industrious individual whom he also had known to have a "loose tongue." He accepted this report from G. S. by writing down everything that she had told him, while trying to be objective so as not to be influenced by what she had told him, and also not to be suspected of appearing to be trying to protect J. He then sent a copy of this report to the regional administrator and to the police.[96]

A police civil servant assigned to the Flensburg Gestapo, hereafter cited as P., went to question G. S. about her complaint, the details of which were not known to him. She told him all of J.'s "political remarks" at this time, and named two additional possible witnesses, hereafter cited as M. and B., who could also testify against him. He then questioned them about what J. had said, and confirmed some of his remarks. J. was questioned thereafter on 7 and 8 February 1944, and was then arrested by the Gestapo on 11 February 1944. He was then taken to Berlin on the next day, and then tried by the People's Court on 6 June 1944.[97]

G. S. and her daughter, M., B., and P. appeared as witnesses at these proceedings, where G. S. gave further incriminating testimony against J., including his deceit about the electricity meter, and reported the amount of livestock in his possession. This court thereafter convicted J. for repeatedly making defeatist remarks in the summer of 1943 and offending the person of the *Führer* in the worst possible means. He was thereby sentenced to death. Petitions that were filed for clemency were unsuccessful, and the sentence was executed on 17 July 1944.[98]

G. S. was tried for perpetrating a crime against humanity of the grounds of political persecution as defined in Article II, paragraph 1c of Control Council Law No. 10. She had turned to a political authority with the undoubted intention and purpose of inflicting injury against another. This led to court proceedings being initiated against J. that led to his execution for having freely expressed his political opinions. Her actions, which had been motivated by feelings of vindictiveness, led to the suppression of this natural and inalienable right through the abuse of political authority in suppressing any political dissent against the National Socialist regime. She was therefore found guilty of perpetrating the inhumane political persecution of another.[99]

G. S. had not hesitated to convey J.'s political remarks as the underlying basis for political persecution and used them as a pretext for settling disputes she had had with him. She maintained what she had heard him say when she was questioned by the Gestapo, and emphasized his alleged misconduct by naming other potential witnesses who had not come forward to take hostile action against him as she had. Although she had not acted out of political convictions, she had exploited political means to bring about inhumane consequences at a time when it was well known that the political authorities dealt with alleged enemies of the regime without mercy.[100]

In evaluating any possible mitigating circumstances in determining the extent of the sentencing, allowance was to be made for the fact that she had not had any prior convictions. On the other hand, the excessively base attitude of the defendant was a crucial factor to be taken into consideration, especially since she had not made any attempt to alleviate the extent of J.'s alleged guilt, even when appearing as a witness before the People's Court where she was aware of what consequences could be for J. The court also took into consideration how, in contrast to J., she did not have a good reputation and that she had not expressed any remorse about her actions, even in the present time. In view of these circumstances and in the interest of not imposing an excessively harsh sentence with respect to occupation policy, she was sentenced to three years' imprisonment.[101]

This case was later reviewed at the Highest Appeal Court of the British Zone on 26 October 1948, where the appeal was rejected. The external circumstances showed how the defendant had perpetrated hostile actions against another, regardless of whether her reporting of J.'s comments were true or not. What remained of decisive importance is that she had consciously and intentionally brought about inhumane consequences for another, an unjustifiable death sentence, by contributing to the abuse of the law at the time for the purpose of serving her personal interests. These actions constituted a crime against humanity in connection with National Socialist violence and tyranny, as was defined through an interpretation of the application of

Article II, section 1c of Control Council Law No. 10. In view of the evidence that had been presented, the conviction and the extent of the sentence were sustained.[102]

There remained considerable reservations in the German courts in the British occupation zone during this time about imposing convictions in certain cases of denunciations. This prohibition against retroactive legislation was the main stumbling block to prosecuting informers, which led to a great deal of judicial inconsistencies that were encountered after 1945. The number of judgments in crimes against humanity had increased considerably in early 1948, when 114 cases were tried in February and March; excluding the March report from the Düsseldorf regional court district, there were a total of 338 cases involving 165 individuals in cases that were tried between October 1946 and 1 May 1948. However, the denunciation cases therein were considered less important. There were only 57 denunciation cases in contrast to the 203 cases involving persecution against Jews and political persecution. In over a year up to 1 May 1948, the numbers of political persecution cases made about 37 percent of the total, with cases involving persecution against Jews making up 28 percent, and denunciation cases constituting only 11 percent. Acquittals in these cases amounted to 33 percent for political persecution, 37 percent for the persecution of Jews, and 60 percent for denunciation cases. Very few denunciation cases as crimes against humanity were tried in the Hamm, Braunschweig and Celle regional court districts in comparison to other districts, which could have been partly attributed to the relative sizes of these districts. The military government therefore demanded to see the files that concerned acquittals in denunciation cases in which the appeals were not pending or had been justified with a detailed summary in the courts' monthly reports.[103] Such cases were thus subjected to further scrutiny on an individual basis while it remained for the public prosecutors and judges to examine the facts of each case as a crime against humanity.

A denunciation case that was heard at the Aurich regional court during this time had political rather than personal motives that were common in such cases. Of the three accused, one of them was found guilty of crimes against humanity on 21 April 1948. He was sentenced to two years' imprisonment and deprived of his civil rights for three years. The two others were acquitted.[104] The defendant, hereafter cited as K., who was found guilty, had been a paid informer for the Gestapo[105] and relayed information about what one of the other accused, W., had told him about what a building contractor they knew had said in 1942. He had said that continuing the fight no longer made any sense, and that soldiers were stupid to return to the front. W. had also told K. that the contractor listened to foreign radio broadcasts, and told foreign workers about the broadcasts. In turn, K. told the police chief in his hometown in October or November 1943 that he wanted to report the contractor for undermining the war effort, and told him in private that, in addition to what W. had told him, the contractor had agitated foreign workers and shifted materials that belonged to the *Luftwaffe*. This information was in turn relayed to the Gestapo office in Wilhelmshaven.[106] The contractor was arrested thereafter, and later brought before the People's Court where he was charged with undermining the war effort and also accused of telling his cousin that America would win the war. On the basis of the witnesses' testimony about what had been said, he was sentenced to death on 25 January 1944 and was executed on 6 March 1944.[107]

The Aurich regional court accused W. and K. of making a political report that led to the judicial persecution of Heinrich A., the contractor, while the defendant S. was charged with having intentionally helped K. with advice that reinforced the report.[108] Upon examining the evidence provided by their testimonies and that of several witnesses, the court acknowledged that W. had had no connection with making the incriminating report and that there was insufficient evidence to convict him.[109] S. was proven innocent[110] in view of evidence provided that he had had nothing to do with the matter.[111] In contrast, although it could not be refuted that K. had made the report against his will, his conduct showed that he had committed a crime against humanity under the terms of Article II, section 1c of Control Council Law No. 10.[112]

As in other such cases, the court could not deny that the application of Control Council Law No. 10 did not contravene the administration of justice. The purpose of Law No. 10 aspired to serve the cause of justice by allowing the prosecution of inhumane criminal actions that were admissible under a criminal regime. Choosing not to prosecute these crimes would be intolerable in the view of civilized humanity.[113] Justice was therefore needed to be seen to work, and was put to work through retroactive application of the law due to the circumstances of the context in which it had to be applied in order to serve the cause of justice by bringing the perpetrators of crimes against humanity to account for their actions on the basis of international legal and moral principles.

The hitherto unprecedented prohibition against administering justice retroactively had been lifted by the judgment of the Nuremberg War Crimes Tribunal on 3 and 4 December 1947. The Allied Control Council for Germany as the highest legislative authority was formally vested with the authority to prosecute violations of international law through Control Council Law No. 10, in combination with the irrefutable force of circumstances involving the moral force of international public opinion and international law. Crimes against humanity that were committed by the National Socialist authorities against Germans were therefore much more serious than violations of existing German law. They were overshadowed by worldwide public opinion and the accepted standards of international law, which removed the moral and legal limitations restricting the retroactive application of justice.[114]

This case followed the interpretation made by the Hamm regional court that had determined in its judgments pronounced on 21 June 1947 and 29 November 1947 that denunciation was considered an inhumane act perpetrated on the civilian population.[115] The definition of inhumane pertained to any action that inflicted considerable suffering and harm upon another without sufficient justification, with a merciless, inhumane, and base disposition in connection with the National Socialist tyranny. This also applied to cases in which the act of denunciation caused concern over the possibility of grievous consequences, such as terrifying distress over the uncertainty of potential consequences of the action at the hands of the regime, in the form of considerable bodily harm and suffering in the absence of legal protection against tyranny.[116] The prosecution of such actions through German courts was upheld through the occupation legislation that made it possible, which ordered the German jurists to apply the law retroactively for the purpose of adjudicating such exceptional cases of political persecution, regardless of whether or not it contravened German law.[117]

This case was thus interpreted as falling under the types of violent actions and offenses outlined in Article 2, section 1c of Control Council Law No. 10. A similar interpretation was made by the Hamburg regional court on 12 November 1947, which ruled that the prosecution of actions on the basis of this law did not necessarily have to have been considered unlawful under German law at the time that the act was committed. Denunciation cases were to be considered crimes against humanity when judging them within the context of the consequences of the external circumstances that had been incurred and the disposition of the perpetrator who had caused them, in addition to the act of denunciation itself.[118]

Although the actual act of denunciation was not explicitly defined as an inhumane act in Article 2, section 1c of Control Council Law No. 10, this act encompassed the actions related to a criminal case. The prevailing jurisdiction over such cases was therefore interpreted as persecution on the basis of political principles, as had been discerned by other courts that had heard such cases, such as the judgment passed at the Berlin *Kammergericht* on Helene Schwärzel on 17 May 1947, and the Freiburg regional court on 12 September 1947. As in other such cases, the defendant, K., had initiated the political persecution of A., since his actions were to lead to severe inhumane consequences by delivering him into the hands of the Gestapo, which had extracted a confession from him with merciless cruelty that later led to his death penalty pronounced by the People's Court. The fact that the defendant had caused his victim to be arrested by an organization and a process by which there was a very high likelihood of violent methods being used against its victims signified the inhumanity of his actions.[119]

The act of denunciation in itself did not directly constitute persecution through an application of power, but it could have led to the injury of human rights. From an objective point of view, informers were to be considered to have indirectly assisted in the process of aiding and abetting political persecution through inciting the abuse of state and political power, and therefore were subject to prosecution in accordance with this interpretation of the law. It was also necessary to note that from a subjective point of view, the informer had been clearly conscious and approved of the potential consequences of their actions that would injure another's human rights, regardless of whether the consequences had occurred or not. Also noted were their motives for taking these actions that had led to inhumane mistreatment at the hands of National Socialist authorities in the absence of the protection of legal guarantees.[120] The underlying factor remained that acts of denunciation constituted extensions of political persecution as political abuses perpetrated by the state.[121]

The basis for persecution at the hands of the political authorities in the present case lay in the fact that the cause for A.'s comments, which could have been considered harmless grumbling, were considered by the authorities of the time to reflect his opposition to National Socialism. The defendant had brought this case to the attention of the judicial organization that had terrorized the civilian population, which meant that he was thus an accomplice to a crime against humanity by having forwarded his report about him. In addition, it was determined that he was an informer for the Gestapo, which reinforced his motivation for persecution on political grounds. This meant that he had intended to persecute an alleged opponent of National Socialism, in contrast to many other cases of denunciation that were made as individual acts against an individual because of personal considerations.[122] It was generally known when the report was made in 1943 that such cases of grumbling would be subject to investigation by the Gestapo and its brutal violence, and that individuals making such comments would either be sent to a concentration camp or brought before the People's Court or a Special Court that would pass a severe sentence. This was clearly known to the defendant, who was conscious of the cruel consequences of his actions.[123] In view of the fact that he was married with children, was at the advanced age of sixty-seven, and suffered from poor health, the court sentenced him to two years' imprisonment and a suspension of his civil rights for three years.[124] The Oldenburg regional court later upheld this decision on 29 March 1949,[125] stating that the report of a criminal act was unjust since the victim of the denunciation was subject to arbitrary force, rather than the law, and was treated inhumanely.

Even truthful reports to the authorities contradicted the rule of law and were an injustice when they were made in the context of the National Socialist administration of justice. Moreover, the defendant had been fully aware of the inhumane consequences that would result due to his actions, and that his victim would be subjected to the violent methods of the Gestapo and inhumane application of National Socialist law.[126] The Aurich regional court had correctly ascertained the defendant's awareness of the inhumane consequences of his actions and his convictions, since, as a paid informer for the Gestapo, he had known and intended that A. be sentenced to death as a result of his report.[127] The precedent of retroactive application of the law that had been set in previous cases and the arguments that were used in previous court judgments for the prosecution of political informers were applied in this case. Thus, the conclusion was reached that even indirect action that led to inhumane consequences for a victim of the National Socialist regime's administration of justice could hereby be considered by the postwar German courts as a crime against humanity. However, this remained dependent on the arguments that could be formulated by the public prosecutors bringing these types of cases to the courts and the judges adjudicating these cases.

The greatest difficulty in dealing with criminal proceedings by this time concerned the prosecution of denunciation cases. There remained high degree of uncertainty in the divergent decisions that were made in these types of cases among the regional courts in North-Rhine Westphalia. Fewer of these types of cases were also indicted in comparison to other types of crimes against humanity. Of those that were brought to court in this *Land,* nearly half of the proceedings had been stayed.[128] Continued prosecution would depend on the severity of the consequences, which would alleviate doubts about the consequences that had been incurred. Further examples of successful adjudications would serve as precedents for similar cases.

A later denunciation case was heard at the Hamburg regional court, where judgment was pronounced on 11 May 1948 on two defendants who were found guilty of crimes against humanity and were sentenced to eight and six months' imprisonment.[129] One of the two accused, the one hereafter cited as P. had a Jewish wife who had evidently suffered from emotional problems for several years, which led to serious conflict with him and the second accused, his sister, hereafter cited as K. This prompted them to report her to the Gestapo for remarks she had made to get rid of her. After receiving an indifferent reception at the Jewish affairs office of the Gestapo in Hamburg in early 1944, K. drafted a long document to the Gestapo about the "Jewess" Mrs. P., their unhappy home life, and what she had said[130] in late 1943 or early 1944. She had said that "the day of vengeance of the Jews will come soon; lists of names of people who will face revenge were already being prepared.

All soldiers were murderers. The many children who had been killed in air attacks were murdered by Hitler himself. The war could not be won,"[131] and brought this letter to the Gestapo office in about the middle of March 1944, accompanied by her brother P., who confirmed the contents of this document and signed it. He initiated divorce proceedings against his wife on 18 March 1944, and Mrs. P. was arrested and imprisoned two days later. The divorce was approved on 5 April 1944. Mrs. P. was later taken to Auschwitz concentration camp in July 1944 where she died at the end of October 1944.[132]

This jury court charged the two accused with having committed a crime against humanity under Article II, section 1c of Control Council Law No. 10, which a German court was empowered with judging on the basis of military government ordinance No. 47. The court determined that the action with which the defendants were charged and their conduct constituted a serious offense against human dignity according to the general feeling of cultured humanity, and aroused a strong feeling of ethical revulsion. It was objectively an accepted fact that denunciation constituted a crime against humanity when it could be interpreted as having been undertaken for the purpose of persecution on the basis of political, racial, or religious grounds, as clarified by a military government instruction issued on 22 November 1946.[133] The defendants had consciously used the law of the time with reprehensible and inhumane motives to report someone of Jewish descent to the Gestapo to resolve a family squabble, thus placing the matter on a racial and political plane, when filing for divorce would have sufficed. What was especially reprehensible was that they knew what the grievous outcome of their actions would be for a Jew at the time.[134]

On the other hand, there were some extenuating circumstances that were considered in their favor. The court granted some clemency on the grounds that the two accused had not hitherto been convicted, and noted how Mrs. P. had to some degree caused the motive for the offense. She had done this by spoiling their home life, especially for P., who endured an unhappy marriage for thirty-five years until he agreed to follow his sister, who took the initiative in getting rid of his wife. The fact that the defendant had brought some necessities to Mrs. P. while she was in prison was also taken into account, in addition to the fact that Mrs. P.'s death weighed on their conscience. In view of these facts, K. was sentenced to eight months' imprisonment and P. to six months.[135] The jury could also have chosen to be rather lenient given their advanced ages, as K. was fifty-nine years old and P. was sixty-seven.

This case was later appealed at the Highest Appeal Court of the British Zone that had been set up to establish uniformity among the judgments of the courts in the British zone, and reinforced the concept of retroactive legislation for the redress of grave injustices in its decisions in cases of crimes against humanity.[136] This court upheld the guilty verdict on 9 November 1948, confirming that the case contained the characteristics of a crime against humanity. The defendant had shown complete disregard for the value and dignity of human rights within the violence and arbitrariness of the National Socialist regime.[137] The Hamburg regional court had correctly assessed that the defendant had consciously intended to bring about inhumane consequences by delivering Mrs. P. into the hands of state sanctioned terror and arbitrariness, especially while being fully aware of the persecution of Jews in Germany at the time, and were thus adjudicated accordingly.[138]

A later case of denunciation was heard at the Itzehoe regional court, where judgment was passed on 28 June 1948 on two accused, hereafter cited as Sch. and S., who were sentenced to eight and six months' imprisonment. Sch. had joined the NSDAP in 1937 in order to secure a public office, and condoned the policies of the National Socialist regime owing to the improved economic conditions of the time. S. had been a member of the NSDAP and the SA from 1 March 1932, and as a convinced National Socialist, later held the offices of *Ortsgruppeleiter* in the NSDAP and *Sturmführer* in the SA.[139]

In the autumn of 1939, Sch. worked on a farm with T., who had been a member of the German Communist Party and had spent two years in the concentration camp after 1933. On the day of the assassination attempt against Hitler in Munich, Sch. overheard T. say to a workmate that if Hitler had been killed, he would celebrate by drinking a week's worth of earnings. This led to an argument between Sch. and T. and other workers. Two months later, Sch. reported T.'s remark to S. in his capacity as an NSDAP official, allegedly as a matter concerning the SA. Although the location in which the incident took place was outside of S.'s jurisdiction, he nevertheless reported the matter with the intention to have T. prosecuted. T. was later investigated by the police, and proceedings were instituted against him. He was brought before the Schleswig-Holstein Special Court in Kiel on 11 June 1940, where Sch. was the leading witness in the trial, and was convicted on an offense against the so-called *Heimtückegesetz* and was sentenced to three years' imprisonment. After serving this sentence, the Gestapo took him to the Neuengamme concentration camp where he remained until near the end of the war. He then died still in custody at the end of April 1945 in the sinking of a steamer that was carrying political prisoners.[140]

Sch. had intentionally made a report against T. in order to have proceedings instituted against him by the "political criminal justice institutions" as he described them, thus undertaking a solely politically motivated action when he reported the matter to S., without there being any personal factors in his decision to do this. Meanwhile, S. thought, according to his own admission, that he deserved to be imprisoned for a year to a year and a half, and therefore reported his remarks in his area of jurisdiction. As a consequence, the persecution that T. had undergone as a result of the contents of a private conversation with his workmates represented a significant abuse of state power on political principles.[141]

The court declared that such persecution on political principles demonstrated a violation of the accepted principles of humanity in all states that were not ruled by dictatorships, as well as a violation against the principles of natural law and all ethical laws, and thus the defendant had to be held responsible for T.'s death. Sch. had a clear understanding of what the consequences of his denunciation would be, as it was common knowledge in 1940 that the remarks that T. had made would be punished barbarically when in the hands of the Gestapo. Moreover, the excessively severe sentences pronounced by the Special Courts were published in the press. Whereas Sch. had acted without the slightest provocation, the facts of the case applied to a greater extent to S. as a political leader. He was shocked by T.'s comments and thus also intended to have proceedings instituted against him by relaying Sch.'s report to the police authorities.

The court ruled that although the defendant could not have necessarily foreseen T.'s death, they were guilty of a crime against humanity in the form of denunciation according to Article II, sections 1c, 2, 3, and 5 of Control Council Law No. 10 in connection with Article I, sections 1 and 2 of Military Government Ordinance No. 47,[142] since it could be demonstrated that the victim of the denunciation had incurred inhumane consequences as a result of this action, and the political persecution that followed could have been anticipated as a consequence of the denunciation.[143] The Schleswig regional court in Kiel later upheld this verdict on 23 March 1949 after examining the facts of the case. The actions of the defendants led to inhumane consequences for T., therefore confirming that they had consciously contravened the principles of humanity that carries and protects the ideals of human value and dignity by delivering him into the hands of the representatives of arbitrary power who did not consider themselves to be bound by the principles of justice and law.[144]

A later denunciation case was heard during this time at the Hannover regional court, where the verdicts were pronounced on 28 and 29 June, and 1 July 1948. The defendant, hereafter cited as S., ran a tavern while he was released from military service from July 1940 to the autumn of 1941, where he became acquainted with a traveling salesman hereafter cited as N. on 17 January 1941, who told him many political jokes and rumors while in a slightly inebriated state of mind. N. had expected that although S. was an old time member of the NSDAP since 1928, he could speak to him freely and that S. would not somehow make use of his remarks. After having listened to N. calmly, S. reported his remarks to the criminal police in Mannheim a few days later on 23 January 1941. These included the following examples. A parrot in Berlin that knew Hitler and other leading personalities was asked whether it knew a uniformed police official. The parrot then asked him: "Where are the rogues?"; Rudolf Hess would get divorced; Mussolini would be guarded by the German military and Germany would occupy all of Italy within eight weeks; Goebbels lived apart from his family, and his wife had lived away from him for seven months, and Berliners laughed when they saw their family reception in the newspaper, saying it had an old and falsified photo; many people gathered before the artillery and procurement office in Berlin one day, and a first lieutenant (*Oberstleutnant*) asked a noncommissioned officer to find out what was going on. People then told him that the English had reported on the radio that the NSDAP leadership was having a banquet there.[145]

The police conveyed this report to the Gestapo and N. was arrested thereafter, and the matter was handed over to the state prosecutor, who began to initiate proceedings against him. N.'s employer approached S. about the possibility of lending his support to N., but S. declined saying there was nothing he could do. Meanwhile, another report was filed against him concerning disparaging remarks about the regime that he had made in a tavern in Stuttgart on 20 January 1944. He was convicted by the Mannheim Special Court on 21 May 1941, and was sentenced to ten months' imprisonment, including six months for the remarks that he had made to S. N. was thereafter released after his sentence that did not involve enduring any especial hardship, which he partly attributed to encouraging Gestapo officials and giving them cigarettes.[146]

S. claimed in his defense that he had reported N. at the prompting of a railroad worker who was present during their conversation, who had asked him a few days after the incident whether he had filed a report, and told him he was obliged to do so as an old time party member. He claimed that he had thus been induced to make this report, hoping to prevent unpleasantries that could be brought on him. The fact that he was a bearer of the NSDAP golden party badge did not make this a sound defense, since he occupied a special position in the party. On the other hand, it could be surmised that as a convinced National Socialist and an "old fighter," he considered himself obliged to file the report as the sole motivating factor.[147]

While S. acted on German criminal law that was in force at the time, the court maintained that this type of action could only be considered a crime against humanity according to Control Council Law No. 10, Article II c, when there were inhumane consequences that had been incurred at the hands of the apparatus of the National Socialist regime and the inhumane cast of mind of the defendant. It could not be determined whether the consequences of the six months' imprisonment was grossly disproportionate with regard to his action, and therefore could be considered inhumane. In addition, the conduct of the defendant could not have been considered to have possessed an inhumane disposition, in view of the consequences of his action. He had been insincere, having told N. that he could speak to him freely, and should have known that drunken talk should not have been taken seriously. He should also have told him to put his chattering to an end and warned N. about the potential consequences of such talk, but there was no evidence of any other reproachable motives, such as envy, resentment, revenge, or hatred that had influenced his decision in filing a report against him. He had only considered the financial disadvantage of losing a well-paying customer. S. had therefore filed a report on the basis of simplistic thinking by which he believed that N.'s talk posed a danger to the regime, and thus had to be prosecuted in view of the prevailing law at the time that served this purpose, without expecting that the consequences for N. would be disproportionate to his actions. It was therefore found that objective considerations of the provisions of Control Council Law No. 10 were not fulfilled, so S. was thereby acquitted of this charge due to insufficient evidence.[148]

He was also tried for another charge, concerning events that took place after he was re-inducted for military service in the autumn of 1941, while he was serving as a truck driver in the motor pool in Mannheim in 1944.[149] The funeral for Colonel-General Dietl took place during this time, which was announced over the radio and was heard in the barracks where S. was housed with a large number of others, including those hereafter cited as K. and Sch. A day after the announcement about this state funeral, K. came to the barracks and told other soldiers who were present there, including S., that he had just come back from their workplace to the headquarters building with Sch. and a non-commissioned officer called Walter. During their conversation, Walter suggested that Dietl had not died from natural causes, and claimed that he "had to go" like Mölders and Udet, since he would no longer "go along with" the regime. In response to K.'s objection that Hitler had been deeply moved at the state funeral and had spoken in a voice broken with sadness, Walter responded that Hitler was an actor, as well as a rogue, an idler, a riffraff tramp, and a villain. When S. heard about these remarks from K., he stated that these were personal affronts to the *Führer* and expected to hear about more such remarks that Walter had made. It turned out that it was generally known in the unit that he had often made disparaging remarks about the National Socialist regime and its leadership. S. then asked Sch. to confirm what Walter had said, which he agreed to do.[150]

On the same day and a few days later, S. turned to the commander of the branch of the motor pool in Landau, hereafter cited as F., who was also the so-called National Socialist leadership officer for the motor pool. S. told him about Walter's remarks, and suggested that he should be "taught a lesson" or "be put in his place," rather than receiving a serious punishment. F. understood this to mean that S. expected Walter to be subjected to disciplinary measures. F. felt disconcertment about the possibility of the danger that could threaten Walter, but nevertheless called in K. and Sch. thereafter to record what they heard, and expressly cautioned them to ensure that what they said was truthful while also ensuring that they were aware of the possible consequences that could follow for Walter. He then conferred with the adjutant of the unit, hereafter cited as B., who agreed that the matter ought to not to be pursued further, as much as it was possible. After reproaching Walter for making disparaging remarks about his highest superiors, especially in front of others who were not completely trustworthy, F. then considered the matter to be settled. The commander of the motor pool, hereafter cited as Major L., also agreed that no further action would be taken against Walter, with the written record of the matter probably having been kept as a matter of protecting his interests.[151]

A few days thereafter, a first sergeant hereafter cited as Be. approached Major L. and brought his attention to how there was talk in the motor pool about the incident concerning Walter's remarks, and how S. was not satisfied with how the matter was resolved. This could have led to difficulties for L., who therefore decided to ask for advice from the divisional military court in Neckargemünd on how to resolve this matter. It was agreed by military court judges and L. and his officers that after questioning about twenty character witnesses speaking in favor of Walter, he would have to face the maximum extent of disciplinary measures, which at best would not lead to court proceedings. Walter was thereafter placed under arrest on 17 June 1944, and was imprisoned for two weeks, which was the severest punishment that he could impose as a brigade commander. He was nevertheless praised by L. for being a good soldier while implying that S. had not acted with an appropriate soldierly bearing in this matter. S. said thereafter that he would not settle for this result. Meanwhile, the matter appeared settled while the record of the incident was forwarded to a higher authority at the general headquarters in Wiesbaden.[152]

In the autumn of 1944, Walter was suddenly arrested again on the order of the central court of the army in Berlin, and was tried for undermining the war effort on the grounds of the evidence that K. and Sch. had forwarded against him, with the additional remark that sometime in the summer of 1944, Walter had told someone in the presence of several soldiers to throw out a picture of

Hitler, and that he had thrown it out the window saying he could not stand to look at it. When S. was asked about the outcome of these court proceedings, he said that "a head would be off and another film would be played in this theatre," meaning that the matter had not yet been resolved since there would be further repercussions for the motor pool leadership. Walter was later executed by firing squad on 6 February 1945 following confirmation of the death sentence by Himmler on 20 January 1945, with a plea for clemency having been rejected.[153]

S. claimed in his defense that he had not reported Walter's remarks to F. in an official capacity, but had rather intended to seek advice on how to deal with this matter. Meanwhile, others had assumed that as an "old fighter" and bearer of the golden party badge, he was obliged say something about it, at the risk of facing severe punishment if he did not do anything. He otherwise argued that he did not forward Walter's remarks to an official NSDAP authority. Although he probably let his intentions be known, he in fact had not taken any action, other than recommending to the commanding officer that Walter ought to be reprimanded.[154]

The court determined that whether S. had actually made an official report to F. was an open question. However, S.'s remarks indicated that he expected that Walter would be called to account in some way and that there would be consequences for the disparaging remarks he had made. He had also considered himself obliged to take action against Walter. However, it could not be established whether he had proceeded with making a further report after he had said he was unsatisfied with how Walter was dealt with by being imprisoned for two weeks, when the record of the incident had been forwarded to a higher authority shortly before the event of 20 July 1944. It could therefore be surmised that the reporting of this incident reached the central court of the army without the instigation of another.[155]

The jury court also could not establish whether S. was the original source of the talk that Be. had told L. that S. was not satisfied with the disciplinary action against Walter, considering that there had been a great deal of gossip circulating at the motor pool, and therefore it could not be proven that S. would proceed to take further action against Walter or report L. if he suppressed the matter. It could only be maintained that he considered the disciplinary action against Walter to have been meaningless. It therefore could not be established that S.'s report to F. had caused the court proceedings that led to the court proceedings against Walter and the subsequent execution.[156]

The question about whether S.'s conduct toward Walter was inhumane when he conveyed his remarks to F. also remained doubtful. Since Walter had often rashly made disparaging remarks about National Socialism in public, it was not surprising that this had attracted S.'s attention as an "old fighter" and a loyal follower of the NSDAP, and had caused him to take great offense in his simplistic way of thinking about how such a comment posed a considerable danger to the nation. The fact that a non-commissioned officer made such remarks to subordinates must have been especially appalling to him. There were otherwise no indications of him having acted on the grounds of any other base motives due to serious personal or professional differences between them, and he had not expressed any intention or approval for a death sentence to be passed against Walter. S.'s remark about "a head" coming off did not necessarily imply expressing satisfaction with the death sentence. The fact that he had turned to F. as a military officer in conveying Walter's remarks so that disciplinary measures would be taken against him, rather than to an NSDAP authority or the Gestapo, was also taken into consideration as a mitigating factor in him not having intended for Walter to face such grave consequences for an offense of a political nature. Meanwhile, although the death sentence was completely unjustifiable in proportion to Walter's futile "grumbling" and his vilifying of the highest wartime leaders, something that he ought to have kept to himself, it was considered that a military court in National Socialist Germany at the height of the war at the end of 1944 would typically take the harshest measures against a non-commissioned officer for allegedly "undermining the war effort," but measures which could not have been considered inhumane.[157]

The jury court therefore could not establish with certainty that S. had intended for Walter to face military court proceedings, or had expected him to receive the death sentence, or had caused the unfortunate chain of events that led to the terrible consequences that followed. While anyone would be appalled at S.'s conduct, neither his conduct nor the causes for his actions could be considered inhumane. He was thus acquitted of this additional charge of having committed a crime against humanity[158] due to the insufficiency of any real incriminating evidence.

This case was later reviewed at the Highest Appeal Court of the British Zone, which quashed this verdict on 8 March 1949 and reverted the case to the jury court at the Hannover regional court for further deliberations. This court ruled that the jury court had misjudged how the death sentence that had been passed on Walter was in fact inhumane, considering that Walter's execution was completely unjustifiable as a typical National Socialist act of inhumanity that resulted from committing an alleged offense against Hitler and his regime, in which the defendant was not allowed any form of defense. The death sentence was therefore unlawful since the military court proceedings excluded the possibility of Walter receiving a fair trial, as would have been the case in the state governed by the rule of law.[159]

The jury court had correctly ascertained that S.'s report to F. had contributed to causing Walter's death. While it began the course of events that led to the death sentence, it could not be determined whether S. had made a second report to another authority, or whether he had first approached F. about imposing some informal disciplinary measures so that at least something would be done about Walter without necessarily putting him into great danger of facing grave consequences. However, there remained far more precise details of determining the extent to which S.'s conduct could be considered hostile, in terms of whether he could have prevented the course of events from continuing further after he had reported Walter to F. S. had put Walter in danger of being prosecuted by a military court from the outset, and therefore, in contrast to the jury court's interpretation, the objective facts of a crime against humanity was fulfilled.[160]

The jury court's dealing with the internal circumstances of the case was also met with disapproval due to the incompleteness of the verdict. It had not taken the intentions of the defendant, or at least his awareness, of the unforeseeable consequences that could follow in connection with the National Socialist system of violence and tyranny, into sufficient consideration. The perpetrator also had to recognize the possibility of the unlawfulness of his actions, which needed to be addressed in renewed proceedings. It had been inappropriate for the defendant to be acquitted on the grounds of determining that his conduct had not been inhumane and that he had acted out of reasonable initiatives, while assuming that he had not wanted or approved of the initiation of court proceedings and subsequently the imposition of the death penalty. Actions that were undertaken out of an inhumane attitude or inhumane motives were equally consequential as the foreknowledge of the concrete results of this hostile action.[161]

Elements of the internal circumstances suggested that the defendant was a so-called old fighter who had proven, as demonstrated in the case with N., that he did not have any misgivings about reporting a "grumbler" to the police. It could hardly be surmised that he could not have known in the summer of 1944 that the reporting of Walter's careless remarks about Hitler himself to a National Socialist leadership officer would normally lead to him facing mortal danger. He would also have known that this officer, whose task was the political supervision of troops, would not risk agreeing with covering up such a case. It was therefore determined that the defendant would either expect F. to call Walter to account for his actions, or the course of events would continue in this regard. This indicated his eventual intention with regard to this possibility, while having expressed dissatisfaction with the outcome of the disciplinary proceedings that had been imposed on Walter. His reaction following the military court proceedings also indicated that he had not been surprised at the outcome, which implied that he had expected to expose Walter to the most serious type of danger. The acquittal was thereby quashed, and the evidence was to be re-examined during renewed jury court proceedings.[162]

Revised verdicts were pronounced at the jury court at the Hannover regional court on 24 March 1950. These proceedings determined that the case involving N. indicated how S. had been prepared to actively intervene against alleged opponents of the National Socialist regime, but he was not convicted due to the insufficiency of any incriminating evidence. When the facts of the case concerning the events that led to the execution of Walter came under further review,[163] new evidence was presented in which it was indicated that S. had attempted to reopen proceedings against Walter after he had been imprisoned for two weeks.[164]

S. had expressed his dissatisfaction about the leniency of this disciplinary measure taken against Walter to another non-commissioned officer, hereafter cited as D. D. had been an NSDAP member who had also heard Walter make disparaging remarks about the National Socialist regime, and had advised him to be more careful and also to think about his wife and child. Since he had though well of him, he determined to prevent the matter from being dealt with by the Gestapo, while he suspected that S. would take further action against Walter as a loyal follower of the NSDAP. S. told him that there was nothing he could do about withdrawing the matter from the Gestapo, which had been aware of the matter, at the risk of implicating himself in this matter, and besides, he chose to act on his conscience as a National Socialist. It thus appeared impossible for D. to exercise any influence on S. on doing anything to save Walter. Soon thereafter on 8 September 1944, Major L. received an order to place Walter under arrest and have him taken to Berlin. Walter was thereafter taken to a prison where he was mistreated by members of the SS, giving L. the impression that he would not return.[165]

S., K., and Sch. had appeared as witnesses at the central military court proceedings in Berlin on 13 November 1944, and did not forward any support in favor of Walter's defense, as they had initiated these court proceedings through their actions against him, even though his life was at stake. When questioned at these proceedings, they reiterated what Walter had said, and added testimony about the incident regarding Hitler's picture in addition to his earlier "grumblings." While a defense witness provided testimony of about seventeen other testimonies in favor of Walter's reputation during these proceedings, S. was visibly annoyed, and in contrast to the defense testimony, provided the court with a provocative testimony against Walter. Despite any of the exonerating evidence, Walter was sentenced to death.[166]

When S. shared a tent in an American prisoner-of-war camp with other former non-commissioned officers after the end of the war, they spoke about

Walter, and S. was asked why he had not reported the matter to the NSDAP since he had not been satisfied with the two weeks' imprisonment that had been imposed on him. He replied that he preferred that others should deal with the matter, and would have let it rest had others not threatened to report him to the party. They thus presumed that that he had reported the matter to the NSDAP after Walter had first been imprisoned, while regretting that the matter had gone so far thereafter.[167]

S. claimed in his defense that he had nothing against Walter and although he had often insulted the NSDAP, he did not have any personal differences with him. The incident involving Hitler's picture had taken place a year before the Dietl incident, and he had not said anything about it although there had been other witnesses present, and that he had only acted against Walter with regard to his remarks concerning Dietl after K. had said he had better put his grumbling to an end. He also said that he did so because others in the barracks said that he had better act as a representative of the NSDAP, rather than let the matter rest. He therefore claimed to have approached F. to recommend imposing disciplinary measures against Walter for this reason, not intending that there be any severe punishment. Additionally, S. claimed that the two weeks' imprisonment had been sufficient, and that he had not contacted any military or political authorities to have a more serious sentence imposed, in spite of the assumptions that were made by the other prisoners-of-war.[168]

In view of the evidence heard from different witnesses, the jury court found that S.'s report concerning the incidents that took place at the motor pool was forwarded to official military channels, which led to military court proceedings in Berlin. This did not exclude the considerable suspicion about the possibility that he could also have taken this matter further in the form of a second report to the Gestapo or another political authority. In evaluating the facts of the case, the court found that the defendant was guilty of a crime against humanity. He had expressed his dissatisfaction with the imposition of disciplinary measures after having initially reported the matter to F., which consequently placed Walter in much greater danger, and did not take any action to alleviate the situation before and during the ensuing military court proceedings in which he displayed a malicious attitude toward Walter. The result of these proceedings ended with Walter's execution, which was completely out of proportion to the remarks he had made. S.'s conduct and the facts of the case thus conformed to the provisions set forth in Article II, section 1c and 2a of Control Council Law No. 10. He had caused Walter's death through his disposition as an "old fighter," and the chain of events that he had initiated with his first report against him that led to his being delivered into the forces of tyranny.[169]

His earlier conduct in the case concerning N. had demonstrated how he had been inclined toward and was ready to deliver "enemies" of the National Socialist regime to the forces of persecution, and showed the same disposition in the case concerning Walter, when, upon hearing what he had said he, was said to have exclaimed: "The glass is full! I'm going to report the matter!"[170] After he had been dissatisfied with the disciplinary measures taken against Walter, a witness in the present proceedings testified how he had objected to withdrawing the matter from being investigated by the Gestapo, saying that it would be against his National Socialist conscience. Other witnesses testified how he had expressed his dissatisfaction without any sense of remorse about the outcome of the military court proceedings, and later boasted about his role in these proceedings. Any remorse he had expressed in the prisoner-of-war camp was interpreted as him having fears about the possibility of being called to account for his actions after the collapse of the National Socialist regime. He had not otherwise expressed any regret during the present proceedings while having been aware of the unjustness of the potential consequences of his actions.[171]

In an examination of any possible mitigating circumstances, the jury court made allowances for the fact that S. did not have any prior convictions, and that these proceedings had extended over several years, thus constituting an emotional burden to the defendant. It was also taken into consideration that he was known to be narrow-minded and unintelligent, which contributed to his politically inflexible cast of mind and his taking the initiative in causing the foreseeable severe consequences. However, these personality characteristics did not deter the court from imposing a prison sentence, especially given the gravity and abhorrence of these consequences. In view of the overall circumstances, he was thereby sentenced to a year and six months' imprisonment.[172]

The successful adjudication of denunciation cases before and throughout this time when such cases were heard in various courts in the British occupation zone would continue to follow the earlier precedents set in applying Control Council Law No. 10. By the end of September 1948, over 2000 cases of crimes against humanity had been investigated by public prosecutors and remained awaiting judgment in the courts of the British occupation zone. The general hesitation in adjudicating these cases was partly alleviated by the institution of jury courts and by the decisions of the Highest Appeal Court of the British Zone, which provided examples that promoted a greater clarity and uniformity concerning the interpretation of Control Council Law No. 10. The underlying factor in all such cases remained the fact that the defendant in such cases had attacked others or violated their human rights as a result of their National Socialist beliefs, and in denunciation cases, they had also intentionally violated the human dignity of another by delivering them into the hands of an illegal and tyrannical system of persecution. Public prosecutors were thereby instructed to continue initiating proceedings in such cases in conformity with the decisions of this court.[173]

A later denunciation case was heard at the Wuppertal regional court, where the judgment was pronounced on 29 October 1948. The defendant, hereafter cited as K., was found guilty of committing a crime against humanity on the basis of Article II, section 1c of Control Council Law No. 10, in that he had persecuted another individual on the basis of their political beliefs.[174] This was another example of how personal political viewpoints could be used as a weapon against another under the guise of upholding the National Socialist regime.

On 15 September 1943, a frontline soldier had returned to his former workplace to visit his former co-workers, where he told them of his wartime experiences. One of the workers there, hereafter cited as St., sharply criticized the successes of the German forces that the soldier had talked about, saying how "German soldiers walked like hares" and "flung lumps." This nearly led to a violent altercation between him and another co-worker who called him a coward who should be at the front. This dispute was taken to be settled by the defendant who was a factory supervisor. He took the matter further with the local NSDAP local authority (*Ortsgruppenleiter*), reporting that St. had caused unrest by making remarks against a frontline soldier.[175]

Two days after the incident occurred, K. wrote a report to the local office of the German Labor Front, with the purpose of getting the matter to be taken up by the Gestapo. He stated that St. had habitually made disparaging criticisms about the government, the army and other institutions of the *Reich* for years in spite of being warned against doing so many times. He went on to claim that St. had said the successes of the German troops were defeats, had mentioned incredible figures for those killed daily, and had claimed that German troops were retreating in greater distances every day, suggesting that the frontline soldier visiting the factory should not return to battle.[176] St. was arrested by the Gestapo shortly thereafter on 20 September 1943. He was later tried by the People's Court in Bonn on 16 December 1943 for undermining the war effort and was sentenced to death and executed on 16 February 1944.[177]

In view of the available evidence and testimonies from the surviving witnesses, the court found that the overall personality and conduct of the defendant indicated that he was clearly aware of the action he intended to take against St. He had insisted on taking the initiative to make the report against him, regardless of the dispute that he had had with his co-worker, and acted alone in intentionally initiating the proceedings against him with conspicuous haste and eagerness. Moreover, he appeared to be pleased about St.'s death sentence, after having made devastating statements against St. as a witness in his trial, which, according to the defense lawyer, had a considerable influence[178] on those proceedings.

The court thus determined that the defendant had committed a crime against humanity given the objective and subjective facts of the case. K. had a hostile attitude toward St., and consciously and coldly set out to persecute him while being aware that his actions would result in the death penalty. Moreover, not being a member of the NSDAP meant that he was not necessarily compelled to act on a matter that could have been considered a personal matter between two co-workers, which could have been settled within their workplace. In view of the facts, the court reached the conclusion that the defendant had persecuted St. on political principles, especially since K. himself admitted that he didn't have any personal differences with St., and recognized him to have always been a competent worker.[179] The only personal difference between them was their differences in political opinions that led to an atrocity being committed at the hands of a regime characterized by violence and arbitrariness where the law was used as a weapon against non-conformists within the population, rather than safeguarding the rights of every individual.

It was inconceivable for any fair-minded individual to imagine that St., who had hitherto never been prosecuted and enjoyed a good reputation, had deserved to be executed for his remarks that would not have caused the slightest disadvantage for the state and its institutions. He had made a purely personal insult that led him to incur the death penalty as a consequence of the denunciation by the defendant, whose action represented an attack on humanity as a bearer and defender of the ideals of human dignity. This had been made possible in the existing administration of justice at the time, in which denunciation made it possible for individuals to contravene the rule of law.[180]

In view of the facts that the defendant had hitherto never been prosecuted and enjoyed a good reputation according to witnesses, the sentence was reduced to a certain degree. On the other hand, given his basic convictions, his persistence in causing St.'s death, especially since it involved a matter not concerning him as he was not a member of the NSDAP, the cowardly manner in which he disputed the facts of the case while trying cast the blame on another, the court determined it was deemed necessary to impose a sentence of a year and six months' imprisonment, in view of the unlawful form of the action and its terrible consequences.[181]

The next such case was heard at the Paderborn regional court. Judgment was pronounced on 2 November 1948, where the defendant, hereafter cited as F., was sentenced to two years and ten months' imprisonment for crimes against humanity as defined by Article II section 1c of Control Council Law

No. 10.[182] A businessman who had had a long-standing membership in the NSDAP used his influence to act against a former business partner with whom he had had a falling out. He not only brought his political influence to bear on a business in which he was interested in taking part, but also used the law to his advantage for personal gain.

The defendant, hereafter cited as F., had joined the NSDAP in 1931, and eventually became able to wear the Golden Party Badge and also occupied several positions in industry after the National Socialist takeover. These positions included the economic advisor to the local *Gauleiter* (regional leader) for Westphalia and Lippe, the councilor for the province of Westphalia, a board member of the Ruhenstroh GmbH. wood production factory. He also served as trustee for the Prussian mining company, Hibernia, for its share in the former company, as a member of the board of the German trade chamber, and as the president of the industrial and trade chamber of Münster until 1945.[183]

He became involved with helping manage a formerly Jewish owned plywood factory in Wiedenbrück, one of the largest in Germany whose owners had fled to Switzerland, and was nationalized in 1938. The manager of this firm's sales office in Berlin, Dr. Bresser, thereafter became the trustee for the national government. Meanwhile, the defendant in his capacity as the local regional economic advisor, was involved in the decision to keep this factory running, rather than closing it down, and trying to find a suitable buyer.[184]

Dr. Bresser expressed his intention to take over the management of the factory, but he could not do so outright without the support of the defendant who intervened in this matter by using his position in the government to put pressure on Dr. Bresser by saying that he would not be able to do so without his involvement in the firm's management. Following negotiations with the authorized representatives of the *Reich* Ministry of Finance and various other branches of local government, they started managing this business from 1 May 1939. While Dr. Bresser was responsible for managing business matters, F. would be primarily concerned with dealing with governmental and NSDAP authorities.[185] The firm made considerable progress under Dr. Bresser's management, and the relationship between these two partners was initially quite good with the occasional unavoidable differences of opinion that were always resolved. More serious discords later took place during 1943, that led to a power struggle between them, in which both tried to push the other out of the firm.[186]

The personal rift between them began in the summer of 1943 when Dr. Bresser had a hunting lodge built using the firm's building materials and labor, which aroused indignation among the local population in view of the shortages of housing and wood. This led to an investigation by the local

Gau (administrative region) inspector, and a fine of 5000 RM. Dr. Bresser suspected the influence of the party behind the legal proceedings that had been instituted against the firm, although it could not be determined whether F. had played a part in this matter. Relations between Dr. Bresser and F. continued to deteriorate after F. moved with his family from Münster to Wiedenbrück. After he had resigned from his position as the economic advisor to the local *Gau* and his home had incurred bomb damage, which probably provided a pretext for him wanting a greater involvement in the firm's business, he laid claim to a company-owned guest house in which the company secretary, Dr. W., was living. Dr. W. had to move out on short notice after being threatened with being forced to move out at the NSDAP's prompting if he did not do so willingly. As a partner in this firm, F. also considered himself entitled to use the garden on Dr. Bresser's property, which Bresser took as a personal injury.[187]

In view of the worsening relationship with F., Dr. Bresser sought to make himself independent of F. through other than political means. He had joined the NSDAP in 1940, but was expelled from the NSDAP in 1941 for having been a Freemason. Therefore, he sought to strengthen his position in the firm by finding large business contracts with the air force, thereby supporting the war effort, and thus gaining support from the Air Ministry and the Armaments Ministry. Political interests prevented him from doing so in the summer of 1943, as the *Gauleiter* of Westphalia in Münster tried to prevent him from making the necessary contacts, claiming his personal conduct had instigated civil unrest, alluding to the matter of the construction of the hunting lodge.[188]

Meanwhile, F. sought to take advantage of his own worsening relationship with Dr. Bresser. Knowing that Bresser depended on him to prove so-called political reliability after taking over the management of the firm, F. had proven to be helpful, until he started to act against him in the summer of 1943. F. had prior knowledge about Bresser that he acquired about him from the *Gau* economic advisor in Berlin, where Bresser had lived, which stated that he was "not considered worthy of Aryanization." Between 23 June and 20 July 1943, F. again asked for a copy of this information, thus starting to collect damaging material that he could use against Bresser.[189]

Further events continued to give rise to the escalating tension between them. While Bresser was on holiday at a sanatorium in Constance, F. took advantage of his absence to continue collecting material against him. In an attempt to weaken his position in the firm, he took the unusual measure of ordering a company audit by an outside auditor, Dr. Schumacher, who F. knew was not on good terms with Bresser. This audit revealed a number of complaints, such as how Dr. W. had received a loan of 4000 RM for moving expenses and had 3000 RM reimbursed to him, the payroll expenses for company-paid domestic servants exceeded the agreed extent, and the expenses for the hunting lodge were not filed, ending with a strong criticism of Bresser, to which he necessarily objected.[190]

The recriminations between them continued thereafter. During a business trip to Vienna where he met Dr. V., the manager of another wood production company and an industry advisor, Bresser told him that he was having difficulties with F. and reiterated that it was not necessary for him to take part in the management of the firm, other than for political reasons and to keep the NSDAP "off his throat." V. later repeated this to F. while they were in the bomb shelter of the Kaiserhof Hotel in Berlin in late November 1943 after suspecting that Bresser may have been responsible for him losing his position of advisor in his industrial group. Meanwhile, the difficulties between them became known to the local NSDAP authorities, in addition to causing a division between the staff at the firm itself,[191] which became divided on political lines.

Two groups of employees had emerged after F. had started taking greater interest in the firm after taking up residence in Wiedenbrück. A part of the workforce supported Dr. W., Bresser's former Masonic lodge brother, while another sided with R., the chief engineer and a member of the NSDAP who suspected that Bresser begrudged the considerable income that could have been attained by his patents. R. had said to Dr.W. in February 1944 that one must position oneself on the side of the more powerful, and sided with F. against Bresser. R. told F. how he intended to push him out of the firm, and that they just needed him in the meantime as political window dressing for as long as it was necessary. He thus asked F. to exert influence on Bresser to change his attitude, even proposing a form of pressure to be used against him.[192]

Bresser had said, when he received a letter concerning his expulsion from the NSDAP because of his prior membership in the Masonic Lodge, that he thought that this letter was worth more than 50,000 RM, since he could later use it to prove at any time that he had not been a Nazi. R. obliged F. with a handshake agreement to not make this information public, and to only use it to bring pressure to bear on Bresser in order to force him to change his attitude against them.[193] This agreement would not stand up under the pressure of later events when F. used it against Bresser, ostensibly to protect himself in the context of the new difficult circumstances that had suddenly arisen.

At the end of 1943, rumors, false or otherwise, had started circulating again after Bresser and F. had taken over the management of the company. It was said that F. was corrupt, and had abused his position in the NSDAP in order to take possession of the factory in Wiedenbrück. Bresser was suspected to be the source of these rumors. The SD reported to the local *Gauleiter* in Hamburg that Bresser had said to different wood dealers in Hamburg that he only needed F. as a "National Socialist advertisement," and would throw him out when he was no longer necessary.[194] This led to F. being questioned about these rumors about him being corrupt.

Upon being confronted about what had been said about him by the deputy *Gauleiter* in Hamburg, F. accused Bresser of being the source of what had been said, in addition to saying what he had said about his letter being worth 50,000 RM, without mentioning the source of this information. He was again accused of the same charges of corruption in the office of the Berlin *Gauleiter* shortly thereafter, and reiterated the same in his defense. The *Gauleiter* there then got in touch with the Gestapo. Meanwhile, V. and R., who F. had named as witnesses, were questioned by criminal commissioner Diehl about whether they had heard Bresser make defeatist remarks. With some hesitation, V. admitted to what had been said at the Kaiserhof Hotel, saying he intended to learn about their "division of their work," while R. was thereby forced to state what he had told F. under the threat of being arrested.

The *Gauleiter* thereafter began recommending that punitive measures ought to be taken against Bresser. Sometime later, he decided to send a report to Speer's Ministry of Armaments, in which he recommended that Bresser be recalled from his office for special tasks for the plywood industry and be removed from his position as a company manager. He added the reports of what he had said in Hamburg and Vienna, and details about his letter of expulsion from the NSDAP being worth over 50,000 RM. At the same time that honor court proceedings were requested for this purpose, a letter containing the contents concerning this matter arrived at Speer's Armaments Ministry in mid-March 1944.[195]

During a routine meeting with the local *Gauleiter* that was attended by F., S., the representative of the *Gauleiter,* M., the economic advisor to the *Gauleiter* who had succeeded F., the local government president (*Regierungspräsident*) Fr., and the leader of the Münster secret police headquarters, senior government advisor (*Oberregierungsrat*) and *SS-Oberstürmbannführer* Landgraf, he brought up the matter of dealing with Bresser. After discussing it for some time, M. later sent a copy of the report to the Armaments Ministry with a cover letter to Landgraf, who in turn sent the documents to the local responsible office in Bielefeld. The official in charge, criminal commissioner Diehl, thereafter ordered that Bresser be placed under surveillance. The report about him, signed by the *Gauleiter* and the *Reichsverteidigungskomissar,* stating that he was no longer politically reliable, had made defeatist statements, quoting the remark about the 50000 RM, and naming R. as a witness and referring to initiating proceedings against Bresser, was in Berlin at the same time, and the machinery of the political police action began to operate soon thereafter. Diehl drove to Wiedenbrück on 31 March

1944, where he examined different company employees as witnesses and arrested W. Diehl arrested Bresser the next day and took him to Bielefeld. Bresser and the others who were questioned at the firm also incriminated R., saying he had made defeatist remarks, and he was consequently also arrested on 3 April. He admitted to doing so when confronted about it while being questioned, and he later also admitted to listening to foreign broadcasts together with Bresser.[196]

Evidence against Bresser and R. was gathered following the questioning of various witnesses at the firm with whom Bresser and R. had contact, and the date for a trial at the People's Court was set for 4 August 1944. They would stand accused of the additional charge of listening to foreign broadcasts and disseminating what had been heard, and would also be held accountable for making the remark about the 50000 RM, and other remarks about Hitler being mentally ill and that the war could no longer be won.[197] As was common in such cases, they were both sentenced to death,[198] but extenuating circumstances concerning the war effort delayed the date for their execution.

After their arrests, a meeting of representatives of the Air Ministry and the Armaments Ministry was called at Speer's ministry to discuss whether they could be released from prison owing to the importance of their work for the war effort. F. tried to defend R. by telling the Gestapo then and again later that he was indispensable for the war industry due to his inventions, while also stating that he could run the firm by himself without Bresser. Nevertheless, the efforts to secure a pardon were unsuccessful and both remain imprisoned.[199]

Different parties acting on the side of the defense managed to file a stay of execution, in which F. was also involved. On 10 August 1944, he sent the two defense lawyers his written support to file for clemency, and drove to Berlin in September or October in his anxiety to garner personal support from a contact at the Air Ministry, Dr. V., to repeat his appeal to the Justice Ministry in support of R. He managed to have a meeting at a Justice Ministry representative tasked with appeal matters, who asked F. whether he also supported an appeal for Bresser as well as R. due to his technical capabilities. F. maintained that Bresser was merely a salesman without similar valuable technical knowledge, and thus only a few phrases were spoken about him during about a half hour of negotiations.[200]

F. continued to seek advantages for his interests thereafter. At the beginning of September 1944, he launched a case in the Bielefeld regional court against Bresser with the purpose of removing him from the company following his judgment by the People's Court. After Bresser called for a suspension of the proceedings through his lawyer, arguing it was not necessary for the war effort, F. maintained that the *Gauleiter* urged Bresser's removal, and added through his lawyer that he had known Bresser to have made other defeatist statements that also implicated his wife.[201]

Further discussions took place at various levels concerning the possibility of a pardon. Dr. V. himself tried to intervene on behalf of Bresser with the same Justice Ministry representative, while both were of the opinion that if one of the two accused were to be pardoned, the man on the street would have the impression that a party member had shot his partner down. Meanwhile a message that the defense had sent to the *Führer*'s Chancellery was returned with the response that a request for clemency was within the jurisdiction of the *Gauleitung* (regional leadership) of Northern Westphalia, where only the *Gauleiter* could order a pardon for a death sentence. He found no reason for him to do so, and communication with the *Führer*'s Chancellery came with the response that this plea for a pardon called for "benevolent discretion."

The *Gauleiter* later received a personal letter from the *Reich* Minister of Justice Otto Thierack dated 13 January 1945, in which he personally commented on this application for appeal by stating he proposed changing the sentence to a ten-year prison sentence for Bresser and twelve years for R. The *Gauleiter* delayed making a decision himself, not being able to decide whether they could yet play an important role in the development of a new high performance aircraft,[202] and therefore sent copies of this letter to various parties, including F., the *Gau* economic advisor, and others on 10 February 1945 to ask for their opinion.[203]

F. responded to this message with a slightly changed opinion that included his first indication of support for a pardon for Bresser. He wrote a letter to the *Reich* Minister of Justice on 17 February 1945, in which he argued for an appeal for R. in almost three pages of text with a mention of his personal feelings for him, and added a short page about Bresser. In this page he said that since R. had not fulfilled the *Gau* economic advisor's requirements for the development and construction of a high performance aircraft, he recommended a pardon for Bresser also if only so that the population would not wonder why two parties convicted of the same crime would not both be pardoned.[204] However, the deliberations for their pardon that in the end did not come did not make any difference. Their health conditions decreased continually, especially Bresser, whose condition worsened from day to day during the time of his imprisonment in Dortmund while being fettered for most of the time. After being transferred to Magdeburg on 8 April 1945, Bresser died upon arrival there from severe debilitation of strength due to dysentery, thyrotoxia, mesentiritis, and swelling of the liver. He was buried hurriedly since the seizure of Magdeburg by American troops was imminent, and the corpse was not found in spite of extensive searches[205] thereafter, thus making it possible to speculate that his death was brought about by causes that the authorities did not want to see revealed.

The facts and circumstances of the case were determined on the basis of the testimony of the defendant that was corroborated with other sources of evidence, including the confirmation of statements made by examined witnesses and the relevant documentation. The examination of the facts that were entered into evidence refuted some parts of F's testimony. It became evident that his testimony was interspersed with his interpretations of the events which could not stand up to examination.

His claim that he was involved in the acquisition of the firm in his capacity as the *Gau* economic advisor was refuted by the testimonies of two different witnesses, who maintained with more credibility that the local president (*Regierungspräsident*) could not sanction such an acquisition and that it could not have been made without his support while he occupied this office. Furthermore, Bresser had told them that he needed to accommodate F. in the firm to allow the acquisition. In addition, his claim that Bresser did not possess the financial means for the acquisition was also refuted, since another maintained that the Hardy & Co. bank had assured him that the financing was forthcoming.[206]

It could also be demonstrated that F. had intentionally and maliciously gathered material to be used against Bresser. When asked about why he had repeatedly looked to obtain Bresser's political assessment in Berlin in 1938, F. had claimed that he sought to procure documents by which he could testify in favor of Bresser when he had anticipated he would be taken to task about the hunting lodge affair. This claim was contradicted by the contents of a letter that F. had written to the Berlin *Gau* economic advisor dated 23 June 1943, in which he described Bresser as "unworthy," following an assessment dated 22 November 1938 that could only be conceived as bad, and therefore he did not have Bresser's best interests in mind. It could only be concluded that his purpose for looking for the assessment was to collect any unfavorable political material to be used against Bresser, which as confirmed by other witnesses, was passed on to S. F.'s claim that the audit by Schumacher was a routine matter also proved to be evidence of him seeking material to discredit Bresser by looking for possible financial offenses to be used against him. Schumacher was not the firm's bookkeeper, and an audit would normally have not been made in Bresser's absence, and the unusualness of this audit required that Dr. W. had to be urgently called back to his office.[207]

In contrast to the evidence that indicated how F. had acted against Bresser, the witnesses examined by the court could not provide any clear proof that he had counted on his high-level office in the NSDAP or exercised his influence on the different departments that were in the background of the proceedings against Bresser. It could only be determined that F. had considerable differences with Bresser, and was most interested in removing him from the firm. As a consequence, he helped instigate the proceedings against him by collecting politically incriminating material against Bresser and conveying these materials to different parties who could use them against him. He also called the Gestapo in Bielefeld two or three times, as well as other individuals in positions of political responsibility.[208]

The court noted how the suffering that had been inflicted on Bresser and his family by the Gestapo and the People's Court which had terrorized the population was typical of the violence and arbitrariness of the National Socialist regime. Anyone who had dared to have a political opinion or attitude that was detrimental to the regime's authorities, the NSDAP, or the prosecution of the war were subject to extreme violence and brutality. It was thereby clear that the judgment that had been passed by People's Court on the deceased Dr. Bresser made him a victim of persecution on the basis of political principles in the spirit of Control Council Law No. 10 as an example of the general disregard for the ideals of humanity.[209]

The measures that had been carried out against him and their consequences—arrest, death sentence, months of imprisonment in fetters, and death in prison, were the results of what had been considered criminal activity in view of the legislation of the time, albeit completely out of humane proportion to his so-called crime. The retribution that had been meted out by the regime against him was representative of the regime's flagrant contravention of humanity as a repository of the legal rights of personal freedom, well being, and life. This was interpreted by the court as a coarse degradation of what the entire civilized world acknowledged to be natural law in the sphere of personal rights. F. brought about a course of events by making the allegations against Bresser, which in turn led to his arrest by the Gestapo and then his appearance before the People's Court,[210] leading to further inhumane treatment thereafter.

After Bresser was placed under investigation by the Gestapo, there also emerged the new charge of his listening to foreign radio broadcasts that was an indirect consequence of this investigation in which R. also became implicated, albeit without F.'s instigation. However, had F. not raised the matter about the 50,000 RM, in all probability this new charge would not have been uncovered. It thus remained that because F. had intended that Bresser be removed from the firm, he set in motion the process that delivered Bresser into the National Socialist machinery of arbitrary violence and persecution, which was particularly onerous in the last years of the war, when the terror apparatus of the NSDAP in the form of the Gestapo, Special Courts, and the People's Court took especially aggressive measures against perceived political offenders.[211]

F. was undoubtedly aware of the consequences that would be incurred in view of the fact that he was a prominent National Socialist, and had also known that the *Gauleiter* of Westphalia at the time was notorious for being a ruthless defender of the prestige of the NSDAP and an individual who took stern measures against actions that were detrimental to the party when they came to his attention. F. had firsthand experience with his disposition when this *Gauleiter* ordered enquires to be made about him to examine the claim that he was corrupt. Given these circumstances of the time, considering his high-level position, and in view of the fact that F. had approved of the possibility of Bresser being accused of being a political offender, the court did not find any subjective grounds on which he could be exonerated, and ruled that the facts of the case constituted a crime against humanity.[212]

F. claimed that he had to defend himself against suspicion by the *Gauleiter* concerning the allegations of corruption, and suspected that Bresser had initiated these accusations. The court nevertheless ruled that he had deliberately decided to report Bresser and that he was not compelled to do so in spite of what he claimed, which meant that it was neither an act of necessity nor of self-defense. Regardless of the reproaches about him being corrupt, he could still count on acquiring control of the firm with the approval of the *Gauleiter*, and he would not be impeded in doing so by charges of alleged corruption that could have been easily dismissed as he was a high-standing member of the NSDAP. Hence, denouncing his opponent on political grounds was unnecessary and, like anyone else, he was obliged on the basis of common humanity to have considered the consequences of making the report against Bresser and if necessary, act against his conscience to prevent harm that would come to another as a result of his actions. It was therefore without a doubt that he was guilty of a crime against humanity as was defined by Article II, section 1c of Control Council Law No. 10.[213]

In determining the severity of the sentence to be imposed, it was taken into consideration that F. did not have any prior convictions, and was of an advanced age. He also was not a radical National Socialist, and according to the testimonies of unobjectionable character witnesses, he had protected fellow citizens that had come into conflict with state or NSDAP authorities in the National Socialist regime, and had repeatedly helped Catholic nuns. Another mitigating factor taken into consideration was that he had already spent a lengthy amount of time in internment. The jury court also did not overlook the fact that both F. and Bresser were guilty of promoting a power struggle between themselves. Bresser had sought the advantage of political protection by employing F., and it was to be added that after the death sentence had been passed, he sought to alleviate the severity of the sentence in his attempts to secure a pardon, which was a separate matter from keeping him out of the firm. Although he had caused the death of another and also inflicted suffering on his wife, the court was not concerned with exacting retribution in political matters to take revenge as compensation for National Socialist brutality. Dr. Bresser's widow had also requested that the jury not impose a vengeful judgment. In considering all of the circumstances, the court therefore ruled that a prison sentence of two years and ten months to be adequate and sufficient, which would include the time that had already been served.[214]

This case was later entered into appeal at the appeal court of the British occupation zone on 2 May 1950, where the appeal was overruled. This court found upon its re-evaluation of the evidence entered by one of witnesses' testimonies that any objections to existing law were unfounded. In reviewing the facts of the case, the jury court was also found to have applied the terms of Control Council Law No. 10 objectively and appropriately.[215] The appeal court thus did not have anything further to review following the adequate evaluation of the subjective facts of the case and the objective application of the law. F. had in fact delivered Bresser into the hands of the National Socialist regime's apparatus of repression that had inhumane repercussions for him. The victim in this case had reckoned with partnering himself with a politically influential individual who could have helped him maintain his position in business, until this partner used the system against him while unjustifiably claiming to have acted in self defense against the same system of repression.

The defendant in this case acted entirely on self-centered materialistic rather than political considerations. Namely, his intention was to seize control of a large firm without regard for the consequences that his actions would entail for the victim of the increasingly radicalized National Socialist administration of justice when it appeared that Germany was losing the war. Whether the other possible motive for his act of denunciation was to clear any suspicions of corruption that could have undermined his standing in view of the authorities who could judge him was secondary, considering that the former far outweighed the latter, and there was no evidence that was collected and brought to the authorities to take action against him. He could only have regretted that his actions indirectly led to the arrest and imprisonment of R. who became involved in the events of the Gestapo taking action against Bresser, and also became incriminated in the process. Unfortunately, F. had lost control of the situation after the investigation process by the Gestapo had begun, and the attempts to gain a pardon to compensate for what would later take place were unsuccessful.

As in other cases of denunciation, the mutual recrimination between these two business partners had tragic consequences for the partner who held a weaker hand in dealing with the National Socialist authorities. F. had already acquired numerous advantages from his long-standing membership in the NSDAP, and continued to exploit his standing in the government to acquire a business opportunity that did not necessarily require his expertise. His greed added to his political connections led to Dr. Bresser being sacrificed for his personal interests, and consequently also led to inadvertent tragic consequences for an innocent bystander who was otherwise on his side, but was caught up in the matter as a result of recrimination that had begun as a result of the initial round of recriminations. Only their personal connections with highly placed individuals enabled them to survive the fate that had come sooner to those who were deemed less important by those who could afford them some measure of protection from the regime whose laws they had violated. This type of case took place in all levels of society, in which individuals sought to benefit themselves by exploiting the laws of the regime for their self-centered purposes.

A later denunciation case was heard at the Münster regional court, where judgment was pronounced on two defendants on 11 February 1949. This case was also characterized by personal considerations under the guise of political devotion to the National Socialist cause. The first accused, hereafter cited as K., had served in the constabulary from January 1924 to 1945, acting as the chief of the Hoetmar branch from 1940. He had joined the NSDAP in March 1936, and was appointed the local *Organisationsleiter* of the *Ortsgruppe* there from 1937 until the end of the war. The second defendant, hereafter cited as M., had been a NSDAP *Kreisleiter* from February 1933, and held this position in Münster from 1936 to 1945, the jurisdiction of which included the 67 *Ortsgruppen,* including Hoetmar.[216]

K.'s responsibilities had involved promoting the NSDAP's political interests among the population, and particularly limiting the influence of the local clergy insofar as it had a detrimental effect on the party's interests from his point of view. He therefore sought to cause difficulties for the local clergy's activities in order to undermine the connection between the population and the clergy, by repeatedly taking it to task to make reports about insignificant incidents. On one such occasion, he criticized a local pastor for not decking his house with flags early enough. On another occasion, K. wrote a police record about how a rector from the neighboring town of Ahlen had organized a soccer outing in the Hoetmar region.[217]

K. was particularly opposed to the *Dechant* W. serving as the priest in Hoetmar while always seeking an opportunity to take action against him, maintaining in his view that he exceeded his pastoral duties and thus strongly impaired NSDAP political life in Hoetmar. He therefore repeatedly took actions against him, such as often subjecting him to police interrogations, and making several reports about him for insignificant reasons. The stated reasons for interrogating the pastor included questioning him about why the swastika flag at the parsonage was allegedly smaller than the church flag, and whether receiving members of the church choir there was a forbidden assembly. Further to these forms of harassment, K. drafted a detailed written complaint on 21 October 1938 to the co-defendant M. who was the *Kreisleiter* in Münster, saying how this priest's conduct was damaging to National Socialism. K. appears to have been particularly appalled by how the priest allegedly exceeded his official capacity with a growing amount of building reconstruction at the pastorate that led to the creation of a large assembly room and reception room. These spaces could be used for assemblies of religious formations and associations in which training could take place, which he considered to be unacceptable to the public. He therefore called on the *Kreis* administration to prevent these developments, following years of reporting about the priest's conduct, as K. considered him to be an opponent of National Socialist movement who was not to be underestimated and had to be treated with extreme caution. K. also objected to how W. had already organized the apostolate and the mothers' association that corresponded to and thereby allegedly conflicted with the National Socialist block and cell system. He had also allegedly sabotaged the work of the NSV while accommodating children from Catholic associations. He was therefore apparently an incorrigible troublemaker.[218]

Further to these complaints, K. also reported to the Kreisleitung in Münster that the priest had also attended to foreign laborers who were working on farms in and around Hoetmar, and had preached to them in a foreign language. In addition to being opposed to his concern for foreign laborers, K. also reported his objections about there not being any National Socialist flags on the parsonage, and the scheduling of church celebrations so that local residents were prevented from taking part in the NSDAP functions. In 1941 when K. found out that W. needed to use a bus for an excursion that he would take with young women of his congregation, he took advantage of this situation by requiring two of the participants on this excursion to write a report about it to be forwarded to the Gestapo in Münster. Shortly thereafter, the Gestapo there then subjected him to questioning about this event and reproached him with a warning. The local Gestapo thus became aware of the reports made about him, and further reports came to them from Hoetmar thereafter.[219]

K. continued to compile evidence that he intended to use against W. After he had found out in the summer of 1942 that W. had been involved in offering clothing to foreign laborers, he questioned witnesses about it and send a written report to the Gestapo in Münster. A notorious local Gestapo agent questioned W. about this record thereafter on 18 July 1942. During this questioning, W. explained that he "loved all people," perhaps spoken as an act of ministration, as could be expected from a member of the clergy, rather than indiscretion as in other cases of denunciation that proved to have dire consequences. The Gestapo agent falsified his statement as saying, with regard to W., "all people in his view are the same, whether they are German, English, French, Russian, Poles, or Jews."[220] This information provided the pretext for him to arrest W. and take him to Münster where he remained in custody.[221]

While he was imprisoned, W. told his sister as she was visiting him that he had been arrested on the basis of a report that K. had made about his providing clothing items to foreign laborers, which had been shown to him along with other reports about him that had been sent to the Gestapo from Hoetmar. Some were from individuals he did not know, but they were signed by K. W. was thereafter taken to Dachau concentration camp in September 1942, where he died from typhus fever in March 1945.[222]

K. tried to exonerate himself when called to account for his actions when the facts of this case were examined as a potential crime against humanity by dissociating himself from his previous conduct, and concocting new evidence in his defense testimony. After W. had been arrested, K. claimed that he had not intended for him to be arrested. He also maintained he had repeatedly although unsuccessfully petitioned different authorities, such as the *Kreis* administration, the local *Landrat,* and the Gestapo in Münster for his release. He also denied that he had ever taken action against W., having acted only on behalf of his supervisor or other individuals in matters relating to this priest, and otherwise denied ever having directly reported about him to the *Kreis* administration or the Gestapo in Münster. Further to the document dated 21 October 1938 that was entered into evidence, K. claimed that it was a draft that was given to him by the *Ortsamtsleiter* of the time for signing and forwarding. He claimed that rather than passing it on, he locked it in a closet in his apartment without signing it. This document was later stolen from the closet by a thief who possessed a duplicated key. He did not report the theft at the time, since he did not know who the thief was until he found out his identity while he was in internment in 1945. The thief allegedly remained in possession of the unsigned original document. K. would not name the thief, for fear of bringing misfortune onto his family, and had sworn not to name the person who had revealed the thief's identity.[223] Further to his defense, he claimed that the report he had made about the priest's outing with the young women of the congregation was made on behalf of one of the witnesses in this case, and that the report about handing out clothing was made upon the insistent prompting of another witness.[224]

The court rejected these claims in their entirety upon an examination of his testimony. He could not deny that the reports he had made about W. and had sent to the *Kreis* administration in Münster were merely a part of the discharge of his functions as a police official. He had not denied that he had given the report dated 21 October 1938 to M. in its original form, although, according to a witness, he probably was incapable of writing it himself in such an elegant manner. After much hesitation, K. admitted the letter had been drafted by the former *Ortsamtsleiter*. The court also dismissed the testimony about his not having forwarded the unsigned report that had been stolen from a locked closet as a "fairy tale." Witnesses could testify that K. had been anxious about working to prevent W.'s activity and influence in Hoetmar, and therefore it was unrealistic to consider that K. would not forward a report against W. in view of his hostile disposition toward him. Why he would not expose the identity of the individual who allegedly knew the identity of the thief he had spoken about was more incomprehensible, since doing so would have cleared up the suspicion that he had signed the report and sent it to the *Kreis* administration in Münster. The sentence for this alleged theft would greatly diminish his considerable incrimination for denunciation. Finally, it could be proven without any doubt that, although he may not have drafted it himself, he had certainly signed and sent the report against W., since the court had a carbon copy of this document in its possession after it had been recovered from a National Socialist office at the end of the war that also matched the contents of another copy. This report also mentioned that K. had made many reports about W.'s conduct to the local *Kreis* administration for years, thus having long denounced him in malicious manner. This was confirmed by several witnesses who had worked at the *Kreis* administration office.[225]

K. made the report dated 21 October 1938, and it was made without him being instructed to do so by either the administrative or NSDAP political authorities. Witnesses who had served as the local administrative authorities from 1935 to 1945 testified that they had not instructed K. to subject W. to questioning, with there being only one possible exception that occurred in 1936 involving the *Amtsbürgermeister* at the time who was not present as a witness, and no one had required K. to make a report about him. Hence, the many reports that K. had made about W., in addition to those concerning the incidents in 1941 and 1942, were made on his own initiative. However, it could not be established whether these reports were sent to the Gestapo by the Münster *Kreis* administration.[226]

K. had made a considerable number of reports that had reached the Gestapo, but apart from those relating to the 1941 and 1942 incidents, the number of those that he had made could not be determined with complete certainty, since there were other anonymous reports coming from Hoetmar that had been made against W. According to W.'s sister, her brother had told her that he had been shown several reports that K. had signed, apart from the ones relating to the aforementioned incidents that were entered into evidence in the present case in view of the available witnesses. These bore his signature, and according to the cross-examination of the testimonies of witnesses to the events, it could be maintained that he had at least freely forwarded these two reports to the Gestapo without the intermediary approval of the local authorities and without any compulsion to do so, which followed his earlier attempts to undermine W.'s influence on the local population. Hence, it was concluded that K. was guilty of having committed a crime against humanity in both objective and subjective respects as defined by Article II, section 1c of Control Council Law No. 10 in connection with using National Socialist tyranny to attack and harm another, and consequently contravening the rights of humanity.[227]

In view of the objective facts of the case, K. had exploited his position as a police civil servant while serving in his capacity as *Ortsgruppenleiter* to persecute W. in an inhumane way on the basis of political and religious principles. He had made several disparaging reports against him since 1937 to the *Kreis* administration in Münster, and at least two reports thereafter in 1941 and 1942 to the Gestapo there. These led to this priest's arrest by the Gestapo, and ultimately led to his death at Dachau concentration camp in March 1945. K. had intended to undermine W.'s religious influence in order to strengthen National Socialist political life, and thus called on the Gestapo to help in this undertaking by taking action against W. It was therefore to be surmised that K. had willingly and maliciously intended for W. to be arrested and imprisoned.[228]

K. had acted unlawfully, considering that even if his reports formed the basis of the circumstances of the case under the National Socialist law of the time and were subject to prosecution, even in view of wartime exigencies, they resulted in W.'s considerable degradation of being arrested, and then taken to a concentration camp without the case first being heard in criminal legal proceedings. Moreover, the consequences of K.'s reports were completely disproportionate to the alleged injustice of W.'s actions. Regardless of whether W. had ostensibly contravened the laws of the time, which were devoid of legal validity in the view of civilized states, K. was called to account for his conduct that had brought about inhumane consequences. It was also noted that his planned efforts in taking actions against W. were separate from his duties as a police civil servant, and therefore he was not under any obligation to do so. Even if he did not intend for W. to be taken to a concentration camp, he must have at least expected this possibility. He had known that the earlier reports he had made about W. to the *Kreis* administration would be forwarded to the Gestapo, and the reports that had been made directly to the Gestapo in 1941 and 1942 indicated that he approved of their taking action against him. He was therefore held completely responsible for the consequences of his actions.[229]

K. was also held responsible for his actions from a subjective point of view, even if his conduct did not result from inhumane convictions. In spite of his calling attention to how he intended to fulfill his official duties, it could not be denied that he was aware of the fact that his actions would lead to W. being subjected to the arbitrariness of the Gestapo. Neither his position as a police civil servant nor his position as an *Ortsgruppenleiter* obliged him to send the reports, and not doing so would not have caused him to incur any professional or other disadvantages. He could have avoided any potential disadvantages by sending the reports to the usual police authorities through the *Amtsbürgermeister,* or he could have chosen to not make reports about W. or convey them[230] to those who were empowered with leading someone to dreadful consequences simply because he had acted on his beliefs that were in contradiction to the views of National Socialism.

K. was therefore found guilty of committing a crime against humanity as defined in Article II, sections 1c and 5 of Control Council Law No. 10. The mitigating circumstances that were considered prior to the sentencing were that K. had not been convicted prior to his actions in this case and the lengthy gap between the present and the time of the actions. He had also endeavored to try to secure W.'s release, and had spent almost three years in internment after the end of the war. On the other hand, his repeated reports and police interrogations that did not have any valid causes had been made against an irreproachable and respectable priest who was only interested in the exercise of his spiritual activity and helping others. It was also considered that his actions had supported National Socialist tyranny that had considerably damaged the reputation and name of the German people in the view of the world. The court therefore sentenced K. to a year and six months imprisonment.[231]

The co-defendant M was accused of having intentionally and unlawfully persecuted W. on political and religious principles by conveying K.'s denunciation to the *Gauleiter* in Münster. He testified in his defense by arguing that as the *Kreisleiter* for Münster and Warendorf, Hoetmar had been one of sixty-seven *Ortsgruppen* for which he was responsible from 1 April 1938, and was thus responsible for handling reports on various issues from all of them before summarizing all of them in a report to the *Gauleitung*. Following the outbreak of the war, he assigned some important reports, such as those containing accusations, to be evaluated by an official advisor. Although he was under suspicion, he was acquitted due to the lack of evidence[232] that could be used to incriminate him.

This case was reviewed on 17 January 1950 at the Highest Appeal Court of the British Occupation Zone. This court restated that M. had striven to eliminate the influence of the clergy hindering the interests of the NSDAP among the local population from 1933 until the end of the war. He had claimed that he had not known about W., as he had not received any reports from K. about him, and did not forward reports about him to the *Gauleiter*. Nor did he have any direct connection with the Gestapo, which came under the jurisdiction of the *Gauleitung*. This court noted that these claims could not be refuted with complete certainty. Although it seemed improbable that he did not personally read the report dated 21 October 1938, witnesses' testimonies showed how this could have been possible, since he had not read all of the reports emanating from the areas for which he was responsible, especially after the beginning of the war. There was the possibility that M. had known about K.'s reports about W. or his personal impressions about him, and could have recommended to the *Gauleiter* in Münster that he should take corresponding measures against W., considering the number of petitions and reports that the local Gestapo had received that accused him of conduct that was hostile to the state.[233] However, there was insufficient evidence to prove that he had been directly involved in a crime against humanity perpetrated against W.

After considering all the evidence brought forward, the court ruled that there were not any grounds for reversing or modifying the verdict previously pronounced against K. This court sustained that the verdict for a crime against humanity was justified in accordance with the provisions of Control Council Law No. 10, and in view of the facts of the case that had been entered at the Münster regional jury court. This court absolutely agreed with the judgment of the jury court that K. could have chosen not to interrogate W. about looking after Russian laborers. In both the 1941 and 1942 incidents, he had acted on his own initiative, rather than under the auspices of a higher authority, and did not forward his reports to the authorities in the local government or to his superiors in the police administration. It also could not be ascertained whether the reports concerning these incidents and several other reports were conveyed from the *Kreis* administration to the Gestapo in Münster, since he sent reports about the two incidents directly himself. It was therefore surmised that K. had avoided sending these reports to the *Kreis* administration before they were forwarded to a higher authority. This thus proved that K. had primarily caused W. to be delivered to the forces of tyranny, regardless of the possibility of the *Kreis* administration also being involved, since the reports had originated with K. and he had sent them himself[234] on his own initiative. He was therefore called to account for these actions, and the earlier verdict remained unchanged after further examination.

Another denunciation case was heard at about the same time at the Wuppertal regional court, where judgment was pronounced for a second time on 11 February 1949. This regional court had previously sentenced the defendant, Marianne Koll, to seven years imprisonment on 28 August 1948 and three years deprivation of her civil rights for crimes against humanity in five different cases of denunciation. However she was not convicted of two additional counts that had not been included in that case by the state prosecutor's office,[235] which concerned two workers who were sentenced to death and executed for undermining the war effort.[236]

This case came under further review at the regional court in Düsseldorf on 16 December 1948, where the disputed judgment was referred back to the jury court at the Wuppertal regional court. This court accepted that the defendant was justified in testifying that she could have expected difficulties with the Gestapo after having been reported for having had illegal dealing with foreigners, and therefore she was acting under some compulsion to cooperate with them to a certain degree. The Wuppertal regional court had argued against this defense since this could be confirmed, which was considered a mistaken interpretation of the burden of proof since it was admissible for the defendant to enter truthful evidence in their defense, provided that the defendant could establish its accuracy. It would otherwise need to be taken into consideration as being relevant, unless the court could establish why it should not be taken into account, and then needed to be determined how it could be refuted. In this case, it was admitted that whoever had been reported to the Gestapo about their illegal dealings with foreigners could expect to suffer some considerable personal disadvantages. Renewed proceedings would therefore have to establish whether the defendant had been pressured into becoming an informer for the Gestapo, and could therefore not be found guilty on the basis of citing urgent necessity in her defense in accordance with an interpretation of Article 54 of the Criminal Code.[237]

Another fault with the judgment was that it had admitted information obtained from the labor office in Remscheid as evidence for the defense, which stated that the defendant was employed by the Gestapo. This did not establish its truthfulness, since this had been merely determined on the basis of her having asked the criminal police office secretary at the time about whether she could work for the police as part of the existing employment agreement. Hence, this condition could not be inferred in justifying the verdict, and therefore the court ruled that there was no evidence proving that the defendant was an agent for the Gestapo. The court was thus required to verify whether she had freely decided to accept this position and fulfill its functions in accordance with the provisions cited in Article II, section 4b of Control Council Law No. 10. The case was henceforth referred back to the Wuppertal regional court for conclusive re-consideration.[238]

After the previous judgment having been quashed, the jury court at the Wuppertal regional court re-examined the facts of the case. The renewed proceedings brought forward essentially the same conclusions that had been made previously during the first time the case was heard. The court reiterated the events leading to the conviction for the first count, in which she was in a relationship with someone, hereafter cited as R., from 1942 to May 1944. She had intended to marry him just after he had lost his second wife in a bombing attack in March 1944, but became angry about how he came to the registry office without the requisite papers. He had apparently changed his mind because she had forbidden him to have any dealings with foreigners, and then reported her to the police for her nightly dealings at the internment camp for foreigners belonging to the Oebels bread factory in Remscheid. She swore she would get her revenge on him when she was arrested, saying she would report him for listening to foreign broadcasts. She in fact reported him to the Gestapo for listening to enemy broadcasts and he was then arrested on 4 July 1944, but his judgment by the Special Court in Wuppertal that was scheduled for 2 September 1944 was postponed due to doubts that had been revealed about the accuracy of her statements, and he was therefore released on 21 December 1944. However, he was then re-arrested by the Gestapo two days later and remained in custody.[239]

During this time, she started a new relationship with another, and went with him and his acquaintance, F., to a pub in Remscheid on 9 July 1944, where, upon the announcement of military reports on the radio, F. said that it should be switched off since it was all nonsense. The defendant reported this and other disparaging remarks that F. had made as early as 1940. F. was thereafter arrested by the Gestapo on 2 August 1944 and criminal legal proceedings were instituted against him. He was killed during an air raid while he was being taken to prison in Arnsberg.[240]

In another instance, she reported another individual for his indiscretion. She and an acquaintance, a soldier on leave hereafter cited as E., had a conversation about politics in a pub on 16 June 1944. Among other things, E. expressed that he was an opponent of the National Socialist government, and would gladly "break its neck" if it were possible. He also added that he had admitted to a Russian commissar that the "V" weapons were essentially a bluff, and then drank to the future government. She reported what he had said in a written statement to the Gestapo in Remscheid, which arrested E. on 29 September 1944. Since he was a soldier, charges for undermining the war effort were to be brought against him by the central court of the army in Berlin, with proceedings later continuing at the People's Court. However, the military collapse took place while he was detained at the infamous Fort Cinna in Torgau before proceedings could begin. He was able to return to Remscheid in June 1945, but was hospitalized three weeks later since he had incurred a serious lung and kidney disease while he was imprisoned, which eventually led to his death on 11 February 1947.[241]

Another example in which someone's indiscretion led to fateful consequences took place soon after the last assassination attempt on Hitler on 20 July 1944. Two later after the events of that day, the defendant joined three of her friends at one of their apartments where they had a small party. While in a drunken state, one of her friends, a police reservist hereafter cited as He., loudly insulted the National Socialist government and said that the Russians were not far from Berlin, and the war would be over in a month's time. The defendant agreed with him. Being concerned about eavesdropping neighbors, one of the other friends suggested that they go to a pub. After they arrived, He. commented on a picture of Hitler there, saying that it was unfortunate that the assassination had not been successful since it would have meant getting rid of "the brown head" (*Brunkopp*). The defendant reported what she had heard him say to the Gestapo afterward. He. was later arrested on 8 August 1944, and was sentenced to death for undermining the war effort by the SS and police court in Düsseldorf on 9 December 1944. However, the files about this case were lost as a result of wartime events and therefore the death sentence was not executed since it lacked the necessary confirmation from Himmler.[242]

The evidence presented in this case at these proceedings was derived from the sworn testimonies of several witnesses, as well as former Gestapo agents who were interested in exonerating themselves, and whose testimony was corroborated by other witnesses. The defendant no longer disputed during these proceedings that she had been a Gestapo agent since the middle of 1944, with the added objection in her defense that she acted on instructions on particular cases that were assigned to her by her superiors, rather than on her own initiative. This testimony was disproven under examination of witnesses, whose statements indicated that she was charged with finding and reporting on whomever had made statements that were considered hostile to the state, and she had sent confidential written quarterly reports to the Gestapo office in Wuppertal. She had also said that her employment with the Gestapo excused her from being employed by the women's labor conscription office in Remscheid. She added in her defense that she was under pressure to work for the Gestapo due to having been charged with having had forbidden contacts with foreigners. This claim was also refuted, as she had been cleared of the charges of slipping foodstuffs and tobacco to prisoners of war in 1943 or earlier. Hence, her functions as an informer for the Gestapo and the results they had yielded could not allow her to evade the charge that she had done all of this willingly, rather than due to some form of compulsion. In view of the evidence, she was found guilty of all five counts of denunciation as crimes against humanity in accordance with the terms of Control Council Law No. 10.[243]

The defendant was conscious of how her actions would result in delivering her victims into the violent and arbitrary hands of the Gestapo, and since she was in their paid service, she had intended for these consequences to take place. Her aggressive conduct was practically an example of her base and inhumane convictions. While the defense argued that she was unaware of the unlawfulness of her actions, this was unfounded since the law did not demand that she act as she did. Her statements indicated that she had also played a significant role in the two additional cases that had led to terrible consequences for those she denounced. She had gained their trust in an underhanded manner, and then used this trust to betray them. Besides, she was proud to be part of an authority whose very name brought terror. She was thus fully devoted to serving as an instrument of an unlawful regime while not having any consideration at all for the lives of others and their claims to the right of freedom of expression, and her appalling actions were thereby characterized as being directed against all people as the result of a system that degraded humanity.[244]

In considering the sentencing, this jury court gave considerable attention to the fact that the defendant had been employed by the Gestapo for some time while evaluating the scope of the consequences of this employment. She had been emphatically made aware of the urgent need for deterrence by the Gestapo and she had carried on her traitorous activities that showed her irresponsibility with regard to the lives of other people, which did not arise from a false readiness to act on behalf of the interests of the NSDAP. Her actions were far from being driven by high or ideal considerations. They were instead motivated by cold material gain and contemptible hatred. Besides, her conduct in these new proceedings showed that she did not have even the slightest remorse for the shameful reprehensible nature of her actions in the past.[245] In terms of any possible mitigating circumstances in her favor, the court considered the possibility of her being rehabilitated along with the fact that she had not had any prior convictions, and in recognition of her reduced physical condition after nineteen months of imprisonment the court sentenced her to six years' imprisonment with the deprivation of her civil rights for an additional three years.[246]

A later denunciation case was heard by a jury court at the Düsseldorf regional court, where judgment was pronounced on 23 April 1949. In comparison to other such cases, the court imposed a particularly heavy sentence of life imprisonment along with a lifelong deprivation of civil rights.[247] Unlike other cases of denunciation in which mitigating circumstances were taken into account, the conduct of the defendant did not merit any leniency.

The defendant, hereafter cited as Wienhusen, had been appointed to serve as the sales director of Birresborn-Mineralbrunnen AG on 1 January 1939 by the sole member of the executive board, hereafter cited as Leo S., who the defendant had known since 1930. He had applied to join the NSDAP from 1 March 1933 and had been a member of the party since August 1937, although this could have been mainly for opportunistic reasons, since his testimony stated that he did not have any political convictions. In 1941, he had spent three weeks in detention while under suspicion of a charge of breaking wartime economic regulations. He was released on account of his mother's serious illness, and the proceedings were adjourned until 1945 at the instigation of the Gestapo in Trier, where he and another defendant, hereafter cited as L. were being held. Both defendants were involved with a black market ring in Luxemburg, in which a criminal secretary of the Gestapo at the time was also involved. In the course of the following months and years, Wienhusen and L. had acted as informers for the Gestapo. They were so successful in this undertaking that the Gestapo had arranged for the then pending legal proceedings against them to be repeatedly suspended. In one of these cases, Wienhusen acted as an informer against Leo S., an act which was the subject of the present proceedings.[248]

On 22 July 1943 S. visited the defendant in Trier where he was employed by their company in order to meet with their clients. The defendant thus informed the Gestapo about where they would meet, and recommended that they send some agents there in order to hear things that could be of interest to them. He would himself write a report about the matter after traveling to Düsseldorf. When they met at the canteen of the local military base, the defendant invited two Gestapo agents at a neighboring table to join them for drinks as they were having a birthday celebration for the hostess and for S.'s birthday that had taken place a few days previously. One of these two agents, criminal commissioner Schütz, wrote down any interesting remarks in the spaces of the newspaper he had with him while eavesdropping on the conversation at the next table. Having been bombed out in Düsseldorf three times, S. made some disparaging remarks about the wartime situation and the National Socialist regime in the course of the conversation. The two unknown civilians at the next table seemed suspicious to the canteen hostess, so she remarked to S. and the others at the table that they appeared to listening in on their conversation and that they must surely be Gestapo agents. The birthday celebration continued, and sixty-nine glasses of schnapps were consumed while S. continued making derisive remarks in front of the soldiers that he had invited to join them while getting into an increasingly drunken state of mind.[249]

A few days later on 2 August 1943, the defendant made a report to the Gestapo agent Schütz about the events in the canteen. The defendant had written that Leo S. was an outspoken enemy of the state, and then reproduced a verbatim record of the words of parts of the conversation he had with S.

about the wartime situation. The report said how S. had said the defendant could not tell the difference between reality and propaganda, questioning whether the war could be won and drawing attention to the situation in Sicily. The defendant also reported that S. had told him how one could receive anything if one had connections, saying how he was able to receive ten times more building materials than before to build a new house, and although he was considered eligible for military service, this was postponed due to him having a good friend, who the defendant suspected was a colonel in Düsseldorf. Reporting about his remarks continued with the defendant also quoting S. as having said that they had lost the war as soon as they had started it. He said that living in Germany at that time was miserable, and that they would be better off living at the mercy of Europe and America. Germany had started the bombing war, and therefore he could no longer stand complaining about the heavy bombing of German cities that would not have happened if Germany had not inflicted a great deal more damage on England. He also reported about him allegedly defending Russia by saying that communism was not as it had been described, since the squalor in Russia was not worse than in Germany. Russian workers worked willingly, and nothing was known to German soldiers about places of cultural interest in Russia. When the two sergeants joined them at their table, S. went on to say that Hitler was a "wretched corporal," and that they were not fighting for any good cause. The defendant further added that S.'s secretary in Düsseldorf must have heard many more such things about what S. had said since she was surprised that he had not already been locked up. The defendant ended this report by asking the Gestapo to not mention his name as having made this report since S. was his employer and he would then have to leave his position.[250]

This report became the basis for criminal proceedings that were henceforth initiated against S. He was arrested by the Gestapo in Trier on 1 September 1943, and then interrogated and taken to the local prison, and then to the Berlin-Moabit prison on 17 September 1943. The proceedings at the People's Court were initiated immediately thereafter. The main proceedings under the presiding judge Dr. Friesler began on 27 September 1943 in which the defendant and others were called as witnesses to testify against him. At the end of the proceedings, when Friesler asked the defendant whether he was drunk on the day in question, he answered that he was in control of his mental capacities. When he was asked whether his witness testimony about the entire matter contained any exaggeration, he answered that what had been said could have been worse. S. was then sentenced to death for being a "subversive propagandist of the enemy" and was executed on 1 November 1943.[251]

The ascertainment of the facts of this case were drawn from the examinations of twenty-three different witnesses, including the canteen hostess, the records of the People's Court proceedings, and the testimony of the defendant insofar as the evidence could be confirmed or did not refute the basis of the judgment. In his defense, the defendant claimed that he was not the Gestapo agent mentioned in the files since he disputed the authenticity of the files. He also disputed having named Leo S. to the Gestapo as an enemy of the state in a report about him, and disputed having given an incriminating testimony about him at the People's Court.[252] These contentions that the defendant proffered were individually examined in these jury court proceedings.

One of the witnesses who testified in these proceedings was one of the two Gestapo agents that had been present at the evening at the canteen. According to his testimony, he had been employed with the Gestapo in Trier since 1934 and had known the defendant, and had also handled the personnel files as part of his duties. The court examined the personnel file of the defendant, which it had obtained from the French police in Koblenz. An examination of these documents showed that they were completely genuine. The authenticity of this file was proved beyond a doubt that it contained a nearly verbatim record of what had been said in the canteen on the evening of 22 July 1943, which was reproduced in the People's Court indictment and verdict.[253]

The defendant had admitted that he had often been approached by the Gestapo agent Feick to find out information in another case concerning an individual named Terhoeven, and the court revealed a Gestapo file dated 21 June 1943 that disclosed how he and L. had been the most successful informers working for them. Their reports had hitherto made the initiation of a total of forty-five different proceedings, included the one the defendant had mentioned. This most especially established the authenticity of his personnel file,[254] and provided documentary evidence of the considerable dealings that he had had with the Gestapo despite his attempts to absolve himself of these charges.

The court also refuted the defendant's second assertion in his testimony that he did not denounce S. He claimed that the Gestapo had questioned him about the events in the canteen some time afterward, but tried to explain it away by saying that he had gotten so drunk that he could not remember anything. He also claimed that the Gestapo questioned him a second time and pressured him to make a report after confronting him with the facts that were known to them, and threaten him by stating that he would also be implicated in the matter. He therefore maintained that he merely confirmed what he was told without adding anything further.[255]

The Gestapo file dated 22 July 1943 proved that the defendant had notified them that he would meet S. at the canteen and informed them about his hostile attitude to the state, and that they should send agents there for the purpose of listening in. The same piece of evidence indicated that the defendant had a meeting with Schütz on 30 July 1943, which mentioned in turn his report dated 1 August 1943. The defendant's Gestapo personnel file also mentioned that he had made a detailed report about S.'s derisive remarks on 2 August 1943. Moreover, the Gestapo file contained a report they had made to the *Reich* central security office in which it was indicated that S. was arrested and interrogated on the basis of the defendant's report about him. Further to this documentary evidence, a credible witness testified that she had overheard the defendant say to Feick before S.'s arrest that he was likely to blurt everything out after he got somewhat drunk.[256] In addition to these facts, the defendant was the only witness to have heard S.'s disparaging remarks in their entirety, and had also appeared as a witness testifying against him at the People's Court.[257]

The court further examined the credibility of the defendant's disputing of the contents of his testimony at the People's Court. Four other witnesses who were present at those proceedings confirmed what the defendant had said at this time. One of the two sergeants who was also present as a witness could not remember the defendant's testimony, which the court surmised could have been because he was preoccupied with his own fate. He had come to realize during those proceedings that he had been expected to have reported S., and therefore thought his neglecting to do so could lead to his own arrest. As a result, he ceased paying attention to Wienhusen's testimony after the court had questioned him. The defendant's responses to Freisler's questions otherwise had the effect of exacerbating the evidence that was used against S., in addition to having reported his defeatist statements about the political and wartime situations of the time.[258]

Wienhusen had thus committed a crime against humanity as defined by the provisions in Article II of Control Council Law No. 10, with an objective view of the facts demonstrating how his report constituted an act of political persecution. The degrading consequences of how it led to an individual's dignity being violated would arouse a strong feeling of revulsion in any decent-minded person, knowing that the statements that S. had made about the war and the wartime situation were very serious and subject to prosecution. The high level of disproportionality of the punishment in comparison to the potential unlawfulness of the statements S. had made had to be examined in the context of the rule of law.[259]

S. had been feeling depressed after having lost his home three times due to bombing attacks, and spoke frankly while in a drunken state of mind. The fact that he was sentenced to death and executed demonstrated an excessively harsh and undeserved punishment that was in itself a flagrant violation of the human right to free expression, even under wartime conditions. Hence, there was not any underlying doubt that these consequences of the defendant's report about S. had violated his human right to a fair trial a judgment according to just laws, which is guaranteed to every individual under the rule of law. The arbitrariness of the state that was directed against any alleged dissident, as S. had experienced, violated humanity itself by disregarding the principles of the rule of law. It was without a doubt that the defendant approved of bringing about such inhumane consequences, having long been a member of the Gestapo and knowing, by 1943, the worst possible consequences that could arise as a result of the report he had made. He did so without hesitation, as was indicated by his conduct.[260]

The court considered his reprehensibility as having exceeded the normal scope of decent conduct. His former employer had appointed him to a financially favorable position and had especially trusted him while they had a good personal relationship. Rather than having been grateful, he delivered S. into a violent fate while knowing he had been opposed to the state and how easily he could expose this attitude while under the influence of alcohol. He used this knowledge in a most underhanded manner, and ensured that S. would suffer the consequences of his hostile attitude to the state by documenting his disparaging remarks in detail at a time that he knew S. had recently been completely bombed out of his house. His testimony against him at the People's Court ensured that the death sentence would be inevitable, and also eliminated any doubt about the reproachfulness of his conduct[261] during these proceedings after the rule of law had been restored.

In an attempt to find justification for what he had done, it was assumed that perhaps he thought his action against S. would demonstrate evidence of his thorough support of Gestapo in its struggle against "enemies of the state," so that the criminal proceedings that were initiated against him for the charges of black marketeering would be stayed. The defendant could not claim that he had acted out of political conviction, since he had testified that had never supported National Socialist ideas, which to a certain extent could have been an understandable cause for his conduct, however unpardonable. In view of these circumstances as well as the repulsiveness of his conduct, the court could find nothing that could exculpate him of contributing to S.'s death, or justify exculpating the extent of his guilt to any degree. The court therefore sentenced him to a deprivation of civil rights and life imprisonment as the second highest admissible punishment, having decided against imposing the death penalty.[262] It can be surmised that this court took his "successful" career as a Gestapo agent into account, without evaluating each of the processes that had resulted from his other activities for them.

The facts of this case came under further review at the Highest Appeal Court of the British Zone, where a motion to quash the Düsseldorf regional court verdict was rejected on 6 February 1950. This court determined that the facts of the case fulfilled all of the requisite conditions in accordance with an interpretation of Article II, section 1c of Control Council Law No. 10.[263] They then addressed any potential weaknesses in the judgment.

While the consequences of the defendant's conduct constituted a crime against humanity, the jury court did not stress the extent to which S. had made himself subject to prosecution as a result of his remarks. More importantly, the jury court had correctly ascertained that the death sentence judgment that had been pronounced on S. was excessively out of proportion to his actions in view of the rule of law. The jury court was also justified in determining that the defendant had acted in a hostile manner by which he consciously and willingly caused S.'s death, knowing that S. would not be judged according to the principles of the rule of law. Having thus delivered S. to the forces of tyranny, the court also interpreted Article II, section 1c of Control Council Law No. 10 correctly.[264]

The defendant found fault with the jury court's judgment. He argued that this court was required to provide evidence to support the assertion that the defendant had unhesitatingly accepted and approved that S. be threatened with the worst form of punishment. The Highest Appeal Court maintained that although this experienced Gestapo agent had known what had generally happened in such cases, it sufficed to say that the perpetrator had delivered the victim to the tyranny of the apparatus of National Socialism. Any further evidence of his consciousness and willingness to cause this criminal action could prove to be significant, and was thus required to be proven as a fact.[265]

The defendant also perceived another error in the jury court's reasoning in conclusively verifying the authenticity of his Gestapo personnel file. This charge was refuted on the grounds that there was no evidence to establish proof of such a mistake. More importantly, the jury court had emphasized that its judgment was made independently of this file while relying on other sources of evidence that had been entered during the trial.[266] Other objections concerning the credibility of one of the witnesses, the extent of his cooperation with the Gestapo in this case, with references to the contents of a letter S. had written in prison, and the incomplete testimony of another witness, were dismissed as irrelevant. It was determined that the jury court had carefully examined the evidence and had clearly demonstrated how the defendant had cooperated with the Gestapo against S., and there was therefore no just cause for re-opening the proceedings, regardless of whether or not he had been an informer for the Gestapo. There was also no cause to dispute the extent of the sentencing to life imprisonment, which the Highest Appeal Court did not reject in view of the discretion being allowed to the judge in this case, and thus respecting judicial independence insofar as the court had not made any judicial errors. Given the absence of any errors in the verdict or the sentencing, the jury court's judgment was upheld.[267]

The defendant was proven to have willingly taken hostile action against S., but may have taken the chance to dispute the evidence while not expecting that there would be surviving evidence that could be used against him. His conduct during the National Socialist regime had demonstrated how he had not only conformed to its tyranny, but had also willingly acted against those who were perceived to be hostile to its interests. In view of the evidence that was used to convict him, this court conclusively demonstrated its objectivity in calling him to account for his actions and the consequences he had brought about for alleged enemies of the regime. The Highest Appeal Court also ensured that the jury court at the Düsseldorf regional court pronounced its verdict with the appropriate judicial conditions, thus also demonstrating the effectiveness of the post war administration of justice in which all those convicted were afforded the right to a fair trial when an objective and impartial application of the law had been restored.

A later denunciation case was heard at the Hamburg regional court, where judgment was pronounced on 2 June 1949. This case involved several defendants who had been Gestapo officials or served as their subordinates. Out of the twelve defendants, those hereafter cited as Alfons P., Köhler, M., W., Georg P. and G. were accused of having committed crimes against humanity on the grounds of political and racial persecution by having been spies for the Gestapo who had denounced alleged enemies of the National Socialist regime.[268]

Alfons P. had first been arrested in Prague on 27 March 1939 where he was the intelligence director for an organization of German émigrés, before this organization was dissolved after the advance of German troops.[269] He was then taken to Hamburg where he was accused of undertaking activities against the National Socialist regime with a Czech émigré organization, and incurred several incidents of mistreatment at the hands of police inspector Knuth, who also threatened to intern his family and have medical experiments conducted on them. This led him to try to commit suicide on two occasions, and then go on a hunger strike to evade having further pressure put on him during interrogations to extract information from him and be recruited to work for the Gestapo. He was kept alive and remained in custody when he was not hospitalized for both physical and mental conditions, and later agreed to work for the Gestapo, initially by reporting on other prisoners who were shifted to his prison cell. He was later placed on trial for preparation to commit high treason in June or July 1941, and was sentenced to six years' imprisonment. He served three months of this sentence until he was released in November 1941 at the instigation of the Gestapo, and began to work for them at this time while reporting to Knuth.[270]

He was provided with a list of about a hundred names of former members of the German Communist Party that he had known, and was given the task of finding them and reporting on their activities and dispositions upon the threat of facing repercussions for himself and his family if he was not cooperative. He looked for some of the individuals on this list and gave weekly verbal reports to the Gestapo criminal secretary Heinrich Wilhelm Teege in Department IIa of the Gestapo regional headquarters in Hamburg, which was charged with suppressing leftist opposition, which was later renamed Department IV 1a of the *Reichssicherheitsamt* (RSHA).[271] Alfons P. received an initial weekly salary of 50 RM for reporting on the members found on the list. He also found normal employment through his brother, Georg P., working as a messenger carrying files and canvassing for a magazine distributor run by its owner hereafter cited as Rec. .This also gave him the opportunity to speak to the people he was spying on, and he was also instructed by Knuth to make general "morale reports." After Rec. was removed from being the owner of this business, the Gestapo appointed Georg P. as a trustee and set up an office on the business premises where he kept card files on suspected individuals that Alfons P. spied on, and later engaged M. as a typist, among others, as his activities became increasingly extensive.[272]

Georg P. had known Rec. since 1939, and had been hired on a provisional basis for his magazine distribution business from the end of that year, and later expressed interest in becoming a partner, to which Rec.'s wife was opposed. The Gestapo later took an interest in this enterprise after Knuth acknowledged during conversations with Alfons P. that a reading circle would be an effective means of spying on individuals. They therefore obtained the means to allow Georg P. to set up his own independent business in the late summer of 1943 while Rec.'s was being operated by a trustee while he was in the army.[273]

He later turned against Rec. by reporting to the Gestapo on 9 September 1943 the remarks that he had heard Rec. make that were hostile to the state and defeatist, which included disparaging remarks about racial legislation, in addition to the comment that Germany could never win the war against the Allies in view of their economic power. He said the NSDAP had consciously led the German people into a "mess" and that it was high time to get rid of the "scoundrel." Although he had grown up in the National Socialist worker youth, his fondest wish was for an early defeat of the Third *Reich*. He had also spoken disparagingly about Germany's chances of winning the war in view of the defeats in Russia, the British-American landings in North Africa, and the bombing attacks in Germany, and had advised Georg P. upon being called in for his medical examination to deceive the physician into certifying him to be unfit for military service. Rec. was thereafter placed in custody in the army on 21 September 1943, and his ownership of his business was removed from him and his wife by the Gestapo headquarters on 23 September. Georg P. was thereafter appointed as trustee while running his own shop at the same time. Rec. was later tried before the central court of the army on 2 June, where Georg and Alfons P. and Helms appeared as witnesses, but he was later exonerated on 8 June due to insufficient evidence.[274]

Throughout this time after he was released from imprisonment, Alfons P. became an informer working under Henry Helms, a criminal secretary for the Gestapo and an independent official in charge of cases,[275] and became his best assistant and was entrusted with a rather free hand. In one of the cases in which he was given the task of finding information, P. was charged with contributing to finding a Soviet agent named Fellendorf who had emigrated to Russia before later being parachuted into Hamburg. Observation of his mother's apartment led to ascertain that a Mrs. Priess would have had contact with him, and P. was ordered to find her, while he claimed that he intended to prevent her arrest. Fellendorf, his bride Erna Eifler, and Mrs. Priess and others involved in the Fellendorf group were arrested some time later, and were sentenced to death by the People's Court. Most of these death sentences were executed. However, the extent of his involvement in these arrests could not be established.[276]

In an early case of Alfons P.'s involvement with the Gestapo, Knuth charged him in the middle of 1942 with spying on the activities of the Svornost association, an organization composed of German citizens of Czech heritage that was under the suspicion of the Gestapo of conducting anti-National Socialist propaganda. He was chosen to be its librarian, and joined its meetings. On one such an occasion, one of its members, Ratzmann, made disparaging remarks about two Czechs who were there wearing German labor service uniforms, criticizing them for their cooperation with the regime. He thereafter wrote a report about how Ratzmann and a former Communist called Smok, who was a member of its executive committee, were ill disposed toward the regime, and that they had expressed their views accordingly in a meeting. Both were later arrested by the Gestapo and were taken to the Neuengamme concentration camp. Their names were placed on a "liquidation list" of inmates who were in custody at the Fuhlsbüttel prison and then taken to Neuengamme. All of them were later executed on 23 April 1945.[277]

In a different case, he was instructed to make contact with the Kr. Group of Communist resistance in the autumn of 1942, with whom he had already been acquainted at the beginning of the year, and was gathering incriminating material against its members. Kr. and P. met again during this time on one evening when many had gathered to offer their farewell to a soldier named Lübbers who was returning to the front and who later became an informer for the Gestapo. The conversation turned to political matters and resistance against National Socialism, and Alfons P. spoke again as he had earlier in the year about his experiences in fighting with the international brigade in the Spanish civil war and the decisions of the Seventh World Congress, where it was resolved that resistance fighters were to join National Socialist organizations in order to reach leading positions to undermine them. This could be done according to the Trojan Horse theory, which Lübbers recommended attempting while the others declined. There was also a letter written to a soldier in the field named Hellbach, which included seemingly innocuous references that were meant by those present at this time to be inferred as reinforcing the will of resistance. P. later composed a report to Helms about the events that took place during this evening, which mentioned this letter to Hellbach. Hellbach and all of those present during that evening were later arrested on the grounds of this report.[278]

Helms arrested Kr. on 6 May 1943, following with a so-called intensified interrogation for having attempted to influence youth and soldiers with Communist ideology, which involved brutal physical mistreatment that was reminiscent of medieval torture methods.[279] He later remained imprisoned in Fuhlsbüttel until he was transported to Auschwitz concentration camp where he perished on 18 July 1944.[280] Two others who also were present during the same evening, Hugo Hecht and Max Löwe, were also arrested in connection with being members of the Kr. Group, and were also taken to Auschwitz at the same time as Kr., where they also perished. Ada Löwe, another member of this group, was taken to Ravensbrück concentration camp, where she remained until she was freed in April 1945.[281] Another, cited in these proceedings as Schö., was arrested by Helms in May 1943, and remained imprisoned without trial in Fuhlsbüttel until the end of the war.[282] Two others, Lisbeth Rose and Hampel, were sentenced to death by the People's Court and were later executed. Hellbach remained imprisoned in Fuhlsbüttel for a long time, before later being taken to Neugamme concentration camp. P. was also accused of being responsible for several other arrests of individuals belonging to the Kr. Group.[283]

Alfons P. was also accused of causing the arrests of the members of another Communist resistance group, members of which are hereafter cited as C., Dol., and Hundert, by the Gestapo. The Gestapo had prior knowledge from another former Communist turned informer that Mrs. C.'s sons from her first marriage were in a school for parachute agents in Russia. P. met the C. couple and their daughter Dol. and her godmother Mrs. Hundert through a long-acquainted fellow Communist cited as Jö. P. told them a great deal about his experiences in Spain, and they met rather frequently thereafter. Since he gave them the impression of being an old and convinced Communist, they spoke about politics that tended to be against the regime. They also listened to foreign broadcasts, and P. told them how to tell others about what they had heard without arousing suspicion while he asked that they tune in to them.[284]

P. made regular reports about those present at these meetings that he forwarded to Helms. The C. couple and Dol. were later arrested on 16 June 1943, believing that P. had betrayed them when they were confronted under questioning with details of conversations that had only been known to their relatives and to P.[285] Mrs. Hundert and others who had interactions with the family were later arrested at the beginning of July 1943. They were then imprisoned in Fuhlbüttel. In order to prevent P.'s identity as an informer being revealed in ordinary court proceedings, the three women were later taken to Ravensbrück concentration camp in April 1944. Mrs. Hundert was later taken to Oranienburg concentration camp where she was killed through mistreatment. Mr. C. was taken to Neuengamme concentration camp until he was evacuated shortly before the end of the war, and then perished in the sinking of the Cap Arcona.[286]

Alfons P. was also engaged in the re-arrest of members of another Communist resistance organization known as the Bästlein Group; he had personally known a large number of its members. There had been great deal of unease at the Gestapo headquarters in Hamburg after the bombing attack of July 1944, after the public prosecutor had ordered the release of political prisoners from police custody, including a large majority of the members of this group. It had been the first thoroughly organized resistance movement, which had been discovered in connection with the "Red Orchestra" spy ring in Berlin. The Gestapo therefore channeled all of its available resources on the re-apprehension of its members who had been released, of which only a small part had complied with reporting back to the authorities, while most of them had gone underground.[287]

A former KPD member approached P. with the question of whether he could harbor an "illegal," and allowed one of the leading members of this organization, Gustav Bruhn, to stay at his home for about two months, and he reported this to Helms. Information about Bruhn's movements led to his arrest. He and three other of the most important members of the Bästlein Group were later taken to Neuengamme concentration camp where they were executed upon a special order from Himmler. P. also met other leading members of this group, and arranged to meet one of them cited as Boh., and informed Helms about this planned meeting where he could arrest Boh. It all went wrong when Boh. seized Helms's handgun and was killed in an exchange of gunfire with other Gestapo agents.[288] P. also reported to Helms about the other members of this group, including how they had been armed, how political instructors were brought into businesses, and where some members listened to foreign broadcasts, which led to seven further arrests. Six of these were executed at Neuengamme concentration camp on 23 April 1945 while one of them survived the internment there.[289]

P. was also made responsible for reporting to Helms and B., Helms's colleague and Gestapo commissioner,[290] about another Communist resistance group. Knuth send him to make contact with Heinrich Schröder, an old Communist, and he start talking to him about experiences in the Spanish Civil War in order to gain his trust and sound out his political activity. He then found out about the existence of an alleged resistance group, and later learned about its leader, hereafter cited as Sch. He later eventually gained his trust by professing to be an active resistance fighter, and found out about the scope of this group. He also persuaded Sch. that this group, which apparently extended throughout the *Reich* and consisted of more than a thousand members, was not organized thoroughly enough. Upon P.'s recommendation, this group was named the KdF (*Kampf dem Faschismus*). He also produced identification cards for the leading members with Sch.'s approval, and provided them with a seal.[291]

P. reported to Helms and his Gestapo headquarters colleague B. about this group and its activities, while realizing it was not a genuine resistance movement, which he considered to be ludicrous and exaggerated. Nevertheless, the leading members of this organization were arrested at the beginning of April 1945, in spite of Helms's and B.'s objections. It could not be established whether this took place on the basis of a report that P. had made against them, and it was also recognized that he was not prepared to act against them in view of his description about them.[292]

In another case, he had become acquainted with Mrs. Rosenkrantz through an old Communist acquaintance hereafter cited as Ru. She made no secret of her disposition that was hostile to National Socialism during their frequent political discussions in which her fiancé Ladewig also joined in. On one occasion, she gave him a book manuscript to read that made disparaging criticisms about Hitler and hoped to publish it after the war. P. then passed this manuscript on to Helms and made a report to him about Mrs. Rosenkrantz's and Ladewig's political dispositions. They were arrested by the Gestapo at the beginning of 1945 and were executed on 23 April 1945.[293]

While it could not be established whether he had also denounced two other former fellow Communist party members named Langer and Vogt to the Gestapo, it was determined that Alfons P. had met with many individuals who were opposed to the National Socialist regime, including those mentioned and many additional others, some of whom were actively engaged in the resistance movement. Although Knuth had instructed him to spy on these individuals, he also made inconclusive reports or no reports at all about them, and they were therefore spared in spite of their activities. Those spared included Ru. who had not been politically active since 1933, but had made disparaging remarks about National Socialism in P.'s presence.[294]

Due to his extensive activities, P. requested a typist from the Gestapo, and recommended a friend of his, hereafter cited as M., who was his former sister-in-law, to work with him. She started working for the Gestapo in this capacity on 15 June 1943 and received the same amount of income as an informer, receiving 60 RM per week for typing reports for Alfons P., Georg P., and several other informers, as well as writing general "morale reports." B. also later charged her with spying on two suspects, Ni. and Mrs. Hey, but this activity did not yield any results.[295] She also mentioned someone in a morale report who had been aggressive toward women in an air raid shelter and had made remarks that were hostile to the state, but he was later released from custody since he was found to be mentally disabled.[296]

The Gestapo also charged her with spying on Mrs. L., the widow of Boh., who was living illegally with the Schill couple. Since it was known that she was armed, the Gestapo did not want to arrest her in her apartment in order to prevent another exchange of gunfire, as was the case when they had attempted to arrest her husband. For this reason, M. was instructed to meet with Mrs. Boh. so that they could achieve the element of surprise when they arrested her. After this incident, M. requested B. to not give her such assignments anymore, preferring to keep to typing work.[297]

Another former Communist functionary in this case, Karl Köhler, also consented to work for the Gestapo after he was arrested in April 1941. He had worked as a Communist functionary distributing propaganda material from the KPD northern leadership group in Copenhagen into Germany through Harburg.[298] Police inspector Knuth who interrogated him offered to release him from custody if he agreed to lead the Gestapo to the members of the KPD leaders in Copenhagen, and attempted to make it clear to him that illegal activities against the National Socialist regime no longer served any useful purpose. They brought forward six veterans of the Spanish Civil War who spoke badly of the Soviets who had refused to grant them asylum in Russia. A week later, Köhler agreed to cooperate with the Gestapo on the condition that he and his wife and his group in Harburg would remain unmolested.[299]

Köhler then led the Gestapo to Wiatrek, the leader of the KPD leadership in Copenhagen, and other members of the leadership by arranging to meet with them through resistance circles in Berlin, giving Gestapo agents the times and places of these meetings. Wiatrek and two other leaders were arrested after the Gestapo had established their identities. Other arrests of members of the Copenhagen resistance group followed, but it could not be established whether they were related to the information that Köhler had provided, or whether the source had come from other members of this group, most of whom received the death sentence.[300]

Köhler continued working for the Gestapo after he returned to Hamburg, mostly writing so-called morale reports before he was conscripted into the army in March 1944.[301] Before this time, he was also involved in spying on active Communists hereafter cited as Gr. and J., the wife of one of the leaders of the Bästlein group, in order to find his whereabouts. This contributed to determining his location, as well as that of J. and another fugitive named Saefkow. Gr. and J. were arrested on 8 July 1944 and sentenced to ten years' imprisonment by the People's Court.[302] Another informer, cited as G., was also charged with spying on J., and was accused of having caused Gr.'s arrest that later led to her conviction. However, there was insufficient evidence to establish a conviction on this charge.[303]

Another informer, hereafter cited as W., was also charged with contributing to re-apprehending members of the Bästlein Group. B. employed her to be the trustee of a soap business at the end of October or beginning of November 1943. Its former owner, Mrs. Thürey, had been arrested since it was suspected that members of this group often went there.[304] The Gestapo made three different arrests while she was in charge of this business, and had contact with those fugitives.

When she began running this shop, Le., who was living illegally after being released from prison, went there with his wife and enquired about Mrs. Thürey. W. responded as she had been instructed to do, saying that she had gone to Berlin and that she was representing her during her absence. Le. then left shortly thereafter, as he felt suspicious, while his wife stayed to place orders to be picked up on the next day. Helms appeared at the shop soon thereafter and arrested her after seeing her papers and those of her husband.[305]

After a second arrest was made in the shop, W. wrote a note saying: "Careful! The police are here!" and kept it in her pocket. In another incident a few days later, an individual named Hornberger came to the shop looking for Mrs. Thürey, whereupon W. gave him the expected response. He then asked her if she was arrested, to which she admonished him to be careful, knowing that Helms was behind a curtain in an adjacent room. Hornberger then threw his handgun onto the shop counter and said he was not afraid, while giving her reason to fear an exchange of gunfire. After a brief conversation that Helms had overheard, he suggested they meet to go for a walk the next day, which Helms demanded that she do. While they were walking together, Hornberger told her a great deal about his illegal work while Helms followed them. As he came closer, she tried to tell Hornberger to escape by taking a departing streetcar. Helms nevertheless kept on his tracks and followed him to his home, and arrested Hornberger some time thereafter.[306]

W. was also charged by the Gestapo with spying on Mrs. Hey, with whom she had been acquainted, and whose husband was a fugitive, having been one of the leaders of the Bästlein Group who had been released from prison after the bombing attack on Hamburg in July 1943.[307] In the course of their conversations during her frequent visits to her home, she mentioned to her that her husband had perished in a concentration camp and that her father had suffered from National Socialist persecution. Mrs. Hey let it be known to her that her husband was sought by the authorities, and asked her to bring food ration coupons for him. She reported this to the Gestapo, without giving them any other information about his whereabouts, which his wife had not disclosed to her and she did not ask her. The Gestapo otherwise did not find out either, while she tried to hinder or prevent Mrs. Hey's arrest by avoiding mentioning anything that could bring danger to her in subsequent reports, which did not give the Gestapo any grounds for an arrest to be made. She was nevertheless arrested on the order of criminal director Hintze.[308]

In reviewing the facts of the case and passing judgments on the defendants, Alfons P., was found guilty of a crime against humanity according to Control Council Law No. 10, Article II, section 1c on the grounds of political persecution in several cases. These included his hostile conduct leading to the arrests of Fellendorf and five members of his group, who underwent serious suffering thereafter. It could not be established whether he was responsible for the arrests of members of the Kr. Group through his reports about them, as well members of the Bästlein Group, the KdF Group, and the cases of Ladewig and Langer, among the other cases evaluated in these proceedings. However, it could be established that he was very active in many cases, acting according to what was defined as hostile conduct according to the Highest Appeal Court of the British Zone's interpretation of Article II, section 1c of Control Council Law No. 10. His hostile conduct had entailed providing Gestapo officials with the names of enemies of the National Socialist regime who they had not known about, people who had made disparaging remarks about the regime, or had reported about their dispositions and actions against the regime, which caused their persecution and injuries inflicted at the hands of the Gestapo.[309]

He was responsible for the death of one fugitive from the Gestapo who was shot and killed while attempting to evade arrest, and for the arrests of twenty-two others, of which fifteen were killed and the rest of them imprisoned for several years in prisons and concentration camps. They were also subjected to the most severe forms of physical and mental mistreatment and torture while under interrogation by Gestapo officials. He was also responsible for their brutal mistreatment, having been aware of how he had intentionally delivered them into the hands of violence and tyranny and the consequences that would follow for the victims of his actions. Moreover, he could not evade responsibility by claiming to have acted under orders from superiors, and Article II, 4b of Control Council Law No. 10 stated how perpetrators were to be called to account for their actions in all such circumstances.[310]

This conclusion was drawn from a similar case, in which the Bielefeld regional court sentenced a Communist to a year's imprisonment for denouncing seventeen KPD members to the Gestapo after he and five of his relatives had been arrested by the Gestapo in October 1933, who were then released in return for his cooperation in spying on the KPD. In reviewing the facts of this case, the Hamm regional appeal court had ruled in its judgment passed on 5 August 1948 that a political denunciation was to be judged on the basis of the overall conduct of the defendant, in view of their having perpetrated a crime against humanity as defined in Article II, section 1c of Control Council Law No. 10. This did not necessarily require that a statement denouncing another had been made on one's own initiative. The question of the defendant's unwillingness could be addressed in § 52 and § 54 of the criminal code concerning having acted out of necessity or under duress, if these factors could be taken into consideration as mitigating circumstances, depending on the how the evidence of the defendant's conduct could be examined. Hostile conduct was not precluded by unwillingness, just as conduct could not be justified by the claim of having acted on the impetus of a higher authority, as was stated in Article II, section 4b of Control Council Law No. 10. It was therefore ruled that an informer could be subject to prosecution when they had been conscious of and intended to expose and deliver another, either directly or indirectly, to the tyranny and violent methods of the National Socialist regime.[311] An indirect perpetrator of a crime against humanity was thus to be held responsible, without being able to claim that they had acted under orders as a means of justifying their hostile conduct against others.

In taking this earlier verdict into consideration, the Hamburg regional court excluded the possibility that P. had acted under duress. He had claimed in his defense that Knuth had threatened his life and well-being, as well that of his relatives. Acting under duress and necessity outside of the law were overruled, since the violence and physical mistreatment that was inflicted on him and the threats that were made against him while he was in custody related to his activities as a Communist functionary took place in the country and abroad. Having occupied a prominent position in the KPD since before 1933 and sometimes undertaking illegal activities, he had known that he would eventually face persecution. This had been especially clear after the NSDAP had come to power and he had emigrated abroad. He thus accepted the inherent dangers of being engaged in activities against the state.[312]

He only could not be charged with having consented to spy on fellow prison inmates in view of Control Council Law No. 10, since this was presumed to have resulted from being under continued psychological pressure. Nevertheless, he remained subject to prosecution for his actions from mid 1942 and thereafter as instances of evidence of hostile conduct, when he could no longer claim to have remained under psychological pressure during this time, after he had consented to work for the Gestapo. He himself had not claimed that he had been under pressure from Helms or B. He was also Helms's best informer, who held his activities in high regard and had given him a free hand. There was otherwise no evidence of pressure on him after Knuth was killed in July 1943, and the evidence cast doubt on his having acted under duress in view of his conduct in undertaking acts of persecution on behalf of the Gestapo against others before and after this time. His claim that Knuth threatened to make his relatives subjects of medical experiments was also unlikely, considering that such mistreatment of concentration camp inmates, as well as extending the liability of all members of a family for crimes of a relative, were only undertaken later, after he had allegedly made this threat. It was thus maintained that he had betrayed others for the sake of preserving his own interests when threatened with facing an uncertain future after having been released from serving a six-year prison sentence, while being aware of the consequences for those he had denounced to the Gestapo.[313]

All of his actions for the duration of the time he had been employed by the Gestapo from 1942 to 1945 were considered to be the same form of crime against humanity according to an interpretation of Article II, section 1c of Control Council Law No. 10. In determining mitigating circumstances, there was no evidence to indicate that he suffered from any form of mental illness or weakness that could have affected or diminished his ability to reason. .[314] His actions also indicated a considerable lack of character, especially since he had exploited his personal relations with like-minded individuals, the consequences for whom had been clear to him due to his personal experiences of having been politically persecuted. It could have been expected of him to warn them. In view of any possible mitigating circumstances, his lack of prior convictions was taken into consideration, and the fact that he had undergone considerable suffering under the influences of the Gestapo, and therefore was under a certain degree of pressure. He was thereby sentenced to twelve years' imprisonment,[315] with six years' deprivation of his civil rights.[316]

In reviewing the facts against Köhler, the judgment was similar to that for Alfons P., although the extent of the damages inflicted were not to the same extent.[317] Evidence of his hostile conduct against He. could not be fully established. Although he had spied on him and reported the contents of his conversations to the Gestapo, it could not be ascertained whether these actions caused the injuries that He. had incurred. However, the court determined that his hostile conduct was confirmed with regard to Wiatrek,

Hel., and Nieter, who were members of the KPD's northern leadership group and were sentenced to death. Nieter was executed, while Wiatrek and Hel. endured severe mental anguish during their imprisonment until they were liberated at the end of the war. P.'s hostile conduct was also established in the case of Gr., whose illegal activity was revealed as a result of his report to the Gestapo in Berlin, which resulted in her being sentenced to ten years' imprisonment. He had also known of the potential consequences of his actions in delivering them to the persecution of violence and tyranny, and was thus found guilty of a crime against humanity as defined in Article II, section 1c of Control Council Law No. 10.[318]

He claimed in his defense that he had acted against Wiatrek in part of his conspiracy to save several members in his group in Hamburg. Nevertheless, the court maintained that he had not acted out of duress, and that while these conspiratorial means may have had political value, they were insignificant in the eyes of criminal law. Moreover, he was also responsible for the arrest of Hel. and Nieter as well as Wiatrek, after having agreed to cooperate with the Gestapo, and he had not been acting under an intolerable threat to his life and limb and therefore was not under any heavy psychological pressure. His overall conduct also indicated how he had coldly calculated the possibilities about how to best serve his own personal advantages.[319] He was thereby sentenced to four years' imprisonment[320] with four years' deprivation of civil rights.[321]

Georg P. was also found guilty of a crime against humanity in accordance with Article II, section 1c of Control Council Law No. 10, for reporting Rec. to the Gestapo in September 1943. This constituted hostile conduct in the circumstances at a time when the accusations he had made against Rec. were very serious and placed his life in danger. P. had been aware of the potential death sentence that could have been imposed on Rec., who had been imprisoned for nearly nine months. The fact that P. had weakened his hostile testimony in the military court proceedings was taken into consideration in his favor, which contributed to averting the death sentence as this court recognized how he had a personal interest in acquiring Rec.'s business while P. appeared to try to exonerate Rec. to a certain degree.[322] The fact that he had also later offered financial compensation was also taken into consideration in his favor.[323] However, these facts did not undermine the results of his hostile conduct in the form of the harm that was inflicted on Rec. in the form of imprisonment and serious mental anguish, which meant that his situation was not any safer than being a soldier deployed at the front, as the defense counsel had tried to maintain, and otherwise he could not claim to have acted under duress.[324] He was thereby sentenced to a year's imprisonment.[325]

M. was acquitted, since it could not be established that she had committed a crime against humanity. She had shown hostile conduct by occasionally observing Ni. and Mrs. Hey, but she did not do any "successful work" for them in these two cases, and therefore could not be held even partly responsible for having caused any injury that they later incurred. Although she had been involved in L.'s arrest, she had been instructed to help prevent unnecessary bloodshed. This could not be considered unlawful hostile conduct, and her actions were not motivated by the same causes as those of Alfons P. and Köhler. It also could not be determined that she had been aware of the unlawfulness of her actions.[326] G. was also acquitted in view of insufficient evidence. She had given signals to Gestapo officials while observing Gr. and J., but it could not be established that her actions had led to the injuries they had incurred. It thus could not be established that she had committed a crime against humanity.[327]

W. was also acquitted due to insufficient evidence. It could not be established that there was any evidence of hostile conduct against Le., and nothing could be derived from the fact that she was prepared to take over as trustee for Mrs. Thürey's shop, since she had not known how this business could be used to serve the Gestapo's purposes. It also could not be ascertained whether she had contacted Helms about Le. coming to the shop or had known that he would return there.[328] Hostile conduct also could not be established in the case of Hornberger, and in view of the circumstances of the facts of this case, it could not be reasonably expected that she should have given him a warning. She also could not be held responsible for the injuries that Hornberger had later incurred. It was possible for Helms to have known about his presence at the shop while they were both there,[329] without having received prior notice from her. In addition, she could not be held responsible for Mrs. Hey's arrest, which was ordered by Hintze, the criminal director at the time. It also could not be refuted that W. had intended to warn her about her impending arrest, so evidence of hostile conduct could not be established.[330] It was also known that she had warned several other individuals who were in danger of being arrested by the Gestapo, and when she was charged with writing "morale reports," she did not mention names of individuals whose remarks were recorded in these reports. She included only those that were considered to be hostile to the state, and did not report an individual she had known who had listened to foreign radio broadcasts.[331]

Three of the accused in this case, Helms, Alfons P. and Karl Köhler, filed an appeal, in which judgment was pronounced by the Highest Appeal Court of the British Zone on 5 September 1950. The verdicts for Helms and Köhler were maintained, while the verdict for Alfons P. was reverted to the jury court at the Hamburg regional court for further deliberations in renewed proceedings.[332] This court ruled that the evidence presented in the verdict against Köhler sufficiently sustained that he had intentionally persecuted four others while being conscious of the consequences of his actions, which justified the sentencing on the basis of formal and material law in relation to Article II, section 1c of Control Council Law No. 10. It was also maintained that there were no mitigating circumstances in his favor.[333] Possible mitigating circumstances remained subject to further examination in the case of P.

P. cited hardship as the grounds for contesting the earlier verdict, which had been ruled as being inadmissible. This court ruled that the application of Control Council Law No. 10 was justifiable, and he otherwise could not maintain the claim of having acted under duress after having been released from prison in return for agreeing to cooperate with the Gestapo. On the other hand, he had also been aware of the potential consequences of his actions, and was therefore justifiably convicted of having committed crimes against humanity.[334]

However, there was a flaw in the reasoning concerning the definition of psychological pressure, with the possibility that the jury court may not have sufficiently addressed the issue of his having acted under duress. The extent of his having acted under duress and his implied reasonable ability to resist this remained to be determined with greater probability in order to establish the extent of his responsibility. It was thus to be determined to what extent had he freely expressed his willingness to work for the Gestapo after the middle of 1942, and whether he was actually in a position to refuse to cooperate while facing the possibility of further severe mistreatment, or even his death. This question of his willingness thus remained to be answered without being subject to any objective or at least subjective doubt about his having acted out of compulsion that could have had affected his reasoning ability, which could then be taken into consideration as a mitigating factor in determining the sentencing.[335]

A further judgment was pronounced on Alfons P. at the Hamburg regional court on 8 December 1951. After Ordinance No. 234 of the High Commission of the U.K. of 31 August 1951 had abolished Control Council Law No. 10 from 1 September 1951, this case was therefore heard on the basis of German law. The charges included aiding and abetting unlawful imprisonment, murder, bodily injury resulting in death, dangerous bodily injury in connection with extortion, as well as serious bodily injury in view of criminal negligence. The previous judgment was upheld in view of the evidence and his considerably hostile conduct, which were maintained in accordance with German law. The earlier verdict and sentencing were thereby sustained on the basis of the evidence that had been presented at the regional court.[336]

Another denunciation case was heard during this time at the Bückeburg regional court, where judgment was passed on 24 June 1949. The defendant, hereafter cited as K., had been a brick worker who had worked for a Jewish manager of a brick works, hereafter cited as Oskar P, until 1932, when he and his brother took over the management of another branch of this same business in Stadthagen, along with seven other brickworkers and a new manager hereafter cited as U. Since this business would eventually be "aryanized," P. managed to relinquish it to his son Ewald who was half-Jewish, but since even he could not manage the business alone, he leased it to the newly-established U. and Co. limited partnership in Stadthagen, with the workers and U. becoming partners. Before the lease began, K. had approached Oskar P. about selling or leasing the brick works to him, which P. refused to do since it was a family business that he wanted to leave to his son; otherwise he felt morally obliged to adhere to the limited partnership arrangement. No disputes arose between them as a result of this decision.[337]

From 1933 onward until he was conscripted for military service after the outbreak of the Second World War, the brick works business was booming. While he was posted in southern France, a fire broke out in the factory, but the cause could not be determined, especially since there was hay and straw used in the production process. When K. was on leave in early 1943, he spoke to U. at the branch office where he was told that the younger P. had made threats against the defendant shortly beforehand, saying that he would "settle up" with him sometime in the future. Learning this caused great consternation with K., and he swore not to forget what P. had said. [338]

K. told an *Ortsgruppenleiter,* hereafter cited as B., about this incident shortly thereafter, who advised him that this matter lay outside his jurisdiction, and that he could write a report about it. A letter then arrived at the local *Ortsgruppe* a few days later, which was forwarded to the Gestapo in Bielefeld. Although this letter was no longer available, witnesses could testify to the contents that told something to the effect that Ewald P. had threatened K. with calling him to account in the future. He also wrote that he was concerned that a Jew was free while he was a front line soldier whose family could not be protected from this threat. He also noted that there had been a fire at K.'s brick works, and it was hoped that it would be investigated to see if P. could have caused it. He also stated that the local population was agitated about P.'s attitude.[339]

The local police chief questioned U. and Ewald P. thereafter, which led to P. losing his position as the factory manager. He was then arrested by the Gestapo on 21 July 1943, and was imprisoned in Hannover and then Bielefeld. He was then taken to a forced labor camp on 24 August 1943 where he later died on 8 October 1943, with the official cause of death apparently recorded as a hemorrhage. According to a witness who was working there, hereafter cited as L., P. was savagely beaten by guards before being killed with a gunshot to the neck.[340]

K. denied having referred to P. as a Jew being free while he was serving at the front, saying that perhaps someone had mentioned this in a different report that led to P.'s arrest. However, the court found that the available written evidence and the testimonies of witnesses proved that K. had in fact emphasized that his life as a front line soldier was more worthwhile preserving than the life of a Jew who often expressed his craving for revenge. His desultory attitude was thus considered his justification for reporting P. to the authorities. He was thus found guilty of committing a crime against humanity as defined by Article II, section 1c of Control Council Law No. 10.[341]

The court reiterated how the retroactive application of the law in crimes against humanity did not violate legal certainty since it was applied to the contravention of moral law, and thus was restoring the principles of the rule of law. K. did not hesitate to mercilessly deliver P. into the hands of the National Socialist system of repression while being aware of the consequences that would follow at that time, when the principles of justice and respect for the dignity of individuals was incompatible with the practices of a brutal and despotic regime. As in other cases of denunciation that were considered crimes against humanity against the civilian population, his disposition was found to be characterized by the typical contempt and malice that prompted someone to denounce another without regard for their well-being, which in itself established that he had approved of the consequences of his actions.[342]

The court also denied K.'s objection that he sought to defend himself against a forthcoming dangerous act of revenge. The court ruled that considering that this revenge would only come in the unforeseeable future and was so vaguely worded, that there was no genuine reason for fear, and they noted that P. did not have the means or ability to do anything to K. or his family at the time. Moreover, K. was deemed to be intelligent enough to realize that he had not been in any danger of reprisal from P., and therefore his claim did not have any credibility. It was more accurate to state that he had acted more out of rage than fear in response to P.'s disrespectful affront, which did not merit the dire consequences that would be incurred for someone whom the regime was merely tolerating. He was half-Jewish, which meant that K. would have known that any complaint he made would result in something much more than a mere reprimand.[343]

It was also irrelevant for him to have referred to P.'s Jewish background, as if to have implied that he should have been imprisoned, as well as adding his suspicion that he had caused the fire in the brick works, as U. had not shared this suspicion. Moreover, the claim that the local population was outraged about P.'s conduct was untrue, since people there did not know anything about it. K.'s report was thus an attack on P.'s integrity, rather than K. allegedly taking action to defend himself. Hence, it was further reasoned that there were racial motives for K.'s report, as there had not been any personal differences between them before that time.[344]

P. was called to account for having rashly made threatening remarks by being exposed to the terror apparatus of the NSDAP and the Gestapo, which led to dire consequences for him because of his racial background. K. had known of consequences that would arise from his report, which was the primary cause of P.'s eventual violent death by initially setting the intervention against him into motion. He had thereby contributed to the persecution of this particular victim of the regime's extermination apparatus as a result of P.'s minor indiscretion. As P. himself had said to his secret love while he was imprisoned, he had been arrested for having a big mouth. The fact that he was expecting times to change would have sufficed for him to be sentenced to imprisonment in a concentration camp for making a defeatist remark. His half-Jewish background also contributed to his fate after K. had handed him over to the authorities and their arbitrary practices of suppression, which were not subject to any law, human or moral. K. had knowledge of these practices and had had a sufficient amount of time to consider the consequences of his actions, and was thus held accountable for them. Although he testified that he was neither a National Socialist nor a racist, he was responsible for initiating the official state persecution himself while being aware of the measures that the regime was capable of taking against its alleged enemies, and he chose to willingly contribute to perpetrating an offense against humanity itself.[345]

An appropriate basis for the sentencing was not found in Control Council Law No. 10, and there were difficulties in applying the norms set in the criminal code for this type of offense, which did not apply to a typical case of National Socialist denunciation. The defendant could be considered guilty of having caused P.'s unlawful imprisonment, but the criminal code did not take the element of the defendant's guilt in this form of offense into consideration, since there was the added aggravating circumstance of the unscrupulous conviction of delivering a victim to powers of extermination. Judging a broadly defined crime against humanity also entailed extending considerations into other forms of offenses, such as injury and death that denunciation had made possible, in addition to all the mitigating circumstances in comprehensively examining the facts of such cases.[346]

In determining the extent of the sentencing, the court considered the possibility that the defendant did not think that his report would result in P.'s certain death, or that he did not intend to cause his death. He may have hoped to have rendered P. harmless, without necessarily anticipating him sustaining bodily harm. He was also known to have saved others from drowning at the risk of his own life. In addition, he enjoyed a good reputation and, apart from paying a fine as financial compensation, he did not have any prior convictions. In view of these considerations, K. was sentenced to a year's imprisonment.[347]

A later denunciation case was heard at the Hamburg regional court, where judgment was pronounced on 2 September 1949. One of the two accused in this case, hereafter cited as B., had been a member of the NSDAP from 1 May 1933 until the capitulation. He had also served as a *Blockleiter* for the DAF from the end of 1933, and later served in this position for the NSDAP until the end of July 1943, when he was convicted by a Hamburg county court on 22 July 1943 for engaging in illegal exchanging and trading in rationed goods for personal gain. The other accused, hereafter cited as P., had been a seamstress who worked with him at his bandage business, and had never been a member of the NSDAP or one its affiliated organizations.[348]

Both came under the attention of the Gestapo following a search by two agents, hereafter cited as S. and G., conducted in the apartment belonging to one of B.'s employees, hereafter cited as Oskar L., who B. had employed since 1930. This house search did not uncover any incriminating material other than some books written by Jewish authors and a novel by Thomas Mann, which led to queries. L. was not arrested, but was placed under further investigation, which led to B. being questioned on 8 May, and P. on 10 May 1943. Their statements that they had made while being questioned were recorded, and signed by them to confirm the accuracy of the contents. These statements were used as evidence to incriminate L., who was arrested by the Gestapo on 10 May 1943. Files concerning the investigations about him were forwarded to the local public prosecutor's office and then to the People's Court. On 24 July 1943, L. was prosecuted at this court for intentionally listening to foreign radio broadcasts from 1942 to February 1943, and undermining the war effort by perpetrating malicious agitation.[349]

The public prosecutor's indictment at these preliminary proceedings cited evidence that had been drawn from his conversations with P. whom he had trusted to be discreet. He had also commented on a poster that had been hung in the company that said 1941 would be the year that Germany would crush Bolshevism, saying to her: "When the chief arrives, I'll point out to him that we still haven't beaten Bolshevism. Therefore, I'll have the poster hanging so that Mr. B. will see that I'm right and not him."[350] After the battle for Stalingrad, he had told P. that Germany was governed by a crazy person. He said it had been proven that Hitler had gone crazy, as he dances on a carpet and fights like a crazy person. He also told her that he regularly listened to English radio broadcasts, since one would then know the truth about what was really happening. He also remarked that the German newspapers only reported lies, such as about losses reported by army reports that were much greater than was admitted, and the large extent of material the Americans were supplying the Russians, adding how it was hopeless to think that Germany could win the war. When P. mentioned in a conversation with L. in March 1943 that evacuees who had been bombed out would be able to move into apartments from which Jews had been vacated, he said that there would be bitter revenge for having removed Jews from their homes. The Nazi fat cats (*Bonzen*) that were responsible for this would each be hanged for doing so, and he hoped to live to see the day when this would happen. When the firm had put up flags on Hitler's birthday and a swastika flag had fallen to the ground, L. asked what that "thing" was and refused to raise that "lousy flag" (*Scheißfahne*) up again. When the press reported news of the dead in Katyn forest, he told P. that it was propaganda, saying how they had murdered the Polish officers but the "Bolsheviks" were blamed for it as an excuse.[351]

This indictment also cited excerpts of a conversation he had allegedly had with B. as evidence that was used against him, saying how he had also had discussions about political events with him, and likewise trusted his discretion.[352] With reference to the aforementioned poster, L. had apparently told him in 1942 to look at it and consider that nothing had changed since the previous year. After the defeat at Stalingrad, L. was said to have told B. that Germany had practically lost the war. When B. turned away from talking about this at this time, L. maintained that he was certain that Germany was losing the war and that blood would flow in the country in three months, adding what that would mean for a political leader such as B. In a later conversation with B., L. made emphatic references to English radio broadcasts saying that the losses that the German army reported did not correspond to the facts, adding how the numbers were much higher, as well as reporting the accurate higher number of German ships that had in fact been sunk. He also told B. about when he listened to the English broadcasts and which frequency he used, as well as adding how he should listen to a broadcast of a section of a speech that Hitler had made containing his prophecies, which he ought to compare to the present situation. L. further added that what was in the newspapers was not the truth, saying how press freedom no longer existed, and therefore he could only believe what he heard that was sent on the English transmitter. With regard to political measures taken against Jews, L. told B. how Jews had their mission to fulfill in the entire world, just like the Germans, and therefore he could not understand from a humane point of view why they had to be exterminated in Germany while they live in other countries. B. was also cited as having repeatedly warned L. to refrain from making such statements to him and P.[353]

After being released from custody from prison in Hamburg by the state prosecutor's office after the large scale air attack in July 1943, he was allowed to return to work as a bandage maker. Since he was bombed out of his apartment, he was granted permission to move to Heidelberg, and later found employment in his trade in Kaiserslautern. He was later re-arrested by the Mannheim Gestapo on 21 October 1943 and taken to Berlin. The main proceedings of the People's Court were to be held on 31 January 1944, in which both P. and B. were to appear as witnesses, but these proceedings were cancelled due to an air attack on the night of 30-31 January 1944 that caused severe damage to the building in which they were to be held. Their witness statements that were sworn under oath were therefore recorded in writing on 31 January, and therefore they were not asked to appear in the postponed proceedings on 7 February. L. was sentenced to death at this time, and was executed on 20 March 1944.[354]

P. and B. were thus held responsible for jointly and continually contributing to this crime against humanity in view of the events of May 1943 in Hamburg and 7 February 1944. It was assumed that P. had reported L. to the Gestapo at B.'s instigation, and that their statements to the Gestapo and at the People's Court made the death sentence possible. They both denied having reported L. to the Gestapo or having caused a report to have been made, admitting only to have repeated what they had heard L. say to them. They also claimed to have made their statements under pressure, and were thus coerced into doing so out of fear of the Gestapo.[355]

Evidence to prove the attestation that one or both of the defendants reported L. to the Gestapo or to another authority, or gave the impetus for an investigation to be undertaken against L., which in turn led to the People's Court proceedings, could not be provided, since these People's Court files were destroyed. All that remained of them was the foil of the bill of indictment against L., which contained the enclosed attested copy of the arraignment. There was only the indication that B. had brought about a report being made about L., but who had actually made the report could not be inferred from this arraignment, since the bill of indictment did not refer to the source. The public prosecutor therefore determined that the bill of indictment dated 24 July 1943 that stated P. had made the report against L. was incorrect, since it could not be corroborated by another source, other than the accusing authority. The validity of this claim therefore could not be verified. The existing People's Court files did not reveal whether a report was made against L., or who had made it, or who had arranged for it to be brought about. The bill of indictment was missing the facts about whether B. had actually determined to make a report against L. Since this information cited in the bill of indictment could not be verified, the simple claim therein was insufficient evidence to convict him.[356]

The evidence cited in the indictment also could not be corroborated by the testimony proffered by L.'s defense lawyer, hereafter cited as D., who was appointed by the People's Court and was present when B. and P. were questioned as witnesses on 31 January 1944 and at the main proceedings on 7 February 1944. He could only state that he was under the impression that the report against L. had come from them, and otherwise could no longer recall whether B. had made the report or had arranged for it to be made.[357]

Another source of potential evidence was a draft of a petition for clemency that B. and P. had drafted, to which L.'s widow had later added that B. had made the report in cooperation with P., whom B. had told to do so. However, D. could not provide clear information about how he could make this interpretation, saying he probably looked at the files and arrived at this conclusion. It also remained opened to question whether this witness had actually seen the People's Court files. He had been an official defense lawyer for this court while maintaining his law practice in Nauen, and estimated that he had been involved in approximately 250 cases before this court. According to his testimony, the news of this case reached him on 30 January 1944 when he received a copy of the bill of indictment, and did not see anything further until the main proceedings were held, and thus possibly saw the files while dealing with another case at this court. It was therefore possible that D. may not have actually seen the files dealing with L. Perhaps he did not deem it necessary to do so after a meeting with L., which took place after B. and P. were questioned on 7 February 1944, since the indictment stated that L. had made a confession. Considering that he had received a copy of the indictment as well as the testimonies offered by B. and P., he was therefore sufficiently familiar with the facts of the case.[358] Not having prior knowledge of the contents of the files, D. therefore could have mistakenly assumed that B. had made the report about L., and he could have done so merely on the basis of the contents in the indictment about B.'s remark about arranging that a report be made about L. It could be that he acceded this information to the clemency appeal while thinking that only P. could have made the report, as she was also incriminated by the contents of the clemency appeal. The court therefore established that D. could not be considered a credible witness to present concrete evidence against the two accused.[359]

One of the aforementioned former Gestapo agents cited as S. was called as a witness in this case who testified in favor of the defendant. He could not remember with certainty whether the proceedings against L. were initiated following a report, or an official message from Hintze, the director of the criminal political affairs department of the Gestapo criminal counsel who had since committed suicide. S. told the court that there had been a Gestapo file on L. in his department that included information about L. having concealed illegal reading material in his home, and having made remarks that were hostile to the state. Hintze had therefore ordered S. and G. to search L.'s apartment on the basis of this information. In view of this evidence, it could not be ascertained whether P. had made a report at the instigation of B. It also could not be proven that Hintze had acquired information from B. about L. Moreover, it could not be refuted that although B. was a political leader, there was no evidence to indicate that he had any contact with Hintze or had provided incriminating information about L. It appeared that the information that B. and P. had told the Gestapo about L. was only imparted after the two agents had searched his home and did not find any evidence that could be used against him.[360]

The court therefore ascertained that the defendants had not taken action to denounce L. since they had neither made a report to incriminate him nor had caused it to be made. Their testimony could not be refuted, in view of the evidence that suggested that they were questioned by the Gestapo while proceedings against L. were already pending. They were therefore considered witnesses in the Gestapo investigation and the People's Court proceedings who were obliged to provide their testimonies, and who could have faced being prosecuted if they did not convey the complete truth in cooperating with the authorities.[361] Hence, they were not considered to be informers who had initiated the action taken against L., but could be considered guilty of having cooperated with the ruthlessly unlawful authorities of the time so that they would not face dire consequences at their hands.

An objective interpretation concerning Article II, Section 2 of Control Council Law No. 10 did not absolve them from prosecution, which would depend on how they had conducted themselves. Although the two witnesses had proffered truthful testimonies about what they had known about L., there remained the question whether they had planned to provide incriminating evidence due to some hostile motives. It was determined that B. was implicated in this respect while P. was not. Although the files of the People's Court proceedings were no longer available, the wording of the testimonies that they provided to the Gestapo indicated the accuracy of the evidence that they had provided against L. Of the surviving People's Court files, an attested copy of the bill of indictment from the state prosecutor at the People's Court dated 24 July 1943 was found on 5 October 1948, which confirmed that the contents of the copy found in the available foil were the same. It presented the remarks that P. and B. had made about L. in quotation marks, with comments in the margins of the bill of indictment that provided further references. This attested to how the contents of their verbal testimonies to the Gestapo and the People's Court were exactly the same, although they had made these testimonies at two different times.[362] Their testimonies incriminated L. in the worst possible way by describing him as an outspoken rabblerousing opponent of the National Socialist regime. The contents of these testimonies formed the basis for the most appalling form of possible consequences. Both of the accused admitted they were fully aware that their remarks would result in the most serious form of punishment.[363]

P. cited in her defense that after receiving written notification from the Gestapo on Sunday, 9 May 1943, she was ordered to appear the next day for questioning. She was told at that time that there had been a report submitted about L., and she was ordered to report what she knew about L. and what he had spoken to her regarding political matters. She initially tried to resist talking about this, saying that she did not talk to L. about politics at all and did not care about politics as well, but the Gestapo agent questioning her then became very agitated and shouted at her saying that she was obligated to speak out. The agent then said that the Gestapo was already aware of L.'s rabblerousing talk, and that since she was already implicated as a witness, she ought to consider writing down what she knew. He also threatened to use "other means" against her and place her in detention if she did not tell what she knew within ten minutes while she was left alone. Being in a state of distress about being subject to arrest and prosecution because of what she had heard L. say, she only then admitted after some hesitation about what she knew about what L. had said to her about politics, and how he had made disparaging remarks about National Socialism and the regime. Meanwhile, the agent compared the details about what she said with notes he had on hand, which dispelled any doubt that he had already questioned someone else about L., thus confirming her fears that she would have faced severe consequences if she had not betrayed what she had known.[364] Since she did not have hostile intentions against L., the only measure she could take to have him spared was her hesitation, which could not be endured under severe presure.

The court did not dispute her testimony, as it was known what methods the Gestapo had used to bring the reluctant accused and witnesses to speak. It therefore was not denied that P. could have hesitated to tell what she knew until she was put under pressure with the threats of the interrogating agent, and thus she acted out of a helpless fear at that time and afterward. Her distressed disposition after this interrogation was confirmed by her fiancée at the time, hereafter cited as Br., whom she had told that the Gestapo had put incriminating material about L. before her and demanded that she tell them what she knew, or else face the consequences if she continued to hesitate. Her state of mind at this time was also confirmed by an acquaintance of hers, hereafter cited as Li., to whom she also expressed remorse about having contributed to incriminating L. by confirming what the Gestapo had known about him. Following that event she provided a written testimony to the People's Court; this acquaintance also told the court how P. was in such a complete state of nervous despair about "having to put the noose around L.'s neck" that she became ill as a result.[365]

It could also be added that B. was interrogated before P., as he was notified on Friday, 7 May 1943 to appear the next day, and his testimony was thus recorded before it could be confirmed by P.'s testimony two days later. It followed that in these circumstances, any reservations could have been detected in view of the contents of B.'s testimony, so she was under pressure to confirm. Given her initial hesitation to do so, as was confirmed by two witnesses Br. and Li., this refuted a potential indication of hostile intent against L., as defined in Article II section 1c of Control Council Law No. 10, since she was not immediately willing to make a report against him. Moreover, there was also no evidence of hostile intent upon the questioning at the People's Court thereafter, in which she said that the examining judge repeated the testimony she had given to the Gestapo. She could only confirm those contents while fearing being prosecuted if she did not speak the truth about what she had said earlier. In view of the evidence, she was therefore acquitted due to insufficient evidence to produce a guilty verdict.[366]

The evidence with regard to B.'s behavior stood in contrast to P.'s experiences and conduct. B. also argued in his defense that he was under placed under pressure from the Gestapo to make his statement, after having initially hesitating to do so. The interrogating agent had also been "energetic" with him while reminding him about his responsibilities as a political leader to speak the whole truth, and therefore he did not see any other way out of this dilemma. These claims were countered with the argument that this testimony was insufficient for him to be exonerated, since it was determined that his intention was to incriminate L. due to a hostile attitude against him, rather than merely acting of out fulfilling his duty to speak the truth.[367]

Additional evidence indicated that there was reason to believe there were grounds for B.'s hostile intentions. B. had employed L. since 1930 and they had come to be on familiar terms for many years until their relationship became strained in April 1943, when B. found out that L. embezzled small amounts of money from customers. Although the amount of 15 RM in one such incident was hardly significant, in the opinion of the court, this constituted a great breach of trust that made B. disassociate himself from L., whom he had trusted completely. This prompted B. to denounce him during his questioning by the Gestapo. He became much more agitated at this time when it was revealed to him that when they had searched L.'s home on 7 May 1943, they had found that he had misappropriated a roll of very difficult to procure leather from his business, which was to be used for producing bandages. The court further believed that upon hearing this, B. thought that L. did not deserve to be spared in any way from receiving the punishment he thought he deserved, due not only to the misappropriations, but also because of his disparaging remarks about the regime, and therefore he did not hesitate to tell the Gestapo everything that he knew.[368]

The court had arrived at this conclusion by considering that until L.'s arrest on 8 May 1945, the Gestapo had not known about the derisive remarks that L. had made about the regime to B. and P. since the search of his home did not uncover anything incriminating. Moreover, they had the facts to use against L. to initiate legal proceedings after they had first interrogated B., who could have easily denied knowledge of L. having said anything disparaging, which they had not known before this time. Instead, he made a coherent detailed report about what L. had said, which was recorded in writing by the Gestapo and was copied verbatim into the bill of indictment dated 24 July 1943. B. had completely acknowledged that these statements were serious offenses at the time, but did not have any inhibitions about telling the Gestapo everything that he remembered in its entirety, in spite of the fateful consequences that would follow for L. As a political leader, he did not have any doubts about how opponents of National Socialism would be dealt with as a result of his actions in dealing with an authority as merciless as the Gestapo, and how L.'s remarks would cost almost anyone their head. He therefore did not act out of his obligation to fulfill his duty, but out of a willingness to act against L. as a result of his hostility toward him.[369]

His hostile attitude was also expressed before and after his interrogation by the Gestapo. When the Gestapo had called him on 7 May 1943 to inform him that he was to appear for questioning the next day, he was informed in reply to his query that this concerned something political. He was told thereafter that this questioning was made as part of the process of an ongoing investigation concerning a political matter, and that L.'s home had been searched. Considering that B. had frequently heard L. make disparaging remarks about National Socialism and was called to be a witness for the Gestapo, he must have known that it concerned these remarks. An objective, rather than malicious, third party would have contacted L. to tell him that he was under the Gestapo's suspicion, and that investigation proceedings were being undertaken against him. According to his testimony, B. did not do anything to let him know what had happened before offering his incriminating testimony on 8 May 1945.[370]

He also acknowledged calling L. after the questioning and telling him that the Gestapo had told him about the roll of leather that was found during a house search, but did not tell him in any way that proceedings were being undertaken against him for political matters, or that he was questioned by the Gestapo and gave a destructive testimony against him. Moreover, when L. told him that he and P. were summoned by the Gestapo on the morning of

10 May 1943 and needed to close the shop, B. did not take this opportunity to tell him anything about the ongoing proceedings. The court interpreted that this withholding of what he knew, without giving L. the slightest hint about the impending danger he was in, while only offering the possibility of it merely concerning the roll of leather, was evidence of his obvious maliciousness. This was further compounded by further malicious actions. After this telephone call on 10 May 1943, B. went to the criminal police to report L. about a charge of embezzlement, as indicated by files drawn from the Altona county court. This behavior further demonstrated B.'s hostile attitude against L., knowing that he would not come back from the Gestapo office. He then continued to demonstrate his malicious attitude. After learning that L. had been arrested, he wrote a message to his wife telling her that she was not welcome to go to his shop, and threatened to report her to the police if she did so. He continued to display complete indifference to L.'s fate hereafter, such as not enquiring about the conclusion of the People's Court proceedings; he only learned about his death sentence and execution during the present proceedings initiated against him.[371]

B.'s hostile conduct against L. as a result of his embezzlement and misappropriation of goods also led him to find incriminating evidence against him on his own initiative. He had asked some acquaintances who had been customers at the bandage shop that L. had managed to compile evidence to be used against him, shortly before the Gestapo had searched his home. Hence, B. had determined to disassociate himself from L. and take action against him for having abused his trust, and therefore did not want to see him spared from fateful consequences, and this was reinforced by their political differences, for which he thought L. ought to be duly punished and delivered him to the Gestapo.[372]

B.'s claim that he was compelled under pressure of threats to offer testimony against L. could therefore not be justified. The evidence indicated that he had not been threatened, as he had said only that the interrogating agent had questioned him "energetically." There was otherwise no evidence proffered to suggest that any pressure was put on him, other than a reminder that was obliged to speak the truth as was his duty as a political leader. It was therefore determined that he had consciously and willingly offered to give his testimony against L. in view of his hostile attitude against him. Meanwhile, he was also aware and approved of the fact that L. would be subject to tyranny, rather than law and justice, at the hands of the People's Court, where according to L.'s defense lawyer, he did not express any interest in what could be presented as mitigating circumstances. He was therefore to be held at least responsible for the death sentence and execution, and was held accountable for crimes against humanity according to Article II, section 1c of Control Council Law No. 10.[373]

The verdict that had been pronounced against B. later came under review by the Highest Appeal Court of the British Zone on 6 June 1950. It was found that the facts of his hostile conduct did not comply with the provisions of Control Council Law No. 10, Article II, section 1c. The earlier judgment at the jury court presented the view that witnesses speaking the truth could be judged for their hostile conduct if their testimony was made with a hostile purpose in mind. This was inferred from B.'s attitude toward L. at the time, as a result of him having discovered his embezzlement and the misappropriation of merchandise that was difficult to procure at the time. However, it did not take into account that B. had been summoned as an "involuntary" witness by the Gestapo who had spoken the truth about what he had heard L. say to him.[374] Hence, the jury court did not demonstrate that B. had taken the initiative in delivering L. to the Gestapo, even though he was well aware of the consequences that his testimony would have.

While this appeal court acknowledged that the jury had emphatically emphasized that the defendant was partly responsible for the consequences of his actions, the means by which it arrived at its judgment would lead to unacceptable legal consequences. Control Council Law No. 10 Article II, section 1c required providing evidence on the motives as well as the *unsolicited* facts that were *voluntarily* given in a truthful statement by the defendant, or when the defendant *caused* the events under scrutiny. It was ruled that this was not ascertained in the jury court hearing.[375]

This court continued to reason that pronouncing a guilty verdict in this case would set a negative precedent in hearing cases involving the entering of evidence of hostile conduct. It was the duty of a summoned witness to provide truthful and complete testimony, regardless of whether they were drawing the attention of the investigating authority due to their hostile intentions, and whether they wanted or approved of the defendant's conviction. It would also entail verifying whether a witness could be considered hostile if they approved of the prosecution. A merely guilty way of thinking as their motive was inadmissible, since the court was required to support its verdict with external evidence. Prosecution for crimes against humanity would otherwise be extended to all those who were not conscious of offenses or made a contribution to persecution and did not talk about it, rather than taking the responsibility to testify against the incriminated. Meanwhile, it was for courts in the present as well as in the future cases to call on witnesses who could be considered sufficiently credible, while maintaining the objectivity of the facts of the case as a separate matter of consideration. What was of decisive importance was to determine whether the defendant had fulfilled his obligation as a witness, or whether he had also consciously and willingly demonstrated his hostile intentions by causing an offense to be brought about through a report or other means. In view of the facts of the case and what was considered to be the jury court's misinterpretation of B.'s hostile conduct in his capacity as a witness, he could not be convicted of having committed a crime against humanity, and was therefore acquitted.[376]

P. was acquitted in view of the fact that the charges that were leveled against her were proven unfounded due to the paucity of the available evidence that could be used to convict her. This case contributed to maintaining that those accused of making denunciations in the National Socialist regime were to be held accountable for this type of crime against humanity, and also demonstrated how the reconstituted post war German courts administered justice fairly and objectively in all of such cases, with any errors being re-evaluated at a higher instance appeal court. B. had been found guilty like others before and after him, having been judged to have acted against another as a result of their self-centered political differences that had prompted him to ensure that dire consequences would ensue as a result of indiscretions at a time when the rule of law had been negated. However, his later acquittal demonstrated how the law remained subject to objective interpretation for all who were brought before the courts, which took precedence over subjective considerations concerning the suspicion or even evidence of a defendant's motives. Concrete evidence of hostile conduct by taking the initiative in acting against another had to take precedence for such cases to be subject to prosecution.

The Highest Appeal Court of the British Zone, which had hitherto clarified contentious judicial issues, had made it clear in numerous judgments that retroactive application of the law did not contravene the principles of the rule of law. It also left no doubts about the criminal responsibility of informers as having perpetrated crimes against humanity, describing denunciation as an attack on victims that formed an integral part of National Socialist violence and tyranny. It was the view of this court that the perpetration of a crime against humanity through hostile conduct was always an injustice. This also applied to truthful reports of incidents since it served the purpose of maintaining the injustice of the regime,[377] which was maintained in several different verdicts pronounced by this court. Evidence presented in cases involving crimes against humanity necessitated that such cases be prosecuted in view of the circumstances in which they had taken place, in which victims were handed over to be prosecuted by a judicial organization that served the purpose of terrorizing the population into submission to the power of the state, and had cruel consequences for those who had been denounced.

Those who had denounced others were called to account for their actions in contributing to acts of inhumanity that had been committed in the name of National Socialist justice that served the purpose of upholding the regime, rather than the civilized norms of justice defined under international law. It was shown how such cases of indirect political persecution mostly arose out of personal considerations by those who exploited the political situation for selfish gain, and out of political conviction in some other cases. Underlying all of these cases in which the defendants were convicted was how they had inflicted suffering through causing unlawful imprisonment, and in many cases the deaths of those they had denounced, by having willingly exposed their victims to the tyranny of the National Socialist regime while having been aware of the consequences of their actions during this time.

The first such cases that were heard thereafter set the precedent for similar cases that were brought before the reconstituted German courts, subject to regulations that were imposed by the respective occupation power that granted German courts the jurisdiction to prosecute cases of crimes against humanity that were committed by Germans against Germans. These crimes were prosecuted whether they were committed directly or indirectly, as accomplices to crimes against humanity after the administration of justice had been restored. In order to bring perpetrators of National Socialist crimes to justice, unprecedented retroactive legislation was passed to serve this purpose under Control Council Law No. 10, which overrode prior sanctions against the legal principle of *nulla poene sine lege*, and reservations against it in German law.

Those who had assisted indirectly in the perpetration of the crimes committed were judged to be responsible for crimes against humanity and were judged accordingly under the provisions of Control Council Law No. 10 where legislation opened the way for their prosecution. These cases were heard in the restored courts in Berlin and the areas of the British, French, and Soviet occupation zones, where the occupation authorities empowered the German courts with jurisdiction over such cases. In spite of discussion about whether to try such cases in the US occupation zone, the US military government did not empower the German courts with adjudicating denunciation cases as a matter of administrative concern in the interest of caution about the possibility of opening a floodgate of litigation. This proved unfounded in comparison with the adjudication of these types of cases in the British and French occupation zones.

While there were successes in bringing indirect perpetrators of crimes against humanity to justice, there remained shortcomings in the broader context of this process. Many of the victims of the National Socialist regime did not file charges against informers, and therefore only a small proportion of them were in fact called to account for actions.[378] An inspection at the Düsseldorf regional court and public prosecutor's office there noted the difficulties with prosecuting cases of crimes against humanity due to a lack of sufficient evidence. A large number of the files had been destroyed by the Gestapo, and many witnesses either could not be found, or were not prepared to provide what could have been incriminating testimonies. On average, only ten indictments were initiated out of every hundred cases, and the numbers of acquittals were excessively high. According to the general public prosecutor, this was attributed to the judges who were not sufficiently stringent in their judgments.[379]

It remained for the German judiciary in the British and French occupation zones to apply the spirit and letter of Control Council Law No. 10 in view of the objective and subjective facts of these cases whenever the evidence was present. Those who had willingly denounced others and had been aware of the consequences of their actions were to be prosecuted and judged according to the conditions of the rule of law, which occupation law had begun to institute after the end of the National Socialist rule of tyranny. There were theoretical reservations among the judiciary about how the broadly defined range of crimes cited in Control Council Law No. 10 could be justifiably applied retroactively. The judiciary was to be reconciled with a new legal standard that was introduced in view of hitherto unprecedented circumstances to overcome the shortcomings in codified German law. The application of Control Council Law No. 10 made it possible to necessarily rectify the politically motivated injustices of the recent past while the provisions of German criminal law were insufficient for achieving the purpose of prosecuting crimes against humanity. The prosecution of cases of indirect political persecution through denunciations would continue after the end of the military occupation.

Chapter 5

Prosecution of Denunciation Cases in the Federal Republic of Germany

Denunciation cases continued to be prosecuted after the end of the military occupation following the establishment of the Federal Republic of Germany where there was evidence and a willingness to take these cases to trial. The creation of a West German state on 21 September 1949 led to legal developments in western Germany that included continuing to adjudicate crimes that were perpetrated during the National Socialist regime. Legal issues under the jurisdiction of the new Federal Republic of Germany were defined in the Occupation Statute. The Allied High Commission that had superseded the military government issued Law No. 13 of 25 November 1949 on "Judicial Powers in the Reserved Fields" withdrew the occupation powers' right to withdraw cases from the jurisdiction of the German courts that had been imposed under military government legislation enacted by the western occupation powers, and defined the new delineation between Allied and German judicial responsibilities.[1] Since the German courts in the American occupation zone were only granted jurisdiction in crimes against humanity and war crimes in individual cases, criminal prosecution in such cases were only possible under German criminal law.[2] Denunciation cases would therefore be sentenced according to the provisions of German criminal law.[3]

Allied legislation that had governed the application of Control Council Law No. 10 was abrogated through new legislation enacted by the Allied High Commission. These conditions went into force in the French occupation zone through Ordinance 171 of the French High Commission of 31 August 1951.[4] The German federal government had expressed the view for some time that the *obligation* for the German administration of justice to apply Control Council Law No. 10 ought to be eliminated, in order to establish a uniformity of jurisprudence in western Germany. Crimes against humanity would thereafter be judged according to the provisions found in German law.[5] The application of the German criminal code in proceedings against informers would be based on a consideration of the consequences of the act of denunciation, as cited in Article 239 of the criminal code concerning unlawful imprisonment and death related to murder.[6] The same conditions took effect in the British zone through Ordinance No. 234 of the British High Commission on 31 August 1951.[7]

German jurists were thereby alleviated of the burden of applying the law retroactively, and they would continue adjudicating National Socialist injustices in accordance with German criminal law. However, the number of prosecutions dropped rapidly, with prosecutors palpably diminishing their investigation proceedings[8] in such cases. These included the prosecution of denunciation cases that could only be adjudicated in accordance with German criminal law. If these cases had previously been adjudicated solely on the basis of Control Council Law No. 10, the judgment would have to have been quashed and re-examined for adjudication under German criminal law in accordance with § 264 of the code of criminal procedure.[9] In practice, the prosecution of these types of cases became much more narrowly limited than before, as it became more problematical to interpret cases of denunciation as crimes against humanity.[10] Fewer such cases were therefore prosecuted as a result of the inherent deficiencies in the law that made it more difficult to maintain the standards of justice in the much more widely encompassing concept of crimes against humanity in the provisions of Control Council Law No. 10.

There had already been difficulties with determining the appropriate sentencing in accordance with interpreting the broad provisions cited in Control Council Law No. 10, as had been stated in the Bückeburg regional court judgment of 24 June 1949, since the typical circumstances of a denunciation case did not conform to the norms of the German criminal code. Passing sentences in such cases thus became much more difficult after this law was abrogated.[11] Denunciation cases could only be subject to prosecution when it could be proven that an informer had been conscious of the serious consequences that would incur as a result of denunciation, such as imprisonment in a concentration camp or execution, and had acted with intent and premeditated approval.[12] This could serve to explain why the number of sentences passed in such cases on the specific basis of inhumane persecution, rather than the more narrowly defined terms of the criminal code, exceeded the number of sentences that were imposed after September 1951. Although increasingly greater numbers of jurists overcame their reservations about applying the law retroactively,[13] other circumstances undermined interest in prosecuting such cases.

The inconsequential denazification program and the increasingly reduced political influence from the western occupation powers had a negative impact on the earlier and later efforts to deal with the politically motivated injustices of the past. The legal division of the British military government had expressed concern in late 1948 that the goal of re-establishing a sound and independent judiciary in the British occupation zone appeared to have become discredited by what they considered to be a "renazification" of the judiciary and the administration of justice. This was due to the increasingly lax denazification standards that were being applied by the denazification panels, and included passing excessively liberal sentences on former judges and prosecutors who served in the Special Courts and who had been known to be staunch supporters of the National Socialist regime. They no longer applied the original spirit of the earlier denazification legislation, and the military government's power to dismiss unacceptable personnel would no be longer be possible after the promulgation of the Occupation Statute. It thus appeared that the previous political cleansing of the administration of justice in the British occupation zone became nullified[14] as a result of the declining denazification standards.

Soon after the Federal Republic of Germany was established, the French military government reported an example of this trend in the Rhineland-Palatinate. Although judicial reform was considered satisfactory, two Ministry of Justice officials who were known for their nationalist sentiments disposed of or discriminated against jurists who had been favored by the military government, and tried to replace them with former National Socialists whom the military government had dismissed, including those who had been Special Court prosecutors and had been interned for this reason in 1945 and 1946.[15]

The adjudication of crimes against humanity continued to be undertaken after the abrogation of Control Council Law No. 10, but the consensus among jurists that denunciation cases ought to be prosecuted had begun to weaken in 1948 and 1949. The occupation powers themselves placed less and less emphasis on the prosecution of National Socialist crimes, and entrusted the German administration of justice to deal with such proceedings after having seen that the initial resistance against doing so had greatly declined. Meanwhile, both the occupation powers and the German public had considerably lost interest in executing the denazification program due to the weaknesses of its implementation. There was also a renewed focus on the new priorities of addressing the necessities of the reconstruction and restoring the economy in view of the advent of the Cold War, as well as a diminished interest among the German population to address the National Socialist past.[16]

The earlier consensus at the highest levels of judicial authority that prosecuting denunciation cases corresponded to restoring the rule of law had weakened by 1949, which was characterized by an increasing hesitation to prosecute such cases.[17] This conservative tendency resulted in a decline of cases sparing many informers from being charged in many cases. Unless a denunciation case had led to an intervention from the Gestapo or the public prosecutor, or the consequences were relatively slight, the defendants were often not convicted.[18] In some cases in 1948 and 1949, courts implemented a positivist interpretation by which lawful conduct during the National Socialist regime was hardly considered to be punishable, in contrast to the spirit of Control Council Law No. 10 that called for the National Socialist law to be considered invalid, since it contradicted the basic principles of the law.[19] The scope of this law had allowed for a wide-ranging interpretation on the grounds of the concept of persecution of those who were reported to the authorities, subject to the perpetrator's consciousness and even approval of the potential consequences of their actions. This was in contrast to the scope of the German criminal code, by which judgments were governed by the provisions cited for unlawful imprisonment, and aiding and abetting manslaughter or murder. As a result, informers who were guilty of crimes against humanity under Control Council Law No. 10 could no longer be convicted under the provisions of German law.[20]

In contrast to the heavy sentence that had been imposed on Helene Schwärzel for her role in the apprehension of Karl Goerdeler, two paymasters who were involved in this case were not prosecuted for their involvement. Proceedings begun against them in the Lübeck regional court ended in their acquittal on 20 March 1948. The public prosecutor instituted an appeal against this verdict to the Highest Appeal Court of the British Zone, which quashed this judgment on 5 December 1949 and reverted the case back to a jury court for review at the Lübeck regional court.[21]

The two defendants had arrested Dr. Görderler at the incitement of Helene Schwärzel in Konradswalde on 12 August 1944, and had handed him over to the criminal police in Marienweder; he was later tried by the People' Court and then executed on 2 February 1945. According to the interpretation of the Lübeck regional court, the defendants had carried out the external but not the internal facts of the case as defined in Article II, section 1c of Control Council Law No. 10, which diverged from the interpretations made by the Highest Appeal Court and was not sufficiently substantiated to allow for an alternative judgment. This court had neglected to recognize that the facts in a case of crimes against humanity demonstrated that a perpetrator had consciously intended to inflict injury on the human rights of another by exposing them to National Socialist violence and tyranny through their hostile conduct. The external circumstances of arresting Gördeler and handing him over to the police constituted hostile conduct as political persecution, given the circumstances of how the National Socialist regime dealt with its political enemies with indiscriminate violence and tyranny. Considering that the victim in this case was exposed to inhumane political persecution, the external facts of the case fulfilled the requirements as defined by Control Council Law No. 10. The Lübeck regional court had not taken Article II, section 1c of this law and the conduct of the defendant into sufficient consideration in its interpretation of the subjective facts of the case. In addition, the death sentence was an especially severe sanction that was intolerably disproportionate to the alleged guilt of the victim in relation to a regime under the rule of law.[22]

The internal facts of the case as demonstrated by Gördeler's arrest and the handing of him over to the police also constituted a conscious intent of hostile conduct. The defendants had known about and approved of the consequences of their actions, which they also had known would lead to severe consequences for the victim of these actions, regardless of whether they could anticipate the details of what would take place and whether they considered their conduct to be lawful. They were therefore to take responsibility for their actions while being able to recognize the injustice of the unjustifiable consequences they would bring about.[23] They also could not claim in their defense that they had acted out of a sense of duty to take action against Gördeler lest they themselves face the consequences of National Socialist tyranny. They did not have any legal obligation to arrest him, and they could not claim that they had acted out of urgent necessity in order to avoid exposing themselves to danger to ensure their personal safety.[24] Their claim that they were under pressure to arrest him and turn him over to the police therefore could not be taken into consideration as a mitigating factor.

The re-opened proceedings at the Lübeck regional court were stayed on 24 December 1951. A judgment on the grounds of a crime against humanity could no longer be applied, since Ordinance No. 234 of the British High Commissioner of 31 August 1951 abrogated Control Council Law No. 10 and its implementation through Military Government Ordinance No. 47. The actions they had perpetrated were not crimes under the jurisdiction of German law, as defined under Article 206a of the code of criminal procedure.[25]

The limitations of interpreting German criminal law in denunciation cases were further constrained by new interpretations concerning mitigating circumstances in favor of the defendant. Many courts perceived the subjective facts of a case to have been fulfilled according to the intention of the perpetrator having consciously accepted and approved the consequences of their actions. On the other hand, this did not entail the perpetrators being aware of the unlawfulness of their actions, which was considered a separate element in the judgment. This was an interpretation that was later adopted by the Federal Supreme Court. Hence, some jurists would not pass sentences on those who had been motivated by an excessive sense of duty, rather than self-centered motives.[26] Hence, cases that resulted in serious consequences for the victims of denunciations were judged as crimes against humanity, while other denunciation cases may not have been judged with sufficient severity since the perpetrators lacked the sufficient sophistication in being conscious of the difference between law and justice. The spirit of Control Council Law No. 10 had also allowed for a much wider interpretation than the letter of the provisions of the German criminal code, which also contributed to the weakening of the effort to adjudicate denunciation cases.[27]

The public prosecutor's office in Detmold that was responsible for the Lippe region exemplified how informers were not prosecuted to the full spirit of Control Council Law No. 10 as defined by Article II, section 1c. Forty-seven cases of denunciation involving twenty-six individuals were investigated as crimes against humanity, but investigation proceedings were only initiated against one case in 1945, two in 1946, twenty-eight in 1947, two in 1948 and 1949, and one in 1950. These were initiated in response to individuals coming forward to file reports about National Socialist crimes with the police authorities following an announcement in the local press and an official announcement posted on a sign at the local city hall. Thirty-five of these were forwarded from the police to the public prosecutor. Investigation proceedings were stayed in thirty-two of these cases. Two of the cases were forwarded to the Berlin regional court,[28] while the Detmold regional court instituted an indictment against denunciation as a crime against humanity as defined by Control Council Law No. 10 in only one case on 8 April 1949.[29]

The defendant had reported an acquaintance to the NSDAP *Ortsgruppe* of South Detmold because she had expressed great satisfaction about the assassination attempt on Hitler on 20 July 1944 and regretted that it had failed. The report was conveyed from the local *Kreisleiter* to the Gestapo and then arrived at the People's Court. Having doubts about what she had initiated, she tried to call off the proceedings by contacting the *Kreisleiter,* and after being unable to do so, wrote a letter to the People's Court to try to avert the proceedings or at least mitigate the sentencing, claiming that she had intended for her report to lead to a reprimand, rather than such drastic consequences. The victim of this denunciation was freed from a "murderous imprisonment" due to the advance of American troops on 4 April 1945, and she filed charges against the defendant in 1946. The defendant was charged with crimes against humanity as defined by Article II, section 1c of Control Council Law No. 10, but these proceedings were stayed on 30 June 1947. A new indictment was filed on 6 April 1948, which led to the new proceedings also being stayed on 21 July 1948. A new appeal was filed on 7 August 1948, and led to the proceedings being re-opened on 8 April 1949 prior to the main proceedings at the jury court of the Detmold regional court on 10 and 11 October 1949, which again led to an acquittal. The public prosecutor eventually abandoned further attempts at appeal after this case was reviewed at the Highest Appeal Court of the British Zone, and was reverted to the Duisburg regional court for revision. This case was conclusively stayed on 17 February 1950 on the grounds of the Immunity from Prosecution Law of 31 December 1949,[30] by which crimes that included those that were perpetrated before 15 September 1949 were to be stayed if the sentencing was not more than six months' imprisonment.[31]

This law concerned a matter of political policy[32] that superseded judicial considerations. The newly-established Federal Government of Germany had justified the drafting of this law as a means of breaking with the past and marking the beginning of a new phase in the development of the state. Its purpose was to implement legislation to conclude years of hardship during which there had been customary judgments and confusion of legal concepts, and thereby forfeit the opportunity to bring to trial the lesser offenses and injustices that had been perpetrated. This specifically concerned criminal offenses of an economic nature that had been perpetrated and prosecuted for years, specifically criminal offenses which would not have taken place under normal economic circumstances. Passing an amnesty would be the simplest possible solution in representing the interests of those who were involved in such relatively insignificant offenses and misdemeanors, and would simplify matters for the administration of justice.[33] This law in its enacted form did not specify that this amnesty only applied to crimes and misdemeanors with economic motives. While this law was intended to serve as an amnesty for black market delinquents and petty criminals during the immediate post-war years, its provisions would also exempt perpetrators who had committed offenses during the National Socialist regime.[34] These offenses included crimes against humanity, which became obscured through the increased prevailing unwillingness at this time in German society to face up to and deal with the National Socialist past.[35] It also had the effect of reducing the number of convictions for denunciation cases.[36]

The acquittal pronounced at the Detmold regional court was met with a public outcry. This was a justified response to such a strict application of the letter of the law that led to such excessive leniency, which ensued from the argument that the defendant allegedly could have foreseen the consequences of her actions. The judgment stated that the objective facts of the case were fulfilled in the sense that the defendant had reported another to an NSDAP authority on political grounds. From a subjective point of view however, the defendant had intended to warn the victim of the consequences of her actions, and therefore thought she could avert the course of events that had taken place. In order for her to be convicted, it had to be proven that she had intended for the potential consequences to occur and thought they were possible. In the view of this court, this could not be determined with absolute certainty.[37] This proved to be a very narrow interpretation that did not take the circumstances of the time into consideration, considering that the consequences of such statements and the National Socialist regime's methods of suppression had been commonly known to the population at that time and were publicized in the press.[38]

An analysis of the thirty-three cases that were stayed in the Detmold public prosecutor's jurisdiction demonstrated there were two types of cases. In eighteen cases, numerous files, especially those concerning the Special Courts, had been destroyed, and therefore the necessary sufficient amount of evidence to institute proceedings was lacking. In the remaining fifteen cases, the court did not consider the evidence to qualify for prosecution as a crime against humanity on the basis of Control Council Law No. 10. It was argued in six of these cases that denunciation could only be prosecuted if it had been undertaken for personal gain or advantage in cooperation with the Gestapo or a similar organization.[39]

The public prosecutor argued that a denunciation case could be prosecuted as a crime against humanity if a report had been made with a reproachable and malicious disposition emanating from either hatred or revenge. Two proceedings against denunciation cases were stayed on this justification due to an insufficient certainty about these preconditions. In one of these cases, someone was denounced by a business partner for criticizing the regime after having threatened to report them for fraud. The Hannover Special Court sentenced them to four years' imprisonment in 1941 as a result of this denunciation. In the other case, a *Kreis* inspector reported a subordinate in 1942 for making disparaging remarks about the regime in 1942, and the subordinate was consequently sentenced by the same Special Court to a year and three months' imprisonment. He claimed in his defense that his intention was to have his subordinate transferred to another department, rather than denounce him because of his way of thinking.[40]

Other investigation proceedings were stayed since it was the view of the court that an accused could only be prosecuted according to Control Council Law No. 10 as perpetrating a crime against humanity through reporting another. However, the public prosecutor also stayed proceedings in such cases when it was concluded that they could only be tried as crimes against humanity if those who were denounced were treated inhumanely. Hence, those who reported them could not be prosecuted for causing consequences for others that were not especially severe. In one such case, a so-called half-Jew was reported for having a relationship with an "Aryan," and was forced to end this relationship or else face arrest and imprisonment in a concentration camp. In another case, the Gestapo had confiscated a radio and had forbidden its owner to listen to any broadcasts.[41] Hence, not all proceedings that were stayed were done so for unreasonable causes. Such minor cases also could have been the cause for concern about the possibility of a floodgate of litigation regarding denunciation cases. It remained the responsibility of regional state prosecutors and the courts to establish justifiable reasons for putting legislation into practice with the purpose of serving justice as well as the law when it could be reasoned that the perpetrators had inflicted severe disadvantages onto others.

There were other such regional differences in the adjudication of National Socialist crimes in the regional court districts of Schleswig-Holstein, consisting of Kiel, Flensburg, Lübeck, and Itzehoe. Proceedings were initiated by the public prosecutor against 239 cases of denunciation in this state between 1945 and January 1965 out of 384 suspected cases, of which 45 were heard in court proceedings.[42] Fifty-four of these cases were dismissed as a result of the 1949 Immunity from Prosecution Law.[43] In one such case at the Izehoe regional court, an accused who had denounced another for making defeatist remarks or remarks that were allegedly hostile to the regime was amnestied as a result of a sentence of less than six months since the victim had "merely" been taken into custody,[44] which was not interpreted as a crime against humanity. Another 326 other cases were dismissed due to lack of evidence.[45] Many proceedings in various types of crimes were stayed due to a lack of evidence, outright acquittals, dismissal of cases before they went to court, or were cases belonging to other regions of jurisdiction. Others were stayed because the alleged perpetrators were unknown to the investigating authorities or the public prosecutors, or because the defendant was deceased.[46] The numbers of cases in which court proceedings were initiated for various types of crimes against humanity were in sharp contrast to each other concerning denunciation cases in the four regional court districts: 1 at the Kiel regional court; 5 at the Itzehoe regional court; 117 at the Flensburg regional court; and 116 at the Lübeck regional court.[47] The extent of the sentences that were passed also varied between these courts.[48] These differences in the results of prosecuting cases of denunciation as well as other types of crimes against humanity in the different jurisdictions could have been caused by the subjective decision making of various judges and public prosecutors. There was also the possibility of being influenced by their own involvement in the National Socialist regime, which could have resulted in them passing lenient sentences or even dismissing a case altogether in their capacity as judges or public prosecutors,[49] thus protecting themselves from discussions about the role they had themselves played in the regime.[50] The lack of uniformity could also be attributed to a lack of consensus and a lack of an exchange of information between the different public prosecutors that could have led to judgments according to different standards, as well as a hesitation among jurists to apply Control Council Law No. 10.[51]

Another example at the Osnabrück regional court demonstrated the reduced interest in the prosecution of denunciation cases. Thirty-eight out of forty-three cases of crimes against humanity concerning denunciations, mostly heard between 1948 and 1951, were stayed. Seven of the cases were heard in court proceedings, of which two were stayed and four others resulted in acquittals. Only one case in September 1949 resulted in a sentence of two months' imprisonment, which was later overruled by the Highest Appeal Court of the British Occupation Zone in January 1950 on the basis of the amnesty for lesser offenders promulgated on 31 December 1949 that granted them immunity from prosecution. The defendant of this case heard at the Osnabrück regional court was given a light sentence since the victim of his report was "merely" sentenced to three months' imprisonment by the central military court. The standards for judgments in denunciation cases had changed toward becoming more and more ambivalent than had previously been the case.[52]

In contrast to judgments in earlier cases in which the act of denunciation itself was subject to prosecution as an indication of premeditated intention, judgments in later cases took the consequences of denunciations into greater consideration. In some cases, the informers' motives were considered as having acting on what they had perceived to be their duty. This was accepted as a mitigating circumstance.[53] Regardless of possible deficiencies in calling every guilty party to account for their actions, informers were prosecuted in spite of the considerable reservations among German jurists to apply Control Council Law No. 10.[54] The effort to call them to adjudicate these cases was reduced after 1 September 1951 due to the limitations in applying German criminal law.

Judgments became less subjective than before in favor of the defendant, which served to justify sentences becoming less severe than they had been before 1949. A comparison of the prosecution of denunciation cases by the German courts after 1 September 1951 indicated that the extent of the sentencing had changed. The prison sentences that were imposed in accordance with Control Council Law No. 10 in cases of denunciations had been relatively high in certain cases, including life imprisonment and two sentences of fifteen years' imprisonment, while most of the sentences that were passed in accordance with the German criminal code mostly ranged from eight months to two years. Both before and after 1 September 1951, the heaviest sentences were imposed on defendants who were directly employed by the Gestapo or whose reports led to proceedings before the People's Court.[55]

One of the first denunciation cases to be heard in the Federal Republic of Germany was at the Hamburg regional court, where judgment was pronounced on 28 August 1950.[56] The two accused, hereafter cited as S. and von W, were called to account for having caused the arrest of a schoolteacher hereafter cited as Yvonne M. by the Gestapo and her internment in a concentration camp where she later perished. They were thereby charged with a crime against humanity, unlawful imprisonment, and having caused death by negligence. Von W. was also accused of committing the same crimes against another hereafter cited as Ho., having reported him to the Gestapo for making defeatist remarks; Ho. later died while in their custody.[57]

The two accused had been colleagues in the Hamburg school administration after life in that city had been shattered by the bombing attack in July 1943. The governor of Hamburg at the time called on S. to reorganize the school administration there as its administrative superior.[58] Von W. later assumed the position of legal advisor to S.[59] Both of them were charged with a considerable amount of organizational tasks in the school administration after they took office. In addition to directing and supervising minor administrative matters, von W. was also responsible for matters concerning personnel, as well as being the director of the legal division, which also involved handling disciplinary measures involving school supervisors and teachers who did not comply with special requests.[60] The execution of his responsibilities in this latter task led to grave consequences for a teacher who had proven to be excessively stubborn in asserting her personal and professional interests. Von W. resorted to abusing the authorities of the time that resulted in those consequences, and S. gave him a free hand without giving sufficient consideration to the implications thereof.

Yvonne M. had been employed as a teacher in Hamburg from 1 April 1938 until the bombing attack of July 1943. Her first disagreement with the Hamburg school administration was in 1942, when she refused to work in a KLV (*Kinderlandsverschickung*) camp, which she considered to be related to the National Socialist regime, to which she remained continually opposed. After she lost her apartment and belongings in the July 1943 bombing, she left Hamburg and moved to Passau, where she began working at a secondary school on 4 September 1943. She did so even though teachers in Hamburg had been previously instructed in writing that they were not allowed to find new positions elsewhere, and she had been informed by telegram on 22 August 1943 that she was to begin work immediately for the Hamburg school administration in a KLV in Austrian Bavaria (*Bayerischen Ostmark*). She replied the next day, saying that she absolutely refused to comply with this demand, as she had done earlier, and preferred to be dismissed from the school. While planning for a leave of absence from the Hamburg school administration, she also refused to comply with the written demands that were sent to her on 7 September and 5 November 1943 to return to Hamburg. Her income was halted, and von W. ordered the Bavarian Culture Ministry to dismiss her from the Bavarian school administration. This was followed by a long exchange of correspondence that ended with an ultimatum demanding that she return to her position by 20 January 1944. An added inducement was later made on 25 May 1944, by which the governor imposed a 200 RM fine for her being away from her position.[61]

She claimed that she had applied for dismissal or being granted leave from the Hamburg school administration before she began working in Passau, but had not received a reply. She also claimed knowledge that most of the teachers in Hamburg had been ordered to leave or were granted leave to work outside the school system, and that many other teachers were granted leave to work outside Hamburg. She was therefore under the impression that those who had lost everything in the bombing were allowed to take up work elsewhere, as she had done in Passau, where she also found new accommodation, and therefore claimed she was treated unfairly for not having her circumstances taken into account. The governor's administration's personnel office considered her objections unfounded in their reply on 25 September 1944.[62]

Rather than returning to Hamburg after leaving her position in Passau, she moved to Wittstock an der Dosse where she began work at another school on 1 February 1944, and faced more unsatisfactory conditions that took the form of a so-called open KLV camp. In this camp, the pupils and teachers were accommodated privately, and teachers were obliged to spend time with the pupils outside the classroom. She did not feel at home in her accommodation there, where she considered the monotonous landscape to be unpleasant and did not have any contact with the other teachers who were also the landlords. There was also a shortage of teaching materials and schoolbooks, and teachers needed to spend their free time with students. Shortly before the beginning of the summer of 1944, she considered not returning to teaching work after the summer holidays and leaving Wittstock, since there was an insufficient amount of necessary books for basic preparation, and felt that the work there was also not sufficiently intellectually challenging.[63]

During the summer holidays, M. wrote her resignation notice to the Hamburg school administration on 15 July 1944, stating it was impossible for her to reconcile her conscience with the teaching work without the necessary books and her own home, and remained unable to cope with KLV requirements. Meanwhile, she also expected to face a serious confrontation with the authorities as well as a difficult future for not conforming to their demands. Refusing to listen to any admonitions to be reasonable from relatives and acquaintances, she chose not to return to her teaching position in Wittstock after the summer holidays, saying it went against her conscience.[64]

She received a written notice from the school administration that was signed by von W. on 26 July 1944, stating that her notice was inadmissible, as she did not have sufficient justification to leave her position during this time of urgent need for staff for the school service. It was also brought to her attention at the same time that her refusal to go back to work could not only result in disciplinary measures, but also criminal court proceedings and police sanctions if she did not return to her position in Wittstock by 1 August 1944. Von W. wrote a subsequent letter on 27 July 1944 threatening her with all possible official disciplinary and police sanctions in response to this new undisciplined refusal to fulfill her duties. He also wrote to a member of the city council on the same day to order preliminary measures of suspending her income and examining the possibility of further criminal court proceedings to be initiated against her with regard to this breach of work contract.[65]

M. met with a school supervisor and von W. on 1 August 1944, and maintained at this time that she had intended to leave the school service for the last six months, saying that she could not work under the present circumstances. The necessary books were not available in Wittstock, she did not feel at home there, and did not have enough contact with other people, and added that she could not tolerate the landscape there. She therefore accepted the possibility of facing disciplinary measures as well as criminal court sanctions if she did not return to work for the school service.[66]

Von W. did not consider these to be valid reasons, but instead merely excuses for not returning to her teaching position. He tried to explain to her that it was not always possible for someone like her to leave the civil service during wartime, especially since she was legally bound to her duty as a civil servant and to her humane duty as a teacher to fulfill her duty. He also said that the KLV was an especially responsible organization affecting the interests of the natural welfare of children, and the catastrophic personnel situation could hardly be overcome through the increasing demands on the KLV, and that every resource was required from capable individuals. Her refusal to work therefore put him in a very awkward position of having to institute disciplinary measures. He then calmly implored her to return to work, threatening her to be imprisoned for a day to think about this matter. If she continued to refuse, she would have to be prepared to go into a concentration camp, which would be worse than doing her work in Wittstock. At the end of this conversation, he gave her until 3 August 1944 to go back to work. Nevertheless, she informed him in writing that she maintained her refusal.[67]

Before taking any further action, von W. made enquiries with the general state prosecutor and with the representative of national work trustee about the possibility of initiating some sort of intervention. The general state prosecutor replied in writing on 4 August 1944, stating that the first report about so-called idlers not going to work, or of employees in private enterprises and the public service workers who were accused of breaching a work contract, would lead to them paying fines or facing imprisonment in some cases. In cases of repeated offenses, the reported individual would be taken to a work education camp supervised by the Gestapo for three to eight weeks. In cases of repeated or serious offenses, the employment authority could initiate criminal court proceedings, which could usually result in prison sentences of three to four months. The work authority preferred to send the offending individual to a work education camp, since they could only be spared from their normal employment for a short time, and these measures would not be cited in the criminal register. Whether they would be imprisoned in a work education camp or a concentration camp also depended on what the work authority considered to be the simplest solution for accommodation and cost for hard labor. In fact, a witness at the present proceedings cited as He. who was the director for dealing with violations of work contracts from 1940 to 1945 did not know of any instances in which anyone had spent a maximum of eight weeks in custody.[68]

Von W. took action against M. by drafting a report to the governor concerning taking official disciplinary measures, to which S. gave his approval by signing it on 4 August 1944. The school administration recommended dismissing M. from the civil service immediately, and stopping her salary from 23 July 1944, as a result of her groundless and completely unjustifiable refusal to work. They also recommended imposing sanctions on her for having set a negative precedent for other civil servants to leave their positions. While employees in private enterprises and the public service were subject to fines and even imprisonment in some cases of violating their work contracts, this was not applicable to civil servants. However, this was considered a legal situation in view of a sense of justice, whereby civil servants were immune from having sanctions imposed on them for not having fulfilled their oath of office and their duty. They therefore petitioned that the governor institute criminal law proceedings in view of this situation, as well as in accordance with healthy popular emotions.[69]

A preliminary enquiry with the general state prosecutor revealed that he would be prepared to raise an indictment. In order to prevent M. from being completely unpunished on legal grounds in the event that an indictment would be quashed by a court, the school administration requested the district 1 of the NSDAP for M. to be ordered to take part in clearing air raid damage. If she refused to comply, as was to be expected, the school administration recommended that she appear before a court. If she complied with this demand and a sanction on the basis of Article 330c of the criminal code on failure to render assistance, as was recommended by the general state prosecutor, was not possible, the school administration petitioned that she be taken into police custody and then to a concentration camp. It was also added that her personnel file mentioned her inclination toward insubordination and of being the prototype of an individualist, which ran counter to the necessary demands of the community, and that she had not joined the NSDAP.[70]

Von W. had meanwhile arranged through the employment office for M. to work in a clothing mending facility of a district women's association, which she accepted, and she was also happy to help those who were affected by the war. Before the governor made a decision about the report of 4 August 1944, the director of his main office spoke to von W. on the phone about the school administration's recommendations. During this conversation, von W. clarified that rather than recommending that M. be taken into police custody and taken into a concentration camp, he intended for her to spend a short time, possibly four weeks, in a work education camp, and also hoped that this potential measure should be brought to her attention. The governor then made his decision about this report on 17 August, which the personnel office of the central administration sent to the school administration on 22 August, and was received by S. on the following day. It was decided that M.'s status as a civil servant was hereby revoked, and her income was suspended from 23 July 1944. This matter was hereby to be forwarded to the Gestapo for some possible intervention if it would be deemed necessary after examining her file. M. would also be informed, and was officially dismissed from the civil service on 31 August 1944.[71]

The school administration conveyed the matter to the Gestapo on 29 August, handing them a copy of the report of 4 August and the letter of 22 August from the main administration. A short description of the matter was also added, which was signed by S., reiterating a summary of the school administration's earlier recommendations with the recommendation that M. ought to be prosecuted. A criminal assistant of the Gestapo questioned M. about this matter on 7 September 1944, and was taken to the prison in Fuhlsbüttel. She was questioned again by the same official on 4 October 1944 in the presence of Gestapo officials. On both occasions, she admitted to having refused to work for the school administration, and after prior consideration preferred to face sanction rather than return to work in the KLV organization. The Gestapo then sent her file to the state prosecutor on 6 October 1944[72] while she remained imprisoned.

The magistrate who studied the file came to the conclusion that keeping her in custody was not justifiable due to the fact that no criminal act had been committed. Nevertheless, he arranged for the public prosecutor to apply for an arrest order in order to forestall returning the matter to the Gestapo if possible, and to clarify whether there was the possibility of court-imposed sanctions in the criminal code for breach of work contract. Both she and a county court judge assigned to the public prosecutor's office hoped that it would be possible to persuade the Gestapo to allow this matter to be adjudicated in a court, and spare M. from facing further Gestapo intervention. The magistrate questioned M. on 11 October 1944 and had her released on 18 October 1944 since he did not see any possibility of initiating court proceedings in this matter through the employment office, which could not claim jurisdiction in this matter. Besides, he also considered her dismissal from the public service and four weeks' of imprisonment to have been sufficient punishment, and that further prosecution was not in the public interest. The general state prosecutor sent the file back to the school administration, stating that further measures would not be undertaken.[73]

The school administration then returned the file to the general state prosecutor, along with a letter signed by von W. on 27 October 1944, which gave his view that it was hardly possible for court proceedings to be initiated, and further measures were not worthwhile, given the length of time that M. had spent in custody. However, it was also requested that the public prosecutor should advise M. that although she was not prosecuted, this case was not be allowed to give a false impression to teachers that she had been released from custody as if she were innocent. If such an explanation were not given to her, the school administration requested that M. ought to be handed back to the Gestapo so that she could face about another month of imprisonment with punitive work. She was not instructed in this manner. File memorandums at the public prosecutor's office on 6 and 7 November 1944 indicated that M. was arrested by the Gestapo and returned to Fuhlsbüttel prison, and was not to be released. Proceedings were hereafter initiated by the general state prosecutor on 30 November 1944.[74]

At about the same time, von W. phoned the Gestapo to request that she be released from custody. After this request went unheeded, he arranged for S. to file a complaint with the governor. S. received the governor's verbal approval to secure her release thereafter. However, the Gestapo could not accept a verbal rather than a written message. S. then went to the governor as von W. recommended, to get from him in writing a request that the Gestapo release M. The governor then drafted a message for this purpose, which was sent by his main office on 15 December 1944. Meanwhile, the Gestapo questioned M. again at around the same time, when she was told she would be taken to Ravensbrück concentration camp. She arrived there in late December 1944, where she very soon became afflicted with severe enteritis, and died there on 6 January 1945.[75]

Von W. claimed that he had intended to persuade the governor to have M. taken to a concentration camp in the event that criminal court sanctions could not be imposed as a possible punishment for her stubborn refusal to work. His decision to take this potential course of action was confirmed by how he had received a reply to his query in early 1944 to a representative of the national education ministry, who had told him that such refusals to comply with disciplinary measures could be dealt with by the Gestapo.[76] There remained the question whether he had intended to bring about severe consequences for M.

The court found that it could not be established that von W. had persecuted M. on political grounds, since it could not be proven that he intended for her to be imprisoned in a concentration camp for an indefinite length of time. It could not be concluded that M.'s opposition to work for the KLV was an indication of her political opposition to National Socialism, or that she was expelled from the school service for this reason. Von W. thus could hardly be accused with political persecution on this basis since there were a number of reasons for her conduct while he demanded that she fulfill her duties as a civil servant. Different witnesses testified how M. had not been interested in party politics, although it was evident that she was against the NSDAP. Regardless of her political dispositions, she had repeatedly stressed the same reasons for being unable to fulfill her teaching duties as she saw fit with an uncompromising attitude, which could not be judged as political grounds for her conduct.[77]

The public prosecutor argued that the letter of 4 August 1944 constituted political persecution, given the wording found therein, including emphasizing a civil servant's oath and obligation to the *Führer,* and that criminal proceedings ought to be initiated for her refusal to fulfill her duties. The jury court interpreted these facts differently. A civil servant's required devotion to their duty related to how official civil service at the time required that references be included to the demands of the Four Year Plan. Meanwhile, M. was obliged to fulfill her duties to the state as a civil servant and was bound by oath to do so as well. The wording in this letter was thus the standard that von W. was obliged to use in those circumstances. Hence, it could not be concluded that this wording indicated political motives in his intentions to report her to higher authorities, especially since it was applied in a completely professional connection.[78] The court also found that rather than reporting the matter directly to the Gestapo from the outset, he intended to bring about court imposed sanctions against M. as a last resort in accordance with the provisions of the criminal code, without attaching political importance to this matter. The letter that was sent to the governor for his decision in this matter was taken into consideration, and it could not be proven that he thought that this would later eventually lead to police persecution. This countered von W.'s claim that he intended for her to be temporarily interned in a work education camp for two or three months, rather than be put into political custody in a concentration camp for an indefinite amount of time. However, this did not appear in the ensuing correspondence between the school administration and other authorities, including the Gestapo, the governor, the main administration, and the public prosecutor. Nevertheless, there remained a great degree of probability that this testimony could not be disputed in view of other evidence.[79]

The public prosecutor had argued that the greatest indication that von W. had acted out of political motives was his request that M. be taken into police custody and taken to a concentration camp. However, it was found upon scrutinizing the past events that the recommended extent of the disciplinary measures due to her stubborn insubordination for several months was very lenient, in view of how the school administration was facing a very difficult situation for months after August 1943. She had been made aware of the application of measures of compulsion in response to her refusing to return to her duties in the letter of 26 July 1944, and had been reminded about her duties again on 1 August 1944, and had been given a few days to think about it. The letter of 4 August 1944 to the governor recommending criminal court sanctions and police custody if necessary was written after other possibilities for disciplinary measures had gradually been exhausted, or were no longer appropriate after she had been dismissed from the civil service.[80] There was also the possibility that the term "work education camp" may have been misinterpreted at the time with the phrase "concentration camp," while he had recommended that M. ought to be imprisoned for a short and limited amount of time. The fact that he had tried to secure her release from custody was also taken into consideration as evidence that he had not intended for her to be taken to a regular concentration camp. It was therefore surmised that he could not have foreseen the consequences that later transpired.[81]

S. claimed the same facts in his defense as von W., also saying that he did not intend for M. to be handed over to the Gestapo. He had only been involved in this matter after von W. had brought it to his attention, and did not give it any consideration other than confirming von W.'s decisions. In view of the psychological circumstances of being excessively overworked while being undernourished, of air raid alerts and the dangers associated with them, and of having to be in a constant state of readiness while being faced with immediately having to deal with the problems resulting from bombing damages affecting the school administration, there was a certain degree of probability that S. was prevented from giving this case sufficient consideration. There was therefore a considerable degree of probability that he had not known that he had signed a report denouncing M. to the Gestapo. The instances in which he had energetically intervened with great courage in many cases in protecting others persecuted by the Gestapo, including two cases of individuals who were held in their custody, were also taken into consideration as decisive mitigating factors. He was thereby acquitted.[82]

The conduct of both accused fulfilled the external circumstances of having officially caused unlawful imprisonment, as defined in §§ 239 and 341 of the criminal code. The letter of 4 August 1944 to the governor prepared for M.'s arrest, and was further brought about by the letter of 29 August to the Gestapo. She was later arrested as a result of these letters, which von W. had drafted and S. had approved, and later perished while imprisoned due to the highly unsatisfactory health conditions therein.[83] Her imprisonment and the conduct of the defendants were unlawful, since her actions were not subject to prosecution according to existing law and therefore could not be justified.[84]

Von W.'s conduct was nevertheless found to have resulted from extra-legal necessity, and was therefore justifiable. The legal justification for this conduct was justified whenever duties that were imposed or recognized by the law were contravened in the interest of being compelled to serve higher values that necessarily injured lower values. M. could have fulfilled the duties toward the education and welfare of children that had been expected of her, especially during wartime conditions, and therefore deserved punishment. Hence, von W.'s demand for a court to impose sanctions against M., or when this measure was not feasible due to a gap in the law that did not apply to civil servants, and that she ought to be taken into custody in a work education camp with the agreement of the governor.[85] Meanwhile, von W. had not expected that there would be a risk to M.'s life and limb while she was in custody in a work education camp, and therefore the intention of causing bodily injury or death could not be established, nor could it be established that he had known that she would not be released after a limited period of time[86] as he had recommended. He had believed that this would be a reasonable punishment for her neglecting to fulfill her duties, although the law did not sanction this course of action in normal circumstances.

Both defendants were acquitted on the indictment of having caused unlawful imprisonment due to their having acted out of extra-legal necessity, while not having been conscious of having acted in an unlawful manner. Evidence to the contrary was insufficient. Sanctions on the grounds of having caused death through negligence were also inadmissible, as they had not envisaged the possibility of this consequence resulting from their actions. Hence, their conduct could not be considered to have emanated from hostile intentions on political grounds in connection with National Socialist tyranny.[87]

Von W. was also accused of causing the death of another individual, hereafter cited as Ho., who was a trade school teacher in Hamburg. He had unmistakably remarked to other teachers at the school where he was employed that he no longer believed that Germany could win the war. On 25 August 1944, he told members of the staff several remarks to this effect, such as saying that whoever did not believe at that time that Germany was losing the war was an idiot; if Germany lost the war, they would at least be able to speak freely again; the Bolsheviks would not go there, since the British and the Americans would not allow it; and that if Germany lost the war, it was guaranteed that they would be able to drive a car again within two years. One of his colleagues, hereafter cited as Heu., had concerns about and took offense at these remarks, fearing that if they were heard outside the school, political discredit would be brought upon the entire teaching staff, as this had already happened a year before when a teacher was arrested and sentenced to death and later executed for making political remarks. This fear was increased when one of his students had asked him during a class whether he believed that victory could still be achieved, and after having given a positive response, he encountered a different opinion among the teaching staff, as could be inferred from the unambiguous remarks that he had heard in the teachers' office. He also feared that the caretaker, Drews, who served as a cell leader for the NSDAP and was reputed to be a spy for the Gestapo, had heard about such conversations about politics among the teaching staff, and as a result, the entire staff could be persecuted for being politically unreliable. He had also heard how Drews had commented on what Ho. had said, and wondered whether Ho. would incur the same consequences as had resulted from a previous teacher having made similar remarks.[88]

Heu. then turned to Fe., who was a representative of the director of this trade school, and asked him whether he possibly knew about this incident without mentioning Ho.'s name, so that he could address the teaching staff about it so that they would refrain from such dangerous conversations in the future. Fe. inferred from the details that he was referring to Ho. He believed that he did not have the necessary authority among his colleagues to make such an address successful, and therefore turned to the local school supervisor, hereafter cited as Schlo., and asked him for advice. However, he was unsure about how to deal with this matter, and thus discussed it with S. and von W. All three of them agreed that this matter could not be concealed from spies. Von W. then took over dealing with this matter, without S.'s further involvement.[89]

Fe. conferred with Schlo. after it was known that the matter would be subject to official examination. They agreed that the questioning of those involved should be directed as much as possible toward diminishing the accusation as far as possible in its written form so that it would become too inconsequential to pursue any further. Schlo. also told another colleague, cited as San., to also be careful about what he would tell the authorities, who in turn told the same to Heu. Von W. questioned Ho. and Heu. thereafter.[90]

Having been warned about telling the truth about the events under scrutiny, Heu. gave von W. an account of what had happened without concealing anything while feeling self-conscious about this questioning and feeling intimidated by a superior authority. He also felt apprehensive about this matter since he also shared Ho.'s opinions, about which he was being questioned. Von W. then questioned Ho., who initially denied having made the remarks he was said to have made while von W. urged him to tell him the truth. The results of these questionings were inconclusive, and since it appeared to von W. that the matter could not be concealed, he believed he had to make a report about it since he expected that the Gestapo would find out about Ho.'s remarks through other means. He feared that in the event that he would not report this matter, there would be considerable difficulties for the leadership of the school administration, and that he and the top directors, including S., would be removed from office. He also feared that he could be called to account by the Gestapo for acting in favor of a defeatist. It was also known to him from conversations with the governor that leading Gestapo officials and high-ranking local NSDAP official had clearly made it known that the school administration was not being led in the spirit of National Socialism, and he feared for his own life and limb if he did not report this matter. He therefore decided to act against Ho. for having made defeatist remarks, which would be adjudicated by a Special Court as a clear case of undermining the war effort, and was fully aware of how this would lead to the imposition of a heavy sentence on Ho.[91]

The governor initiated official criminal proceedings against Ho. on behalf of the school administration on 7 September 1944. A few days later, two Gestapo officials came to von W.'s office and reproached him in threatening tones about this matter, asking why it had not been hitherto forwarded to the Gestapo and what the school administration had done about it. They left after von W. told them a report had been filed, as they had been unaware that proceedings were underway, and later apologized a few days later after the file had been found.[92]

Formal disciplinary proceedings were initiated until the matter was also forwarded to either the public prosecutor or the Gestapo, with the Gestapo taking precedence. He was charged on the suspicion of having made defeatist remarks, as well as the suspicion of having had illegal dealings with prisoners-of-war during 1944, which had been revealed from the Gestapo questioning Heu. and Ho. during September 1944. Ho. was arrested during this time, and was taken to Neuengamme concentration camp, where he remained imprisoned without trial, until he died there of enterocolitis on 3 December 1944.[93]

The public prosecutor argued that von W. had sought to have Ho. convicted from the outset on the basis of his suspicions about information he had acquired from Heu. On the other hand, the jury court disputed this assertion. Schlo.'s testimony along with the testimonies of both defendants refuted this interpretation of the facts, by which it was shown how the matter was brought to the attention of a third party, rather than hushed up as it could have been if Fe. had not discussed the matter further with Schlo. It was thereby indicated that those involved in this matter were capable of causing a dangerous situation, which they had resolved to avoid by not reporting it to the school administration, while there was the possibility of the caretaker getting involved by reporting Ho. This was evident to von W., who as a jurist recognized that he would be faced with a dangerous responsibility if he did not take official action immediately, especially in view of the existing tensions between the school administration and the Gestapo. He thus did not willfully act with malicious intentions in pursuing this matter.[94]

Von W. claimed in his defense that he had feared that if he did not convey this matter to the Gestapo, the administrative directors of the school would be replaced with radical National Socialists. He was therefore concerned about the unforeseen consequences for the school administration as well as his personal safety, and could therefore claim to have acted under duress. He also maintained that reporting Ho. to the Gestapo was unavoidable, and neglecting to do so by suppressing the matter could result in S. and himself being accused of harboring an enemy of the state. This could be expected in view of their previous experiences, when von W. had tried to intervene with the Gestapo to secure the release of a teacher who had been accused of preparing to commit high treason. The jury court considered this explanation to be plausible, especially during this highly tense time during the summer of 1944.[95]

It remained for the court to determine whether he had committed a crime against humanity by having caused Ho.'s unlawful imprisonment and death through negligence and through his report to the public prosecutor or the Gestapo. It was found that there was insufficient evidence to establish grounds for a conviction, considering that the Gestapo had already had prior knowledge about Ho.'s defeatist remarks from another source, presumably from an informer in the trade school, before von W. had conveyed his report. It was also surmised from this incident that the Gestapo had expected the school administration to take action against Ho., to which they had attached considerable importance. Hence, it could not be ascertained with complete certainty whether von W.'s report had caused Ho.'s arrest, and therefore raised the possibility that he did not have hostile intentions against him.[96]

This jury court determined that a conviction on the grounds of causing unlawful imprisonment and death through negligence could not be justified. The fact that neglecting to report Ho., whose remarks had already been known to the Gestapo, would result in his dismissal and being replaced by radical National Socialists in the school administration leadership was also taken into account. This danger, as well as danger to his personal safety, could only be averted by filing a report. He had also acted out of necessity to preserve his own life and limb, having already been under suspicion by the Gestapo for having acted in favor of an enemy of the state, as well as being under added suspicion for belonging to the old aristocracy that was considered especially unreliable after the 20 July conspiracy. In view of these circumstances, there was a considerable threat of persecution. He was thereby acquitted on the grounds of having acted under duress as defined in § 54 of the criminal code.[97]

The Federal Supreme Court of the Federal Republic of Germany quashed the jury court's judgments on von W. on 16 January 1953, and returned these cases for further deliberations. It was determined that the jury court's judgment that von W.'s conduct was justified by extra-legal necessity, since his duty to the school administration was a greater value than M.'s unlawful imprisonment, was erroneous. This court argued that if an action that fulfilled the external circumstances was the only means to safeguard either a legally protected right or fulfill a duty that was imposed or recognized by law, then it was therefore not unlawful to fulfill the higher duty at the cost of the lower value, or to protect the highest value at the cost of the slightest. This was not the case in this matter, in which it was argued that M.'s freedom, which was a legally protected right, and her duty that she was to respect, were misinterpreted as being less important than the education and upbringing of children in the KLV organization, which was not protected by criminal legal regulations. M. had not done anything unlawful, and as a civil servant she could not be prosecuted for breach of contract. However, von W. wanted her to be punished and had her delivered into the hands of the Gestapo since he believed there was no other recourse. However, this assumption could not be established under legal examination, since the element of acting out of necessity was unfounded. It could not be established that depriving M. of her freedom was unavoidable in order to prevent endangering the interests of the KLV, such as other teachers following her example of refusing to work and jeopardizing the proper education of children.[98]

This court also reproached the jury court's verdict with regard to the potential consequences that M. could incur as a result of von W.'s conduct. It had been argued that von W. had expected her to be sanctioned with forced labor in dealing with a non-political matter, rather than imprisonment in a concentration camp as a means of political persecution. However, the jury court overlooked how her refusal to work could be interpreted as being resistance against the National Socialist regime. In addition, von W.'s intention for M. to be imprisoned in a labor camp was a clear violation of the law. The jury court also could not establish the circumstances about the possible misunderstanding about whether he had intended for M. to be taken to a work education rather than a concentration camp, in view of how the written record in the letter of 4 August 1944 indicated that he had recommended custody in a concentration camp to the Gestapo. However, this had been disregarded by the jury court, and would therefore have to be addressed in renewed proceedings. If this could be established, there would be hardly any doubt that he had caused her death through negligence, regardless of whether this had been his intention.[99]

Von W.'s intentions were also to be examined in the case of Ho., in which he had also been familiar with the Gestapo's behavior. The jury court had made the assumption that the Gestapo had prior knowledge about Ho.'s remarks, and thus he would be subject to persecution without the contributing factor of von W.'s report about him. This court disputed the jury court's judgment that it was justifiable for von W. to convey this report and was obliged to take this action in the exercise of his official duties. He could not justify subjecting another to criminal prosecution when it would lead to persecution by the tyranny and violence of the political police in the National Socialist regime, which would lead to inhumane treatment and unforeseeable consequences in a concentration camp. As an administrative superior, von W. also was not legally obliged to report suspicions of criminal actions. The jury court's judgment was thereby considered deficient. Moreover, it could not necessarily be argued that Ho.'s remarks were subject to prosecution as having undermined the war effort, since they had been made within a narrow circle of teachers who had all known each other and had shared the same opinions, rather than in public. This, therefore, did not constitute a danger to the interests of the war effort. The jury court's presumption that von W. had acted under duress was thus not to have been influenced by Ho.'s remarks.[100]

The facts of these cases were reviewed in renewed proceedings at the jury court at the Hamburg regional court from 1 to 8 June 1953.[101] The court maintained that M.'s imprisonment was unlawful, since she had not violated any criminal law. Although she had breached the work contract, she was not subject to prosecution under existing labor law as a civil servant. There was also no justification for her arrest for having refused to resume her teaching duties, in terms of endangering the KLV enterprise in Wittstock or undermining the KLV organization by causing many other teachers to follow her example in refusing to work for the KLV. There was also no cause for Gestapo intervention, which was theoretically charged with investigating activity that was hostile to the state, and was an organization not bound by the rule of law.[102]

Von W. had intentionally had M. arrested by the Gestapo and recommended her imprisonment in a concentration camp, as he had stated in writing in the letters of 4 August and 29 August 1944, as a positive alternative measure to disciplinary measures that had proven to be ineffective, and court sanctions that would be impossible to impose. His intentions were thereby unlawful, since he knew that M. could not be prosecuted after having investigated the possible extent of criminal jurisdiction, and had therefore known that her arrest was unlawful. Her imprisonment in a concentration camp for breach of her work contract also was not justified by moral, social, or disciplinary considerations in the interest of serving the urgent demands of the state.[103]

Von W. claimed that his conduct followed so-called urgent extra-legal necessity. However, this could only be justifiable when the perpetrator acted after careful consideration to fulfill higher values at the cost of causing injury to lower ones, which was in conflict with the duties that were imposed or recognized by the state. It followed that the injury of slighter-valued duty was the only means to fulfill higher values, and that legally protected rights could not be in danger of being eliminated through the higher-valued duty. The evidence demonstrated that von W. faced a conflict of duties. He was responsible for the implementation of KLV functions, which he misjudged to be a higher duty than the value of M.'s personal freedom. He was thereby found guilty of having caused unlawful imprisonment that led to death.[104]

In determining whether von W. had intended to cause M.'s death or was responsible for this charge as a result of neglect, this court re-examined his motives for bringing about M.'s imprisonment. He claimed that he had intended for her to be imprisoned in a work education camp for a period of a few weeks, and had verbally conveyed this message to the director of the central office of the governor a few days after his letter of 4 August 1944. However, the court could not accept this claim that the Gestapo would consider this case as being of an exceptional non-political nature, and there was no written record of there having been a misinterpretation of the difference between a work education and a concentration camp. Von W. claimed he used the term "concentration camp" as a phrase to describe any penal institution that was under Gestapo jurisdiction while knowing that the Gestapo dealt with all prisoners in a different manner, depending on the cause for their arrest. His intention was to have M. put to work for a limited period of time, as was prescribed according to regulations at the time for labor violations, without having had any direct or determined intention to have her killed. Meanwhile, there remained the possibility that the Gestapo would treat this case as a political matter, even though von W. did not make any mention about a politically based offense. Hence, it could not be determined that he had consciously caused her death through negligence, or had been aware of this possibility. He was therefore to be acquitted of this charge.[105]

Upon reviewing the charges in the case regarding Ho., the court reviewed von W.'s claim that Ho.'s remarks constituted a violation of wartime regulations for undermining the war effort that could not be concealed. He therefore considered himself obliged to convey the matter to the Gestapo, while being concerned that suppressing this matter could result in him being brought before the People's Court or summarily taken to a concentration camp. This seemed a possibility since he was already under suspicion by the Gestapo after January 1944 for having attempted to protect a teacher from the charge of preparation to commit high treason.[106] In view of the evidence, he was to be acquitted on the charge of having caused unlawful imprisonment that led to death through negligence.

It could not be determined with certainty that von W.'s report about Ho. had led to his arrest and imprisonment by the Gestapo that later led to his death. The evidence presented demonstrated that the Gestapo had had prior knowledge of the incident concerning Ho.'s remarks before von W. filed a report about this incident on behalf of the school administration. Hence, although von W. had intentionally attempted to cause unlawful imprisonment that was unjustifiable, it could not be established whether this action contributed to the subsequent measures that the Gestapo took against Ho.[107] There was also evidence to sufficiently demonstrate that there was a risk for his personal life and limb if he did not file this report, as had been presented in the earlier proceedings. The court therefore accepted that he had faced the unavoidable circumstances of having to act out of necessity, which excluded the possibility of his intention to have Ho. killed. He was thereby acquitted of this charge due to insufficient evidence.[108]

In evaluating the extent of the sentencing in case regarding M., the court found that von W. had played an inauspicious role in those circumstances, which led to an inevitable conflict ensuing from their major personality differences. Von W. was descended from an old Prussian officer and civil servant family and was instilled from childhood with the virtues of discipline, devotion to duty, and service to one's homeland, which unfortunately may have led to his inability to consider other points of view. Meanwhile, M. placed high demands on herself in undertaking her duties very conscientiously, while thinking independently with such an uncompromising attitude that it must have appeared to von W. as the highest degree of insubordination that went beyond the reach of his comprehension.[109]

He therefore resorted to excessive means to see M. punished for her refractoriness, considering fulfillment of duty to be a greater value than one's personal freedom, and only realized that he had gone too far after learning that she would not be released by the Gestapo. The remorse he had shown thereafter was also taken into consideration as a mitigating circumstance, as well as considering that he had acted out of an excessive sense of duty, rather than hatred or other base motives or political reasons. His irreproachable background and often proven helpfulness, especially toward non-members of the NSDAP and Jews, his brave advocacy for such people who had fallen into the hands of the Gestapo, and his energetic assistance to the population of Hamburg with relentless effort during the bombing attack of July 1943 were also taken into consideration. In view of these factors, he was sentenced to eight months' imprisonment.[110]

One of the next denunciation cases was heard at the Würzburg regional court jury court, where judgment was pronounced on 5 December 1953. The defendant was sentenced to six years' imprisonment for attempted murder and unlawful imprisonment, with her civil rights being suspended for the same length of time.[111] This was also the only case of denunciation in the Federal Republic tried on the grounds of attempted murder that was also clearly motivated by base private interests.[112] The defendant, hereafter cited as H. B., had been known to have deceived her husband, hereafter cited as M. B., many times during his absence while he was a soldier during the war by having many different extramarital affairs, and had entertained thoughts of getting rid of her husband altogether so that she could be free to carry on living her dissolute lifestyle. She was provided with the opportunity to do so when her war-weary husband was at their home on leave in the autumn of 1944, when he privately expressed his thoughts about the war and leading state personalities, saying that when the Russians were going to arrive, the bastards would have their throats cut; Goebbels was a rogue; and that if the 20 July conspiracy had succeeded, the war would be over. His letters to his wife also contained bad-tempered remarks about the war, such as if Hitler had been killed on 20 July 1944, the "pigsty" the country was in would be over, while being totally unaware of her debauched lifestyle during this time and maintained marital relations until 1944.[113] Nevertheless, she took hostile action against her husband before this time.

While her husband was serving in October 1944, H. B. had approached the *Sturmführer* of the SA in their community of Gemünde, hereafter cited as A., and told him about her husband's remarks and offered to show him his letters. A. recognized that she was acting out of personal considerations rather than political convictions, and returned the letters to her unread with a serious warning about how his remarks could cost him his head. She replied that whoever spoke in this manner about Hitler did not deserve to live, and therefore A. ought to report him to the authorities. She later repeatedly demanded the same after that first conversation, and then to his relatives while he continually refused to file a report about her husband and repeated the same warning. He only spoke to the *Ortgruppenleiter* H. about the matter, who also refused to have anything to do with this matter due to H. B.'s bad reputation.[114]

The NSDAP *Kreisleiter* R. later confronted H. about not having reported the matter, having heard about it from unknown sources, and demanded a written report about it. H. neglected to do so, being as familiar as A. was with the fact that H. B. was not prompted to act out of political tendencies. She was not a member of the NSDAP or any of its affiliated organizations, and was not in the least politically active or even interested in politics. It was evident that she only intended to have her husband arrested for his disparaging political remarks through her incessant insistence so that he would punished for making them, or at least so that as a soldier he would be sent to the foremost part of the front. Her motive was to be rid of him, rather than give up her immoral lifestyle.[115]

Her husband came home unexpectedly at the beginning of February 1945 for a two week leave and realized that a soldier had been staying overnight in their apartment. When he confronted his wife as to whether she had been engaged in relations with another soldier during this time, there was a dispute between them on the night of 9 February. She claimed that during this dispute he had hit her with his waist belt and threatened to move out and shoot her and her mother. H. B. then reported this incident to A. the next morning, who advised her to turn to the local *Ortsgruppe* or *Gendarmerie* if she needed personal protection. She then turned to H., who told her that she should go to the police or the *Kreisleiter*. The local police arrested M. B. soon afterward on the instructions of the *Kreisleiter* on 10 February.[116]

He was then handed over for trial by a military court in Würzburg for having made disparaging remarks against the regime, without any mention made about the personal altercation between him and his wife. H. B. came forward as the leading witness testifying against him before and during his trial for undermining the war effort on 17 February 1945, in spite of having been repeatedly admonished by the presiding trial judge that she had the right to refuse to make a statement against her husband that could lead to a death penalty. During the trial, she repeated his earlier remarks while acknowledging that they did not merit the death penalty, but that she also expected the court to pass this sentence after her testimony. This would wrongfully allow her to maintain her immoral lifestyle after perpetrating an injustice.[117]

After the presiding judge ruled following deliberations that a conviction could not be reached due to a lack of evidence, H. B. heatedly swore that she would provide the necessary evidence. The judge again urged her to reconsider putting her husband's life at risk by refusing to testify against him, but she insisted on giving her sworn testimony under oath. This sworn testimony consequently led M. B. to be sentenced to death, which his wife welcomed with sneering laughter. She also did not try to make any contact with him while he was imprisoned or accept a relative's suggestion that she file for a pardon with the support of NSDAP functionaries and the police, and only asked for continued support after her husband was executed. The sentenced was not executed during a time of uncertainty about whether M. B. would be pardoned or the death penalty would not be confirmed before the end of the war. He remained imprisoned until April 1945, when he was released for deployment, and was then imprisoned as a prisoner-of-war until 1947.[118]

H. B. was tried by the local denazification tribunal in Gemünden on 7 June 1948 for having denounced her husband, which sentenced her to two years' imprisonment in a labor camp along with sequestration of 15 percent of her property in accordance with Article 7, part II, paragraph 8 of the Law for Liberation. She served fourteen months and eighteen days of her sentence from 14 June 1948 until 30 August 1949, and was then held in custody for those proceedings from 31 August 1949 to 21 November 1950. The jury court at the Würzburg regional court pronounced judgment on 6 February 1950 on the charge of attempted murder and unlawful imprisonment, sentencing her to fourteen years' imprisonment and ten years' deprivation of civil rights.[119]

She appealed this decision, which was quashed by the Bavarian highest appeal court on 11 October 1950, and the case was reverted to the jury court at the Würzburg regional court for reconsideration in renewed proceedings. This appeal court determined that the members of the previous jury had been insufficiently instructed about legal action being taken twice for the same cause of action, or "double jeopardy" (*ne bis in idem*). It was not to have taken the sentence passed by the denazification tribunal into account in reaching the verdict and needed to have applied the law independently of the sanctions imposed under the Law for Liberation.[120] This court also reproached the jury court for having passed a sentence that was excessively harsh. The jury court also had not taken the denazification tribunal's sentence into sufficient consideration as a mitigating circumstance in passing its judgment.[121]

She was later acquitted by the jury court at the Würzburg regional court on 29 November 1950 due to insufficient subjective evidence[122] that was needed to be evaluated to determine how the law could be applied to make her subject to prosecution in criminal proceedings. The public prosecutor appealed this decision to the Federal Supreme Court, which quashed this verdict on 8 July 1952 and remanded the case back the jury court at the Würzburg regional court for further reconsideration.[123]

This court determined that anyone who had made a truthful report that led to the imprisonment or death sentence of another was subject to prosecution for aiding and abetting unlawful imprisonment or death. Judgment was to be rendered accordingly when the earlier judgment was unlawful, with regard to when the provisions of criminal law did not sanction the death sentence, or this sentence was disproportionate to the act that was perpetrated and therefore did not warrant this sentence, and when the informer had known that this possible judgment contravened the true legal situation, but nevertheless intended to cause this outcome.[124] The jury court had correctly ascertained that the military court's ruling had been typically National Socialist with there having been the possibility of a cruel sentence to serve the law through deterrence. However, it had not been determined whether the defendant was aware of the unlawfulness of her actions, and had been involved as an indirect perpetrator in this case of attempted murder by having initiated the proceedings that led to the unlawful sentence against her husband.[125] The court also indicated that since the defendant's husband's remarks were not made in public, the death sentence was unlawful under military law. The jury court had not taken into consideration how military law had been abused, and how the defendant's actions against her husband led to the passing of an unlawful death sentence during a time when violent political repression was prevalent. It also followed that his imprisonment was also unlawful.[126]

The conduct of the defendant was likewise to be judged in view of these circumstances, since she had willfully intended to cause these unlawful consequences. She refused to claim the legal right to refuse to testify against her husband, and demanded that the court impose an unlawful sentence, which was of decisive significance in determining the unlawfulness of her actions. Her actions had made her intentions clear, and she had prior knowledge of the potential consequences of imprisonment and death that would incur as a result of her actions. This had not been made sufficiently clear in the earlier jury court verdict, and therefore the acquittal of the defendant was not tenable in view of her personal intentions that also served the purpose of political terror.[127]

During the second revised proceedings at the Würzburg regional court, the court ruled that while they were not to take the denazification trial sentence into account, it conformed to an interpretation made by the federal appeal court that the death sentence passed by the military court was objectively unlawful since M. B.'s remarks were not made in public, and therefore this death sentence was not justifiable in military law, and his imprisonment was likewise unlawful on the grounds of the charge made against him. As a result, H. B. was guilty of having intentionally indirectly contributed to these unlawful actions by having envisaged these unlawful consequences of her actions, and was subject to prosecution accordingly.[128] Her reaction of outrage to the court's ruling that the evidence to establish a conviction was lacking, her demand to give sworn testimony that would lead to the imposition of a death penalty, and her obvious callous reaction at this result were striking indications of her hostile intentions and expectations due to her base motives.[129]

On 5 December 1953, these revised proceedings ended with the ruling that M. B.'s wife was guilty of having been indirectly involved in the attempted murder of her husband as a result of the imposition of the unlawful death penalty. She had been aware of the unlawfulness of this judgment, and intended for her husband to be unlawfully imprisoned and killed, for which she could not provide any justification other than that she would be unhindered from continuing to engage in extramarital activities.[130] In evaluating the extent of the sentencing, the court took into consideration that she had not been previously convicted and had had a harmonious marriage before the outbreak of the war, before it disintegrated during wartime conditions and she projected her excessive maliciousness toward him through her extraordinary callousness about an unnecessary loss of life. The term of imprisonment that had been imposed by the denazification tribunal and her ostracism by others in her community for nearly nine years were also taken into consideration as mitigating factors. In view of these circumstances and the offenses she had committed, she was thereby sentenced to six years' imprisonment with her civil rights being suspended for the same amount of time.[131]

The Federal Supreme Court upheld this verdict on 8 June 1953, ruling that making a truthful report about another that led to unlawful imprisonment and death was subject to prosecution on these grounds when the conviction was unlawful, and the informer consciously had prior knowledge of being able to anticipate this unjustifiable outcome. The defendant could not deny that she had been aware of the potential consequences of her actions during this time, and was therefore convicted accordingly while her motive for her conduct had been unlawful.[132] It was therefore found that she had abused the law of the time and how it could be administered against alleged enemies of the regime to serve her base motives as a pretext for political persecution.

The application of German criminal law taking precedent over occupation law led to acquittals for defendants who had been convicted under the provisions of Control Council Law No. 10 after this law had been abrogated. Some cases indicated the limitations by which German law could not adjudicate National Socialist unlawfulness[133] in the administration of justice. Although fairness and objectivity were maintained while respecting the rights of those accused of indirectly perpetrating crimes against humanity, interpreting events in accordance with German law could prove to be less extensive than the broader interpretations that could be made under Control Council Law No. 10, which could make convictions more difficult to justify in spite of the evident injustices that had been perpetrated.

A later denunciation case at the Duisburg regional court demonstrated these limitations in German criminal law in such cases. On 6 November 1952, the Federal Supreme Court quashed an earlier verdict passed by this jury court that had sentenced a defendant on 25 September 1950 to two years' imprisonment and three years' deprivation of civil rights. This case was reverted to the jury court for review, since a conviction could no longer be maintained on the grounds of Article II, section 1c of Control Council Law No. 10.[134] It thus remained to be determined whether this judgment could be upheld in accordance with the provisions of German law that had since superseded occupation law.

The defendant had been a convinced follower of the NSDAP since 1933, while his brother, hereafter cited as K. H., was a Communist and a harsh opponent of the National Socialism who repeatedly criticized the regime during the war, and expressed his views about the unfavorable prospects of the course of the war to workmates and relatives. At one time at the end of 1942, he told his brother how he could not understand how he could still be in the NSDAP. He thought Germany would lose the war, and then party members, along with their wives and children, would be the first to have their throats cut. In another incident, K. H. said in his brother's presence that everyone who still kept making the "Heil Hitler!" greeting was mad. The Gestapo received knowledge about what he had said, and he was arrested at the beginning of December 1943.[135]

He was later convicted by the People's Court, where he was charged with undermining the war effort. During these proceedings on 8 March 1944, in which the defendant was summoned to appear as a witness, he was informed about his right to refuse to give testimony. He told the court that he wanted to and would testify against his brother, since people such as him had to be eradicated so that they would never again have to live through another 1918. He then repeated the above-cited remarks that his brother had made. One of K. H.'s workmates also testified against him, saying that he had told him that German soldiers in Russia should throw their rifles away and take up Russian ones. The wife of one of his workmates also testified against him, saying that he had said that the war was lost and that the Bolsheviks would soon be in Hamburg. In view of the evidence that was presented in these proceedings, he was sentenced to death on the same day, and was later executed on 20 May 1944.[136]

The Federal Supreme Court ruled that since a conviction on the basis of Control Council Law No. 10 could not be maintained after its withdrawal from the jurisdiction of German courts, the jury court had to determine whether the defendant intentionally caused the unlawful death of his brother according to German criminal law. This followed from a debate as to whether the death sentence had been objectively unlawful in accordance with the existing law and circumstances at the time. It was established that the People's Court had arbitrarily abused its powers of discretion and that the death sentence on K. H.'s brother was excessively harsh and unjustifiable while serving as a means of intimidating alleged enemies of the regime.[137]

The defendant had contributed to this unlawful killing though his conduct. The fact that it could not be proven that he had filed a report against K. H. and that other witnesses had also testified against him did not preclude the possibility that it was his testimony that led to the death sentence, and he had otherwise not made use of his right to refuse to testify. The judgment was passed on the basis of his testimony and those of the other witnesses, as had been set forth when the conviction was pronounced at the People's Court. He also could not claim that his conduct was justified while he had possessed the legal right as well as the duty to prevent an unlawful sentence from being passed.[138]

The defendant had known that he had exposed his brother to an uncertain fate at the hands of National Socialist authorities that would proceed against him with arbitrariness, and had exploited this possibility to inflict this injury, while having known that being charged with undermining the war effort was punishable by death. Whether he had considered the death sentence as a potential consequence of his actions, and whether he had been aware that this judgment would be unlawful, and whether he had approved of this possible consequence would have to be reviewed in new proceedings where it would be determined whether he was guilty or not guilty of aiding and abetting manslaughter.[139]

The jury court at the Duisburg regional court passed a revised verdict on 15 September 1953.[140] Although he had not refused to testify against his brother, the defendant disputed having had intentionally contributed to his brother being killed, and had done everything possible to prevent a death sentence from being imposed. He also denied any knowledge of having perpetrated any unlawful act. This testimony was hereby taken into consideration, and the court concluded that a conviction could not be maintained in the present proceedings.[141]

This court ruled that whether the defendant could be incriminated on the charge of aiding and abetting manslaughter first required an examination regarding whether the action to which the perpetrator had contributed was unlawful. This precondition of the death sentence and the subsequent execution could not be established with sufficient certainty. It was determined that the People's Court judgment was in fact justified in accordance with wartime legislation, as set forth in the special wartime criminal law ordinance (*Kriegssonderstrafrechtsverordnung*, KSSVO) Article 5, section 1, number 1 that was applicable at the time. Although the possibility that this court had exceeded its powers of discretion could not be dismissed, it was also found to have not misused the application of this law since K. H. had made his remarks in public for the intended purpose of dissemination, which warranted this sanction as the heaviest possible sentence.[142]

The court also examined whether the defendant had intended to contribute to a death sentence by not declining to refuse to give testimony, or had considered this possibility. Moreover, it was to be determined whether he had approved of this verdict, and whether he had been aware of the unlawfulness of his conduct. His remark about having to "eradicate such people" could not necessarily be proven to have been an accurate indication of his intentions. Such expressions were used in different ways during the National Socialist regime, and did not necessarily mean to kill, since it could also have meant to eliminate or remove or render harmless through imprisonment. There were otherwise no conclusive arguments that the defendant had wanted his brother to be killed, considering that he had not filed a report against his brother for making disparaging political remarks. Also, it could not be established whether he had persuaded another to take this action, and he had tried to dissuade his youngest brother from filing a report with his SS commander. He had also tried to protect his brother from facing political persecution by warning him to exercise more discretion about making such remarks in public. It was thus determined that there was insufficient evidence[143] to demonstrate hostile conduct. There were also additional mitigating circumstances that influenced the court's verdict. The examination of the evidence also had not shown that the defendant had been a fanatical National Socialist who had not tolerated those with different political viewpoints.[144]

Examining whether the death sentence was excessively harsh was limited by the lack of any sufficient available evidence that remained from those People's Court proceedings. The files concerning the written death sentence, its purport, and the decisive grounds for the judgment could not be found. Additionally, the record could not be completely and sufficiently reconstructed from the witnesses' testimonies in the present proceedings, as their capacities to remember the details of the proceedings and the contents of the judgment that was pronounced at that time were dulled by this time. In addition, it could be established that K. H. had openly expressed his political disposition, and had therefore expected and approved that his political remarks would be disseminated among the public. Hence, the People's Court judgment could not be proven to be unlawful in view of the prevailing law at the time. Whether the death sentence was harshly disproportionate to K. H.'s remarks and was thereby unlawful could not be established with absolute certainty due to the lack of existing written evidence.[145] In addition to determining whether the People's Court judgment could be considered lawful during the prevailing circumstances during wartime conditions, the court found that the defendant could not be convicted for the act of aiding and abetment. Although the defendant's testimony had contributed to and consequently caused K. H.'s conviction at the People's Court, it could not be established with sufficient certainty whether he had demonstrably intended to bring about the allegedly unlawful death sentence and had prior knowledge of having contributed to unlawfulness.[146]

The defendant had been known to respect the political views of others, including those of his workmates who were hostile to the National Socialist regime before and during the war, and had often refused to accept to the position of *Ortsgruppenleiter* and had been reproached for not doing so, and had not allowed his children and his wife to join NSDAP organizations. There was otherwise no evidence to indicate that he had intended to have his brother killed. It could only be established with certainty that he had spoken the truth in his testimony at the People's Court, but it could not be established with certainty that he had envisaged an unlawful death sentence as a possible consequence for his action, or that he had approved of this possibility.[147]

The court found that this possibility was not supported by the overall impression of his personality, whereby he was not very sophisticated in his way of thinking and could not imagine that a high court could pass an unlawful death sentence. This was representative of large segments of the German population that had not known about the unlawful practices of the People's Court, just as they had not known about the cruelty found in concentration camps and the murder of Jews. He had known that making disparaging political remarks in public was subject to prosecution when he had warned his brother about his indiscretions, but had not known that they could result in a death sentence. He therefore had not envisaged this possibility when appearing as a witness to testify against him, and therefore did not have reservations about taking this action as a result. He had expected his brother to receive a term of imprisonment and was later shocked when the verdict was pronounced, as another witness in the present proceedings had testified. This reaction was taken into consideration as part of the court's interpretation of his conduct, and was further evidence that he had not intended or approved of this verdict, or had knowledge of having acted unlawfully.[148]

This court thereby ruled that there was insufficient evidence to establish that he had intentionally aided and abetted an unlawful killing. An acquittal could not be granted since he had been convicted for the same act under Control Council Law No. 10 as a crime against humanity, which had been withdrawn from the jurisdiction of German courts, and therefore could be subjected to reconsideration. These proceedings were therefore stayed as no sentence could be imposed using German criminal law, so the court could only record him a moral reproach on him for his actions which would hereafter have to weigh on his conscience.[149]

The moral duty of an individual in the face of averting potential inhumane consequences and what could be cited as ignorance regarding what could be construed as being unlawful were thus not taken into consideration in this case. Occupation law had proven to be more extensive than German criminal law, which was again confirmed at a later case, in which a conviction that had been reached under Control Council Law No. 10 was later subjected to revision under German law. The earlier verdict could not be maintained due to limitations in determining the extent of how the evidence could be interpreted theoretically, in contrast to stressing the circumstances of unlawfulness. This had hitherto been accomplished through occupation law, which demanded that the element of inhumane consequences resulting from acts of denunciation that led to setting arbitrary proceedings into motion against those who were denounced to National Socialist authorities. Earlier interpretations of this broad precondition were taken into less practical consideration in establishing convictions when the evidence was interpreted through the provisions of conventional criminal law. Thereby the accuracy of the evidence in view of the judicial process took precedence over questions regarding inhumane consequences, and how they could be averted through an individual's actions by choosing not to act against another in view of the potential consequences of their actions.

The jury court at the Wuppertal regional court passed judgment on two defendants, hereafter cited as B. and M. on 6 and 8 June 1950 for crimes against humanity for having persecuted two other employees at a lock factory in Heiligenhaus on political grounds.[150] At the end of November 1943, M. spoke with his workmate P. who told him that their workmate Frerichs had made disparaging remarks about Mussolini's overthrow, saying that one was out and the other, Hitler, would be next, and that if the Third *Reich* was at an end, he would be ashamed of belonging to the NSDAP. M. then asked P. whether he had reported this matter, to which he responded that he would report it to B., the DAF enterprise representative. M. then went to B. himself and told him what P. had heard. B. thereupon spoke to the personnel department director, hereafter cited Mo., who arranged for P. to be called into his office. P. thereupon repeated what he had told M., which was typed into a written record, which both P. and M. were asked to sign. About two weeks later, Frerichs was arrested by the Gestapo in Verlbert, He was charged with undermining the war effort by the People's Court on 28 July 1944, and was later executed on 28 August 1944.[151]

M. claimed in his defense that he had not filed a report against Frerichs, and that there had been a third party present when P. talked about what Frerichs had said. He had also thought at the same time that what P. had said could not be true and had reproached him for whether he could reconcile such a severely incriminating incident with his conscience. P. maintained that what he said was true and would report the matter, knowing he had been a

Communist and what would happen to him after reporting him. M. henceforth thought it was his duty to help Frerichs and decided to forestall P. by calling on the third party to hold P. to what was not truthful. He thereafter went to B. to report the incident so that he could pursue this matter with the third party, while being aware that he was taking a serious risk, expecting that Frerichs had not made this remark and that it would not be confirmed.[152]

In the view of this court, which questioned the credibility of this testimony, he had in fact acted under his obligation as a member of the NSDAP to report remarks that were derisive of the regime. Moreover, he had known that Frerichs would have proceedings initiated against him that would result in a conviction of terrifying harshness if this matter was not settled within the firm. He had also known that legal proceedings would not be initiated against him if he had had reported a matter that he may not have known would result in a death sentence for Frerichs.[153]

Whether his report to B. had led to proceedings being initiated against Frerichs could not be established with certainty, since it was not known how the Gestapo had received knowledge of this matter. It was only suspected that P. had filed the report with the Gestapo in view of his comment to Bu. after Frerichs was arrested, saying that he would not come back. Three months after Frerichs was executed, P. had also told Ho. that "he had seen to it."[154]

However, the court determined that M. had acted against Frerichs before P. had acted against him, having told M. that if P. did not report him, he would do so himself, and had not waited for P. to take this action, having gone to B. immediately after they had spoken about it, thinking that this was his duty. He had thereby set the cause for the Gestapo to receive a report about this incident. He and others who had known about it would thereby not come under suspicion from the NSDAP for not reporting it, while also having been aware of and accepting the severe consequences that would follow for Frerichs at the hands of the Gestapo. The harsh consequences that followed for Frerichs were disproportionate to the wartime conditions of the time, and represented an affront to the dignity and honor of all of humanity. These subjective and objective circumstances were thus interpreted as persecution on political grounds in accordance with Article II, section 1c of Control Council Law No. 10.[155]

In another incident at the end of November 1943, M. overheard a Russian worker at the factory tell another worker, hereafter cited as Bar., that the barracks where she was housed had been damaged by bombing the night before. Bar. said that the target of the bombs was the Third *Reich,* while M., who overheard their conversation from his workplace, reproached her, having understood her to say the bombs were coming through the Third *Reich*, and told her that she ought to be happy that the war was not being fought in

Germany. Shortly thereafter, he told the local DAF cell representative in the department, hereafter cited as Bu., about this remark. When Bu. confronted Bar. thereafter about what she had said, she disputed what M. thought she had meant, while claiming that M. had reported this incident to him out of spitefulness. M. disputed this reproach and asked Bu. to consider the matter to be settled.[156]

As a DAF representative, Bu. was responsible for settling this matter and reporting all ill-considered remarks, and conveyed this matter to Bar.'s department foreman, hereafter cited as H. They thereupon agreed to report the matter to B. Although he did not consider it to be a serious matter, he in turn reported it to Mo. About two weeks later on 9 December 1943, Bar. was summoned to the Gestapo office in Velbert where she was arrested. She remained imprisoned until June 1944 when she was then prosecuted for making a hostile remark against the state, and was sentenced to a year's imprisonment.[157]

It could not be proven in this case whether M. had filed the report with the Gestapo, nor could it be determined how they had acquired knowledge about it. Evidence of hostile conduct on his part lay in the fact that M. had been conscious of how his words that he had spoken to Bu. and this incident would be interpreted. However, it could not be established whether he had consciously and intentionally attributed a false remark to Bar., since he had heard what was allegedly spoken from some distance. There was therefore the possibility of having misheard what she had said. It therefore could not be established with certainty that he had consciously distorted her words to cause her injury.[158]

It could also not be established with certainty that M. had reported the incident to Bu. with the intention and consciousness that he or another employee would forward it to the Gestapo. According to the witnesses' testimonies, it appeared that Bu. and H. had decided to forward this matter further to B. since they had known that M. was a convinced National Socialist, and therefore feared they would incur disadvantages if they did not do so after receiving knowledge about this incident. However, it could not be established whether there was evidence to indicate that they considered themselves obliged to report the matter to B. as a result of M.'s conduct. Proof could not be established that M. intended for Bu. or another individual to forward his report to the Gestapo, and it could not be proven that he had been unaware that his conversation with Bu. about the incident concerning Bar. would lead to her inhumane persecution. However, both cases constituted concurrent action that warranted prosecution under Article II, sections 1c, 2, and 3 of Control Council Law No. 10.[159] In view of the evidence presented, he was thereby sentenced to a year's imprisonment for having perpetrated a crime against humanity.[160]

In his defense, B. disputed that he had filed a report against Frerichs and Bar., claiming that as an enterprise representative, he was forbidden from conveying information about incidents within the firm to outside authorities, and was also charged with the duty to report all incidents within the work-force to the firm's management. Since the owner of the firm, hereafter cited as K., was often not present, he had mainly dealt with Mo. about any incidents of grousing or political frictions in the workplace, which were settled internally. No other case had hitherto been forwarded from the management to an NSDAP or state representative. Such matters had been mediated by K. or Mo. or an independent mediator who had issued instructions or warnings. After the incident concerning Frerichs was brought to his attention, he had consulted Mo. who required a written report as in other such cases in the past. K. and Mo. thereafter recommended that this matter was then to be settled by an independent mediator. B. was therefore surprised that Frerichs had suddenly been arrested, not having attached much significance to this matter, just as he had been surprised about Bar.'s arrest.[161]

B.'s conduct could have been interpreted as having been hostile by having accepted the report about Frerichs, if he had later expressed the view that the two cases were serious enough to be dealt with by authorities outside the firm. It could only be established that he had reported the matter about Frerichs to Mo. without any additional documentation. There was otherwise no other plausible testimony to constitute evidence of any hostile intentions. There was therefore insufficient evidence to demonstrate that he had expected that the information he had conveyed about this incident to the firm's management would in turn be forwarded to other authorities, and that Frerichs would be subject to arbitrary measures, rather than intending for the matter to be settled within the firm.[162]

The testimonies of witnesses also confirmed during these proceedings that he had not attached much significance to the incident regarding Bar. It could also not be determined that he had expected his conveying of the information about this incident to the firm's management to be further forwarded to outside authorities. Nor could a causal connection be made between his conduct and the proceedings that were later initiated against Frerichs and Bar. He was thereby acquitted due to insufficient evidence.[163]

The Federal Supreme Court quashed this verdict on 6 November 1952, and reverted the case concerning Frerichs back to the jury court for revision. The judgment could not be maintained after the abolition of Control Council Law No. 10, but he could still be prosecuted under the provisions of German law by taking the pretext of intentional killing into consideration. The jury court had hitherto determined from a legal basis that the defendant had initiated the series of the events that had taken place, by having at least contributed to

Frerichs's death sentence by having reported his alleged remarks to B. before P. may have done so. However, the judgment also mentioned that this report could have been conveyed by another party, which thus constituted a contradiction. Moreover, the judgment also necessitated establishing the contents and basis of the report in bringing a charge against Frerichs.[164]

It remained to be determined whether a third party other than the defendant had filed a report against Frerichs with the police, and thereby remove doubt that the defendant was responsible for causing the events that led to the death sentence. It was also to be determined whether Frerichs had made his remarks not only to P., but also to other workers at the firm, and had expected them to be circulated among them, or that he had merely made them to one person in private, which could determine whether the death sentence was unlawful in accordance with the existing law at the time. The charge of having aided and abetted manslaughter could come into consideration if the People's Court judgment could be demonstrated to have been unlawful, and if M.'s conduct had caused this sentence to be imposed on Frerichs through his report, rather than that another individual had reported him to the authorities. With regard to internal circumstances, it was also necessary to determine whether the defendant had also envisaged and intended an unlawful death sentence to be passed, and whether he had approved of the possibility of his report being forwarded to the police, which would later lead to that result. It was also necessary to determine whether he had been reasonably conscious of his conduct being unlawful.[165]

Renewed proceedings at the Wuppertal regional court led to a revised verdict on 23 September 1953.[166] M. protested his innocence in this matter regarding Bar., testifying that he had only been aware of the dangers of reporting this incident after having seen Bu. become agitated about what he had told him, and had expected his assurance not to cause any unpleasantness for Bar., to which Bu. had agreed with the condition that she was to receive a reprimand. M. had otherwise thought that this matter was settled after the discussion between Bu. and Bar. He maintained that the report to B. was made without his knowledge or his intention, and that he did not know who would have forwarded the report to the Gestapo. He said that he had not intended that this happen, and did not have any hand in contributing to this action.[167]

This testimony could not be refuted with the necessary certainty in view of examining the evidence, and therefore a conviction could not be made. After initial hesitation, Bu. testified in the main proceedings that M. had asked him to give him his word not to cause any disadvantages for Bar., which appeared plausible since he admitted to his own guilt about not having made this report at M.'s instigation. Given these circumstances, it could not be ruled out that M. had conveyed Bar.'s alleged remark in a conversation without intending to inflict injury on her, and did not expect Bu. to pass the remark on to B. Furthermore, it could not be proven that M. had made the report to the Gestapo or had known about this in any way. How they had received this information was otherwise impossible to ascertain in view of the available evidence. He was therefore acquitted in this case due to insufficient evidence.[168]

M. also pleaded innocence in this matter concerning Frerichs, claiming that P. was feared throughout the firm due to his intolerant National Socialist disposition, and had expressed his intentions to report Frerichs's alleged remark. He also did not believe what P. had told him and he did not know Freirichs. His intention was to forestall P. by reporting the matter to B. so that B. would investigate what had been said within the firm and reveal the untruthfulness of P.'s claim, and also to avoid being told to file a report, before being accused of neglecting his duty. He said that he did not know who filed this report with the Gestapo, and that he had neither contributed to, nor wanted, nor approved of this action. When he was questioned by the Gestapo and later appeared as a witness at the People's Court, he had merely spoken the truth about what P. had told him about Frerichs's alleged remark, without having said anything more to Frerichs's disadvantage, especially since he was convinced of his innocence while being aware of the potential death sentence that could be passed on him, and hoped that he would receive a prison sentence.[169]

In view of the evidence presented in this case, M. could also not be convicted on the charge of aiding and abetting murder or manslaughter, considering that he had not incriminated himself through reporting the matter to B. or as a result of his conduct as a witness at the People's Court. It could not be established with certainty that his report about Frerichs's alleged remark had caused the unlawful death sentence that was imposed on him. Whether his remark would not spread throughout the firm without reporting it to B., and how it had then been conveyed to the Gestapo thereafter could not be determined. Moreover, P. and Ba. had known about this remark before he talked about it to B., and it was assumed that it was P. who forwarded the matter to the Gestapo. This possibility followed the witness Ho.'s testimony that Frerichs was executed; P. said: "I saw to it." It also could not be determined whether M. had expected and approved of a possible death sentence at this time in 1943.[170]

In view of M.'s conduct as a witness at the People's Court proceedings, it was considered that he had contributed to causing the unlawful death sentence, which was confirmed during the second proceedings in this trial after only P. had been summoned to appear as a witness. The significance of his statement was slighter than the testimony presented during the first proceedings, when the verdict would be apparent. After he had already set

Gestapo proceedings into motion through reporting the matter to B., he could not retract his earlier statement in this report. However, he also had not given any additional evidence when it could have been possible to avert or mitigate the pending death sentence. However, it could not be sufficiently established that he had been aware that he was potentially able to influence the outcome of those proceedings. He was thereby acquitted due to insufficient evidence.[171]

Another of the first denunciation cases in the Federal Republic of Germany had originally been heard in the British occupation zone at the Braunschweig regional court, where a revised judgment was pronounced on 22 June 1950. This jury court had previously passed its sentenced on 28 October 1948, before this case came under further review at the Highest Appeal Court of the British Zone on 20 April 1949, where the disputed judgment was referred back to the jury court for further consideration. The Federal Supreme Court ruled that the jury court had correctly ascertained that the defendant had violated the human rights of another by having denounced his seventy-three year old father-in-law, hereafter cited as F., for listening to foreign radio broadcasts. This denunciation had resulted in an excessively harsh three-year prison sentence imposed by the Braunschweig Special Court, and he later died while imprisoned as a result of his earlier diagnosed intestinal illness that required him to have medical attention.[172]

This court questioned the earlier verdict that had been passed by the regional court, and made several criticisms about the judgment. Whether the National Socialist regime was justified in prohibiting its citizens from listening to foreign broadcasts and spreading the news about what they heard, and what penalties could be imposed for these actions remained open to question. What remained decisive in the external facts of this case was the example of a widely-used practice of imposing inhumanely severe punishments for actions that were not commensurate to the illegal actions that were committed.[173]

This court criticized the jury court's earlier judgment for making an irrelevant comparison to legal developments in England, Switzerland, and the United States concerning laws regarding undermining the war effort. The National Socialist regime had unscrupulously subordinated human rights to its despotic purposes, and it could not be compared to how undermining the war effort was interpreted in a state governed by the rule of law, protecting its interests while prosecuting the war. The jury court had thus misjudged the fundamental principles of the rule of law that had been completely disregarded by the National Socialist regime with its cruel and arbitrary measures for eradicating opposition. This court therefore failed to recognize that the instruments of state power served the purpose of protecting human rights without resorting to using political violence. As a result, the court's assertion that F. could have been considered to have been justly punished for his actions was untenable, considering that these legal consequences were not derived from the principles of the rule of law.[174] The jury court had also cited how the defense lawyer at the Special Court proceedings did not file for an appeal, fearing that F., being older and ill and most probably not fit to be kept in prison, would be exposed to life threatening danger at the hands of other state organs. It had also cited that the defendant had been subject to unpleasantness from F. and his family. The Federal Supreme Court also deemed these mitigating circumstances to be irrelevant.[175]

The fact remained that the defendant had intentionally brought about injury to F. through his report about him. While the motive for his actions was not altogether conclusive, the jury court citing F. and his family's unpleasant disposition toward the defendant was irrelevant, since criminal law always took the action of the perpetrator into consideration, as well as their attitude and conduct. The evidence indicated that the defendant was undoubtedly responsible for taking action against F., with the intention of causing the consequences of political measures being taken against F. Like anyone who willingly reported a political offense committed by another in connection with the despotism of National Socialism, the defendant was to be held responsible for violating Control Council Law No. 10, Article II, section 1c by giving the Gestapo reason to initiate action against F. In addition to the facts of the case, the jury court also appeared to have neglected the possibility that the defendant had deliberately acted against F. with hostile intentions, rather than being motivated by the belief that he was obliged to comply with the law.[176]

The Federal Supreme Court further criticized the jury court's irrelevant statements that by the autumn of 1944, most Germans were aware of the criminal character of the National Socialist regime and questioning whether most Germans did not listen to foreign broadcasts. This court had always maintained that the facts of a denunciation case followed the perpetrator considering and approving another being subjected to arbitrary practices. It was therefore irrelevant to question whether it was conceivable that listening to foreign broadcasts could be prohibited, and whether information about what was heard could be conveyed, and combining this matter with knowledge about the criminal character of the regime. The systematic terror measures used against opponents of the regime from 1933 onward that later culminated in the inhumane criminal practices that were used as means of deterrence characterized the arbitrariness of the regime.[177]

Although an interpretation of Control Council Law No. 10, Article II, section 1c did not necessarily imply that political denunciation was the worst product of the regime as the jury court had implied, in view of the many kinds of inhumane atrocities that had been perpetrated, it would suffice for that court to maintain that the defendant was aware of how the state could arbitrarily violate the fundamental rights and legal security of an alleged political opponent after a denunciation had been made against them. It would also suffice for the jury court to state that the defendant believed that his report about F. would cause him to be arrested, and that this would result in considerable injury.[178]

Another weakness in the previous jury court verdict was that it did not acknowledge one of the aggravating circumstances of the case. The proceedings had indicated how the former criminal secretary, cited as K., warned the defendant about the gravity of the expected consequences of his report, and had advised him that this matter lay outside the jurisdiction of the ordinary criminal police. The defendant therefore could not cite in his defense that he did not intend to bring about serious consequences. He was also given the opportunity to retract his report when he was asked by a criminal police officer whether he had thought all of the contents were precise. The defendant insisted on maintaining in writing that F. was an incorrigible defeatist who brought danger upon his family and therefore requested Gestapo measures to be initiated against him. He was there therefore conscious of the arbitrary actions that would be imposed on K. This case was therefore to be heard again in reopened proceedings.[179]

The proceedings were reopened at the Braunschweig regional court, where judgment was pronounced on 22 June 1950. The court reiterated how the defendant had been severely wounded several times in the early days of the fighting on the western front in May 1940, which included a shot to the head. The court therefore entered medical experts' opinions into evidence, considering the implication of the defendant's possible brain damage and consequent soundness of mind at the time that he had denounced his father-in-law in September 1944, which could have influenced the course of events involving the accusation.[180]

The defendant, hereafter cited as H., recovered in a military hospital until February 1941, and met his future wife there. Their marriage plans were initially troubled to a large extent because his father-in-law, hereafter cited as F., was of noble birth, and thus did not consider others, such as H. who was the son of a worker, to be equal to his social status. These tensions continued when he and his fiancée were married in July 1941, with events such as K. disallowing H.'s parents to be present at the wedding. However, he tried to gain his father-in-law's approval through military experiences. While recovering from the wounds he had incurred and serving with reserve troops, he was sent to officer candidate school in May 1944 and became an artillery officer in Italy. The events that would lead to his father-in-law's denunciation took place while he was on leave in August and September 1944 after suffering from bouts of malaria that he had caught in May.[181]

F. had initially been enthusiastic about the outbreak of the war and the early successes of the German army, but later fell into a deep pessimism about the military situation, especially after the defeat at Stalingrad, following information that he heard on foreign radio broadcasts. He thought the war was lost and criticized the conduct of the war, and shared his opinions and what he had heard on the foreign broadcasts with his family at mealtimes. H. was present at these times while spending time with his wife who lived with her parents at their home in Goslar. This led to reciprocal aggravation between him and his father-in-law due to their differences of opinions, since he believed that the war could yet be won, and pointed out that F.'s opinions would bring disaster on them.[182]

F. also continually added to the discord between them by repeatedly making snobbish criticisms about H.'s humble origins, even though he had worked his way up to becoming an officer. H. also had the impression that his father-in-law tried to persuade his daughter to divorce him. The contention and mistrust between them culminated in F. hoping that H. would not come back from the front.[183]

H. denounced F. in the midst of this charged atmosphere.[184] The earlier tensions reached a new high when H.'s mother and pregnant sister-in-law arrived unexpectedly in Goslar on 13 September 1944, seeking refuge there after leaving their homes in Aachen that was under attack. K. objected to allowing them to stay in his apartment there while making derisive remarks about refusing to associate with them, which brought about great distress. H. later went to the police to report this ongoing domestic dispute on 16 September. What he had said at the police station could not be verified in detail. It was surmised that he mentioned K.'s earlier political remarks, since the criminal secretary, hereafter cited as K., told him that offenses of a political nature lay outside his jurisdiction, and referred H. to his Gestapo colleague criminal secretary R. in Bad Harzburg, who had jurisdiction over such matters in Goslar.[185]

R. met with H. when he arrived in Goslar later that day, and asked him whether he had considered everything that he had said earlier to K. about the contents and background of the domestic dispute. He reiterated how F. would not recognize his achievements, along with the cause for the dispute that was caused by his mother's arrival and what F. had said about her presence, and continued with F.'s political attitude and thoughts about the war situation. R. then summarized what H. had brought forward about F.'s political offenses, and asked him to sign this record that said his father-in-law had been making defeatist statements for about one and a half years. This included repeatedly saying that the war could no longer be won and that the party clique would not admit defeat and therefore sacrificed many soldiers and all the German cities. Three days earlier, he had told H.'s mother and sister-in-law that they should have stayed in Aachen, since the situation during the occupation would not have been bad, and anyway all of Germany would have to be evacuated since the English would be there between two to three months. This last statement threw the domestic situation into complete disarray, and he therefore requested that the necessary Gestapo measures be initiated against his father-in-law. H. signed this record knowing that this meant reporting a political offense to the Gestapo.[186]

H. soon regretted what he had done, but there was nothing that could be done to remedy the consequences of the situation. Later that evening, he was exceptionally despondent and told his wife that he believed he had said something stupid. Meanwhile, R. questioned F. about the contents of the report and was subsequently arrested. He had told R. outright during this questioning that he had listened to foreign radio broadcasts, and in subsequent interrogations had admitted that he had regularly listened to broadcasts from England and Switzerland, and had talked about what he had heard with his family, even though his stepdaughter, H.'s wife, had warned him against it. He also later admitted to listening to these broadcasts with a couple in Goslar who were then also arrested.[187]

On 19 January 1945, the Braunschweig Special Court sentenced the seventy-three year old mentally and physically shattered F. to three years' imprisonment, and sentences of three years and one and a half years were imposed on the couple he had mentioned while under interrogation. Having betrayed them caused him agonizing mental anguish, as did thinking about what would happen to his wife. These thoughts aggravated his already weak stomach and intestinal conditions that worsened his physical state while he was imprisoned. Nevertheless, his defense lawyer advised him against appealing for clemency due to his advanced age and ill health, for fear of being arrested by the Gestapo upon being released and then taken to a concentration camp. He soon died on 11 March 1945 in Wolfenbüttel prison as a result of stomach and intestinal enteritis and heart trouble.[188]

The defendant spoke in his own defense saying that the domestic situation that he was in proved to be intolerable, with the fierce disputes that had taken place that were further aggravated by attacks of malaria and the effects of the earlier brain injury. He therefore sought help from the police to restore order in the home, rather than reach for his weapon. In the midst of this commotion, he inevitably mentioned the political remarks that F. had made while describing the background of the entire dispute, but did not imagine the consequences that would result thereafter.[189]

The jury court found the defendant guilty of committing a crime against humanity in accordance with the provisions of Article II, section 1c of

Control Council Law No. 10. This law did not provide specific details about what characterized a crime against humanity apart from outlined references that concerned persecution on political grounds. According to an interpretation by the Highest Appeal Court of the British Zone, the external factors of such a crime involved hostile conduct in connection with the violence and arbitrariness of the National Socialist regime, which not only affected the victim individually, but also violated their universal human rights to such an extent that it also affected humanity as a whole. In keeping with this interpretation, the jury court disavowed questioning whether K.'s remarks and listening to foreign broadcasts were subject to prosecution in a state governed by the rule of law during wartime. It maintained that the unjust consequences of the report that was made against him were completely disproportionate to his conduct, as well as violated the principles of humanity.[190]

What remained unclear in this case was what H. had told K. in the preliminary questioning in addition to the contents of the signed record that R. had written, which left his motive for his actions unclear. He remained responsible for giving the Gestapo cause to arrest and interrogate F., even if he did consider or foresee the consequences of his actions. The act of making a report against another who would suffer the consequences of the arbitrary measures taken against them constituted hostile conduct, and thus his guilt was proven.[191]

There remained the question of whether his guilt could be justified in view of his soundness of mind at the time of his actions, taking the brain injury into consideration as evidence of a mitigating circumstance. Given the results of different examinations conducted by nerve specialist physicians between the end of 1945 and January 1950 and the expert witness in the present proceedings, the answer to this question remained uncertain, apart from maintaining that brain damage had most probably been sustained.[192]

In view of this possibility, the medical experts explained that such individuals were likely to be psychologically frail, excitable, and sensitive. In emotionally tense situations, they were likely to suffer from thought disorders, weaknesses in decision making, and excitability that temporarily changed their personality. The jury court took this type of severe mental health dysfunction into consideration as it was accounted for in Article 51 of the criminal code. The court accepted the conclusions of the medical expert at these proceedings that H. was of sound mind at the time that he made his report to R., but was probably lacking in the ability to reason at the time.[193]

It remained to be determined whether H. had possessed sufficient ability to foresee the consequences of his actions and his incentives for those actions while under the influence of mental inhibitions. H. had undoubtedly known, regardless of his brain injury and time spent at the front, that there were very serious repercussions for making so-called defeatist and political remarks that were hostile to the state, which had long followed the arbitrary persecution that had begun in 1933. This was further indicated by his having repeatedly warned his father-in-law about making such statements, and how he had suggested that "state political measures" be taken against him.[194] It had been determined that the brain injury had weakened his reasoning ability to a considerable extent. This was further aggravated by the attendant circumstances of frontline fighting during a tense military situation and his malaria attacks, which were later further aggravated by the events of the tense domestic situation after his mother and sister-in-law had been evacuated from Aachen.[195]

The jury court accepted the medical expert's proposition that H. had not necessarily been in control of his reasoning during his initial contact with the police. He was suffering from an agitated state of mind, which most probably did not completely dissipate by the time he later made his report to R., even though his ability to reason had recovered to a certain extent. When R. questioned him about matters of a political nature, such as which foreign radio stations his father-in-law had listened to and whether he had any connection with the 20 July conspirators, he was sufficiently aware of the dangers of these questions and therefore did not say everything he knew, although he had known that his father-in-law had listened to foreign broadcasts since 1942 and had been acquainted with Count von Helldorf, who had been implicated in the conspiracy. On the other hand, he had been aware that the political contents of his report would lead to the Gestapo becoming involved in taking action against his father-in-law.[196]

In view of the circumstances, the jury court concluded that after the initial intense state of agitation, the defendant recognized that willingly signing a report about his father-in-law constituted a political attack, and at least possibly accepted and approved that arbitrary Gestapo measures would be taken against him. Although his reasoning ability was considerably undermined at the time of these actions, this influence was not absolutely decisive to the extent that he was unable to have acted differently, and therefore he remained accountable for his conduct. The motive for making the report thus constituted a crime against humanity.[197]

It had been completely unnecessary to resolve a domestic dispute by calling on the Gestapo and making a political report against an elderly individual who had belonged to another generation and considered himself entitled as the head of a household to speak his mind to his family. Hence, the defendant had not always shown the appropriate understanding in finding justifiable ways to reduce the domestic tensions, rather than take such hostile action against his father-in-law that led to tragic consequences that contravened all ideas of justice. Meanwhile, the father-in-law was also not completely blameless for the enormous tensions that contributed to the defendant turning against him. This was taken into consideration as a mitigating circumstance, along with the fact that the defendant had hitherto not been prosecuted, and had given the court the positive impression that he felt remorse for the consequences of his actions, along with the extenuating circumstances of his mental disability as defined in Article 51, section II of the criminal code. In evaluating all of the circumstances in this case, the very wide range of possible sentences in Article II, section 3 of Control Council Law No. 10, and the provisions of Article 3 of the Law on Granting Immunity from Prosecution of 31 December 1949 regarding excessive sentencing, the court found it unnecessary to impose a sentence of imprisonment higher than six months. The proceedings were therefore stayed on the grounds of this law, and the defendant was hereby acquitted on the grounds of this amnesty.[198]

Another denunciation case was heard at the Hamburg regional court jury court on 27 November 1950, where judgment was passed on two defendants, hereafter cited as K. and D., for a crime against humanity relating to the denunciation of their workmate.[199] They had worked together at a Hamburg dockyard with Kr. during 1943 and 1944, where they had sharp differences in their political opinions. Kr. had been a member of the German Communist Party (KPD) from 1933, and had never changed his political views. He also knew that D. had been a communist and tried to influence him accordingly. On one occasion, Kr. said that it did not matter to him whether he continued working or arrived for work on time, since the hours he neglected would contribute to Germany losing the war, which would mean a victory for Communists. At another time, he boasted to D. that that the war was as good as won for the Communists. On another occasion, he claimed that the alleged killing of 600,000 ethnic Germans in Poland should be blamed on Germans rather than Poles. Kr. also continually argued that the bombing of German cities would essentially lead to a timely end of the war, and told his workmates about details of the bombing targets and the extent of the damage as well as the numbers of those killed. D. and K. surmised that this could only have come from his listening to foreign radio broadcasts, while he repeatedly expressed his hope that the bombing could be intensified with sadistic satisfaction with regard to the amount of damage that could be still be inflicted.[200]

These remarks caused considerable commotion in the workplace, but did not strain the relationship between Kr. and his workmates. However, K. began to feel considerable indignation and hatred toward Kr. after his wife was very seriously wounded by phosphorus in the fire bombing of Hamburg, and D. had worked as a volunteer fire fighter all night before going to work at the dockyard on the same morning. The situation became further aggravated by Kr. making political remarks about Germany losing the war and expecting the Communists would come to power, which K. considered to be a personal threat to his own life.[201]

D. and K. later discussed how Kr. was to be dealt with and how his conduct could no longer be tolerated on the dockyard. After an initial hesitation, D. decided in May 1944 that he was oath bound as a marine soldier to make a report about Kr., and he also considered himself responsible for reporting subversive acts in accordance with the dockyard regulations. He then first reported Kr. to the local police station, and the matter was conveyed to the SD in Holstenglacis. D. was thereafter questioned about the matter there by a SS *Obersturmführer*.[202]

D.'s report led to Kr.'s arrest and imprisonment by the Gestapo on 8 May 1944. The general state prosecutor at the Hanseatic regional court instituted an indictment against him on 26 August 1944 for preparation to commit high treason, patronizing the enemy, and undermining the war effort. Proceedings were initiated at this court on 27 October 1944, where D. and K. appeared as witnesses and told the court about Kr.'s remarks. Kr. was sentenced to death on the same day, and nothing came of a plea for clemency and commuting the sentence to imprisonment. He was later executed on 14 December 1944.[203]

D. claimed in his defense that he was both bound by oath as a soldier as well as his position at an enterprise that was vital for the war effort to report Kr. to the authorities. Kr. had not restrained his conduct in spite of constant exhortations, which would have considerably disrupted comradeship at work, and if he had not filed a report, his workmates could have been called to account for not having taking this action. He had hesitated to take action against Kr, and had only done so after he did not change his conduct, especially after he had felt personally threatened by some of his remarks. Moreover, he claimed that as a simple dockyard worker, he had not been at all certain that his report would lead to a death sentence, rather than one of imprisonment.[204]

In view of such previous cases, this court resolved that D. had demonstrated hostile intent and actions in connection with the National Socialist tyranny that led to an unlawful death sentence, and they could not accept that he had been unaware of the potential consequences of his actions. The court found him guilty of crimes against humanity as defined in Control Council Law No. 10, Article II, sections 1c and 2a. His testimony could only be taken into consideration in determining the extent of the sentencing, but not for justifying an acquittal.[205]

In evaluating possible mitigating circumstances, the court considered in his favor that he had hitherto not had any prior convictions and had acted out obedience to his oath as a soldier and a worker in an enterprise vital for the war effort. In addition, Kr.'s remarks had greatly affected his judgment by agitating him to significant extent, especially after the time of the fire bombing of Hamburg, which must have given him cause for his excessive indignation at Kr.'s remarks. His claim that he did not expect Kr. to receive a death sentence was also taken into consideration. He was thereby sentenced to two and a half years' imprisonment.[206]

K.'s conduct could not be judged using Control Council Law No. 10, and the report filed against Kr. had come from D., who had testified that he had done this without being influenced by K. . He had therefore not taken part in making this report, and was unaware of D.' actions. K. had only known about the report having had been made after D. had gone to the authorities. He was therefore acquitted.[207]

One of the next denunciation cases was heard at the Bonn regional court, where judgment was pronounced on 5 April 1951. The three accused had inevitably caused the death of another by taking personal advantage of the National Socialist racial legislation. One of the defendants, hereafter cited as Sch., had rented a ground floor flat and an attic in the house of a seventy-year-old, severely diabetic widow of Jewish heritage, hereafter cited as Eva Merkelbach, who had lived in the house in Bonn with her two sons Rudolf and Oskar until June 1944. The other accused lived in the same house. One of them, hereafter cited as P., had rented a large furnished room in the basement, while the other, hereafter cited as K., rented a separate furnished room. Each of the defendants had known that Mrs. Merkelbach was a so-called full Jew in the National Socialist definition of this term at the time, and that her two sons were so-called half-Jews. Although she had been subject to the racial policies against Jews, her son's intervention at the Gestapo on the grounds that she had been twice married to so-called Aryans had saved her from incurring official disadvantages because of her heritage, and she was stricken from a list of people marked as being Jews. The defendant and Mrs. Merkelbach otherwise enjoyed an amicable arrangement, until some personal differences occasionally arose between them that resulted from Mrs. Merkelbach's diabetic condition, which, as was expected, affected her reasoning.[208]

A greater quarrel began in early 1944 about a subletting arrangement for the attic between P. and Sch. to make room for P.'s friend, without first doing so with a required prior agreement with Mrs. Merkelbach's sons. Mrs. Merkelbach's son Rudolf thereafter lost his apartment in Cologne, that he had lived in with his wife and daughter, in March 1944 as a result of an air raid, and he had hoped to be able to move into this attic with his family, but could not. The two brothers then tried to cancel the tenancy for the attic on 16 May to claim it for personal use, but they could not because they were "half-Jews," and as a result of this they were not be legally entitled to claim this right. They were instead to be satisfied with the support of their "full

Jewish" mother for their living requirements. It was surmised that Sch. had told the lawyer dealing with this case about the brothers' and their mother's social status at this time. During these pending eviction proceedings, the local Gestapo received a letter about Mrs. Merkelbach. This letter reproached her with being quarrelsome and having forced her way into the tenants' apartments, and mentioned how the defendant could no longer be expected to live under the same roof with a "Jewess." This letter, which had been written by a third party, was signed by the three accused, and by a fourth person whose identity could not be established.[209] The Gestapo arrested Mrs. Merkelbach thereafter on 9 June 1944. She was first imprisoned at the Gestapo prison, and then taken to a so-called work camp in Bonn, and later taken to a "reception camp" in Cologne-Müngesdorf. She was then sent to the Theresienstadt concentration camp where she was presumed to have perished, not having been afforded the required medical attention for her serious diabetic condition and insulin injections. Her son's attempts at intervention with the Gestapo came to no avail.[210]

Mrs. Merkelbach would have remained unmolested had the defendant not reported her to the Gestapo. After having sent a letter about her to them, they then allowed themselves to be subject to questioning about the relations in the house, whereby they confirmed verbally she had been nagging, quarrelsome, and cantankerous. These actions inevitably led to her to being exposed to arbitrary proceedings that led to severe mental and physical suffering and her inevitable death. The defendants were to be called to account for their hostile conduct that caused these consequences of National Socialist violence and tyranny, having intended to get Mrs. Merkelbach out of the house and no longer face her annoying habits, as well as to forestall the eviction process. In view of these considerations, the defendants were found guilty of committing a crime against humanity on racial grounds according to Article II, paragraphs 1c and 2 a-d of Control Council Law No. 10.[211]

In evaluating any possible mitigating circumstances, the court acknowledged that the defendants, especially K. and P., had helped Mrs. Merkelbach at a time when this had been forbidden for so-called Aryans under the threat of serious punishment. The court also made allowances for how their report had not expressed the consequences they expected to her to incur, but they also took into consideration that the victim of their actions had been an old and ill person who was sentenced to imprisonment and death. Sch. and P. were to be held responsible for these consequences. They were therefore sentenced to eight months' imprisonment. K.'s guilt was considered secondary to that of the others, in view of her own interests and the extent of her disputes with Mrs. Merkelbach. However, she had also sanctioned the Gestapo taking action against her by signing the letter about her. She was sentenced to six months' imprisonment that was commuted under the law for the guarantee from criminal prosecution of 31 December 1949.[212]

A later judgment in a denunciation case was reviewed by the Federal Appeal Court, where judgment was pronounced on 10 June 1952 upon the appeal on the grounds of an erroneous application of Control Council Law No. 10, which could no longer be administered through German courts after 1 September 1951, and the apparently unfounded conviction and sentencing according to valid German law. Renewed proceedings would thereby evaluate the record and determine the verdicts according to German law.[213] The jury court at the Hamburg regional court II had earlier convicted and sentenced the three accused, hereafter cited as K., to a year and three months' imprisonment, L. to a year and two months' imprisonment, and A. to a year and six months' imprisonment, for crimes against humanity on 11 February 1950.[214]

K. had heard from her friend, hereafter cited as Ro., one day in 1943 that Ro.'s landlord, Ferdinand von Reichel, who had been married to a Jew since 1930, had often made disparaging remarks about the National Socialist system. After a heavy bombing attack in the summer of 1943, his wife made critical remarks about the war and the regime, and was denounced by a well-known SA leader in Hamburg-Winterhude. She was then arrested by the Gestapo and was imprisoned in the police prison in Hamburg-Fuhlsbüttel, until she was taken to the Ravensbrück concentration camp where she later perished. After her arrest, von Reichel openly made his anti-National Socialist disposition clear to Ro. Unbeknownst to Ro, K. visited von Reichel and warned him against making disparaging remarks too often in front of Ro., who she had known to speak her mind as well. They later developed a good friendship, and he accepted her recommendation for her friends, Mr. and Mrs. A., to live in his apartment.[215]

During a visit by A. at K.'s home where L. was also present, there was talk about von Reichel's frequent disparaging remarks about the National Socialist regime, and they expressed their apprehension that they could all be implicated by these remarks and be in danger of being taken to a concentration camp. The situation became further aggravated in August 1944, when von Reichel told A.'s wife that the Russians would be there soon. He said he would be protected as an opponent of National Socialism, and that he would speak for her and her husband. This caused her a great deal of distress, and she told A. what von Reichel had told her.[216]

A. had long time unwillingly heard von Reichel's disparaging remarks against the National Socialist regime and the war it had started, and therefore allegedly decided to put it to an end by having L., then employed by the SD in Hamburg during this time, report him to the Gestapo.[217] A. then first told K. what von Reichel had told his wife shortly afterward, who conveyed the same remarks to L thereafter.[218]

Both K. and L. were outraged about von Reichel's remarks, and agreed to pass the matter on to the Gestapo. L. then called the Hamburg Gestapo and told them what von Reichel had told A., which K. then confirmed during the same phone call and arranged to meet them for questioning on the next day. The Gestapo arrested von Reichel a few days later. K. later told A. about the phone call they had made to the Gestapo that led to his arrest, to which he reacted with a great deal of consternation, asking them if they had gone insane. This incident caused him a great deal of concern, since he feared that the Gestapo's investigation could lead to difficulties for him, since he lived with his wife in von Reichel's apartment.[219] Their investigation could also possibly reveal how he had secretly brought a Jew to the Romanian border to escape persecution after hearing that the Jews would be taken into a ghetto.[220] Meanwhile, von Reichel was eventually taken to Neuengamme concentration camp where he later perished.[221]

This verdict was quashed and the case was reverted to the Hamburg regional jury court for further review.[222] On 10 June 1952, the Federal Supreme Court resolved that his imprisonment in a concentration camp was unlawful, and constituted an inhumane contravention of law and justice with a complete deprivation of the rights of human dignity that threatened bodily and mental injury in the worse possible means. The institutionalization of von Reichel at the Neuengamme concentration camp was hence unlawful, especially due to the fact that his remarks were not made in public and therefore reporting them was also unlawful in accordance with an interpretation of the law at the time, according to § 5, part 1, No. 1 of the KSSVO. New proceedings were therefore to take the German criminal code provisions regarding unlawful imprisonment into consideration, as defined in § 239, part 2 and 3, § 47 and § 222 of the German criminal code, along with the provisions regarding unlawful death defined in § 341 in connection with 239, parts 1 and 3, in connection with his death that was incurred as a result of the imprisonment. It was thus resolved that whoever had reported another to the Gestapo for having made a remark that was allegedly "detrimental to the state," or had taken part in doing so in August 1944, had acted unlawfully, having caused persecution through the all-powerful political police of the National Socialist regime that was characterized by arbitrariness and violence. Anyone who had been named as an enemy of the state was thereby placed in danger of being taken to a concentration camp where they would face inhumane treatment und unforeseeable consequences without being afforded the protection of the law.[223]

It was apparent that K. and L. had contributed to von Reichel's persecution by the Gestapo. New proceedings were to establish with greater accuracy the question and extent of A.'s involvement in this persecution, and whether he had intended to initiate these consequences by agreeing with K.

and L. about their making a report against von Reihel. He had been obligated to do whatever was possible and reasonable to save von Reichel from the Gestapo prior to the occurrence of these events. The jury court was to determine whether he had prior knowledge of this report before von Reichel was arrested, whether he had had the opportunity to warn him about his impending arrest, and whether he could have exercised an influence in exonerating him when he and his wife were questioned by the Gestapo without risking life and limb through giving false information. This evidence would thereby establish whether he was directly involved, or had directly aided and abetted in von Reichel's unlawful imprisonment. The Hamburg jury court was thereby instructed to review the facts of the case concerning the three defendants under all possible considerations under German law with regard to this charge, including also the possibility of a verdict according to an interpretation of murder in accordance with § 212 of the criminal code.[224]

The Hamburg regional jury court passed a new judgment on 11 November 1952,[225] reviewing the evidence on the basis of German law after the abolition of Control Council Law No. 10. The evidence revealed that the Gestapo had already possessed an extensive file against von Reichel prior to the report that K. and L. had made about his remarks, since he had long been under investigation and had incriminating material compiled against him before this incident because he had been married to a Jew. The hitherto incriminating material that the Gestapo had allegedly compiled did not suffice to make an arrest appear necessary until K. and L. took action against him, which then led to his arrest and imprisonment. However, it could not be determined whether this report led to his death. He had been an older person and could have died of natural causes that were not related to the period of imprisonment. A conviction on the grounds of murder or aiding and abetting an unlawful death according to §§ 212, 222, and 239 part 3 of the criminal code were therefore overruled.[226] This jury court also ruled that von Reichel's imprisonment was unlawful, since his so-called remarks that were hostile to the state were not made in public. His arrest by the Gestapo was therefore unlawful, thereby making K. and L. subject to prosecution for this charge on the grounds of § 341 of the criminal code for having taken hostile action against him, which they undoubtedly anticipated and accepted would lead to his arrest and a lengthy period of imprisonment.[227]

They claimed in their defense that they had not been aware of the unlawfulness of their actions and had not wanted to cause von Reichel's arrest. However, the court was not convinced, as everyone in Germany in 1944 had known how the Gestapo had proceeded against any so-called defeatists with merciless severity, and those who were denounced as enemies of the state would be taken to a concentration camp. This had been especially clear to L.

who had been employed by the SD, and therefore had a detailed knowledge about the local Gestapo's tasks and methods, which had a separate department in Hamburg for dealing with remarks that were hostile to the state. K., who possessed above-average intelligence, was likewise completely aware of the consequences of her actions, having been able to judge the circumstances of the time from her life experiences.[228]

Both of them had also known that von Reichel's wife had been imprisoned in a concentration camp for months at this time, solely because of the so-called hostile remarks she had made, and had also heard A. express concern about how von Reichel's disposition and their mere association with him would endanger all of them. They therefore took action to bring about von Reichel's imprisonment, while also having been aware of the unlawfulness of their actions that would expose von Reichel to the tyranny and violence of the National Socialist regime. They also had prior knowledge that their actions could lead to the unforeseeable potential dangers of the worst forms of inhumane physical and mental suffering that he would face, having been acquainted with two different people who had been imprisoned in a concentration camp, and had known of von Reichel wife's bloodstained clothes that had been sent from the concentration camp. K. and L. were thus found guilty of contributing to unlawful and severe imprisonment under § 239, sections 2 and 49 of the criminal code.[229]

The previous jury court had not established whether A. had contributed to von Reichel's unlawful imprisonment. Although the fact that A. had told K. about von Reichel's disparaging political remarks had signaled her decision to take action against him, A. could not have anticipated this reaction. He had told her about his remarks many times beforehand, and had also known that von Reihel had made no secret of his anti-National Socialist disposition in front of her. In addition, K. herself had made disparaging remarks to A. about the regime several times. It therefore could not be assumed that the remarks that von Reichel had made to A.'s wife had provoked K. and L. to denounce him. It also could not be established that A. had knowledge of their report against von Reichel until after he was arrested. He also had not added to the incriminating evidence that had already been compiled against von Reichel when the Gestapo questioned him and his wife after von Reichel's arrest, and they could not have forwarded any exonerating facts during those prevailing circumstances. He was thereby acquitted due to a lack of incriminating evidence that could be brought forward against him.[230]

In evaluating the sentences that that had been imposed on K. and L., this court found that they had inflicted the greatest form of injustice on an irreproachable individual. They had filed a report against him for having made a harmless remark in his home to a housemate, while knowing that he was greatly afflicted by the arrest of his wife. This was in addition to having known from their contemporaries about the Gestapo's methods and the conditions in a concentration camp. In considering possible mitigating circumstances, it was noted that they had not had any prior convictions and that K. had previously saved another from persecution by the Gestapo. However, she had been the driving force behind von Reichel's arrest and imprisonment, and thus L.'s sentencing was to be considered in a more favorable view. The previous sentences were thus to be sustained.[231]

A later judgment in a denunciation case was reviewed by the Federal Supreme Court, where judgment was pronounced on 4 December 1952 and the case was reverted to the Essen jury court for further review of a previous judgment on crimes against humanity that had been pronounced on 26 January 1950. One of the defendants, hereafter cited as P., had been convicted and sentenced to ten months' imprisonment. The second accused, hereafter cited as D., had also been convicted, but the sentence was suspended on the grounds of the 31 December 1949 amnesty law. The public prosecutor filed an appeal for P.'s conviction.[232]

P. and Wilhelm Ricken had worked together as directors at the Rhineland-Westphalian electricity works, where Ricken made his opposition to the National Socialist regime conspicuous. He had remarked that the war would end the same way it had ended in 1918. Sometime later after Italy's fall in the autumn of 1943, Ricken asked P. what he thought about it. P. had replied that the traitors, including the Vatican, ought to be hanged. Ricken retorted that others who thought like him, namely fascists and National Socialists, ought to be hanged. Soon after this conversation, P. turned to D., who was a high-level leader in the SS as well as the mayor of Essen and co-chairman of the firm's board of directors. P. told him about Ricken's remarks, and demanded that D. file a report against him and have him removed from the enterprise. P. also unhesitatingly reported Ricken to the Gestapo, which forwarded the report to the People's Court, where P. appeared as a hostile witness against him. Ricken was sentenced to death on 8 March 1944 and executed on 2 May 1944.[233]

The public prosecutor's pending filing for the suspension of P.'s and D.'s convictions for crimes against humanity could not be sustained on the grounds of the abolition of Ordinance No. 47 of the British military government through Ordinance No. 234 of the British High Commissioner of 31 August 1951. This court took into consideration that jurisdiction over such cases had not been subsequently withdrawn as a result of this abolition, and it therefore did not have the jurisdiction to circumvent the verdict and the sentencing passed by the jury court according to Control Council Law No. 10. New proceedings would have to be henceforth judged according to German criminal law.[234]

The court resolved that the killing of Ricken was unlawful. Although this was the execution of a sentence, the guilty verdict passed by the People's Court was an arbitrary and obviously unjustifiable interpretation of positive law, making the sentencing unlawful and in complete disproportion to the charges made against the defendant. The sentencing was also unlawful in view of the interpretation of the law of the time, considering that Ricken's remarks were made in private, and therefore the death sentence was both inherently unlawful as well as completely unjustifiable. Both of the defendants had been aware of and had approved of these potential unlawful consequences, but it remained for the Essen regional court to discover with greater clarity the motives of the defendants, and conclusively establish the extent of their intent for causing the death penalty to be imposed.[235]

D. had vainly attempted to intervene in Ricken's favor by trying to get the *Gauleiter* to change his mind. It was to be determined why he had not taken any further measures toward saving his life, such as providing greater support for the petition for clemency that had been signed by several industrialists. P.'s unhesitatingly hostile conduct against Ricken had been made abundantly clear through his testimony at the People's Court. The defendants could be called to account for intentionally having aided and abetted an unlawful death, if it could be established that they had prior knowledge that the court judgment at this court would be unlawful as a means of suppression, and that they did not avoid contributing to this consequence by any possible means. If the court could not establish evidence of the defendant having contributing to the unlawful death of Ricken, the court would have to establish evidence of whether they had caused death through negligence.[236]

Judgment was pronounced in the re-opened proceedings at the jury court of the Essen regional court on 9 March 1953. While P. had died on 17 January 1953, this jury court re-evaluated the evidence concerning D. in accordance with German criminal law after Control Council Law No. 10 had been abolished. He was thereby tried for negligence causing death.[237] This court reconsidered how D. had initially not shown any interest in taking action against Ricken when he first spoke about the matter of his politically unreliable disposition to the general director of the firm, and continued to hesitate in the face of P.'s insistence in demanding that D. take action against Ricken for repeatedly speaking against Hitler and his policies and saying that the war was lost. He eventually relented about reporting the matter, considering that Ricken's remarks could not possibly eventually remain concealed and they feared possible unpleasant consequences if he did not intervene in this matter. He therefore called a Gestapo leader, hereafter cited as N., and after initial hesitation, told him what he had heard P. say about Ricken's remarks. This report then led to a Gestapo investigation against him, in which P. and others were questioned as witnesses. The Gestapo in Berlin then forwarded the matter to the state public prosecutor in Berlin, who in turn filed the bill of indictment with the People's Court. This led to the proceedings chaired by Roland Freisler on 8 March 1944, which ended with the imposition of a death sentence.[238] After this sentence was passed, the chairman of the board of directors of D.'s firm and D. attempted to ask a *Gauleiter* to intervene for clemency for Ricken, who roughly refused to take any action on their behalf. D. also made a petition for clemency that was signed by several industrialists. The Justice Minister, Otto Thierack, made no use of this petition and forwarded it to Hitler himself, who in turn simply ordered that the execution of the sentence was to take place within twenty-four hours.[239]

D. admitted that he did not take responsibility for Ricken's unlawful execution. His message to N. did not in itself lead to the court proceedings against him, as his remarks against the National Socialist regime had hitherto been known to the Gestapo and the *Gauleiter* who had come to the firm. Moreover, he had not expected this terrible fate to come to him, having anticipated a mild sentence and his removal from the firm, which he had thought would have been unavoidable, regardless of his message to the Gestapo, due to Ricken's public indiscretions. Besides, he had to fear for his own position and even his life if he did not convey what Ricken had said, due to his animosity against Himmler and Henze, the police president, which had resulted in his dismissal from his post as the inspector general of the German energy industry in 1942. Moreover, he had intended for N. to talk to P. directly, and had given his report to him verbally during questioning. During this time, N. warned him that he would be in very serious danger if he did not allow himself to be questioned. In addition, he had tried to save Ricken by seeking clemency, citing his indispensable work for the war effort, which he could not sign himself as a member of the SS because this attempt at intervention could have caused him great difficulties.[240]

The court determined that his claim that he had decided to report Ricken's remarks upon having been pressed by P. and N. was not subject to any doubt, thus having acted out of pressure and fear. On the other hand, he had also given a detailed explanation about this matter when he called N., who therefore did not need to put heavy pressure on D. for information, as D. maintained. It was also maintained that this conveying of Ricken's remarks set in motion the course of events that later led to his execution. However, P. had told him about these remarks and testified against Ricken at the People's Court about what he had heard firsthand, whereas D. had conveyed them to N. after P.'s repeated prompting.[241]

The court thus accepted D.'s claim that he did not intend to cause Ricken's death, which was emphasized by his initial hesitation to act against him as well as his especially good reputation. Several witnesses testified how he had made his decisions on the basis of professional rather than political considerations. He had prevented Jews from being called on to do roadwork, and had called the burning of synagogues and other offenses against Jews a crime committed by the Germans that would be a heavy burden for them. According to other witnesses, he had stifled knowledge of remarks that were hostile to the state to prevent them from being conveyed to NSDAP members in the firm, and had intervened in behalf of another, requesting that he be allowed to keep his position at work after he had been expelled from the NSDAP. Another witness further testified that he had been removed from his office as the inspector general of the German energy industry in 1942 due to political considerations having come into conflict with his professional and non-political disposition. He was also known to have tried to protect alleged enemies of the National Socialist regime, by means such as securing the release of a father of one of the witnesses from Gestapo custody. In addition, he played a decisive role in preventing a Catholic children's home from being closed, and tried to have another witness released after she had been arrested.[242]

In view of the examination of his unobjectionable testimony and the evidence presented by various witnesses, the court concluded that D. did not intend for Ricken to be killed, and probably had not anticipated this consequence. In determining whether his actions intentionally led to an unlawful death and thus justified the charge of murder or aiding and abetting manslaughter, it was determined that he had used all possible means to avert Ricken's death after he had reported him to the Gestapo at his own risk while his political position was unstable after he had fallen out of favor with the National Socialist authorities. His actions also could not have been interpreted as negligence causing death. In addition to having tried to save Ricken's life by filing for clemency, he could not have anticipated the death sentence and had recognized that it was unlawful. He was to be reproached for having initiated the process with N., but his guilt of having caused his death through neglect therefore could not be established since it had become impossible for him to avert this danger. D. was therefore acquitted, with the added consideration that he had acted out of duress in accordance with § 52 and § 54 of the criminal code, of having caused unlawful imprisonment.[243]

A later case was heard at the Kassel regional court, where judgment was pronounced on 16 November 1954. This case involved a Gestapo informer, Dagmar Irmgart, who had been active in Gießen and Berlin from 1941 to 1944. She was accused of aiding and abetting murder in two cases, through having provided incriminating materials against two individuals, Heinrich Will and Rev. Dr. Max Josef Metzger, which constituted the basis for their convictions and death sentences passed at the People's Court. She was also accused of nine cases of aiding and abetting severe unlawful imprisonment of individuals, hereafter cited as Renate R., Pastor St., Steffi Ha., S., Bo., Mrs. Falckenberg, Dr. Kaufmann, Elisabeth Will, and Ba., who were arrested by the Gestapo and were tried by the People's Court or the Special Court in Darmstadt and Bremen, and some of them were consequently imprisoned in a concentration camp. She was therefore charged with aiding and abetting attempted murder in the case of Dr. Kaufmann, whose death sentence was not executed; causing death through negligence in the cases of Heinrich and Elisabeth Will, Mrs. Falckenberg, Pastor St., and Dr. Metzger; aiding and abetting severe unlawful imprisonment in the cases of Heinrich Will and Dr. Metzger, and aiding and abetting unlawful imprisonment in the case of Ba.[244]

She had first been called to account for her actions at the Gießen denazification tribunal on 24 and 25 September 1947, which classified her as a major offender and sentenced her to ten years' imprisonment in a labor camp. Apart from being in police custody from 16 October 1948 to 2 February 1949 before these court proceedings, she was imprisoned at the labor camp in Darmstadt from 25 September 1947 to 31 October 1950 when she was released on parole. She was then taken into police custody again following an arrest order by the Limburg regional court, and remained in custody until 1 November 1951, after being acquitted[245] of two charges of aiding and abetting murder, aiding and abetting severe imprisonment in nine cases, and taking part in a murder.[246]

The Federal Supreme Court quashed this verdict in its judgment passed on 29 January 1953, and reverted the case to the jury court at the Kassel regional court for further review. The Limburg regional court had dismissed the charge of criminal responsibility against her for having caused the Gestapo to act against Elisabeth Will, stating it could not be proven that there was a causal connection between her report about the Kaufmann circle and Will being taken to a concentration camp because of her Jewish heritage. The Federal Supreme Court disputed this judgment, arguing that Will had been arrested on the basis of the defendant's report which led to this consequence. She was therefore to be prosecuted for unlawful imprisonment resulting in death. The court had also not appropriately addressed the question of Bo.'s arrest, which was also related to the defendant's report about the Kaufmann circle.[247]

The jury court also had not acknowledged the unlawfulness of the defendant's actions. This included determining the legal basis on which the members of the Kaufmann circle were prosecuted according to the law at the time, especially when the sentences were disproportionately severe with regard to the offenses, such as the death sentences passed against Dr. Kaufmann and Heinrich Will and the heavy prison sentence passed against Elisabeth Will. It was to be determined whether listening to foreign radio broadcasts constituted treason by supporting the enemy, which was not subject to the death penalty. The same consideration was to apply to evaluate the heavy sentence that had been passed against Elisabeth Will for having listened to foreign radio broadcasts as especially harsh. The new proceedings were also to determine whether the other sentences had been excessively harsh, and thereby examine whether the defendant could be charged with unlawful imprisonment with regard to the others who were implicated and taken into Gestapo custody. New proceedings were also to determine whether the defendant was responsible for Ba.'s first arrest by the Gestapo on 7 February 1942 and her second arrest on 5 June 1942, and whether her two terms of imprisonment were unlawful.[248] The fundamental error in the previous judgment was found in evaluating whether the death sentence passed against Rev. Dr. Metzger was unlawful in view of determining whether he was guilty of treason. Her report about him to the Gestapo had led to his arrest by the Gestapo and subsequent imprisonment, but this was not mentioned in the previous judgment. New proceedings were also to determine whether his imprisonment had been unlawful.[249]

The defendant returned to police custody from 15 April to 24 April 1953 on the grounds of the Federal Supreme Court's judgment These proceedings took the earlier denazification tribunal verdict as the basis for re-examining the facts of the case and the events that had taken place before passing a new sentence.[250] The Gestapo had first become interested in her due to her traveling to her native Sweden twice a year, just as they had been interested in all others who traveled to neutral countries during the war who were requested to report on matters of political significance abroad. She also aroused their interest due to her association with the Christian Wingolf association and her membership since 1940 in the *Una Sancta* ecumenical movement led by Rev. Dr. Metzger. By the autumn of 1941, the Gestapo in Darmstadt ordered its branch office in Gieβen to approach her about cooperating with them. She accepted this task, not because of a sense of responsibility to the state and administration of justice or for the political regime of the time or maintaining wartime morals, but because of an innate need for admiration, a certain lust for adventure and intrigue, as well as the personal advantage of being able to travel to Sweden with the Gestapo's visa approval and their provision for her travel expenses. She was initially mainly employed as an informer in Gieβen, assigned to report on so-called church politics. She was later given further assignments by the *Reichsicherheitsamt* (RHSA) in Berlin to be undertaken in Germany and abroad, particularly during her trips to Sweden.[251]

She became acquainted with Dr. Alfred Kaufmann in 1936 through the meetings of the Wingolf association in Gieβen, and formed a group of individuals who were opposed to the National Socialist regime, especially after the outbreak of the war. He organized evening meetings in his apartment where they had political discussions and listened to foreign broadcasts, especially after the flight of Rudolf Hess to England in May 1941, who had been his student at the German school in Alexandria for eight years. Bo., Heinrich, and his Jewish wife Elisabeth Will belonged to this group from its beginning. Other members joined later, including others hereafter cited as S., Ha., Mrs. Falckenberg, R., and Mrs. K.[252]

When the defendant attended these meetings, she always expressed harsh criticisms against National Socialism, and insulted Hitler and his regime. She therefore gave the impression to the others at the meeting that she was a convinced opponent of the regime and gained their trust, suggesting that they read out letters with political contents at these meetings. Sometimes she asked provocative questions, and appeared to support the other individuals' disparaging remarks about the regime while they expressed their opinions freely. She would then immediately give detailed reports about what had been said and done to the Gestapo office in Gießen, whether it was political or otherwise, especially mentioning that they had listened to foreign broadcasts and discussed what they had heard. She also commented that disparaging political remarks had been made, and she eventually urged the Gestapo to arrest the members of this group, which they resolved to do on 6 February 1942, giving her advance notice of their intentions. In turn, she urged S., Ha., and Mrs. Falckenberg to be there. They were all arrested, along with Dr. Kaufmann and Mr. and Mrs. Will, by a large contingent of Gestapo agents from Darmstadt and Gießen. Their apartments were searched at the same time, but not the apartment of the defendant. She was released later that evening after she was shown the incriminating evidence that she had compiled against those who were arrested. Pastor St. and his wife and R. who had not been present during this evening were arrested on the following morning, while St.'s wife was later released to conceal the defendant's release on that morning, after she had also been released the night before, with the pretext that they had to look after the children in their homes.[253]

At noon on the same day, two Gestapo officials came to the homes of two witnesses in these proceedings hereafter cited as K. and Ka., allegedly to question them about Kauffmann. Their apartments were searched while they were taken to and questioned at the Gießen Gestapo office, for having earlier had social contact with Kaufmann. They were later released, not having been members of his group. On the same day, Kaufmann, Mr. and Mr. Will, Mrs. Falckenberg, and Pastor St., as well as S., R. and Ha. were taken to Darmstadt.[254] Pastor St. later died in police custody on 16 March 1942. The Gestapo cited the cause of death as suicide, and it could not be established whether he had died of other causes or was killed through mistreatment. Upon examining the facts of the case against the other defendants who remained in custody, the general state prosecutor at the People's Court raised an indictment against Kaufmann, Mr. and Mrs. Will, Mrs. Falckenberg, Ha., and R. for listening to foreign radio broadcasts, high treason, and treason. The People's Court proceedings later took place on 20 and 21 July 1942.[255] Kaufmann and Heinrich Will were convicted on 21 July 1942 of high treason in supporting the enemy, and were sentenced to death. The other defendants were convicted of listening to foreign radio broadcasts. Elisabeth Will was sentenced to six years' imprisonment, S. to three years, Ha. and Mrs. Falckenberg and R. to three years.[256]

The judgment stated that Kaufmann had listened to foreign radio broadcasts since the beginning of the war. He had also always made disparaging political remarks to R. from the autumn of 1939 to the beginning of 1942, once saying that the war would not last much longer, and that there would be a new nation in which all of the conditions that he criticized would be eliminated. Soon after the war broke out, he said there would not be a war if there were not any "villains and scoundrels." From May 1941 to 6 February 1942, he had arranged for the other defendants to listen to foreign radio broadcasts from London and Switzerland. Heinrich Will had sometimes tuned into them and ensured the reception was clear. Kaufmann and Will had discussed the contents of these broadcasts in the presence of the other accused in a manner that was hostile to the state, often in a spiteful and sneering manner. They had hoped for a military collapse that would lead to a bloody political coup, and had talked about an occupation of Germany after this collapse. They had also insulted the leadership of the regime and disputed the reliability of the German military's news reports. On 23 January 1942, Kaufmann and Will expressed suspicions that General Field Marshal von Reichenau had not died of natural causes, since he did not want to respect Hitler's crazy plans, and talked about how Hitler had killed anyone who did not agree with him. They also claimed that Mölders was also killed for not agreeing with Hitler's plans. In addition, they had spoken about how they anticipated Germany would be divided after the collapse, and that at least a million Germans would be taken to Russia for forced labor for reconstruction, and that all members of the SS and the SA would be killed, and in the small remaining part of Germany, only reliable Germans who had not dealt with the Nazi swindle would remain. Kaufmann had also spoken about the feigned National Socialist disposition of German workers, and Will had spoken about the imminent re-conquest of the Ukraine by the Russians and mutinies by German troops.[257]

The women in this group also occasionally made disparaging remarks. R. was to be convicted for having said that in her view, von Reicheneu was subject to incurring strokes. Mrs. Will and Ha. had often said that the conditions in their native Austria under Schuschnigg had been better, and that there was prevailing discontent. Ha. had said how the reoccupation of Benghazi was meaningless, since it would be lost again. Mrs. Falckenberg had sometimes talked disparagingly about the compulsory collection of clothing by the NSDAP in Nuremberg. S. had spoken about outrages in women's prisons, atrocities in nursing homes, and shootings in concentration camps, and had once made a nasty political joke about Hitler and Göring.[258]

Kaufmann was accused of having dealt with the enemy by inciting others to listen to foreign radio broadcasts, thereby exposing them to enemy propaganda as a result of his "reactionary attitude" and hostile disposition to National Socialism. Heinrich Will was accused of the same, mainly because he was married to a Jew. Both were also accused of intending to demoralize the women in the group, and had expected the news from foreign radio broadcasts to be circulated to others through them, and had thereby implicated them and made them subject to prosecution, as well as being guilty of having caused Pastor St.'s alleged suicide. Elisabeth Will was also especially reproached for having listened to foreign radio broadcasts while being aware that as a Jew, she was especially obliged to respect the law. S. was also given a heavier sentence due to her position as a teacher and being a member of the NSV.[259]

Kaufmann and Will endured inhumane conditions during their imprisonment at the prison in Frankfurt-Preugesheim. Kaufmann was spared being executed, and the sentence was commuted to eight years' imprisonment as a result of an intercession from five universities and many highly influential personalities. He remained imprisoned until he was liberated by American troops on 1 April 1945. A petition for a pardon for Heinrich Will was refused due to his having a Jewish wife, and he was executed on 20 February 1943. Elisabeth Will was imprisoned in a women's prison in Darmstadt until she was taken to Auschwitz concentration camp on 7 December 1942 where she later perished. S. remained imprisoned until 20 February 1945. Mrs. Falckenberg was imprisoned in Darmstadt until she was released for medical treatment and was provisionally released for medical reasons in December 1944, and died of bronchial cancer very soon afterward. R. was imprisoned in Darmstadt until her conditional release on 23 February 1944. Ha. was likewise imprisoned in Darmstadt until her conditional release on 20 February 1944.[260]

The defendant was also implicated in the arrest of Bo., who was arrested in Bremen in connection with the Kaufmann circle. She had taken part in its meetings while was living in Gießen with Mr. and Mrs. Will from October 1939 to February 1940, and had had political discussions and exchanged correspondence with Kaufmann thereafter. Her letters included political questions in which she also expressed herself in ways that were hostile to the state, and the contents thereof were read out and discussed during Kaufmann's meetings. These letters were found in the house search by the Gestapo on the evening of 6 February 1942 and consequently led to her immediate arrest. An intervention by a Gestapo official that she had known led to her imprisonment in Bremen, and therefore she was not taken to Darmstadt to be tried in the People's Court proceedings there. She remained in Gestapo custody in Bremen until 6 March 1942, and then in prison before she was convicted by the local Special Court on 18 May 1942. She was found guilty of making insidious attacks on the state as cited in § 1 of the *Heimtückegesetz*, and three cases of listening to foreign radio broadcasts, and sentenced to a year and six months' imprisonment. She was later released on 2 June 1943.[261]

The defendant was also implicated in another case, in which she denounced an acquaintance hereafter cited as Ba., who had not made any secret of her rejection of National Socialism, and had had several minor run ins with the political authorities for years. After the defendant became an informer for the Gestapo in 1941, she made detailed written reports about Ba., such as mentioning how she had made hostile remarks to the state about political conditions in Germany while she was traveling in Sweden, which led to her mail from Sweden being examined and her being placed under constant observation. The defendant also reported that Ba. and her acquaintance Bö. listened to foreign radio broadcasts together. As a result of the defendant's reports about her, Ba. was arrested on 7 February 1942 in connection with the Kaufmann circle, although she had never gone to its meetings, having declined the defendant's invitation to do so. The Gestapo also confronted Bö. as to whether she could provide incriminating testimony about Ba., since it was known to them that they often had political discussions. Meanwhile, Ba. was imprisoned for a week until she was interrogated on 13 February 1942, when she was questioned about matters that she had discussed with the defendant, such as whether she listened to foreign broadcasts, which she denied. She was then released, not having had any connection with the Kaufmann circle.[262]

Ba. later told various acquaintances about how the accused had denounced her, which she later learned, and wrote a letter to Ba. in the middle of May 1942 demanding that she retract what she had said, and threatened her with telling the Gestapo "everything that she knew." Ba. then employed a lawyer to write a letter in response threatening her with action for slander. The defendant retaliated by filing a new detailed report about Ba. to the Gestapo, which led to Ba.'s re-arrest on 5 June 1942. She was at times sharply and thoroughly interrogated for nine hours about allegedly having made disparaging remarks about Hitler, Göring, and the handing of the Jewish question, which she denied. Above all, she was accused of listening to foreign radio broadcasts, as the defendant had said. She initially denied doing so, but eventually admitted to doing so after repeated accusations. She was then taken to the women's prison in Darmstadt, and was later convicted by the Special Court in Darmstadt on 2 October 1942 for listening to foreign radio broadcasts, to which she had listened alone, and was sentenced to a year and three months' imprisonment. She was conditionally released on 1 March 1943, but was then re-arrested by the Gestapo on the same day. She was imprisoned in Gießen and Kassel and Berlin before being taken to Ravensbrück concentration camp on 11 October 1943.[263]

The defendant was also implicated in a different case involving the *Una Sancta* movement that strove for a convergence between Catholic and Lutheran churches, and was led by Rev. Dr. Metzger until his arrest. The defendant came into contact with his movement, allegedly having been interested in its goals, and later became a member. He had already been under the suspicion of the Gestapo since 1934, and the defendant was given the task of spying on him after she became an informer for them. She invited him to go to Gießen in January 1942 to give a lecture about his movement. He had planned to establish a group there, an idea that foundered after the arrest of the Kaufmann circle; the defendant also then withheld her support, since she had enough to do with the Wingolf association. Nevertheless, he believed she was genuinely interested in the religious goals of his movement and assumed that she was opposed to the National Socialist regime in view of her conduct and demeanor, and he therefore entrusted her with his most secret thoughts, including political ones.[264]

During the adverse course of the war in Russia during the winter of 1941/1942, Metzger had thought about writing to Hitler to ask him for a withdrawal in order to make an acceptable peace treaty possible. He was dissuaded from sending this letter by a pastor friend of his who laughed at this plan and strongly advised him not to send it. At the beginning of 1943, he told the defendant that he had developed a plan to contact the English church leadership through the mediation of the Archbishop E. in Stockholm to possibly approach the English government about imposing tolerable peace conditions on Germany after the expected collapse of the regime. At the same time, he would present in writing how he envisaged the political reconstruction of Germany after the end of the war with the suppression and prosecution of all influential National Socialists. Although he was aware of the danger of this political Endeavour, he nevertheless thought that everything needed to be put at stake for a great matter.[265] The accused showed great interest in this plan. After a Swedish pastor in Berlin refused to speak with Archbishop E. personally for this purpose, Metzger then planned for the defendant to have this memorandum taken to Stockholm, which she accepted, and lent him a typewriter that the Gestapo had provided to her for the purpose of writing his political thoughts and plans, allegedly to conceal his identity by not using his own typewriter.[266]

Metzger typed his political thoughts into memorandum in early 1943 and then gave it to the defendant, allegedly so that she would forward it to Archbishop E. on her next trip to Sweden. She then informed the RASH in Berlin about it, which planned to use it as incriminating evidence against him. On 29 June 1943, she went to visit him, and soon thereafter, six Gestapo officials assigned to the RHSA's religious affairs department arrested him, took the memorandum, and took him to a prison in Berlin-Plötzensee.[267] The general state prosecutor at the People's Court raised the indictment against him on 20 September 1943, in which he was accused of writing recommendations for the establishment of a democratic German federal state under the influence of enemy states after he expected Germany to be defeated, and therefore he was to be prosecuted for preparing to commit high treason in connection with enemy government representatives. He later appeared before the People's Court on 14 October 1943. He was convicted of treason and was sentenced to death on the same day on the grounds of his political memorandum, and was later executed on 17 April 1944.[268]

The defendant disputed the indictment that was raised against her, denying that she had been a Gestapo informer and especially denied that she had written reports against the Kaufmann circle and Ba., or had denounced Rev. Dr. Metzger, or had reported them to the Gestapo.[269] However, her testimony was refuted in view of the evidence that was presented by several witnesses whose credible testimonies disproved what the defendant had claimed in her defense. She was therefore to be convicted for providing the Gestapo with incriminating materials that led to the arrests and convictions of the members of the Kaufmann circle, Ba.'s arrests and conviction, and Rev. Dr. Metzger's arrest and conviction.[270]

The Federal Supreme Court had ruled that it had to be determined whether the sentences that had been passed against those who had been denounced by the defendant were unlawful with regard to the precepts of the law at the time, which would correspond to the unlawfulness of her conduct, and whether she had anticipated this unlawful sentencing and had intended and approved of these consequences of her actions.[271] The judgment that had been passed on Kaufmann had not been considered unlawful in the previous judgment, which evaluated the circumstances of the evidence in accordance with the law at the time. There was also no evidence to indicate that the defendant had expected or wanted and approved of the death sentence that had been passed, having only expected that they would receive a term of imprisonment.[272] The death sentence that the People's Court had passed on Rev. Dr. Metzger was also not unlawful in view of the facts of the case and the prevailing wartime circumstances, and thus was not considered disproportionate to his actions. The defendant's contribution to this death sentence and its execution therefore was not subject to prosecution.[273]

The judgment against Heinrich Will was considered unlawful, as the People's Court had not sufficiently justified why his actions had warranted the death sentence, which was excessively harsh. The fact that he was married to a Jew was most probably a decisive factor in this court's judgment,[274] which was also completely unjustifiable as it was irrelevant to the facts of the case. The defendant's actions in contributing to the deaths of both Heinrich and Elisabeth Will were correspondingly unlawful, especially since she was not obliged to file a report against them, and she considered Kaufmann's and Will's conduct to be harmless. However, it could not be established whether she had intended and approved of an unlawful death sentence, or had expected this judgment.[275]

The six year sentence passed on Elisabeth Will was also unlawful due to its excessive harshness that did not correspond to the extent of the offense, and also in comparison with the sentences passed against R., S., and Mrs. Falckenberg. Her Jewish heritage was an aggravating factor that did not relate to the principles of criminal law, even at that time. The defendant's report about her was also unlawful, considering that, as in the previous cases, she was not under any obligation to file a report. However, it could not be established that the defendant had expected an excessively harsh and unlawful judgment, or that she had wanted or approved of this consequence of her actions. Nor could it be established that she had been able to foresee that Mrs. Will would later be taken to Auschwitz concentration camp, not having known that Mrs. Will was a so-called full Jew. It also could not be established whether the defendant had expected that her report about the Kaufmann circle would result in Bo.'s arrest and conviction, in view of the fact that they had not known each other. She also could not be held accountable for Ba.'s imprisonment at Ravensbrück concentration camp, which was a later consequence that she could not have anticipated, let alone accepted or approved of.[276]

In determining the extent of the sentencing, the court took into account that she did not have any prior convictions, and had been imprisoned in a labor camp for the conduct and actions that were under scrutiny in the present proceedings. In view of all of the circumstances, she was sentenced to a year and three months' imprisonment for intentionally causing the harsh imprisonment of Rev. Dr. Metzger, a sentence that was in addition to the time she had already served, in addition to two years' deprivation of her civil rights. She was acquitted of the other charges,[277] as there was insufficient evidence to bring about convictions in the cases of the Kaufmann circle, Bo., and Ba.[278]

This verdict was later upheld by the Federal Supreme Court on 28 June 1956[279] with certain reservations about some of shortcomings in the judgment. In reviewing the facts of the case relating to Rev. Dr. Metzger, the Kassel regional court was reproached with misinterpreting the meaning of aiding an enemy power, and thereby misjudged how the death sentence that the People's Court had passed on him had been unlawful. The Federal Supreme Court ruled that he had intended to serve Germany's true interests in the face of the collapse that he had anticipated, and therefore he had not been guilty of treason, while the application of the law at the time had been exploited for destroying political opposition.[280] The Kassel regional court had thus misjudged how he had neither supported the enemy, nor had committed any apparent criminal act that could have damaged Germany's war effort, and therefore this court had neglected to examine how the defendant had contributed to Metzger's unlawful killing under the guise of the administration of justice. The unjustified acquittal hitherto passed by two separate jury courts demonstrated the exceptional factual and legal difficulties that were encountered in prosecuting National Socialist judicial crimes after the passage of time had closed minds to injustice.[281] This court had otherwise correctly ascertained that the defendant had aided and abetted unlawful severe imprisonment, in view of how Metzger had endured inhumane conditions in Gestapo custody without any charges made against him. The conviction and sentencing was considered appropriate, and the defendant's appeal was thereby rejected.[282]

The Kassel regional court was also reproached for insufficiently examining how the death sentence passed on Dr. Kaufmann was not apparently justifiable, in view of the principles of the rule of law, and whether Kaufmann and the members of this group had undermined the war effort, and why a death sentence which the Federal Supreme Court ruled to be arbitrary and cruel was justifiable,. The death sentence was thus unlawful and was to have been taken into consideration as an intentional attempt to commit murder. Although taking moderate action against listening to foreign radio broadcasts during wartime may have been legally admissible in preserving the public interests, listening to them as part of a group and discussing the contents did not warrant the death sentence under any circumstances. On the other hand, the Federal Supreme Court confirmed that it could not be established that the defendant could have foreseen the death sentence being handed down in this case, as well as for the case of Heinrich Will.[283]

The case relating to Elisabeth Will was also maintained. The Kassel regional court had correctly maintained that the six year sentence of imprisonment was unlawful, which was imposed on her because of her Jewish heritage. However, no one, including the defendant, could have expected such an arbitrary sentence. The same followed for the case relating to S. She also could not be held accountable for the second arrest of Ba.[284] The defendant was therefore acquitted of these charges, although her actions had set forth the events that led to inhumane consequences for those she had reported to the Gestapo.

This case demonstrated the limitations of German law with regard to prosecuting crimes against humanity, in comparison with the application of Control Council Law No. 10. After the application of this law by the German courts was abolished, National Socialist lawlessness in the administration of justice that had inhumane consequences for those who were denounced and convicted in previous judgments could not be circumvented. While the law was applied with greater objectivity, objective considerations outweighed the more subjective ones, and although there were inhumane consequences that had been incurred, they could not be prosecuted as such. Previous judgments that were considered lawful at the time became obstacles to bringing about convictions under German law, in spite of the inhumane consequences that been incurred by the victims of denunciation. On the other hand, the defendant's conviction by a denazification tribunal had also imposed retribution for her actions that she had taken against others, which likewise served to circumvent the shortcomings that were to be found in the objective application of German law.

A later case heard at the Munich II regional court from 27 to 29 November 1957 proved to be based on political rather than personal motives. The main accused, hereafter cited as S., had been a convinced National Socialist who also was a member of the NSDAP and held positions in two of its affiliated organizations, serving as a group leader of the BDM (*Bund Deutscher Mädel*) and the shop steward for the DAF at the Deutsche Bank where she worked as a bookkeeper from 1939 to 1945. Given her political convictions, she had been very annoyed at remarks made by the director of the bank in 1943, hereafter cited as Mi. He had made critical remarks in his office at the bank about the NSDAP, the German army, the outbreak of the war, and his doubts about the course of the war, which he no longer believed that Germany would win. S. overheard and noted these remarks and was determined to act against him.[285]

She first told her father about these remarks, who had been a NSDAP member for a long time as well as also being a convinced National Socialist and a friend of Mi.'s, and told him to report the matter to M., who was the *Ortsgruppenleiter* of the NSDAP in their local community of Hindenburg in Upper Silesia. Her father was not surprised, having been familiar with her employer's attitude, and told her he would not do anything and told her that she should not to do anything either. She nevertheless continued pressing her father to take action against Mi. by reporting him to M. However, this bank did not fall within this area of jurisdiction and therefore he would not take responsibility for this matter. About three weeks later, S.'s father spoke to M. about Mi.'s remarks as a result of S. continually pressing him about this matter, and he again replied that it lay outside his area of jurisdiction and therefore would not do anything.[286]

Meanwhile, Mi. continued making critical remarks about the NSDAP and what S. considered to be serious defeatist remarks, which prompted her to take action against him by reporting him to M. herself in early August 1943. She gave him written records of what she had heard Mi. say in his office, including: "The *Führer* understands best how to swindle our nation"; "our air force has failed to act against the English one"; "He sees black" (concerning the ill-fated American bombing attack on Romanian oilfields); "When will it be over for us?" (concerning the overthrow of the Italian regime and the institution of the Badoglio government). M. was appalled by these serious remarks, which he said ought to be brought to the attention of J., who held jurisdiction over where these remarks were made. S. continued to emphasize her justification for taking action against Mi., in spite of M. telling her that there could be serious consequences for Mi. if these remarks were made known to the higher level political authorities. [287]

S. was aware of how her reporting Mi. could lead to criminal proceedings being initiated against him at the People's Court and then subsequent imprisonment and a death sentence. Nevertheless, she was determined to report him to J., the local *Kreisleiter,* who she could expect to convey the report to the police. Although M. recognized the unlawful consequences that could transpire, he nevertheless decided to report the matter to J. to demonstrate his loyalty to the NSDAP, and was too cowardly to rectify the matter amicably through a conversation with Mi. J. then questioned S. about this matter at his office the next day, where she repeated what she had told M, which was recorded by his secretary. J. was outraged by what he heard and likewise expected the matter to lead to criminal proceedings, and hoped he would gain recognition for being a convinced National Socialist as well as an energetic *Kreisleiter* for taking action in this matter and personally bringing it to the attention of the police. S. was thereafter questioned by the criminal police and the Gestapo, and confirmed what she had said earlier about Mi.'s remarks, without mentioning anything to exonerate him, adding that she had heard Mi. say: "Everything is going down and under, but that's the way it is when a system is heading to its end."[288] Her insistence on reporting what she had heard him say led to Mi.'s arrest at the bank on 10 August 1943. He appeared before the People's Court with Roland Freisler as the presiding judge on 14

September 1943, where S. appeared as the leading witness and again repeated the remarks she had heard him make. He was sentenced to death, even though the prosecutor did not request it, and was executed on 21 September 1943.[289]

S. claimed in her defense that she had not intended to report Mi. to the authorities, having intended to ask M. for advice on how to prevent Mi. from making disparaging remarks, and believed that M. or J. would reprimand him for making them. However, the hearing of the evidence refuted these claims, as she had never attempted to speak with Mi. about this matter directly. Moreover, she had pursued the matter with the local National Socialist authorities with a great deal of stubbornness while having prior common knowledge of the severe consequences of denouncing him at that time for having made illegal so-called defeatist remarks, including having expected him to appear before the People's Court and receive a death sentence.[290]

M. claimed that his not conveying the report about Mi.'s remarks would have resulted in his being rebuked by the *Kreisleiter,* but this proved untenable. He likewise had prior knowledge of these potential consequences, having read in the newspapers about how the People's Court had imposed death sentences against so-called defeatists, as well as having known about this through his activity in the NSDAP. J. denied having conveyed the report about Mi.'s remarks to the police, only admitting that he had dealt with the matter by questioning S. and keeping a record about it before intending to settle the matter with Mi. verbally. These claims also proved untenable in view of S.'s testimony, having himself said that Mi.'s remarks were serious and were subject to prosecution, and that he would take the matter to the police, which was also proven by an eyewitness account. J. had also been aware of the possible consequences of his actions due to his own activity in the NSDAP.[291]

This court ruled that S. had intentionally killed Mi. by an interpretation of § 212 of the criminal code. Her report that was conveyed through M. and her cooperation in the forwarding of this report had brought about the death sentence, and therefore she intended for him to be killed. Her actions were also unlawful, having been aware that the death sentence was an unusually excessive punishment that was inherently unlawful in view of Mi.'s actions. Moreover, she was not obliged by the law at the time to report her superior's statements to the political authorities, and took the initiative to do so without any justification. Having been a convinced and uncompromising National Socialist, she was fully aware that the possible outcome of her actions would be the People's Court arbitrarily passing a death sentence without her superior being afforded the benefit of a fair trial. She knew this would happen regardless of the unlawfulness of these consequences, at a time when this court was known for imposing excessively harsh sentences without regard for the principles of the rule of law in the interest of killing the alleged enemies of the regime and intimidating the population.[292]

There were not any mitigating circumstances that could have been taken into consideration, and she was found to be of sound mind and completely criminally liable for her actions. She had taken action out of her own free volition in persisting in conveying her report about Mi. to M., and did not do so out of any necessity. She was therefore found guilty of murder under § 212 of the German criminal code and § 239, section III concerning unlawful imprisonment leading to death, having intentionally initiated the course of events that led to these consequences that resulted from the unlawful sentence passed by the People's Court.[293]

Both M. and J. had also willingly contributed to these consequences by conveying S.'s report about Mi. The police had first been made aware of Mi.'s remarks through J., after M. had brought the matter to his attention by conveying information that S. had reported to him. They had therefore supported taking action against Mi. by accelerating and facilitating the process of political persecution that S. had initiated, not having had any justification for or having been under any obligation to support S.'s unlawful actions, regardless of the fact that they were NSDAP functionaries. They had also been aware of the potential unlawful consequences of conveying her report to other authorities, but chose to take this course of action as convinced National Socialists who wanted to demonstrate their loyalty to the NSDAP, rather than rectifying the matter through other means that probably would not have led to Mi.'s unlawful imprisonment and death.[294]

M. and J. also could not cite mitigating circumstances. Both were also deemed to be of sound mind and therefore criminally liable for their actions. They also could not demonstrate they had acted out of any necessity, and they could have taken action by merely warning Mi. about the possibility of criminal proceedings being instituted against him. They would not have exposed themselves to any danger had they dealt with the matter by other means. They had also been aware of the unlawful consequences of their actions in supporting S.'s actions, and were therefore found guilty of intentionally having contributed to aiding and abetting murder under § 212, and unlawful imprisonment resulting in death as defined in § 239, section III of the criminal code.[295]

In determining the extent of the sentencing, the court took into consideration that the three accused did not have any prior convictions and had been considerably influenced by National Socialist propaganda at the time of their actions. The court also considered that S. had only been twenty-two years old at that time, had been influenced by National Socialist ideology throughout her upbringing, her brother had been missing since 1942, and her bridegroom had been killed in the war. On the other hand, she had abused her employer's trust, after he had given her employment, and had been a very good superior, and she had denounced him without any warning. In M.'s favor, it was taken into consideration that he had hesitated to act on S.'s report, and that he had been in an unfavorable situation by having been confronted with making a report by S. who had been a convinced National Socialist. Moreover, he had served respectably in his political office as *Ortsgruppenleiter* and had spent five years in a Polish prisoner-of-war camp. In J.'s favor, it was considered that he had served as a brave soldier who had been wounded six times after having had served as a *Kreisleiter,* and had otherwise acted respectably at other times toward others. In view of these circumstances, S. was sentenced to four years' imprisonment, while M. was sentenced to two years' and J. to three years' imprisonment.[296] The federal appeal court later sustained this verdict on 13 May 1958. This court determined that the evidence presented in the Munich regional court II proceedings was accurate, and therefore revision was unnecessary.[297]

One of the last denunciation cases in the Federal Republic of Germany was heard at the Hamburg regional court, where judgment was pronounced on 8 May 1964. The defendant, hereafter cited as F., had been a consultant for the legal department of the National Socialist propaganda ministry and had written several articles on behalf of the regime. On 6 November 1942, he recorded the contents of a conversation with his wife at the time, hereafter cited as S., that he had earlier that day. S. met an old acquaintance, hereafter cited as T., in a pub in the city centre of Berlin while out with a friend, hereafter cited as B.[298]

After S. told T. about her husband's workplace during their conversation, they started talking about the political situation. T. told them how the German troops in North Africa were beaten and would soon have to leave altogether. All of Italy would then have to be occupied since the Italians would not fight any further. The war would then be lost. S. argued if the war was lost, then one ought to put one's head in a gas oven. T. continued that a cultivated and intelligent lady such as herself must not chatter on about what he called "Nazi claptrap." One would finally be able to breathe again and move about freely after the war was over. The English did not have anything against the Germans, and so only the Nazi bigwigs and the leading gentlemen of the ministries, such as where her husband worked, would be put up against a wall. Hitler was not normal, and was in fact completely mentally deranged while living only on injections. If he were to be taken into an insane asylum, he would not come out again, and the crazy demographic policy would then come to an end. If he could make suggestions for peace terms, he would prescribe that German women not have more than two children, since they would only lead to future wars and Germany would not allow peace. When

S. again objected to his remarks, T. continued further by saying that it was unfortunate that the English were not at the Brandenburg Gate yet, but it would not be too much longer. The members of the SS were the worst sadists when compared to the Russian commissars.[299]

These remarks raised concerns with S. As a result, she asked F. later that evening whether he would consider resigning from his position at the propaganda ministry. After having told him what T. had told her, F. called B. to confirm what had been said, ending their telephone conversation by saying that T. would be dealt with. F. then called another person and told them about what had been said. F. then typed the contents of the conversation that S. had had with T. after the second telephone call. He then read the text to S. and asked her to sign it. She refused to do so, and tried to dissuade F. from taking the matter any further, which caused him consternation, telling her that such people should be made a head shorter. He then signed the form himself, and passed it on the next day to the person he had called the previous evening.[300]

An investigation was initiated against T. thereafter. He was detained for four days following a search of his home on 11 May 1943, and S, B., and K. were questioned by the police. On 30 July 1943, the state prosecutor at the People's Court requested that T. be arrested on the charge of undermining the war effort, but this was overruled and T. remained free. Two days before the initial main proceedings at the People's Court in August 1943, F. met with a Dr. Wo., who was T.'s acquaintance and hoped to intervene in T.'s favor. He told him that since he had saved his father's life from a life-threatening illness, he hoped he could return a favor to him by persuading his wife to mitigate the report with harmless content while implying that if she would not, his wife would be made out to be an unreliable source of information. F. was not amenable to changing his viewpoint, telling Wo. that his request was unreasonable and threatening to cause problems for him.[301]

A few days later, F. visited Roland Freisler, the president of the People's Court, at his home to find out who would hear the case against T. It would be Freisler himself, and he told him that someone would try to cast doubt on his wife's testimony through personal defamation. Freisler reassured F. that his wife's testimony would not be necessary since B. had confirmed everything. The main proceedings that were scheduled to begin the next day were postponed since the notice for B. to appear as a witness could not be delivered, and T. was free to go. Before the newly scheduled proceedings were opened, S. tried to intervene in T.'s favor by contacting Freisler in his office, feeling miserable and distraught about the course of events that had caused friction between herself and her husband. Freisler was outraged by these suggestions coming from the wife of an employee of the propaganda ministry and referred to her duties as a citizen while giving her to understand that things for T. were not very bad since he remained free.[302] Between the first and second scheduled proceedings, T. and his wife took their gold and valuables from Berlin, along with letters of recommendation from English business friends and the bill of indictment, and tried to flee to Hungary, but they were arrested at the border at the beginning of September 1943. New proceedings were opened on 26 October 1943 with Freisler presiding. F., S., and B. appeared as witnesses, but only B. was questioned.[303]

Friesler's judgment reiterated what T. had said to S. and B. In addition to rebuking T. for unscrupulously making defeatist statements in the worst degree, he also added how he had made an extraordinarily bad impression in the proceedings. He castigated him for having a very bad conscience as well, having attempted to go abroad with over 20,000 RM worth of valuables, the bill of indictment from the People's Court, and recommendations from English firms, just as Jewish emigrants would be expected to do to try to set themselves up abroad as political refugees. T. was thereby found guilty of undermining the war effort and patronizing the enemy, and was sentenced to death to serve as an example for others, and was later executed on 10 December 1943. K. had expressed his satisfaction with the verdict, saying that whoever spoke the way T. had done would get what they deserve.[304]

S. was interned in the American occupation zone for about two years while under suspicion of having reported T. Meanwhile, K. lived unrecognized as a farm laborer in Schleswig-Holstein.[305] An investigation was later initiated against him on 4 May 1961, and he was taken into custody for attempting to suppress evidence regarding the pending case against him for aiding and abetting murder by telling two witnesses what they should tell the court. He claimed in his defense during the court proceedings that he could not recall and doubted whether he had approved or demanded, and whatever he had said had been in a state of agitation without prior thought. He claimed that he was very depressed about the military situation in Africa following the retreat from El Alamein, and had been very shocked about what his wife had told him regarding what she had heard T. say and how he should consider leaving his work at the propaganda ministry before something would happen to him. He therefore called someone, whose identity could not be established, who told him that this incident had to be forwarded, or else he would face difficulties for not taking proper action, considering that others could have heard the conversation between T., S., and B. Although K. claimed he did not want to report this matter to his superior, this person recommended that he do so. Therefore, he considered himself obliged to write down the details of the incident and give it to him so that T. would be placed under surveillance, especially in view of the military situation and the gravity of the remarks. He further claimed that he did not exercise any influence on the outcome of the forthcoming events after forwarding the report, without further consideration for the consequences of doing so, thinking only that one had to be prevented from making further such remarks.[306]

The jury court was given the task of ascertaining whether K.'s conduct in November 1942 was subjectively and objectively subject to prosecution according to the criminal laws of the time, regardless of his moral guilt. He was accused of aiding and abetting manslaughter, and therefore the court had to prove at least objectively that this murder occurred at the behest of another. This would only be the case if T.'s execution following the People's Court's death sentence pronounced on 26 October 1943 was unlawful. The view of the jury court was that the People's Court's judgment violated the universal principles of the rule of law and was therefore unlawful.[307]

The jury court also determined that since this judgment was unlawful, it followed that every contribution to this judgment objectively constituted aiding and abetting manslaughter. K. had made such a contribution by reporting T. to the authorities, and thereby initiated the proceedings that were taken against him. In order for the court to convict him, it had to be proven that K. intended for T. to be killed as a result of an unlawful death sentence, or at least consciously approved of this consequence emanating from his actions. It could be maintained with certainty that he had known a death sentence would result at the time he made his report, and had approved of the consequences of his actions, given his background, education as a jurist, and position in the civil service, as well as the remarks he had made regarding the proceedings against T.[308]

In considering possible mitigating circumstances, the court doubted whether K. had actually considered a death sentence to be unjustifiable in view of what he had known and accepted about the law of the time, especially considering his conduct after the death sentence was passed. As a jurist and a convinced National Socialist, it was possible that he did not believe that the judgment of the People's Court had constituted a perversion of the course of justice or manslaughter. He also did not report anything that was false while reiterating T.'s remarks that were punishable at the time. Moreover, it could not be proven that his report was forwarded to the Gestapo, and therefore the proceedings were initially lawful until T. tried to flee abroad. K. also could not have foreseen the extent of the sentence that was imposed at that time, given the high probability that the death sentence was pronounced in reaction to this attempt to escape prosecution, and therefore was outside the range of what K. could have expected. This was taken into consideration in favor of the defendant, with regard to establishing that he was guilty of aiding and abetting manslaughter.[309]

The court thus added that the imposition of the death penalty on 26 October 1943 probably resulted from the worsening military situation at the time and other political considerations that led the People's Court to commit this perversion of justice, which could not be attributed to the defendant who could not have foreseen these consequences in November 1942. Moreover, since he was not questioned as a witness in the 26 October proceedings, he did not express any new malicious intentions or show whether he still intended to see T. put to death. K. was therefore acquitted.[310]

The office of the state prosecutor appealed this decision to the Federal Supreme Court, where the earlier verdict was maintained in its judgment of 27 April 1965. The state prosecutor objected to the earlier judgment, citing F.'s conviction as a convinced National Socialist who may have blindly believed that the courts of the Third *Reich* did not perpetrate any unlawfulness in perverting the course of justice or perpetrate murder. It was inferred from the judgment that F. was merely a political opportunist, and therefore it was not proven that he was not guilty of aiding and abetting manslaughter. However, there was no new evidence that could support this assertion and cause the Federal Supreme Court to diverge from its previous interpretations regarding a defendant's expectation and approval of manslaughter.[311]

The jury court at the Hamburg regional court had examined the facts of this case in view of the events of two separate points in time on two separate matters. K. could have been considered a hostile witness to what had been said who also took the initiative in initiating the proceedings against T., using his political connections to contact the notorious president of the People's Court to ensure that T. would appear before this court, rather than reporting the matter to the Gestapo as other informers had done. By the time that T. appeared before the People's Court, sentencing nearly a year later had become increasingly severe, and the jury court would not blame the defendant for the consequences of the process he had originally set into motion. In spite of his hostile conduct and intentions to inflict disadvantage on another, it could not be proven with sufficient evidence that he had been guilty of contributing to institutional manslaughter, rather than committing a crime against humanity under the provisions of Control Council Law No. 10 that had been open to a much wider interpretation than the application of conventional criminal law.

The courts of the Federal Republic of Germany continued to adjudicate in cases arising from crimes committed during the National Socialist regime for as long as the perpetrators could still be called to account for their actions. The justification for adjudicating in such cases maintained the common element of calling the individuals tried in these types of cases to account for their actions on the basis of civilized legal norms as well as moral responsibility. This was justified by the retroactive application of justice under the terms of Control Council Law No. 10 that was specifically designed to prosecute political crimes that were given free rein in National Socialist Germany. Hence, there was a genuine need to circumvent the basis of established German criminal law, under which the retroactive application of justice was contravened. Conventional criminal law that was found in the provisions of the criminal code was limited to the motivations and actions of individual crimes, which would have otherwise opened the way to National Socialist crimes being left untried.

Conclusion

The rule of law had been nullified by the National Socialist regime that had established a politicized administration of justice that was to uphold its interests. Consequently, this opened up the way for individuals to use it for the promotion of their personal interests to the detriment of others at a time when the law did not serve the purposes that it is meant to serve—to uphold individual interests by protecting them from abuses directed against them by others, in addition to upholding the state and its institutions. The effectiveness of the law also collapsed following the National Socialist takeover of the state, when the regime sought to exploit the law as a means of primarily upholding the interests of the NSDAP and quelling any opposition to the regime. The law was restored after the postwar collapse of the National Socialist regime, and the administration of justice applied retroactive legislation as an extraordinary measure to compensate for the injustices that had been perpetrated. There was also the willingness to make this possible among the western occupation powers and German jurists by implementing the broadly defined provisions of Control Council Law No. 10.

Those who had indirectly taken part in these past injustices by making political denunciations against others were prosecuted by a restored administration of justice governed by the restored rule of law. Extraordinary legislation was enacted by the Allied occupation powers as the highest legislative authority in Germany to open the way for a retroactive application of the administration of justice on the basis of criminal law that could not have been administered at the time of the perpetrators' actions. Whereas the authorization for the German courts to prosecute cases of denunciations as crimes against humanity was not granted in the American occupation zone, these types of cases were nevertheless adjudicated by lay jurors in denazification tribunals. This type of case was prosecuted in the criminal law courts of the French and British occupation zones in order to bring the offending parties to justice for *all* forms of crimes against humanity in the reconstituted German courts. The courts and their staffs and the juries all demonstrated the objective applications of the law in the ways that it was meant to serve, when it became possible for them to administer justice.

There had been objective reservations against the retroactive application of the administration of justice among many members of the judiciary which needed to be overcome. Meanwhile, other jurists put forward arguments considering the necessity of doing so, while expressing their views on examples of its application through several verdicts in cases of denunciations. Those who had denounced others to the National Socialist regime, conscious of the consequences of their actions for those they had denounced to the authorities, now faced the consequences of those actions. The judgments of many German courts left no doubt about how informers who had denounced others to National Socialist authorities were to be called to account for their actions for having perpetrated a crime that constituted an attack on a victim that had led to inhumane treatment of the victim. Those who had undoubtedly taken premeditated action against their victims received the heaviest sentences. Meanwhile, it could be argued that many other sentences may have been too lenient.[1] This could have been partly symptomatic of the psychological reaction to the excessively harsh sentencing during the National Socialist regime, a reaction that led to insufficiently severe sentencing thereafter.[2] Also, it could have been partially attributed to certain cases in which the applying of the letter of the law tended to outweigh considerations of the guiding principles of justice and humanity.

Therein lay the problem of setting forth the rule of law in prosecuting denunciation as a crime against humanity. The range of sentences that were imposed in these cases did not necessarily recognize the consequences of denunciations. While being afforded the flexibility of judicial independence in passing sentences, the jurists primarily took what the law prescribed into consideration and, apart from a few exceptions, passed largely lenient sentences, hesitating to risk passing judgments in cases of a political nature. Control Council Law No. 10 was insufficiently detailed with regard to reconciling the provisions of existing law and the principles of humanity in determining how a crime against humanity could be judged in view of the consequences that had been caused by the indirect perpetrators of crimes against humanity. As a result, such cases could be judged on the basis of different precedents, while it was also necessary for jurists to demonstrate the willingness to sufficiently take the consequences of the informers' actions into consideration in the interest of redressing past injustices that emanated from political circumstances. The question as to whether the law and morality as defined by the principles of humanity could be reconciled would only be decided through the individual court judgments.

The inconclusiveness of the post war denazification program led to suspicions that there had been jurists whose objectivity about past political injustices that had been perpetrated, such as through denunciations, may have been compromised if they had themselves contributed to crimes against humanity during the National Socialist regime.[3] The Highest Appeal Court had always maintained that those who denounced others and caused them to appear before a Special Court were to be judged for committing crimes against humanity, but the jurists of the courts that adjudicated political offenses in the National Socialist regime were not similarly judged for their accountability in these cases.[4] On the other hand, the reconstructed administration of justice demonstrated in individual cases how the law could be applied objectively and fairly to those who stood accused of crimes against humanity. While there were errors made in judgments, these were thereafter reviewed by the appellate courts at higher levels of jurisdiction that continued serving justice.

The willingness to continue prosecuting cases of denunciations as crimes against humanity continued throughout the newly-established Federal Republic of Germany. This followed the initiative for doing so that had been set out during the military occupation, in keeping with the necessity for doing so while evidence for prosecuting such cases could be marshaled to convict those who remained guilty. The original spirit of administering the widely encompassing definition of crimes against humanity under the provisions of Control Council Law No. 10 later had less significance after this law was abolished. Jurisdiction was no longer extended to interpreting the inhumane consequences when such cases came under the jurisdiction of German law. The consequences of the actions had taken precedence over the actual act of reporting another to the authorities when the individual was conscious of the consequences that could inevitably follow. Due to the more narrowly defined scope of interpretation that could be made from the provisions found in the German criminal code, the prosecution of informers became subject to much more narrowly defined circumstances. This made convictions less likely than cases heard under the broad interpretations that had been allowed under the concept of political persecution cited in Control Council Law No. 10. As a result, fewer and fewer cases of denunciation were prosecuted than theoretically could have been anticipated.[5] There were 7674 cases of suspected denunciation in western Germany by December 1964, with 603 convictions. Out of this number, there was one sentence of life imprisonment, 566 prison sentences of varying lengths, 36 fines, and 18 pending cases. Proceedings were temporarily suspended in another 61 cases, and 6992 proceedings ended without convictions.[6]

It remained for the highest appeal courts at the state and federal levels to set the precedent for judgments in such cases emanating from the courts at the lower levels of jurisdiction, and for legislators to set standards of justice in bringing the direct or indirect perpetrators of crimes against humanity to account for their actions outside the rule of law that serves to protect the human rights of every individual. Political conditions following the beginning of the Cold War exercised a negative influence on the willingness for denunciation cases to be prosecuted, and this subjective element exacerbated the problem of judicial limitations in making the law seen to work by the society it served, whereby the willingness to prosecute denunciation cases as crimes against humanity was undermined. As a consequence, there were those who escaped prosecution and conviction due to the way the law was defined, as well as the reduced willingness to serve justice in these types of cases. As with all who live under the rule of law to this day, the principles of humanity are maintained to preserve its values regardless of any statute of limitations after the time that offenses against these principles were committed. Maintaining the precepts of natural law in the form of upholding the rights and dignity of humanity will thus afford all individuals the protection of the law against those who would disregard these rights, whether it would be by other individuals or by the state.

Notes

INTRODUCTION

1. "Anzeigeerstattung bei der Gestapo wegen antinazistischer Äußerrungen kann als Verbrechen gegen die Menschlichkeit bestraft werden," *Deutsche-Rechtszeitschrift* 1946: 126.

2. Hodo von Hodenberg, "Zur Anwendung des Kontrollratsgesetzes Nr. 10 durch deutsche Gerichte," *Süddeutsche Juristenzeitung* (1947) 2: 113.

3. "Law No. 10: Punishment of Persons guilty of War Crimes, Crimes against Peace and against Humanity," *Official Gazette of the Control Council for Germany* No. 3. (31 January 1946): 50–55; Michael P. Hensle, "Denunziantentum und Diktatur als Mittel der Machtausübung und Konfliktsaustragung im Nationalsozialistischen Deutschland," *Zeitschrift für Geschichtswissenscahft* 2003 51(2): 161.

4. Article 2 (1), "Law No. 10: Punishment of Persons guilty of War Crimes, Crimes against Peace and against Humanity," *Official Gazette of the Control Council for Germany* No.3 (31 January 1946): 50–51.

5. Article 3 (1d), "Law No. 10: Punishment of Persons guilty of War Crimes, Crimes against Peace and against Humanity," *Official Gazette of the Control Council for Germany* No.3 (31 January 1946): 52–53.

6. Carl Haensel, "Das Urteil im Nürnberger Prozeß," *Deutsche Rechts-Zeitschrift* 3 (2) 1948: 41.

7. Richard Lange, "Zum Denunziantenproblem," *Süddeutsche Juristenzeitung* 3 (1948): 303.

8. Lange, "Zum Denunziantenproblem," 303.

9. Ernst Boesebeck, "Privatrechtliche Haftung des Denunzianten," *Neue Juristische Wochenschrift* 1947/1948 1: 15.

10. "Zum Kontrollratgesetz Nr. 10," *Neue Justiz* 1947 1 6: 137–138.

11. "Zum Kontrollgesetz Nr. 10," *Neue Justiz* 1947, 137–138.

12. "Zum Kontrollgesetz Nr. 10," *Neue Justiz* 1947, 138.

13. Richard Lange, "Zu neuen Ufern im Strafrecht," *Neue Justiz* 1947 1: 8.

14. Karl-Alfred Storz, *Die Rechtsprechung des Oberstern Gerichtshofes für die Britische Zone in Strafsachen* (Tübingen: J.C.B. Mohr, 1969): 18.

15. "Zum Kontrollgesetz Nr. 10," *Neue Justiz* 1947, 138.

16. Bernhard Diestelkamp and Susanne Jung, "Die Justiz in den Westzonen und der frühen Bundesrepublik," *Aus Politik und Zeitgeschichte* 13 (24 March 1989): 25.

17. Lange, "Zum Denunziantenproblem," 303–304.

18. Lange, "Zum Denunziantenproblem," 304.

19. This principle of "no punishment without law" is expressed by the rules that "the punishment for a crime must not be greater than that which could have been inflicted at the time the crime was committed" and "no act is a crime unless it was a crime at the time when it was committed." Bundesarchiv. Koblenz. Z21/784. Legal/CLO/108. Central Legal Office. Liason Officer, Legal Division. Control Commission for Germany (BE). 23rd October, 1946. Subject: Crimes against Humanity. Appendix A. Nulla Poene Sine Lege.

20. Gisela Diewald-Kerkmann, *Politische Denunziation im NS-Regime oder kleine Macht der "Volksgenossen"* (Bonn: Dietz Nachfolger, 1995): 153.

21. *Entscheidungen des Obersten Gerichtshofes für die Britische Zone in Strafsachen* Vol. 1 (Berlin/Hamburg: Walter de Gruyter & Co, 1949): 56.

CHAPTER 1

1. Karl Loewenstein, "Reconstruction of the Administration of Justice in American-Occupied Germany", *Harvard Law Review* 1947–1948 61: 436.

2. Jeremy Noakes and Geoffrey Pridham, *Documents on Nazism*: 1919–1945 (New York: Viking Press, 1974) 226–227.

3. Karl Loewenstein, "Justice," *Governing Postwar Germany*, Edward H. Litchfield, ed. Ithaca: Cornell University Press, 1953: 252–254.

4. Gustav Ralbruch, "Gesetzliches Unrecht und übergesetzliches Recht," *Süddeutsche Juristenzeitung* (1946): 61–62.

5. Helmut Coing, "Zur Frage der strafrechtlichen Haftung der Richter für die Anwendung naturrechtswidriger Gesetze," *Süddeutsche Juristenzeitung* (1946): 61–62.

6. Radbruch, "Gesetzliches Unrecht und übersetzliches Recht," 105.

7. Radbruch, "Gesetzliches Unrecht und übersetzliches Recht," 105–106.

8. Radbruch, "Gesetzliches Unrecht und übersetzliches Recht," 106.

9. Radbruch, "Gesetzliches Unrecht und übersetzliches Recht," 107–108.

10. Bundesarchiv. Koblenz. Z21/1334. Der Generalstaatsanwalt Gera. 1. Februar 1946. Betr.: Strafverfolgung von Denunzianten.

11. Bundesarchiv. Koblenz. Z21/1334. Der Generalstaatsanwalt Gera. 1. Februar 1946. Betr.: Strafverfolgung von Denunzianten.

12. Bundesarchiv. Koblenz. Z21/799. Vereinigung der Verfolgten des Nazi-Regimes. Denkschrift über Strafverfolgung von Naziverbrechen an Deutschen. Landgerichtsdirektor E. H. 4. Der Denunziant, p. 15.

13. Bundesarchiv. Koblenz. Z21/799. Vereinigung der Verfolgten des Nazi-Regimes. Denkschrift über Strafverfolgung von Naziverbrechen an Deutschen. Landegerichtssdirektor E. H. 4. Der Denunziant, pp. 15–16.

14. Bundesarchiv. Koblenz. Z21/799. Vereinigung der Verfolgten des Nazi-Regimes. Denkschrift über Strafverfolgung von Naziverbrechen an Deutschen. Landgerichtsdirektor E. H. 4. Der Denunziant, p. 15.

15. Bundesarchiv. Koblenz. Z21/799. Vereinigung der Verfolgten des Nazi-Regimes. Denkschrift über Strafverfolgung von Naziverbrechen an Deutschen. Landgerichtssdirektor E. H. 4. Der Denunziant, p. 16.

16. Bundesarchiv. Koblenz. Z21/799. Rechtsgutachten über Article II, 10, 3 und 5 des Kontrollratsgesetzes Nr. 10, erstattet von Dr. Eberhard Schmitt. 1. November 1946, pp. 1–2.

17. Bundesarchiv. Koblenz. Z21/799. Rechtsgutachten über Article II, 10, 3 und 5 des Kontrollratsgesetzes Nr. 10, erstattet von Dr. Eberhard Schmitt. 1. November 1946, pp. 5–7.

18. Hodo von Hodenberg, "Zur Anwendung des Kontrollratsgesetzes Nr. 10 durch deutsche Gerichte," *Süddeutsche Juristenzeitung* March 1947: 113.

19. von Hodenberg, "Zur Anwendung des Kontrollratsgesetzes Nr. 10 durch deutsche Gerichte," 116–117.

20. von Hodenberg, "Zur Anwendung des Kontrollratsgesetzes Nr. 10 durch deutsche Gerichte," 120.

21. von Hodenberg, "Zur Anwendung des Kontrollratsgesetzes Nr. 10 durch deutsche Gerichte," 122–124.

22. von Hodenberg, "Zur Anwendung des Kontrollratsgesetzes Nr. 10 durch deutsche Gerichte," 123.

23. Karl Loewenstein, "Justice," 253.

24. Bundesarchiv. Koblenz. Z21/799. Landgerichtsdirektor Dr. Rudolphi: Zur Bestrafung der Humanitätsverbrechen nach Gesetz Nr. 10. Bestrafung der Humanitätsverbrechen nach Kontrollratsgesetz Nr. 10 und Humanitätsverbrechen und Schadenersatz. Referate gehalten in der Richterbesprechung des Landgerichtsbezirks Essen am 4. Juni 1947: 3.

25. Bundesarchiv. Koblenz. Z21/799. Landgerichtsdirektor Dr. Rudolphi: Zur Bestrafung der Humanitätsverbrechen nach Gesetz Nr. 10. Bestrafung der Humanitätsverbrechen nach Kontrollratsgesetz Nr. 10 und Humanitätsverbrechen und Schadenersatz. Referate gehalten in der Richterbesprechung des Landgerichtsbezirks Essen am 4. Juni 1947: 14–15.

26. Bundesarchiv. Koblenz. Z21/799. Landgerichtsdirektor Dr. Rudolphi: Zur Bestrafung der Humanitätsverbrechen nach Gesetz Nr. 10. Bestrafung der Humanitätsverbrechen nach Kontrollratsgesetz Nr. 10 und Humanitätsverbrechen und Schadenersatz. Referate gehalten in der Richterbesprechung des Landgerichtsbezirks Essen am 4. Juni 1947: 16–17.

27. Bundesarchiv. Koblenz. Z21/799. Legal/CLO/71. British Liason Officer. Central Legal Office. Control Commission, Germany. Subject: Publication of a discussion by the Kammergerichtspräsident Dr. Strucksberg.

28. Georg Strucksberg, "Zur Anwendung des Kontrollratsgesetzes Nr. 10," *Deutsche Rechts-Zeitschrift* 1947 2 (9): 277.
29. Strucksberg, "Zur Anwendung des Kontrollratsgesetzes Nr. 10," 278.
30. Strucksberg, "Zur Anwendung des Kontrollratsgesetzes Nr. 10," 279.
31. "Kontrollratsgesetz Nr. 10," *Monatsschrift für deutsches Recht* 1947 1: 242.
32. Lange, "Zum Denunziantenproblem," 307–308.
33. Lange, "Zum Denunziantenproblem," 309.
34. A. Henneka, "OLG Dresden. Anmerkung," *Süddeutsche Juristenzeitung* 1947 (2): 522.
35. Henneka, "OLG Dresden. Anmerkung," 524–525.
36. Henneka, "OLG Dresden. Anmerkung," 525.
37. M. Güde, "Die Anwendung des Kontrollratsgesetzes Nr. 10 durch die deutschen Gerichte," *Deutsche Rechtszeitschrift* 4 1947: 111–112.
38. Güde, "Die Anwendung des Kontrollratsgesetzes Nr. 10 durch die deutschen Gerichte," 114.
39. Güde, "Die Anwendung des Kontrollratsgesetzes Nr. 10 durch die deutschen Gerichte," 115–116.
40. Güde, "Die Anwendung des Kontrollratsgesetzes Nr. 10 durch die deutschen Gerichte," 117–118.
41. Gustav Radbruch, "Zur Diskussion über die Verbrechen gegen die Menschlichkeit," *Süddeutsche Juristenzeitung* 2 (March) 1947: 136.
42. Diewald-Kerkmann, *Politische Denunziation im NS-Regime*, 157.
43. Radbruch, "Zur Diskussion über die Verbrechen gegen die Menschlichkeit," 133.
44. Radbruch, "Zur Diskussion über die Verbrechen gegen die Menschlichkeit," 134–136.
45. Claudia Bade,"'Das Verfahren ist eingestellt.' Die Strafrechtliche Verfolgung von Denunziation aus dem Nationalsozialismus nach 1945 in den Westzonen und in der frühen BRD," *Historical Social Research* 26 (2001) 2/3: 73–74.
46. August Wimmer, "Die Bestrafung von Humanitätsverbrechen under the Grundsatz '*nullum crimen sine lege*.'" *Süddeutsche Juristenzeitung*, 2 (March) 1947: 128–129.
47. Wimmer,"Die Bestrafung von Humanitätsverbrechen under the Grundsatz '*nullum crimen sine lege*',", 130–131.
48. Wilhelm Kiesselbach, "Zwei Probleme aus dem Gesetz Nr. 10 des Kontrollrats", *Monatsschrift für deutsche Recht* 1 1947: 2–3.
49. Lange, "Zum Denunziantenproblem," 303.
50. Lange, "Zum Denunziantenproblem," 303.
51. Lange, "Zum Denunziantenproblem," 303–304.
52. Bundesarchiv. Koblenz. Z21/799. Zur praktischen Anwendung des Kontrollratsges No. 10. Landegerichtssdirektor Dr. R., p. 1.
53. Bundesarchiv. Koblenz. Z21/799. Zur praktischen Anwendung des Kontrollratsges No. 10. Landegerichtssdirektor Dr. R., p. 1.
54. Bundesarchiv. Koblenz. Z21/799. Zur praktischen Anwendung des Kontrollratsges No. 10. Landegerichtssdirektor Dr. R., pp.1–2.

55. Bundesarchiv. Koblenz. Z21/799. Zur praktischen Anwendung des Kontrollratsges No. 10. Landegerichtssdirektor Dr. R., pp. 3–4.
56. Bundesarchiv. Koblenz. Z21/799. Zur praktischen Anwendung des Kontrollratsges No. 10. Landgerichtssdirektor Dr. R., p. 5.
57. Bundesarchiv. Koblenz. Z21/799. Zur praktischen Anwendung des Kontrollratsges No. 10. Landegerichtssdirektor Dr. R., pp. 5–6.
58. Hans-Georg Meister, "Die Widerspruchlosigkeit der Rechtsordnung" *Monatsschrift für deutsches Recht* 2 1947: 47–48.
59. Bundesarchiv. Koblenz. Z21/799. Appendix "A" to LEGAL/MOJ/52326/1 of 17 July 1947. British Special Legal Research Unit. Biased Articles by German Lawyers on Control Council Law No. 10: 1.
60. Meister, "Die Widerspruchlosigkeit der Rechtsordnung," 48.
61. Meister, "Die Widerspruchlosigkeit der Rechtsordnung," 49.
62. Bundesarchiv. Koblenz. Z21/799. Appendix "A" to LEGAL/MOJ/52326/1 of 17 July 1947. British Special Legal Research Unit. Biased Articles by German Lawyers on Control Council Law No. 10: 1.
63. Bundesarchiv. Koblenz. Z21/799. Appendix "A" to LEGAL/MOJ/52326/1 of 17 July 1947. British Special Legal Research Unit. Biased Articles by German Lawyers on Control Council Law No. 10: 1–2.
64. Bundesarchiv. Koblenz. Z21/799. Legal Division. Zonal Executive Offices. Subject: Control Council Law No. 10: Article in Monatsschrift für Deutsches Recht, May 1947. 17 July 1947.
65. R.H. Graveson, "Der Grundsatz „nulla poena sine lege" und Kontrollratsgesetz Nr. 10,", *Monatsschrift für Deutsches Recht* (1947): 278.
66. Graveson, "Der Grundsatz „nulla poena sine lege" und Kontrollratsgesetz Nr. 10," 278.
67. Graveson, "Der Grundsatz „nulla poena sine lege" und Kontrollratsgesetz Nr. 10," 278–279.
68. Graveson, "Der Grundsatz „nulla poena sine lege" und Kontrollratsgesetz Nr. 10," 280–281.
69. Richard Lange, "Kontrollratsgesezt Nr. 10 in Theorie und Praxis", *Deutsche Rechts-Zeitschrift* 1948 3 (6): 156.
70. Lange, "Kontrollratsgesezt Nr. 10 in Theorie und Praxis,", 160–161.
71. Richard Lange, "Kontrollratsgesezt Nr. 10 und deutsches Recht: Das Kontrollratsgesetz in Theorie und Praxis II,", *Deutsche Rechts-Zeitschrift* 1948 3 (6): 187–188.
72. Lange, "Kontrollratsgesezt Nr. 10 und deutsches Recht," 189–190.
73. Theodor Klefisch, "Die NS-Denunziation in der Rechtsprechung des Obersten Gerichtshofes für die britische Zone," *Monatsschrift für deutsches Recht* 3 1949: 325–326.
74. Heinrich Jagusch, "Das Verbrechen gegen die Menschlichkeit in der Rechtsprechung des Obersten Gerichtshofs für die Britische Zone," *Süddeutsche Juristenzeitung* 1949: 620.
75. Bade, "'Das Verfahren wird eingestellt'," 72.
76. Lange, "Zum Denunziantenproblem," 302.

28. Staatsarchiv Darmstadt. Abt. H 13 Da Nr. 889. Hessisches Staatsministerium. Der Minister für politische Befreiung. Berufungskammer Darmstadt. Darmstadt, den 17.5.47. Aktz.: Erm/St. Tgb. Nr. 6937. An die Staatsanwaltschaft; Hessisches Staatsministerium. Der Minister für politische Befreiung. Berufungskammer Darmstadt. Darmstadt, den 25.5.1948. An den Oberstaatsanwalt bei dem Landgericht Darmstadt. Aktz. Js. 455/46. Betr.: Strafsache gegen A. W. in Bonsweiher und 2. And. Wegen Beihilfe zum Mord; Der Erste Öffentliche Kläger bei der Zentralberufungskammer Hessen. Frankfurt a.M., den 22.12.1950. –C-Ib-Pi. An den Oberstaatsanwalt beim Landgericht Darmstadt. Betr. Ermittlungssache A. W. G. Z. Js 455/46 II.

29. Hoffmann, *Die Verfolgung der nationalsozialistischen Gewaltverbrechen in Hessen*, 145.

30. Ernst Boesebeck, "Privatrechtliche Haftung des Denunzianten," *Neue Juristische Wochenschrift* 1947/1948 1: 14.

31. Diewald-Kerkmann, Politische Denunziation im NS-Regime, 155–156.

32. Diewald-Kerkmann, *Politische Denunziation im NS-Regime*, 156.

33. Diewald-Kerkmann, *Politische Denunziation im NS-Regime*, 156–157.

34. Loewenstein, "Reconstruction of the Administration of Justice," 437.

35. "Gesetz zur Ahndung nationalsozialistischer Straftaten vom 29. Mai 1946," *Gesetz- und Verordnungsblatt für Groß-Hessen* (1946): 136; "Die Rechtspflege in der Gesetzgebung der amerikanischen Zone II. Die gemeinsame Gesetzgebung der drei Länder Bayern, Württemberg-Baden und Großhessen. B. Strafrechtspflege," *Deutsche Rechtszeitschrift* 1946 4: 119.

36. 17/201–3/2 Legal Division, RG 260 OMGUS, Institut für Zeitgeschichte, Munich. Subject: Authorizations granted to Wuerttemberg-Baden Courts for trying offenses pursuant to Control Council Law No. 10. 5 August 1947.

37. Z1/1235A, Koblenz. Niederschrift über die Sitzung der Justizminister am 17. April 1946 in Stuttgart. Besprechungsgegenstand: Gesetz zur Ahndung nationalsozialistischer Straftaten. Stuttgart. 17 April 1946.

38. Adolf Arndt, "Das Recht der politischen Säuberung," *Süddeutsche Juristenzeitung* 1948 3: 110.

39. Z1/1235A, Koblenz. Niederschrift über die Sitzung der Justizminister am 17. April 1946 in Stuttgart. Besprechungsgegenstand: Gesetz zur Ahndung nationalsozialistischer Straftaten. Stuttgart. 17 April 1946.

40. Z45F 17/56–3/7 RG 260/ OMGUS, Koblenz. OMGUS LD, LA Br. La 91 The German Government, German courts. Memo: to Lt. Col. A.S. Brown, Legal Division; Subject: Alleged Violations of Control Council Law No. 10, 4 March 1946.

41. Lange, "Zum Denunziantenproblem," 302.

42. *Bayerisches Gesetz- und Verordnungsblatt*, No. 10 1 Juli. 1946. "Gesetz zur Befreiung von Nationalsozialismus und Militarismus" 1. Abschnitt, Artikel 6, 7 II (8):147

43. *Official Gazette of the Control Council for Germany* No. 11 31 October 1946: 187, 188.

44. Werner Lachmann, "Die Denunziation unter besonderer Berücksichtigung des Kontrollratsgesetzes Nr. 10," (Diss: Ludwig-Maximilians-Universität, 1951): 41.

45. Arndt, "Das Recht der politischen Säuberung," 110.

46. Albert Eberhardt, "Die Denunziation im Spiegel des Kontrollratgesetzes Nr. 10 als Verbrechen gegen die Menschlichkeit," (Munich: Ludwig-Maximilian Universität zu München, 1950): 148.

47. 17/262–3/15 Legal Division, RG 260 OMGUS, Institut für Zeitgeschichte, Munich. Subject: Punishment of Informers. 17 January 1947.

48. 17/262–3/15 Legal Division, RG 260 OMGUS, Institut für Zeitgeschichte, Munich. Subject: Punishment of Informers. 17 January 1947.

49. 17/262–2/15 Legal Division, RG 260 OMGUS, Institut für Zeitgeschichte, Munich. Subject: Trial by German Courts of Crimes against Humanity. 16 September 1947.

50. 17/262–2/15 Legal Division, RG 260 OMGUS, Institut für Zeitgeschichte, Munich. Subject: Trial by German Courts of Crimes against Humanity. 16 September 1947.

51. 17/262–2/15 Legal Division, RG 260 OMGUS, Institut für Zeitgeschichte, Munich. Subject: Trial by German Courts of Crimes against Humanity. 16 September 1947.

52. Lange, "Zum Denunziantenproblem," 302.

53. Lange, "Zum Denunziantenproblem," 302.

54. Blattsammlung der Staatsanwaltschaft betreffend Strafsache gegen G. wegen polit. Sache. Hessisches Hauptstaatsarchiv, Wiesbaden. Abt. 463 Nr. 1191. Hessisches Staatsministerium. Ministerium für politische Befreiung. Spruchkammer Wetzlar. Der öffentliche Klager. 3. August 1947. Betr.: Spruchkammerverfahren gegen J.G.

55. Blattsammlung der Staatsanwaltschaft betreffend Strafsache gegen G. wegen polit. Sache. Hessisches Hauptstaatsarchiv, Wiesbaden. Abt. 463 Nr. 1191. Der Oberstaatsanwalt Limburg/Lahn, der 29. 7. 1947. 2 Js 4951/46. 1. Schreiben: An die Spruchkammer in Wetzlar. Strafsache gegen J. G.

56. Blattsammlung der Staatsanwaltschaft betreffend Strafsache gegen G. wegen polit. Sache. Hessisches Hauptstaatsarchiv, Wiesbaden. Abt. 463 Nr. 1191. Der Oberstaatsanwalt Limburg/Lahn, den 29. 7. 1947. 2 Js 4951/46. Strafsache gegen die Masseuse J. G. aus Wetzlar wegen Verbrechen gegen die Menschlichkeit in Tatenheit begangen mit falscher Anschuldigung und wegen Unterschlagung.

57. Blattsammlung der Staatsanwaltschaft betreffend Strafsache gegen G. wegen polit. Sache. Hessisches Hauptstaatsarchiv, Wiesbaden. Abt. 463 Nr. 1191. Der Oberstaatsanwalt Limburg/Lahn, den 2. 9. 1947. 2 Js 4951/46. An die Amtsgericht in Wetzlar. Anklageschrift.

58. Blattsammlung der Staatsanwaltschaft betreffend Strafsache gegen G. wegen polit. Sache. Hessisches Hauptstaatsarchiv, Wiesbaden. Abt. 463 Nr. 1191. K.H. Bürgermeister i. R. Wetzlar, 25. November 1947. An den Herrn Staatsanwalt Limburg/Lahn durch das Amtsgericht, Wetzar. Betr.: 4 Ds 193/47.

59. Blattsammlung der Staatsanwaltschaft betreffend Strafsache gegen G. wegen polit. Sache. Hessisches Hauptstaatsarchiv, Wiesbaden. Abt. 463 Nr. 1191. Der Oberstaatsanwalt Limburg/Lahn, der 29. 7. 1947. 2 Js 4951/46. An die Strafkammer in Limburg. Anklageschrift.

60. Blattsammlung der Staatsanwaltschaft betreffend Strafsache gegen G. wegen polit. Sache. Hessisches Hauptstaatsarchiv, Wiesbaden. Abt. 463 Nr. 1191. Der Oberstaatsanwalt Limburg/Lahn, der 29. 7. 1947. 2 Js 4951/46. An die Strafkammer in Limburg. Anklageschrift.

61. Blattsammlung der Staatsanwaltschaft betreffend Strafsache gegen G. wegen polit. Sache. Hessisches Hauptstaatsarchiv, Wiesbaden. Abt. 463 Nr. 1191. Der Oberstaatsanwalt Limburg/Lahn, den 29. 7. 1947. 2 Js 4951/46. Strafsache gegen die Masseuse J. G. aus Wetzlar wegen Verbrechen gegen die Menschlichkeit in Tatenheit begangen mit falscher Anschuldigung und wegen Unterschlagung.

62. Blattsammlung der Staatsanwaltschaft betreffend Strafsache gegen G. wegen polit. Sache. Hessisches Hauptstaatsarchiv, Wiesbaden. Abt. 463 Nr. 1191. Hessisches Staatsministerium. Der Minister der Justiz. 9. August 1947. 4107a III 740/47. An der Herrn Oberstaatsanwalt bei dem Landegericht in Limburg. Betrifft: Strafsache gegen J.G. in Wetzlar.

63. Blattsammlung der Staatsanwaltschaft betreffend Strafsache gegen G. wegen polit. Sache. Hessisches Hauptstaatsarchiv, Wiesbaden. Abt. 463 Nr. 1191. Hessisches Staatsministerium. Der Minister der Justiz. 9. August 1947. 4107a III 740/47. An der Herrn Oberstaatsanwalt bei dem Landegericht in Limburg. Betrifft: Strafsache gegen J.G. in Wetzlar.

64. Blattsammlung der Staatsanwaltschaft betreffend Strafsache gegen G. wegen polit. Sache. Hessisches Hauptstaatsarchiv, Wiesbaden. Abt. 463 Nr. 1191. Az. 2 Js. 4951/46. 1. Berichten an den Herrn Minister der Justiz.

65. Blattsammlung der Staatsanwaltschaft betreffend Strafsache gegen G. wegen polit. Sache. Hessisches Hauptstaatsarchiv, Wiesbaden. Abt. 463 Nr. 1191. Strafsache gegen die Masseuse J. G. ... wegen falscher Anschuldigung und Unterschlagung.

66. Blattsammlung der Staatsanwaltschaft betreffend Strafsache gegen G. wegen polit. Sache. Hessisches Hauptstaatsarchiv, Wiesbaden. Abt. 463 Nr. 1191. Der Oberstaatsanwalt. Limburg/Lahn, den 6. Februar 1948 an den Herrn Vorsitzenden der Strafkammer III in Limburg. Berufungsgründung.

67. Adelheid L. Rüter and C.F. Rüter, eds., *Justiz und NS-Verbrechen: Sammlung deutscher Strafurteile wegen nationalsozialistischer Tötungsverbrechen 1945–1966*, Vol. 2 (Amsterdam: University Press Amsterdam, 1969): 105, 108.

68. Rüter und Rüter, eds., *Justiz und NS-Verbrechen*, Vol. 2, 108.

69. Rüter and Rüter, eds., *Justiz und NS-Verbrechen*, Vol. 2, 24.

70. Rüter und Rüter, eds., *Justiz und NS-Verbrechen*, Vol. 2, 125.

71. Rüter und Rüter, eds., *Justiz und NS-Verbrechen*, Vol. 2, 105,109.

72. Rüter und Rüter, eds., *Justiz und NS-Verbrechen*, Vol. 2, 105.

73. Rüter und Rüter, eds., *Justiz und NS-Verbrechen*, Vol. 2, 125–126.

74. Rüter und Rüter, eds., *Justiz und NS-Verbrechen*, Vol. 2, 126.

75. Rüter und Rüter, eds., *Justiz und NS-Verbrechen*, Vol. 2, 126.

76. Rüter und Rüter, eds., *Justiz und NS-Verbrechen*, Vol. 2, 127–128.

77. 17/201–3/2 Legal Division, RG 260 OMGUS, Institut für Zeitgeschichte, Munich. Subject: Authorization to Administration of Justice for Trying Offenses Pursuant to Control Council Law No. 10. 21 August 1947.

78. Rüter und Rüter, eds., *Justiz und NS-Verbrechen*, Vol. 2, 105, 123.

79. Hessisches Hauptstaatsarchiv. Abt. 461 Nr. 30264. 3 Js 381/46. 28.2.46. Betrifft: Strafsache gegen E. M. Frankfurt (Main), wegen falscher Anschuldigung. An der Herrn Justizminister in Wiesbaden; Hessisches Haupstaatsarchiv. Abt. 461 Nr. 30264. Protokoll der öffentlichen Sitzung vom 5. November 1947. Ber. Reg. Nr. 1256. E. M. Ber. Reg. Nr. 1255, E. L. Begründung.

80. Hessisches Hauptstaatsarchiv. Abt. 461 Nr. 30264. 3 Js 381/46. 28.2.46. Betrifft: Strafsache gegen E. M. Frankfurt (Main), wegen falscher Anschuldigung. An der Herrn Justizminister in Wiesbaden; Abt. 461 Nr. 30264. Grosshessisches Staatministerium. Der Minister der Justiz. Az.: 4107a– 52/46. 8.3.1946. An der Herrn Oberstaatsanwalt Frankfurt/Main; Abt. 461 Nr. 30264. Der Oberstaatsanwalt beim Landgericht. Frankfurt (Main), den 28. Januar 1958. 4 AR 1/58. An den Generalstaatsanwalt in Frankfurt/Main. Betr. Tötung des Reichsbahndirektors Z. in Frankfurt/Main.

81. Hessisches Haupstaatsarchiv. Abt. 461 Nr. 30264. Protokoll der öffentlichen Sitzung vom 5. November 1947. Ber. Reg. Nr. 1256. E. M. Ber. Reg. Nr. 1255, E. L. Begründung.

82. RG 260 OMGUS, 17/210–3/3, Hessisches Hauptstaatsarchiv. Wiesbaden. APO 655. Subject: "Reports of Important Trials," 5 November 1947.

83. 71/201–3/2 Legal Division, RG 260 OMGUS, Institut für Zeitgeschichte, Munich. Subject: Authorizations granted to Wuerttemberg-Baden Courts for trying offenses pursuant to Control Council Law No. 10. 5 August 1947.

84. Bundesarchiv. Koblenz. Z21/2213. Legal/MOJ/52340. Ministry of Justice. Legal Division. 11. März 1948. Betrifft: Aburteilung von Verbrechen gegen die Menschlichkeit durch deutsche Gerichte; "A. Anweisung des Zonal Office of the Legal Adviser. Verbrechen gegen die Menschlichkeit – Kontrollratsgesetz Nr. 10," *Zentraljustizverwaltungsblatt* 1948: 250–251.

85. Bundesarchiv. Koblenz. Z21/2213. Legal/MOJ/52340. Ministry of Justice. Legal Division. 11. März 1948. Betrifft: Aburteilung von Verbrechen gegen die Menschlichkeit durch deutsche Gerichte.

86. Bundesarchiv. Koblenz. Z21/2213. Legal/MOJ/52340. Legal Division. 20. April 1948. Betrifft: Aburteilung von Verbrechen gegen die Menschlichkeit durch deutsche Gerichte.

87. 171/201–3/3 Legal Division, RG 260 OMGUS, Institut für Zeitgeschichte, Munich. Subject: Authorization of German Courts to Try Cases under Control Council Law No. 10. 14 September 1948.

88. 17/201–3/3 Legal Division, RG 260 OMGUS, Institut für Zeitgeschichte, Munich. Subject: Trials for Crimes against Humanity in the U.S. Zone. 20 October 1948.

89. 17/201–3/2 Legal Division, RG 260 OMGUS, Institut für Zeitgeschichte, Munich. Subject: Crimes against Humanity – Ex Post Facto Legislation. 19 May 1947.

90. 17/20–3/3 Legal Division, RG 260 OMGUS, Institut für Zeitgeschichte, Munich. Subject: Control Council Law No. 10. 10 October 1947.

91. Bundesarchiv. Koblenz. Z21/1309. Niederschrift über die Tagung der Chefs der obersten Justizbehörden der britischen und amerikanischen Zone in Bad Godesberg am 16. und 17. Juli 1946, pp. 7, 11–12.

92. "OLG Bamberg, Beschluß vom 27. 7. 1949, Ws 152/49," *Monatsschrift für deutsches Recht* 4 1950: 55.

93. OLGrat Dr. Sauer, "OLG Bamberg, Beschl. v. 27. 7. 1949, Ws. 152/49," *Neue Juristische Wochenschrift* 1950 (1): 35–36.

94. "OLG Bamberg, Beschluß vom 27. 7. 1949, Ws 152/49," *Monatsschrift für deutsches Recht* 4 1950: 56; "OLG Bamberg. § 239 StGB", *Süddeutsche Juristenzeitung* 1950: 208–209.

95. "OLG Bamberg, Beschluß vom 27. 7. 1949, Ws 152/49," 55.

96. Hoffmann, *Die Verfolgung der nationalsozialistischen Gewaltverbrechen in Hessen*, 145–146.

CHAPTER 3

1. Archives de L'Occupation Française en Allemagne et en Autriche. Colmar. AJ c.372, p.16. Der Chef der deutschen Justizverwaltung in der französischen Zone Badens. Freiburg/Br. 10 Jan. 1946. Betr. Mitteilung wichtiger Gerichtsentscheidungen.

2. Archives de L'Occupation Française en Allemagne et en Autriche. Colmar. AJ c.372, p.16. Der Chef der deutschen Justizverwaltung in der französischen Zone Badens. Freiburg/Br. 15. Jan. 1946. Betr. Verfolgung von Straftaten, welche während des nationalsozialistischen Regimes begangen wurden; Der Chef der deutschen Justizverwaltung in der französischen Zone Badens. Freiburg/Br. 21 Februar 1946. Betr. Verfolgung von Straftaten, welche während des nationalsozialistischen Regimes begangen wurden.

3. Archives de L'Occupation Française en Allemagne et en Autriche. Colmar. AJ c.3678, p. 8. Ergebnis der mündliche Aussprache am 25. Februar 1946 mit Herrn Oberleutnant S. bei der französischen Abteilung der Justiz. 2. Zuständigkeit der deutschen Gerichte für die Aburteilungen von Kriegsverbrechen.

4. Archives de L'Occupation Française en Allemagne et en Autriche. Colmar. AJ c.372, p.16. Der Chef der deutschen Justizverwaltung in der französischen Zone Badens. Freiburg/Br. 27. Februar 1946. Betr. Verfolgung von Straftaten welche während des nationalsozialistischen Regimes begangen wurden; Archives de L'Occupation en Allemagne et en Autriche. Colmar. AJ 3647/17. Le Directeur Régional du Contrôle et dela Justice à Monsieur le Directeur de la Justice Allemande a Neustadt. 20 Mai 1946. Répression des crimes et délits d'inspiration politiques ou raciale.

5. Zuständigkeit für Aburteilung der Kriegsverbrechen im Sinne des Kontrollratsgesetzes Nr. 10. Anweisung der Militärregierung Baden vom 2. Mai 1946. *Amtsblatt der Landesverwaltung Baden. Französisches Besatzungsgebiet* (1946): 49.

6. Archives de L'Occupation Française en Allemagne et en Autriche. Colmar. AJ 3674/17. Le Directeur Régional du Contrôle et de la Justice à Monsieur le Procureur Générale près la Cour d'appel à Neustadt. 20 Mai 1946. Répression des faits de denunciation politique.

7. Archives de L'Occupation Française en Allemagne et en Autriche. Colmar. AJ 3674/17. Der Generalstaatsanwalt für Hessen-Pflaz an den Herrn Directeur Régional du Contrôle et de la Justice in Neustadt/Hdt. 31. Mai 1946. Betrifft: Verfolgung von politischen Denunziationen. Zum geehrten Schreiben vom 20. Mai. 1946.

8. Archives de L'Occupation Française en Allemagne et en Autriche. Colmar. AJ 3674/17. Oberregierungspräsidium Hessen-Pflaz. Nachrichten- und Presseamt. Zeitungsaussichte. 21.5.1946. Gegen die Denunziaten. Generalstaatsanwalt Dr. K. über die Verfahren.

9. Archives de L'Occupation Française en Allemagne et en Autriche. Colmar. AJ 3674/17. Der Generalstaatsanwalt für Hessen-Pflaz an den Herrn Directeur Régional du Contrôle et de la Justice in Neustadt/Hdt. 31. Mai 1946. Betrifft: Verfolgung von politischen Denunziationen. Zum geehrten Schreiben vom 20. Mai. 1946.

10. Archives de L'Occupation Française en Allemagne et en Autriche. Colmar. AJ 3674/17. Oberregierungspräsidium Hessen-Pfalz. Nachtrichten- und Presseamt. Zeitungsausschnitte. 21.5.1946. Gegen die Denunzianten. Generalstaatsanwalt Dr. K. über die Verfahren.

11. Archives de L'Occupation Française en Allemagne et en Autriche. Colmar. AJ 3674/17. Oberregierungspräsidium Hessen-Pfalz. Nachtrichten- und Presseamt. Zeitungsausschnitte. 21.5.1946. Gegen die Denunzianten. Generalstaatsanwalt Dr. K. über die Verfahren.

12. Archives de L'Occupation Française en Allemagne et en Autriche. Colmar. AJ 3674/17. Oberregierungspräsidium Hessen-Pfalz. Abteilung Justiz. 18. Juni 1946. An den Herrn Directeur Régional de la Justice. Neustadt a.d.Hdt. Betrifft: Bestrafung politischer Denunzianten aus der nat. soz. Zeit.

13. Archives de L'Occupation Française en Allemagne et en Autriche. Colmar. AJ 3674/17. Gouvernement Militaire de la Zone Française d'Occupation. Le Directeur Régional du Contrôle et de la Justice à Monsieur le Generalstaatsanwalt près l'Oberlandesgericht de Neustadt. 26 Juin 1946. Object: Repression des faits de dénoncations politiques.

14. Archives de L'Occupation Française en Allemagne et en Autriche. Colmar. AJ c.3673/p.8. Oberriegierungspräsidium Pflaz. Abteilung III – Justiz -. Neustadt a.d.Hdt. 26. Oktober 1946. Betrifft: Anwendung des Gesetzes Nr. 10, betreffend Bestrafung von Personen, die sich Kriegsverbrechen, Verbrechen gegen den Frieden oder die Menschlichkeit schuldig gemacht haben.

15. Adelheid L. Rüter und C.F. Rüter, eds., *Justiz und NS-Verbrechen: Sammlung deutscher Strafurteile wegen nationalsozialistischer Tötungsverbrechen 1945–1966*, Vol. 1 (Amsterdam: University Press Amsterdam, 1968): 65–66.

16. Rüter und Rüter, eds., *Justiz und NS-Verbrechen*, Vol. 1, 66.

17. Rüter und Rüter, eds., *Justiz und NS-Verbrechen*, Vol. 1, 66–67.

18. Rüter und Rüter, eds., *Justiz und NS-Verbrechen*, Vol. 1, 68.

19. C.F. Rüter und Adelheid L. Rüter, eds., *Justiz und NS-Verbrechen*, Vol. 1, 710–711.

20. Rüter und Rüter, eds., *Justiz und NS-Verbrechen*, Vol. 1, 715–716.

21. Rüter und Rüter, eds., *Justiz und NS-Verbrechen*, Vol. 1, 716.

22. Rüter und Rüter, eds., *Justiz und NS-Verbrechen*, Vol. 1, 716–717.
23. Rüter und Rüter, eds., *Justiz und NS-Verbrechen*, Vol. 1, 716.
24. Rüter und Rüter, eds., *Justiz und NS-Verbrechen*, Vol. 1, 717.
25. Rüter und Rüter, eds., *Justiz und NS-Verbrechen*, Vol. 1, 719.
26. "Zum Kontrollgesetz Nr. 10", *Neue Justiz* 1947 1: 139; "Der Grundsatz „nullum crimen sine lege" wird durch das Kontrollratsgesetz Nr. No. 10 nicht verletzt. Zum Begriff der Verfolgung aus politischen Gründen i.S. des KRG Nr. 10." *Deutsche Rechts-Zeitschrift* (1947) 9: 309.
27. Rüter und Rüter, eds., *Justiz und NS-Verbrechen*, Vol. 1, 711.
28. Rüter und Rüter, eds., *Justiz und NS-Verbrechen*, Vol. 1, 711–712.
29. Rüter und Rüter, eds., *Justiz und NS-Verbrechen*, Vol. 1, 712.
30. Rüter und Rüter, eds., *Justiz und NS-Verbrechen*, Vol. 1, 713.
31. Rüter und Rüter, eds., *Justiz und NS-Verbrechen*, Vol. 1, 722.
32. Rüter und Rüter, eds., *Justiz und NS-Verbrechen*, Vol. 1, 722.
33. Rüter und Rüter, eds., *Justiz und NS-Verbrechen*, Vol. 1, 723.
34. Rüter und Rüter, eds., *Justiz und NS-Verbrechen*, Vol. 1, 723.
35. Rüter und Rüter, eds., *Justiz und NS-Verbrechen*, Vol. 1, 723–724.
36. Rüter und Rüter, eds., *Justiz und NS-Verbrechen*, Vol. 1, 726.
37. Archives de L'Occupation Française en Allemagne et en Autriche. Colmar. 3679/13/1. Wurtemberg. Contrôle Justice 3e Partie. Justice Allemande. Période de Rapport du 20 Mai au 20 Juin 1946. Appreciation sur l'État d'Esprit des Juges Allemands.
38. Archives de L'Occupation Française en Allemagne et en Autriche. Colmar. 3679/13/1. Gouvernement Militaire de la Zône Française d'Occupation. Délégation supérieure pour le Gouvernement Militaire de Rhénomie-Hesse-Nassau. Direction Régionale de la Justice. Rapport Mensuel sur la période du 20 Février 1946 au 20 Mars 1946.
39. Archives de L'Occupation Française en Allemagne et en Autriche. Colmar. 3679/13/3. Gouvernement Militaire de la Zône Française d'Occupation. Délégation supérieure pour le Gouvernement Militaire de Rhénomie-Hesse-Nassau. Direction Régionale de la Justice. Rapport Trimestriel. Sur la période du 20 Mai au 20 Juillet 1946. E. Appréciation sur l'état des Juges Allemands et leur manière d'appliquer la Loi Allemande.
40. Archives de L'Occupation Française en Allemagne et en Autriche. Colmar. 3679/13/4. Wurtemberg. Controle Justice. 3e Partie. Justice Allemande. Période du Rapport du 20 Juin au 20 Juillet 1946. E. Appréciation sur l'État des Juges Allemands et leur Manière d'Appliquer la Loi Allemande.
41. Archives de L'Occupation Française en Allemagne et en Autriche. Colmar. 3679/13/3. Gouvernement Militaire de la Zône Française d'Occupation. Délégation supérieure pour le Gouvernement Militaire de Bade. Rapport Mensuel. Sur la période du 1 Septembre au 30 Septembre 1946. E. Appréciation sur l'état des Juges Allemands et leur manière d'appliquer la Loi Allemande.
42. Adolf Arndt, "Das Strafmaß", *Süddeutsche Juristenzeitung* (1946) 1: 30.
43. Archives de L'Occupation Française en Allemagne et en Autriche. Colmar. AJ 806 p.616. Wurtemberg. Contrôle Justice. 3e Partie. Justice Allemande. Période de

Rapport du 10 Novembre au 9 Décembre 1946. Observations générales sur le fonctionnement de la Justice Allemande.

44. Archives de L'Occupation Française en Allemagne et en Autriche. Colmar. AJ 806 p.616. Wurtemberg. Contrôle Justice. 3e Partie. Justice Allemande. Période de Rapport du 10 Novembre au 9 Décembre 1946. Appréciation sur l'État d'Esprit des Juges et leur Manière d'Appliquer la Loi.

45. Martin Broszat, "Siegerjustiz oder strafrechtlicher 'selbtsreinigung'? Aspekete der Vergangenheitsbewältigung der deutschen Justiz während der Besatzungszeit 1945–1949," *Vierteljahrshefte für Zeitgeschichte* 1981(4): 496–499; "LG Konstanz", *Süddeutsche Juristenzeitung* 1947 (2): 337; "Zur Auslegung des Kontrollratsgesetzes Nr. 10," *Deutsche Rechts-Zeitschrift* 1947 (8): 267–270.

46. Archives de L'Occupation Française en Allemagne et en Autriche. Colmar. 3679/15/2. Gouvernement Militaire de la Zône Française d'Occupation. Délegation Supérieure pour le Gouvernment Militaire de Bade. Rapport Mensuel sur la période du 1 Novembre 1946 au 30 Novembre 1946. F – Observations générales sur le fonctionnement de la Justice Allemande.

47. Archives de L'Occupation Française en Allemagne et en Autriche. Colmar. 3679/15/2. Gouvernement Militaire de la Zône Française d'Occupation. Délegation Supérieure pour le Gouvernment Militaire de Bade. Rapport Mensuel sur la période du 1 Novembre 1946 au 30 Novembre 1946. F – Observations générales sur le fonctionnement de la Justice Allemande.

48. Archives de L'Occupation Française en Allemagne et en Autriche. Colmar. 3679/15/2. Gouvernement Militaire de la Zône Française d'Occupation. Délegation Supérieure pour le Gouvernment Militaire de Bade. Rapport Mensuel sur la période du 1 Novembre 1946 au 30 Novembre 1946. F – Observations générales sur le fonctionnement de la Justice Allemande.

49. Archives de L'Occupation Française en Allemagne et en Autriche. Colmar. 3679/15/2. Gouvernement Militaire de la Zône Française d'Occupation. Délegation Supérieure pour le Gouvernment Militaire de Bade. Rapport Mensuel sur la période du 1 Novembre 1946 au 30 Novembre 1946. F – Observations générales sur le fonctionnement de la Justice Allemande; C3680 P27/1. Synthese des Rapports Mensuels. Justice Allemande – Mars de Novembre 1946.

50. Archives de L'Occupation Française en Allemagne et en Autriche. Colmar. AJ3679/14/2a. Gouvernement Militaire de la Zône Française d'Occupation. Délegation Supérieure pour le Gouvernment Militaire de Bade. Rapport Mensuel sur la période du 1er Décembre 1946 au 31 Décembre 1946. F – Observations générales sur le fonctionnement de la Justice Allemande.

51. Archives de L'Occupation Française en Allemagne et en Autriche. Colmar. 3679/13/5. Circonscription Judiciaire de la Sarre. Rapport Mensuel sur la pèriode du 1 Août au 31 Août 1946. III Justice Allemande.

52. Archives de L'Occupation Française en Allemagne et en Autriche. Colmar. 3674/17/2. Der Oberstaatsanwalt. Landau. Pf, den 28. Januar 1947. An Ladesregierung Rheinland-Pfalz. Der Minister der Justiz. Betr. Durchführung von politischen Verfahren.

52. Rüter und Rüter, eds, *Justiz und NS-Verbrechen*, Vol. 2, 365.
53. Rüter und Rüter, eds, *Justiz und NS-Verbrechen*, Vol. 2, 365.
54. Rüter und Rüter, eds, *Justiz und NS-Verbrechen*, Vol. 2, 366.
55. Rüter und Rüter, eds., *Justiz und NS-Verbrechen*, Vol. 2, 366.
56. Rüter und Rüter, eds, *Justiz und NS-Verbrechen*, Vol. 2, 366.
57. Rüter und Rüter, eds, *Justiz und NS-Verbrechen*, Vol. 2, 366.
58. Rüter und Rüter, eds., *Justiz und NS-Verbrechen*, Vol. 2, 367.
59. Rüter und Rüter, eds., *Justiz und NS-Verbrechen*, Vol. 2, 368–369.
60. Rüter und Rüter, eds., *Justiz und NS-Verbrechen*, Vol. 2, 369–371.
61. Rüter und Rüter, eds., *Justiz und NS-Verbrechen*, Vol. 2, 363–364.
62. Rüter und Rüter, eds., *Justiz und NS-Verbrechen*, Vol. 1, 681.
63. Rüter und Rüter, eds., *Justiz und NS-Verbrechen*, Vol. 1, 682.
64. Rüter und Rüter, eds., *Justiz und NS-Verbrechen*, Vol. 1, 682–683.
65. Rüter und Rüter, eds., *Justiz und NS-Verbrechen*, Vol. 1, 682–683.
66. Rüter und Rüter, eds., *Justiz und NS-Verbrechen*, Vol. 1, 684.
67. Rüter und Rüter, eds., *Justiz und NS-Verbrechen*, Vol. 1, 685.
68. Rüter und Rüter, eds., *Justiz und NS-Verbrechen*, Vol. 1, 685.
69. Rüter und Rüter, eds., *Justiz und NS-Verbrechen*, Vol. 1, 688.
70. "Der Grundsatz „nullum crimen sine lege" wird durch das Kontrollratsgesetz Nr. No. 10 nicht verletzt. Zum Begriff der Verfolgung aus politischen Gründen i.S. des KRG Nr. 10," *Deutsche Rechts-Zeitschrift* (1947) 9: 309.
71. Rüter und Rüter, eds., *Justiz und NS-Verbrechen*, Vol. 1, 688–689.
72. Rüter und Rüter, eds., *Justiz und NS-Verbrechen*, Vol. 1, 689, 693.
73. Rüter und Rüter, eds., *Justiz und NS-Verbrechen*, Vol. 1, 689.
74. Rüter und Rüter, eds., *Justiz und NS-Verbrechen*, Vol. 1, 694.
75. Adolf Schönke, "Unrechtsbewußtsein, Vorsatz und Irrtum," *Deutsche Rechtszeitschrift* 1946 (4): 102.
76. "KRG Nr. 10, StGB § 60", *Deutsche Rechts-Zeitschrift* 1948 (7): 259.
77. Rüter und Rüter, eds., *Justiz und NS-Verbrechen*, Vol. 1, 695.
78. Rüter und Rüter, eds., *Justiz und NS-Verbrechen*, Vol. 1, 695.
79. Rüter und Rüter, eds., *Justiz und NS-Verbrechen*, Vol. 1, 695–696.
80. Rüter und Rüter, eds, *Justiz und NS-Verbrechen*, Vol. 1, 698.
81. Archives de L'Occupation Française en Allemagne et en Autriche. Colmar. 36780/21/2. 2 Kls. 59/47, pp. 1–2.
82. Archives de L'Occupation Française en Allemagne et en Autriche. Colmar. 36780/21/2. 2 Kls. 59/47, p. 1.
83. Archives de L'Occupation Française en Allemagne et en Autriche. Colmar. 36780/21/2. 2 Kls. 59/47, pp. 2–3.
84. Archives de L'Occupation Française en Allemagne et en Autriche. Colmar. 36780/21/2. 2 Kls. 59/47, pp. 1, 3.
85. Archives de L'Occupation Française en Allemagne et en Autriche. Colmar. 36780/21/2. 2 Kls. 59/47, pp. 1, 3.
86. Archives de L'Occupation Française en Allemagne et en Autriche. Colmar. 36780/21/2. 2 Kls. 118/47, p. 1.

87. Archives de L'Occupation Française en Allemagne et en Autriche. Colmar. 36780/21/2. 2 Kls. 118/47, p. 2.

88. Archives de L'Occupation Française en Allemagne et en Autriche. Colmar. 36780/21/2. 2 Kls. 118/47, pp. 2–3.

89. Archives de L'Occupation Française en Allemagne et en Autriche. Colmar. 36780/21/2. 2 Kls. 118/47, pp. 1, 3–4.

90. Archives de L'Occupation Française en Allemagne et en Autriche. Colmar. AJ 3679 p.20 d.2. Gouvernement Militaire en Allemagne. Délégation Supérieure pour le Gouvernement Militaire de Bade. Direction Régionale de la Justice. Rapport juridique. L'activité des tribunaux allemands du pays Bade Durant le mois de Octobre 1947. I. Repression des Crimes contre L'Humanité.

91. Archives de L'Occupation Française en Allemagne et en Autriche. Colmar. AJ 806/p.617. Rapport Mensuel. Rapport du Décembre 1947. Justice/Activité Pénal 1947.

92. Archives de L'Occupation Française en Allemagne et en Autriche. Colmar. 3679/22/2. Gouvernement Militaire de la Zone Française d'Occupation. Délégation Provinciale pour le Gouvernement du Palatinate. Direction du Contrôle de la Justice. Rapport Mensuel. 29 Avril 1948 au 29 Mai 1948. Affaires de Crimes contre L'Humanité.

93. Archives de L'Occupation Française en Allemagne et en Autriche. Colmar. JA 3680/22/1. Délégation Supérieure pour le Gouvernement Militaire de Bade. Direction Régionale du Controle de la Justice. Troisième Partie.

94. Archives de L'Occupation Française en Allemagne et en Autriche. Colmar. C.3680/P.27/12. Direction Générale de l'Activité Mensuelle. Février 1948. B. Justice Allemande.

95. Adelheid L. Rüter und C.F. Rüter, eds., *Justiz und NS-Verbrechen: Sammlung deutscher Strafurteile wegen nationalsozialistischer Tötungsverbrechen 1945–1966*, Vol. 3 (Amsterdam: University Press Amsterdam, 1969): 131.

96. Rüter und Rüter, eds., *Justiz und NS-Verbrechen*, Vol. 3, 131–132.

97. Rüter und Rüter, eds., *Justiz und NS-Verbrechen*, Vol. 3, 132–133.

98. Rüter und Rüter, eds.., *Justiz und NS-Verbrechen*, Vol. 3, 133–134.

99. Rüter und Rüter, eds., *Justiz und NS-Verbrechen*, Vol. 3, 135.

100. Rüter und Rüter, eds., *Justiz und NS-Verbrechen*, Vol. 3, 135.

101. Rüter und Rüter, eds., *Justiz und NS-Verbrechen*, Vol. 3, 136.

102. Rüter und Rüter, eds., *Justiz und NS-Verbrechen*, Vol. 3, 136.

103. Rüter und Rüter, eds., *Justiz und NS-Verbrechen*, Vol. 3, 137–138.

104. Rüter und Rüter, eds., *Justiz und NS-Verbrechen*, Vol. 3, 138, 131.

105. Rüter und Rüter, eds., *Justiz und NS-Verbrechen*, Vol. 3, 139.

106. Rüter und Rüter, eds., *Justiz und NS-Verbrechen*, Vol. 3, 140.

107. Rüter und Rüter, eds., *Justiz und NS-Verbrechen*, Vol. 3, 141, 143.

108. Rüter und Rüter, eds., *Justiz und NS-Verbrechen*, Vol. 3, 143; "KRG Nr. 10, StGB § 60," Deutsche Rechts-Zeitschrift 1948 (7): 259.

109. Rüter und Rüter, eds., *Justiz und NS-Verbrechen*, Vol. 3, 289.

110. Rüter und Rüter, eds., *Justiz und NS-Verbrechen*, Vol. 3, 289–290.

111. Rüter und Rüter, eds., *Justiz und NS-Verbrechen*, Vol. 3, 290.
112. Rüter und Rüter, eds., *Justiz und NS-Verbrechen*, Vol. 3, 290–291.
113. Rüter und Rüter, eds., *Justiz und NS-Verbrechen*, Vol. 3, 291.
114. Rüter und Rüter, eds., *Justiz und NS-Verbrechen*, Vol. 3, 291.
115. Rüter und Rüter, eds., *Justiz und NS-Verbrechen*, Vol. 3, 292.
116. Rüter und Rüter, eds., *Justiz und NS-Verbrechen*, Vol. 3, 292.
117. Rüter und Rüter, eds., *Justiz und NS-Verbrechen*, Vol. 3, 292–293.
118. Rüter und Rüter, eds., *Justiz und NS-Verbrechen*, Vol. 3, 293.
119. Rüter und Rüter, eds., *Justiz und NS-Verbrechen*, Vol. 3, 293–295.
120. Rüter und Rüter, eds., *Justiz und NS-Verbrechen*, Vol. 3, 295.
121. Legal jurisdiction in Berlin under the control of the four powers was divided between the separate occupation powers. The American occupation authorities did not authorize the German courts in their occupation sector to adjudicate crimes against humanity, and the general state prosecutor at the *Kammergericht* expressed that administering the British Military Government Ordinance No. 47 at this court was practically inapplicable. Prosecution of crimes under Control Council Law No. 10 took place when the act was committed in the Soviet or French occupation sectors or when the perpetrator lived in these sectors and with the previous authorization of the occupation sector authority. The French occupation authorities had hitherto set the precedent for prosecuting crimes against humanity in Berlin through their authorization for the prosecution of Helene Schwärzel. The prosecution of cases authorized by the Soviet occupation sector authorities was heard at the *Kammergericht* in the Soviet sector as a separate jurisdiction. Bundesarchiv Koblenz. Z21/784. Abschrift. K., Staatsanwalt. Hamburg, den 11.10.1946. Bericht.
122. Rüter und Rüter, eds., *Justiz und NS-Verbrechen*, Vol. 3, 371.
123. Rüter und Rüter, eds., *Justiz und NS-Verbrechen*, Vol. 3, 371–372.
124. Rüter und Rüter, eds., *Justiz und NS-Verbrechen*, Vol. 3, 372.
125. Rüter und Rüter, eds., *Justiz und NS-Verbrechen*, Vol. 3, 372.
126. Rüter und Rüter, eds., *Justiz und NS-Verbrechen*, Vol. 3, 373.
127. Rüter und Rüter, eds., *Justiz und NS-Verbrechen*, Vol. 3, 373.
128. Rüter und Rüter, eds., *Justiz und NS-Verbrechen*, Vol. 3, 373–374.
129. Rüter und Rüter, eds., *Justiz und NS-Verbrechen*, Vol. 3, 374.
130. Rüter und Rüter, eds., *Justiz und NS-Verbrechen*, Vol. 3, 374.
131. Rüter und Rüter, eds., *Justiz und NS-Verbrechen*, Vol. 3, 375.
132. Rüter und Rüter, eds., *Justiz und NS-Verbrechen*, Vol. 3, 375.
133. Rüter und Rüter, eds., *Justiz und NS-Verbrechen*, Vol. 3, 375–376.
134. Rüter und Rüter, eds., *Justiz und NS-Verbrechen*, Vol. 3, 376.
135. Rüter und Rüter, eds., *Justiz und NS-Verbrechen*, Vol. 3, 376.
136. Rüter und Rüter, eds., *Justiz und NS-Verbrechen*, Vol. 3, 376.
137. Rüter und Rüter, eds., *Justiz und NS-Verbrechen*, Vol. 3, 377–378.
138. Archives de L'Occupation Française en Allemagne et en Autriche. Colmar. AJ 806/p.618. Rapport Mensuel de la Justice Allemande du Wurtemberg. Activité du 1er au 31 Décembre 1948. Observations générales sur l'état d'esprit des Magistrats Allemands.

139. Adelheid L. Rüter und C.F. Rüter, eds., *Justiz und NS-Verbrechen: Sammlung deutscher Strafurteile wegen nationalsozialistischer Tötungsverbrechen 1945–1966*, Vol. 4 (Amsterdam: University Press Amsterdam, 1970): 133.
140. Rüter und Rüter, eds., *Justiz und NS-Verbrechen*, Vol. 4, 133–134.
141. Rüter und Rüter, eds., *Justiz und NS-Verbrechen*, Vol. 4, 134.
142. Rüter und Rüter, eds., *Justiz und NS-Verbrechen*, Vol. 4, 134–135.
143. Rüter und Rüter, eds., *Justiz und NS-Verbrechen*, Vol. 4, 135.
144. Rüter und Rüter, eds., *Justiz und NS-Verbrechen*, Vol. 4, 135–136.
145. Rüter und Rüter, eds., *Justiz und NS-Verbrechen*, Vol. 4, 135–136.
146. Rüter und Rüter, eds., *Justiz und NS-Verbrechen*, Vol. 4, 135–136.
147. Rüter und Rüter, eds., *Justiz und NS-Verbrechen*, Vol. 4, 135–136.
148. Rüter und Rüter, eds., *Justiz und NS-Verbrechen*, Vol. 4, 136–137.
149. Rüter und Rüter, eds., *Justiz und NS-Verbrechen*, Vol. 4, 137.
150. Rüter und Rüter, eds., *Justiz und NS-Verbrechen*, Vol. 4, 137–138.
151. Rüter und Rüter, eds., *Justiz und NS-Verbrechen*, Vol. 4, 137–138.
152. Rüter und Rüter, eds., *Justiz und NS-Verbrechen*, Vol. 4, 139.
153. Rüter und Rüter, eds., *Justiz und NS-Verbrechen*, Vol. 4, 143.
154. Rüter und Rüter, eds., *Justiz und NS-Verbrechen*, Vol. 4, 143–144.
155. Rüter und Rüter, eds., *Justiz und NS-Verbrechen*, Vol. 4, 144.
156. Rüter und Rüter, eds., *Justiz und NS-Verbrechen*, Vol. 4, 144.
157. Rüter und Rüter, eds., *Justiz und NS-Verbrechen*, Vol. 4, 144.
158. Rüter und Rüter, eds, *Justiz und NS-Verbrechen*, Vol. 4, 144.
159. Rüter und Rüter, eds, *Justiz und NS-Verbrechen*, Vol. 4, 145–146.
160. Rüter und Rüter, eds., *Justiz und NS-Verbrechen*, Vol. 4, 146–147.
161. Rüter und Rüter, eds., *Justiz und NS-Verbrechen*, Vol. 4, 147.
162. Rüter und Rüter, eds., *Justiz und NS-Verbrechen*, Vol. 4, 144–145.
163. Rüter und Rüter, eds., *Justiz und NS-Verbrechen*, Vol. 4, 663.
164. Rüter und Rüter, eds., *Justiz und NS-Verbrechen*, Vol. 4, 663.
165. Rüter und Rüter, eds., *Justiz und NS-Verbrechen*, Vol. 4, 663.
166. Rüter und Rüter, eds., *Justiz und NS-Verbrechen*, Vol. 4, 663–664.
167. Adelheid L. Rüter und C.F. Rüter, eds., *Justiz und NS-Verbrechen: Sammlung deutscher Strafurteile wegen nationalsozialistischer Tötungsverbrechen 1945–1966*, Vol. 5 (Amsterdam: University Press Amsterdam, 1970): 57.
168. Rüter und Rüter, eds., *Justiz und NS-Verbrechen*, Vol. 5, 58.
169. Rüter und Rüter, eds., *Justiz und NS-Verbrechen*, Vol. 5, 58.
170. Rüter und Rüter, eds., *Justiz und NS-Verbrechen*, Vol. 5, 58.
171. Rüter und Rüter, eds., *Justiz und NS-Verbrechen*, Vol. 5, 58–59.
172. Rüter und Rüter, eds., *Justiz und NS-Verbrechen*, Vol. 5, 59–60.
173. Rüter und Rüter, eds., *Justiz und NS-Verbrechen*, Vol. 5, 59.
174. Rüter und Rüter, eds., *Justiz und NS-Verbrechen*, Vol. 5, 60.
175. Rüter und Rüter, eds., *Justiz und NS-Verbrechen*, Vol. 5, 60.
176. Rüter und Rüter, eds., *Justiz und NS-Verbrechen*, Vol. 5, 60–62.
177. Rüter und Rüter, eds., *Justiz und NS-Verbrechen*, Vol. 5, 62.
178. Rüter und Rüter, eds., *Justiz und NS-Verbrechen*, Vol. 5, 62–63.

179. Rüter und Rüter, eds., *Justiz und NS-Verbrechen*, Vol. 5, 75.
180. Rüter und Rüter, eds., *Justiz und NS-Verbrechen*, Vol. 5, 75.
181. Rüter und Rüter, eds., *Justiz und NS-Verbrechen*, Vol. 5, 76.
182. Rüter und Rüter, eds., *Justiz und NS-Verbrechen*, Vol. 5, 77.
183. Rüter und Rüter, eds., *Justiz und NS-Verbrechen*, Vol. 5, 77.
184. Rüter und Rüter, eds., *Justiz und NS-Verbrechen*, Vol. 5, 78.
185. Rüter und Rüter, eds., *Justiz und NS-Verbrechen*, Vol. 5, 78.
186. Rüter und Rüter, eds., *Justiz und NS-Verbrechen*, Vol. 5, 78–79.
187. Rüter und Rüter, eds., *Justiz und NS-Verbrechen*, Vol. 5, 79–80.
188. Rüter und Rüter, eds., *Justiz und NS-Verbrechen*, Vol. 5, 80–81.
189. Archives de L'Occupation Française en Allemagne et en Autriche. Colmar. 3679/16/1. Rapport Mensuel du Contrôle de la Justice Allemande du 1er mars au 31 mars 1947.
190. Archives de L'Occupation Française en Allemagne et en Autriche. Colmar. AJ 806 p.619. Gouvernement Militaire de la Zone Française d'Occupation. Rapport Mensuel. Contrôle de la Justice Allemande du Wurtemberg. Rapport Mensuel. Activité du 1er au 30 Avril 1949.
191. Archives de L'Occupation Française en Allemagne et en Autriche. Colmar. 3680/21/1. Anlage zum Monatsbericht für Dezember 1947; Rapport Mensuel de mois de Décembre 1947. Justice Allemande. Personnel du Contrôle et Observations, p. 15; AJ c.372, p. 17 Bad. Justizministerium, Freiburg/Br. 16. Juli 1947. Berichte in politische Strafverfahren; 3680/22/1. Gesamtzusammenstellung der Staatsanwaltschaften des OLG-Bezirks Neustadt. Anlage zum Monatsbericht der Gerichte – allgemeine Tätigkeit.
192. Archives de L'Occupation Française en Allemagne et en Autriche. Colmar. 3680/25/4. Gouvernement Militaire de la Zone Française d'Occupation. Rapport Mensuel. Contrôle de la Justice Allemande du Wurtemberg. Rapport Mensuel. Activité du 1er au au 30 Avril 1949. Aperçu sur L'Évolution de La Jurisprudence en Matiere de Crimes contre L'Humanité.
193. Archives de L'Occupation Française en Allemagne et en Autriche. Colmar. 3680/25/4. Gouvernement Militaire de la Zone Française d'Occupation. Dèlègation Provinciale pour le Gouvernment Militaire du Palatinat. Direction du Contrôle de la Justice. Rapport Mensuel. Période du 1 Août au 31 Août 1949.
194. Archives de L'Occupation Française en Allemagne et en Autriche. Colmar. 3680/25/4. Gouvernement Militaire de la Zone Française d'Occupation. Dèlègation Provinciale pour le Gouvernment Militaire du Palatinat. Direction du Contrôle de la Justice Allemande. Rapport Mensuel. Période du 1 Août au 31 Août 1949.
195. Archives de L'Occupation Française en Allemagne et en Autriche. Colmar. 3680/25/4. Rapport d'Activité du Contrôle de la Justice Allemande et de l'Administration Pénintentiaire Coblence, le Septembre 1949. No/49/JUS/JA. Rapport du Contrôle de la Justice Allemande.
196. Archives de L'Occupation Française en Allemagne et en Autriche. Colmar. 3680/25/4. Studio Koblenz. Redaktion. Rheinlandecho 12.45 – 13.00. 8.8.1949. Gouvernement Militaire de la Zône Française d'Occupation. Délégation Générale pour

le Gouvernement Militaire de l'État Rhéno-Palatin. Contrôle de la Justice. Rapport Mensuel. Période du 1e Aout 1949 au 1 Septembre 1949.

197. Archives de L'Occupation Française en Allemagne et en Autriche. Colmar. 3680/25/4. Studio Koblenz. Redaktion. Rheinlandecho 12.45 – 13.00. 8.8.1949. Gouvernement Militaire de la Zône Française d'Occupation. Délégation Générale pour le Gouvernement Militaire de l'État Rhéno-Palatin. Contrôle de la Justice. Rapport Mensuel. Période du 1e Aout 1949 au 1 Septembre 1949.

198. Archives de L'Occupation Française en Allemagne et en Autriche. Colmar. 3680/25/4. Studio Koblenz. Redaktion. Rheinlandecho 12.45 – 13.00. 8.8.1949. Gouvernement Militaire de la Zône Française d'Occupation. Délégation Générale pour le Gouvernement Militaire de l'État Rhéno-Palatin. Contrôle de la Justice. Rapport Mensuel. Période du 1e Aout 1949 au 1 Septembre 1949.

199. Archives de L'Occupation Française en Allemagne et en Autriche. Colmar. 3680/25/4. Gouvernement Militaire de la Zône Française d'Occupation. Délégation supérieure pour le Gouvernement Militaire de Hesse-Palatinat. Contrôle de la Justice Allemande. Rapport Mensuel sur la période du 1e Novembre 1949 au 30 Novembre 1949. Activité du service de la Justice Allemande.

CHAPTER 4

1. Kerstin Freudiger, *Die juristische Aufarbeitung von NS-Verbrechen: Beiträge zur Rechtsgeschichte des 20. Jahrhunderts 33* (Tübingen: Mohr Siebeck, 2002): 317.

2. Ordinance No. 47. "Crimes against Humanity (Control Council Law No. 10), *Military Government Gazette: British Zone of Control* No. 13: 306.

3. Martin Broszat, "Siegerjustiz oder strafrechtlicher 'selbtsreinigung'? Aspekete der Vergangenheitsbewältigung der deutschen Justiz während der Besatzungszeit 1945–1949," *Vierteljahrshefte für Zeitgeschichte* 1981(4): 516.

4. Bundesarchiv. Koblenz. Z21/396. Legal/MOJ/52343/1. Legal Division. 10 September 1946. Subject: Control Council Law No. 10 – Crimes against Humanity; Erlass der Mil.-Reg., Legal Division – Legal/MOJ/52 343/1 - vom 10. September 1946; *Justizministerialblatt Zentraljustizamt für das Land Nordrhein-Westfalen* 1947 (1): 50.

5. Bundesarchiv. Koblenz. Z21/784. Der Präsident des Hanseatischen Oberlandesgerichts an Controller Legal Branch. 4. Oktober 1946.

6. Bundesarchiv. Koblenz. Z21/784. Der Präsident des Hanseatischen Oberlandesgerichts an das Zentral-Justizamt für die britische Zone. 20. Dezember 1946. Betrifft: Kontrollratsgesetz 10.

7. Bundesarchiv. Koblenz. Z21/784. Der Generalstaatsanwalt be idem Hanseatischen Oberlandesgericht an Legal Division, Zonal Executive Offices. 4053 -1-. 8. Oktober 1946. Betr.: Kontrollratsgesetz No. 10. – Verbrechen gegen die Menschlichkeit.

8. Bundesarchiv. Koblenz. Z21/1334. Legal Division. Zonal Executive Office. Control Commission for Germany (British Element). 21 November 1946. Subject: Control Council Law No. 10. Crimes against Humanity – Trial of Informers.

9. Bundesarchiv. Koblenz. Z21/1334. Legal Division. Zonal Executive Office. Control Commission for Germany (British Element). 21 November 1946. Subject: Control Council Law No. 10. Crimes against Humanity – Trial of Informers.

10. Erdsiek, "Das Zentral-Justizamt für die britische Zone," *Deutsche Rechtszeitschrift* 1946 (4): 121.

11. Bundesarchiv. Koblenz. Z21/1334. Legal Division. Zonal Executive Office. Control Commission for Germany (British Element). 21 November 1946. Subject: Control Council Law No. 10. Crimes against Humanity – Trial of Informers.

12. Bundesarchiv. Koblenz. Z21/784. Der Präsident des Hanseatischen Oberlandesgerichts. An: Controller Legal Branch. HQ Mil Gov Hansestadt Hamburg.

13. Bundesarchiv. Koblenz. Z21/784. Legal/CLO/108. Central Legal Office. Liaison Officer. Legal Division. Control Commission for Germany (BE). 23rd October, 1946. Subject: Crimes against Humanity. Appendix A. Nulla Poene Sine Lege.

14. Bundesarchiv. Koblenz. Z21/784. Der Präsident der Rechtsanwaltskammer in Hamburg an das Zentral Justizamt, Hamburg. 4. Februar 1947; Z21/784 Stellungnahme des Hanseatischen Rechtsanwaltskammer zur Frage der rückwirken Kraft des Gesetzes Nr. 10 des Kontrollrates.

15. Bundesarchiv. Koblenz. Z21/784. Legal/CLO/108. Central Legal Office. Liaison Officer. Legal Division. Control Commission for Germany (BE). 23rd October, 1946. Subject: Crimes against Humanity. Appendix A. Nulla Poene Sine Lege.

16. Bundesarchiv. Koblenz. Z21/1352. Legal/MOJ/52316. 17. November 1946. Betrifft: Hamburger Besuch vom 12.-15. November 1946; Z21/784. Der Präsident des Hanseatischen Oberlandesgerichts. 20. Dezember 1946. Betrifft: Kontrollratsgesetz 10.

17. Bundesarchiv. Koblenz. Z21/784. Der Generalstaatsanwalt bei dem Hanseatischen Oberlandesgericht. 4053-1-. 8. Oktober 1946. Betr.: Kontrollratsgesetz No. 10 – Verbrechen gegen die Menschlichkeit.

18. Bundesarchiv. Koblenz. Z21/1352. Legal/MOJ/52343/1. Legal Division. Zonal Executive Office. Control Commission for Germany. 31. Oktober 1946. Betrifft: Kontrollratgesetz Nr. 10 / Verbrechen gegen die Menschlichkeit; Bundesarchiv. Koblenz. Z21/784. Legal/MOJ/52343/1. Legal Division, Zonal Executive Offices. To: British Liaison Officer, Central Legal Office. Subject: Control Council Law No. 10 – Crimes against Humanity.

19. Erlass der Mil.Reg., Legal Division – Legal/MOJ/52 343/1 – vom 21. November 1946 betr. Aburteilung von Denunzianten. *Justizministerialblatt Zentraljustizamt für das Land Nordrhein-Westfalen* 1947 (1): 50–51.

20. Bundesarchiv. Koblenz. Z21/784. Zentral-Justizamt für die Britische Zone. November 22, 1946. To: All Hamburg Newspapers, incl. German News Service and Nordwestdeutsche Rundfunk. Trial by German Courts of Crimes against Humanity.

21. Bundesarchiv. Koblenz. Z21/784. Der Präsident des Hanseatischen Oberlandesgerichts. 401/1c/1/. 17. Januar 1947. Betrifft: Kontrollratsgesetz Nr. 10. Verbrechen gegen die Menschlichkeit: 1.

22. Bundesarchiv. Koblenz. Z21/784. Zentral-Justizamt für die Britische Zone. November 22, 1946. To: All Hamburg Newspapers, incl. German News Service and Nordwestdeutsche Rundfunk. Trial by German Courts of Crimes against Humanity.

23. Bundesarchiv. Koblenz. Z21/424. Legal/MOJ/52316. Legal Division. Zonal Executive Offices. Control Commission for Germany (British Element). 15 January 1947. Subject: Visit to Hamburg 13–14 January 1947. Control Council Law No. 10 – Crimes against Humanity. Tillson [sic] Case.

24. Bundesarchiv. Koblenz. Z21/1355. Legal/MOJ/52318/1. Legal Division. 16. Oktober 1947. Betrifft: Inspektionsreise der Aufsichtskommission für deutsche Gerichte vom 23. September bis 8. Oktober 1947.

25. Bundesarchiv. Koblenz. Z21/1356. Legal Division. Legal/MOJ/52340. 16 January 1948. Betrifft: Verbrechen gegen die Menschlichkeit – Verordnung No. 47.

26. Bundesarchiv. Koblenz. Z21/784. Zentral-Justizamt. 1 February 1947. Vermerk: Betr.: Kontrollratsgesetz Nr. 10.

27. Bundesarchiv. Koblenz. Z21/784. Zentral-Justizamt. 1 February 1947. Vermerk: Betr.: Kontrollratsgesetz Nr. 10.

28. Bundesarchiv. Koblenz. Z21/1354. Legal/MOJ/523434/1. Legal Division. 23. Mai. 1947. Betrifft: Kontrollratsgesetz No. 18 [sic] – Verbrechen gegen die Menschlichkeit – Aburteilungen von Denunzianten; Z21/784. – 401/5 – Iis. 16. Juni 1947. Betrifft: Kontrollratsgesetz Nr. 10, Verbrechen gegen die Menschlichkeit – Aburteilung von Denunziationen; Legal/MOJ/52343/1. 23. Mai. 1947. Betrifft: Kontrollratsgesetz Nr. 10 – Verbrechen gegen die Menschlichkeit – Aburteilung von Denunziaten; Z21/784. Legal/CLO/152. 29. Mai 1947. Betrifft: Verbrechen gegen die Menschlichkeit; Z21/784 -401/5-IIa. 16. Juni 1947. Betr.: Verbrechen gegen die Menschlichkeit – Kontrollratsgesetz Nr. 10-; Z21/784. -401/5-IIa. 16. Juni 1947. Betrifft: Kontrollratsgesetz Nr. 10, Verbrechen gegen die Menschlichkeit.-Aburteilung von Denunziationen; "Ordinance No. 69: Trial of members of Criminal Organizations", *Military Government Gazette: British Zone of Control*. No. 16: 405–407; Erlaß der Kontrollkommission, Legal Division – Legal/MOJ/52 343/1 - vom 23. Mai 1947 betr. Aburteilung von Denunzianten. *Justizministerialblatt Zentraljustizamt für das Land Nordrhein-Westfalen* 1947 (1): 51; "Betr. Kontrollratsgesetz Nr. 10 – Verbrechen gegen die Menschlichkeit", *Niedersächsische Rechtspflege* 1948: 10.

29. Bundesarchiv. Koblenz. Z21/784. Der Oberlandesgerichtspräsident. Celle. -103 III a-. 19. Dezember 1946. Betrifft: Verbrechen gegen die Menschlichkeit (Denunziationsfälle).

30. Bundesarchiv. Koblenz. Z21/784. Der Präsident des Hanseatischen Oberlandesgerichts. 401/1c/1. 17. Januar 1947. Betrifft: Kontrollratsgesetz Nr. 10. Verbrechen gegen die Menschlichkeit: 2–3.

31. Bundesarchiv. Koblenz. Z21/784. Der Präsident. -401/4-Ia. An den Herrn Oberlandesgerichtspräsidenten in Celle, über den Herrn Niedersächsischen Justizminister in Hannover. 23. April 1947. Betr.: Verbrechen gegen die Menschlichkeit – Denunziationsfälle.

32. Bundesarchiv. Koblenz. Z21/784. 401/5-II. 23. Mai. 1947. Betr.: Verbrechen gegen die Menschlichkeit; 401/5–II-. May 24th, 1947. Subject: Crimes against Humanit; -401/5-IIa. 16. Juni 1947. Betrifft: Kontrollratsgesetz Nr. 10, Verbrechen gegen die Menschlichkeit – Aburteilung von Denunziationen; -401/5-IIa. 16. Juni. 1947. Betr.: Verbrechen gegen die Menschlichkeit – Kontrollratsgesetz Nr. 10; Legal/

MOJ/52341/1. Legal Division. 23. Mai. 1947. Betrifft: Kontrollratsgesetz Nr. 10 – Verbrechen gegen die Menschlichkeit – Aburteilung von Denunzianten.

33. Bundesarchiv. Koblenz. Z21/784. Der Präsident der Rechtsanwaltskammer in Hamburg. 800/46. 4. Februar 1947. An das Zentral-Justizamt, Hamburg.

34. Bundesarchiv. Koblenz. Z21/1354. Legal/MOJ/52343/1. Legal Division. Zonal Executive Offices. 7. Mai 1947. Betrifft: Verbrechen gegen die Menschlichkeit.

35. Bundesarchiv. Koblenz. Z21/1354. Legal/MOJ/52343/1. Legal Division. 14. Mai. 1947. Betrifft: Verbrechen gegen die Menschlichkeit; Z21/784. Legal Division, Zonal Executive Offices, Control Commission for Germany (British Element). 14 May 1947. Subject: Crimes against Humanity.

36. Bundesarchiv. Koblenz. Z21/784. 401/5–II-. May 24th, 1947. Subject: Crimes against Humanity.

37. Bundesarchiv. Koblenz. Z21/784. 401/5-II. 23. Mai. 1947. An den Herrn Generalstaatsanwalt in Kiel über den Herrn Landesminister der Justiz in Kiel; "Kiel verfolgt Naziverbrecher", Berlin *Telegraf* 20 May 1947, No. 115.

38. Bundesarchiv. Koblenz. Z21/784. 401/5-II. 23. Mai. 1947. An den Herrn Generalstaatsanwalt in Kiel über den Herrn Landesminister der Justiz in Kiel; "Kiel verfolgt Naziverbrecher", Berlin *Telegraf* 20 May 1947, No. 115.

39. Bundesarchiv. Koblenz. Z21/1355. Legal/MOJ/52316. Legal Division. Zonal Executive Office. 18. Juni 1947. Betrifft: Besuch beim Hauptquartier des Landes Nordrhein-Westfalen am 16. und 17. Juni 1947.

40. Rüter und Rüter, eds., *Justiz und NS-Verbrechen* Vol. 1, 661.

41. Rüter und Rüter, eds., *Justiz und NS-Verbrechen*, Vol. 1, 663–664.

42. Rüter und Rüter, eds., *Justiz und NS-Verbrechen*, Vol. 1, 665–666.

43. Rüter und Rüter, eds., *Justiz und NS-Verbrechen*, Vol. 1, 667–668; "Zur Frage der Anwendbarkeit des Kontrollratsgesetzes Nr. 10 im Falle einer Denunziation," *Monatsschrift für deutsches Recht* 1947 1: 205.

44. Rüter und Rüter, eds., *Justiz und NS-Verbrechen*, Vol. 1, 669–671.

45. Rüter und Rüter, eds., *Justiz und NS-Verbrechen*, Vol. 1, 671.

46. Rüter und Rüter, eds., *Justiz und NS-Verbrechen*, Vol. 1, 672.

47. Rüter und Rüter, eds., *Justiz und NS-Verbrechen*, Vol. 1, 673.

48. Rüter und Rüter, eds., *Justiz und NS-Verbrechen*, Vol. 1, 675.

49. Bundesarchiv. Koblenz. Z21/799. Der Generalstaatsanwalt bei dem Oberlandesgericht. 401a. 24. Oktober 1947.

50. Diewald-Kerkmann, *Politische Denunziation im NS-Regime*, 171.

51. Diewald-Kerkmann, *Politische Denunziation im NS-Regime*, 171.

52. Diewald-Kerkmann, *Politische Denunziation im NS-Regime*, 172.

53. Bundesarchiv. Koblenz. Z21/799. Der Generalstaatsanwalt bei dem Oberlandesgericht. 401a. 24. Oktober 1947.

54. Bundesarchiv. Koblenz. Z21/799. 1. Schreiben Herrn Generalstaatsanwalt Dr. S. Braunschweig. 13. Nov. 1947.

55. "Verordnung zur Durchführung der Militärregierungsverordnung Nr. 98 über die Errichtung eines Obersten Gerichthofes für die Britische Zone. Vom 17. November 1947," *Verordnungsblatt für die Britische Zone* 1947 Nr. 25: 149–153.

56. Bundesarchiv. Koblenz. Z21/2213. Legal/MOJ/52340. Ministry of Justice Branch. Legal Division. 11. März 1948. Betrifft: Aburteilung von Verbrechen gegen die Menschlichkeit durch deutsche Gerichte; Bundesarchiv. Koblenz. Z21/140. Die Tätigkeit der Strafrechtsabteilung des Zentral-Justizamts 1946/49.

57. Bundesarchiv. Koblenz. Z21/1357. 29. KLs 2/46. Beglaubigte Abschrift: 1–2, 10.

58. Bundesarchiv. Koblenz. Z21/1357. Legal Division, Zonal Executive Offices. 15 August 1947. To: Chief Legal Officer, H.Q. Land North Rhine/Westphalia. Subject: Crimes against Humanity: J. M.

59. Bundesarchiv. Koblenz. Z21/799. NRW/LEG/19001. Land Legal Department. HQ Land North Rhine/Westfalen. 9 Sep 47. Subject: Control Council Law No. 10. Crimes against Humanity.

60. Bundesarchiv. Koblenz. Z21/1357. 2 KMs. 18/47 22 a 252/47, pp. 2–3

61. Bundesarchiv. Koblenz. Z21/1357. 2 KMs. 18/47 22 a 252/47, p. 3

62. Bundesarchiv. Koblenz. Z21/1357. 2 KMs. 18/47 22 a 252/47, pp. 3–5.

63. Bundesarchiv. Koblenz. Z21/1357. 2 KMs. 18/47 22 a 252/47, pp. 4–5.

64. Bundesarchiv. Koblenz. Z21/1357. 2 KMs. 18/47 22 a 252/47, p. 6.

65. Bundesarchiv. Koblenz. Z21/1357. 401 E b-77-IIe-4707/48. Betr. Strafsache gegen W. F. A. wegen Verbrechen gegen die Menschlichkeit.

66. Bundesarchiv. Koblenz. Z21/794. Monatliche Bericht über die Hauptverhandlung betr. Verbrechen gegen die Menschlichkeit (Monat Februar 1948.)

67. Bundesarchiv. Koblenz. Z38/653. 3 KLs 3/47: 1–2.

68. Bundesarchiv. Koblenz. Z38/653. 3 KLs 3/47: 2–3.

69. Bundesarchiv. Koblenz. Z38/653. 3 KLs 3/47: 3.

70. Bundesarchiv. Koblenz. Z38/653. 3 KLs 3/47: 3–6.

71. Bundesarchiv. Koblenz. Z38/653. 3 KLs 3/47: 1, 6–8; Z21/794 Monatliche Bericht der deutschen ordentlichen Gerichte über die Verbrechen gegen die Menschlichkeit (Monat Februar 1948.) B. Revisionen Oberlandesgericht Hamm 2. Strafsenat.

72. Z21/794. Monatliche Bericht der deutschen ordentlichen Gerichte über die Verbrechen gegen die Menschlichkeit (Monat Februar 1948.) B. Revisionen Oberlandesgericht Hamm 2. Strafsenat.

73. Bundesarchiv. Koblenz. Z38/653. (2) Ss 469/47 OLG Hamm. 5 KLs. 3/47 Bielefeld; Z21/794: 1–2.

74. Bundesarchiv. Koblenz. Z38/653. (2) Ss 469/47 OLG Hamm. 5 KLs. 3/47 Bielefeld; Z21/794: 3–7.

75. Bundesarchiv. Koblenz. Z38/653. (2) Ss 469/47 OLG Hamm. 5 KLs. 3/47 Bielefeld; Z21/794: 3–7.

76. "Die Denunziation ist nach dem Kontrollratsgesetz Nr. 10 nur stafbar, wenn sie eine unmenschliche Verfolgung aus politischen Gründen ist und der Täter sich dessen bei der Tat bewußt war," *Monatsschrift für deutsches Recht* 1947 1: 307; "Zur Frage der Strafbarkeit einer politischen Denunziation," *Monatsschrift für deutsches Recht* 1947 1: 305–306; "OLG Düsseldorf. Article II 1c KRG 10. Denunziation als Teilnahme an der Verfolgung aus politischen Gründen, Bewußtsein, Vorraussetzungen des Vorsatzes, Vollendung und Versuch," *Süddeutsche Juristenzeitung* 1948: 328–332;

H. Arndt, "KRG 10. – Die wahre Anzeige für sich allein ist keine Verfolgung i.S. des KRG 10. OLG Kiel, StS Beschl. v. 16. 1. 1948 – Ws 8/48," *Neue Juristische Wochenschrift* 1948 1: 393; "OLG Hamm. Article II 1c KRG 10. Denunziation als «Gewalttat» i.S. der ersten Gruppe der Verbrechen gegen die Menschlichkeit, Bedeutung der Tatfolgen." *Süddeutsche Juristenzeitung* 1948: 332–334.

77. Bundesarchiv. Koblenz. Z38/653. (2) Ss 469/47 OLG Hamm. 5 KLs. 3/47 Bielefeld; Z21/794: 2.

78. Bundesarchiv. Koblenz. Z38/653. Der Generalstaatsanwalt beim Obersten Gerichtshof für die Britische Zone. Sts 8/48. Köln, den 17. April 1948: 1.

79. Bundesarchiv. Koblenz. Z38/653. Der Generalstaatsanwalt beim Obersten Gerichtshof für die Britische Zone. Sts 8/48. Köln, den 17. April 1948: 2–3.

80. Bundesarchiv. Koblenz. Z38/653. Der Generalstaatsanwalt beim Obersten Gerichtshof für die Britische Zone. Sts 8/48. Köln, den 17. April 1948: 3–6.

81. Bundesarchiv. Koblenz. Z38/653. Sts 8/48: 1–3.

82. Bundesarchiv. Koblenz. Z38/653. Sts 8/48: 5.

83. "Oberster Gerichtshof. Köln," *Monatsschrift für deutsches Rechts* 1948: 303–304.

84. Bundesarchiv. Koblenz. Z38/653. Sts 8/48: 5–6.

85. Bundesarchiv. Koblenz. Z38/653. Sts 8/48: 6–7.

86. Bundesarchiv. Koblenz. Z38/653. Sts 8/48: 8.

87. Bundesarchiv. Koblenz. Z38/653. 6 Kls 30/48: 1

88. Bundesarchiv. Koblenz. Z38/653. Sts 8/48: 1

89. Bundesarchiv. Koblenz. Z38/653. Sts 8/48: 1–2.

90. Bundesarchiv. Koblenz. Z38/653. Sts 8/48: 4.

91. Bundesarchiv. Koblenz. Z21/794. Monatliche Bericht über die Hauptverhandlung betr. Verbrechen gegen die Menschlichkeit (Monat Februar 1948.) I. Instanz Oberlandesgericht Düsseldorf.

92. "Die Strafbarkeit der Denunziation nach dem Kontrollratsgesetz Nr. 10. OLG Düsseldorf," *Monatsschrift für deutsches Recht* 1948 2: 124.

93. "Urteil des KG v. 13. 7. 49 – 1 Ss 156. 49," *Juristische Rundschau* 1949: 510–511.

94. Bundesarchiv. Koblenz. Z21/794. Monatliche Bericht über die Hauptverhandlung betr. Verbrechen gegen die Menschlichkeit (Monat März 1948.) Instanz. Oberlandesgericht Düsseldorf. Gericht. Landgericht Duisburg III Strafkammer.

95. Rüter und Rüter, eds., *Justiz und NS-Verbrechen*, Vol. 2, 397–399.

96. Rüter und Rüter, eds., *Justiz und NS-Verbrechen*, Vol. 2, 399.

97. Rüter und Rüter, eds., *Justiz und NS-Verbrechen*, Vol. 2, 399.

98. Rüter und Rüter, eds., *Justiz und NS-Verbrechen*, Vol. 2, 399.

99. Rüter und Rüter, eds., *Justiz und NS-Verbrechen*, Vol. 2, 400–401.

100. Rüter und Rüter, eds, *Justiz und NS-Verbrechen*, Vol. 2, 401.

101. Rüter und Rüter, eds., *Justiz und NS-Verbrechen*, Vol. 2, 401–402.

102. Rüter und Rüter, eds., *Justiz und NS-Verbrechen*, Vol. 2, 403–406; *Entscheidungen des Obersten Gerichtshofes für die Britische Zone in Strafsachen* Vol. 1 (Berlin/Hamburg: Walter de Gruyter & Co, 1949): 123–126.

103. Bundesarchiv. Koblenz. Z21/791. 5.5.1948. Bemerkungen zu den bis 1. Mai 1948 vorgelegten Berichten über Verbrechen gegen die Menschlichkeit.

104. Rüter und Rüter, eds., *Justiz und NS-Verbrechen*, Vol. 2, 425.

105. Rüter und Rüter, eds., *Justiz und NS-Verbrechen*, Vol. 2, 427.

106. Rüter und Rüter, eds., *Justiz und NS-Verbrechen*, Vol. 2, 427.

107. Rüter und Rüter, eds., *Justiz und NS-Verbrechen*, Vol. 2, 428.

108. Rüter und Rüter, eds., *Justiz und NS-Verbrechen*, Vol. 2, 428.

109. Rüter und Rüter, eds., *Justiz und NS-Verbrechen*, Vol. 2, 433.

110. Rüter und Rüter, eds., *Justiz und NS-Verbrechen*, Vol. 2, 433.

111. Rüter und Rüter, eds., *Justiz und NS-Verbrechen*, Vol. 2, 432.

112. Rüter und Rüter, eds., *Justiz und NS-Verbrechen*, Vol. 2, 433.

113. Rüter und Rüter, eds., *Justiz und NS-Verbrechen*, Vol. 2, 434.

114. Rüter und Rüter, eds., *Justiz und NS-Verbrechen*, Vol. 2, 434.

115. Rüter und Rüter, eds., *Justiz und NS-Verbrechen*, Vol. 2, 435.

116. "Die Voraussetzungen des objectiven und subjectiven Denunziations-Tatbestandes nach dem Kontrollratsgesetz Nr. 10," *Monatsschrift für Deutsches Recht* 1948 (2): 94.

117. "Zur Frage der Anwendbarkeit des Kontrollratsgesetzes Nr. 10 im Falle einer Denunziation," *Monatsschrift für deutsches Recht* 1947 (1): 205.

118. "Die Strafbarkeit der Denunziation nach dem Kontrollratsgesetz Nr. 10. OLG Hamburg," *Monatsschrift für deutsches Recht* 1948 2: 125–126.

119. Adelheid L. Rüter und C.F. Rüter, eds., *Justiz und NS-Verbrechen*, Vol. 2, 435–436.

120. "Die Strafbarkeit der Denunziation nach dem Kontrollratsgesetz Nr. 10. OLG Düsseldorf," *Monatsschrift für deutsches Recht* 1948 2: 124–125.

121. "Die Strafbarkeit der Denunziation nach dem Kontrollratsgesetz Nr. 10. LG Freiburg," *Monatsschrift für deutsches Recht* 1948 2: 126.

122. Adelheid L. Rüter und C.F. Rüter, eds., *Justiz und NS-Verbrechen*, Vol. 2, 437–438.

123. Rüter und Rüter, eds., *Justiz und NS-Verbrechen*, Vol. 2, 439.

124. Rüter und Rüter, eds., *Justiz und NS-Verbrechen*, Vol. 2, 441.

125. Rüter und Rüter, eds., *Justiz und NS-Verbrechen*, Vol. 2, 442.

126. Rüter und Rüter, eds., *Justiz und NS-Verbrechen*, Vol. 2, 444–445.

127. Rüter und Rüter, eds., *Justiz und NS-Verbrechen*, Vol. 2, 447.

128. Bundesarchiv. Koblenz. Z21/1357. Legal/MOJ/52308. Legal Division. 25. Mai. 1948. Betrifft: Bericht über die Revision der deutschen Gerichte in Nordrhein-Westphalen in der Zeit vom 30. März 1948 bis 14. Mai 1948.

129. Rüter und Rüter, eds., *Justiz und NS-Verbrechen*, Vol. 2, 491.

130. Rüter und Rüter, eds., *Justiz und NS-Verbrechen*, Vol. 2, 492–493.

131. Rüter und Rüter, eds., *Justiz und NS-Verbrechen*, Vol. 2, 493–494.

132. Rüter und Rüter, eds., *Justiz und NS-Verbrechen*, Vol. 2, 492–493.

133. Rüter und Rüter, eds., *Justiz und NS-Verbrechen*, Vol. 2, 494.

134. Rüter und Rüter, eds., *Justiz und NS-Verbrechen*, Vol. 2, 495.

135. Rüter und Rüter, eds., *Justiz und NS-Verbrechen*, Vol. 2, 495–496.

136. Rüter und Rüter, eds., *Justiz und NS-Verbrechen*, Vol. 2, 496–497.

137. Mandy Jakobczyk, "Das Verfahren is einzustellen," *Demokratische Geschichte* (2003) 15: 276; Richard Lange, "Die Rechtsprechung des Obersten Gerichtshofs für die Britische Zone zum Verbrechen gegen die Menschlichkeit," *Süddeutsche Juristenzeitung* 3 1948: 655–660.

138. Adelheid L. Rüter and C.F. Rüter, eds., *Justiz und NS-Verbrechen*, Vol. 2, 498.

139. Adelheid L. Rüter and C.F. Rüter, eds., *Justiz und NS-Verbrechen*, Vol. 2, 498–499.

140, Adelheid L. Rüter and C.F. Rüter, eds., *Justiz und NS-Verbrechen*, Vol. 2, 737.

141. Rüter und C.F. Rüter, eds., *Justiz und NS-Verbrechen*, Vol. 2, 737–738.

142. Rüter und Rüter, eds., *Justiz und NS-Verbrechen*, Vol. 2: 738.

143. Rüter und Rüter, eds., *Justiz und NS-Verbrechen*, Vol. 2 739–740.

144. "Die Strafbarkeit der Denunziation nach dem Kontrollratsgesetz Nr. 10. OLG Braunschweig," *Monatsschrift für deutsches Recht* 1948 2: 125.

145. Rüter und Rüter, eds., *Justiz und NS-Verbrechen*, Vol. 2, 740–742.

146. Adelheid L. Rüter und C.F. Rüter, eds., *Justiz und NS-Verbrechen: Sammlung deutscher Strafurteile wegen nationalsozialistischer Tötungsverbrechen 1945–1966* (Amsterdam: University Press Amsterdam, 1971), Vol. 6: 250–252.

147. Rüter und Rüter, eds., *Justiz und NS-Verbrechen*, Vol. 6, 251–252.

148. Rüter und Rüter, eds., *Justiz und NS-Verbrechen*, Vol. 6, 252.

149. Rüter und Rüter, eds., *Justiz und NS-Verbrechen*, Vol. 6, 252–253.

150. Rüter und Rüter, eds., *Justiz und NS-Verbrechen*, Vol. 6, 250, 253.

151. Rüter und Rüter, eds., *Justiz und NS-Verbrechen*, Vol. 6, 253–254, 243.

152. Rüter und Rüter, eds., *Justiz und NS-Verbrechen*, Vol. 6. 254.

153. Rüter und Rüter, eds., *Justiz und NS-Verbrechen*, Vol. 6, 254–255, 244.

154. Rüter und Rüter, eds., *Justiz und NS-Verbrechen*, Vol. 6, 255, 243, 246.

155. Rüter und Rüter, eds., *Justiz und NS-Verbrechen*, Vol. 6, 256, 243.

156. Rüter und Rüter, eds., *Justiz und NS-Verbrechen*, Vol. 6, 256.

157. Rüter und Rüter, eds., *Justiz und NS-Verbrechen*, Vol. 6, 256.

158. Rüter und Rüter, eds., *Justiz und NS-Verbrechen*, Vol. 6, 257–258.

159. Rüter und Rüter, eds., *Justiz und NS-Verbrechen*, Vol. 6, 258.

160. Rüter und Rüter, eds., *Justiz und NS-Verbrechen*, Vol. 6, 259–260.

161. Rüter und Rüter, eds., *Justiz und NS-Verbrechen*, Vol. 6, 260.

162. Rüter und Rüter, eds., *Justiz und NS-Verbrechen*, Vol. 6, 260.

163. Rüter und Rüter, eds., *Justiz und NS-Verbrechen*, Vol. 6, 260–261.

164. Rüter und Rüter, eds., *Justiz und NS-Verbrechen*, Vol. 6, 241.

165. Rüter und Rüter, eds., *Justiz und NS-Verbrechen*, Vol. 6, 245.

166. Rüter und Rüter, eds., *Justiz und NS-Verbrechen*, Vol. 6, 245.

167. Rüter und Rüter, eds., *Justiz und NS-Verbrechen*, Vol. 6, 245.

168. Rüter und Rüter, eds., *Justiz und NS-Verbrechen*, Vol. 6, 246.

169. Rüter und Rüter, eds., *Justiz und NS-Verbrechen*, Vol. 6, 246–247.

170. Rüter und Rüter, eds., *Justiz und NS-Verbrechen*, Vol. 6, 247–248.
171. Rüter und Rüter, eds., *Justiz und NS-Verbrechen*, Vol. 6, 248.
172. Rüter und Rüter, eds., *Justiz und NS-Verbrechen*, Vol. 6, 248.
173. Rüter und Rüter, eds., *Justiz und NS-Verbrechen*, Vol. 6, 248–249.
174. Bundesarchiv. Koblenz. Z21/1357. Legal/MOJ/52340. Zonal Office of the Legal Adviser. 6. Oktober 1948. Betrifft: Kontrollratgesetz Nr. 10: Strafverfolgung von Verbrechen gegen die Menschlichkeit.
175. Rüter und Rüter, eds., *Justiz und NS-Verbrechen*, Vol. 3, 325.
176. Rüter und Rüter, eds., *Justiz und NS-Verbrechen*, Vol. 3, 325–326.
177. Rüter und Rüter, eds., *Justiz und NS-Verbrechen*, Vol. 3, 326–327.
178. Rüter und Rüter, eds., *Justiz und NS-Verbrechen*, Vol. 3, 327.
179. Rüter und Rüter, eds., *Justiz und NS-Verbrechen*, Vol. 3, 328–330.
180. Rüter und Rüter, eds., *Justiz und NS-Verbrechen*, Vol. 3, 331.
181. Rüter und Rüter, eds., *Justiz und NS-Verbrechen*, Vol. 3, 332.
182. Rüter und Rüter, eds., *Justiz und NS-Verbrechen*, Vol. 3, 332.
183. Rüter und Rüter, eds., *Justiz und NS-Verbrechen*, Vol. 3, 345.
184. Rüter und Rüter, eds., *Justiz und NS-Verbrechen*, Vol. 3, 345.
185. Rüter und Rüter, eds., *Justiz und NS-Verbrechen*, Vol. 3, 345–346.
186. Rüter und Rüter, eds., *Justiz und NS-Verbrechen*, Vol. 3, 346–347.
187. Rüter und Rüter, eds., *Justiz und NS-Verbrechen*, Vol. 3, 347.
188. Rüter und Rüter, eds., *Justiz und NS-Verbrechen*, Vol. 3, 347–348.
189. Rüter und Rüter, eds., *Justiz und NS-Verbrechen*, Vol. 3, 348.
190. Rüter und Rüter, eds., *Justiz und NS-Verbrechen*, Vol. 3, 348.
191. Rüter und Rüter, eds., *Justiz und NS-Verbrechen*, Vol. 3, 348.
192. Rüter und Rüter, eds., *Justiz und NS-Verbrechen*, Vol. 3, 349.
193. Rüter und Rüter, eds., *Justiz und NS-Verbrechen*, Vol. 3, 349–350.
194. Rüter und Rüter, eds., *Justiz und NS-Verbrechen*, Vol. 3, 350.
195. Rüter und Rüter, eds., *Justiz und NS-Verbrechen*, Vol. 3, 350.
196. Rüter und Rüter, eds., *Justiz und NS-Verbrechen*, Vol. 3, 350.
197. Rüter und Rüter, eds., *Justiz und NS-Verbrechen*, Vol. 3, 351–352.
198. Rüter und Rüter, eds., *Justiz und NS-Verbrechen*, Vol. 3, 352.
199. Rüter und Rüter, eds., *Justiz und NS-Verbrechen*, Vol. 3, 365.
200. Rüter und Rüter, eds., *Justiz und NS-Verbrechen*, Vol. 3, 353.
201. Rüter und Rüter, eds., *Justiz und NS-Verbrechen*, Vol. 3, 353.
202. Rüter und Rüter, eds., *Justiz und NS-Verbrechen*, Vol. 3, 354–355.
203. This most probably refers to the He 162 Salamander jet fighter that was built with a wood and steel construction. John Killen. *The Luftwaffe: A History* (Barnsley: Pen & Sword Military Classics, 2003): 271.
204. Rüter und Rüter, eds., *Justiz und NS-Verbrechen*, Vol. 3, 354.
205. Rüter und Rüter, eds., *Justiz und NS-Verbrechen*, Vol. 3, 354.
206. Rüter und Rüter, eds., *Justiz und NS-Verbrechen*, Vol. 3, 355.
207. Rüter und Rüter, eds., *Justiz und NS-Verbrechen*, Vol. 3, 355–356.
208. Rüter und Rüter, eds., *Justiz und NS-Verbrechen*, Vol. 3, 356.

209. Rüter und Rüter, eds., *Justiz und NS-Verbrechen*, Vol. 3, 358.
210. Rüter und Rüter, eds., *Justiz und NS-Verbrechen*, Vol. 3, 359.
211. Rüter und Rüter, eds., *Justiz und NS-Verbrechen*, Vol. 3, 359–360.
212. Rüter und Rüter, eds., *Justiz und NS-Verbrechen*, Vol. 3, 360–361.
213. Rüter und Rüter, eds., *Justiz und NS-Verbrechen*, Vol. 3, 360–361.
214. Rüter und Rüter, eds., *Justiz und NS-Verbrechen*, Vol. 3, 360–361.
215. Rüter und Rüter, eds., *Justiz und NS-Verbrechen*, Vol. 3, 360–361.
216. Rüter und Rüter, eds., *Justiz und NS-Verbrechen*, Vol. 3, 363–364.
217. Rüter und Rüter, eds., *Justiz und NS-Verbrechen*, Vol. 4, 81.
218. Rüter und Rüter, eds., *Justiz und NS-Verbrechen*, Vol. 4, 82.
219. Rüter und Rüter, eds., *Justiz und NS-Verbrechen*, Vol. 4, 82–83.
220. Rüter und Rüter, eds., *Justiz und NS-Verbrechen*, Vol. 4, 83.
221. Rüter und Rüter, eds., *Justiz und NS-Verbrechen*, Vol. 4, 83.
222. Rüter und Rüter, eds., *Justiz und NS-Verbrechen*, Vol. 4, 83.
223. Rüter und Rüter, eds., *Justiz und NS-Verbrechen*, Vol. 4, 83–84.
224. Rüter und Rüter, eds., *Justiz und NS-Verbrechen*, Vol. 4, 84.
225. Rüter und Rüter, eds., *Justiz und NS-Verbrechen*, Vol. 4, 84–85.
226. Rüter und Rüter, eds., *Justiz und NS-Verbrechen*, Vol. 4, 85–86.
227. Rüter und Rüter, eds., *Justiz und NS-Verbrechen*, Vol. 4, 86–87.
228. Rüter und Rüter, eds., *Justiz und NS-Verbrechen*, Vol. 4, 87–88.
229. Rüter und Rüter, eds., *Justiz und NS-Verbrechen*, Vol. 4, 88.
230. Rüter und Rüter, eds., *Justiz und NS-Verbrechen*, Vol. 4, 88–89.
231. Rüter und Rüter, eds., *Justiz und NS-Verbrechen*, Vol. 4, 89.
232. Rüter und Rüter, eds., *Justiz und NS-Verbrechen*, Vol. 4, 89.
233. Rüter und Rüter, eds., *Justiz und NS-Verbrechen*, Vol. 4, 89–90.
234. Rüter und Rüter, eds., *Justiz und NS-Verbrechen*, Vol. 4, 91.
235. Rüter und Rüter, eds., *Justiz und NS-Verbrechen*, Vol. 4, 91–92.
236. Rüter und Rüter, eds., *Justiz und NS-Verbrechen*, Vol. 4, 97–98.
237. Rüter und Rüter, eds., *Justiz und NS-Verbrechen*, Vol. 4, 99, 103 fn. 3.
238. Rüter und Rüter, eds., *Justiz und NS-Verbrechen*, Vol. 4, 104–105.
239. Rüter und Rüter, eds., *Justiz und NS-Verbrechen*, Vol. 4, 105.
240. Rüter und Rüter, eds., *Justiz und NS-Verbrechen*, Vol. 4, 97.
241. Rüter und Rüter, eds., *Justiz und NS-Verbrechen*, Vol. 4, 98.
242. Rüter und Rüter, eds., *Justiz und NS-Verbrechen*, Vol. 4, 98.
243. Rüter und Rüter, eds., *Justiz und NS-Verbrechen*, Vol. 4, 98–99.
244. Rüter und Rüter, eds., *Justiz und NS-Verbrechen*, Vol. 4, 99–101.
245. Rüter und Rüter, eds., *Justiz und NS-Verbrechen*, Vol. 4, 101–102.
246. Rüter und Rüter, eds., *Justiz und NS-Verbrechen*, Vol. 4, 102.
247. Rüter und Rüter, eds., *Justiz und NS-Verbrechen*, Vol. 4, 102–103.
248. Rüter und Rüter, eds., *Justiz und NS-Verbrechen*, Vol. 4, 431.
249. Rüter und Rüter, eds., *Justiz und NS-Verbrechen*, Vol. 4, 431–432.
250. Rüter und Rüter, eds., *Justiz und NS-Verbrechen*, Vol. 4, 432.
251. Rüter und Rüter, eds., *Justiz und NS-Verbrechen*, Vol. 4, 432–434.
252. Rüter und Rüter, eds., *Justiz und NS-Verbrechen*, Vol. 4, 434–435.

253. Rüter und Rüter, eds., *Justiz und NS-Verbrechen*, Vol. 4, 435.
254. Rüter und Rüter, eds., *Justiz und NS-Verbrechen*, Vol. 4, 435–437.
255. Rüter und Rüter, eds., *Justiz und NS-Verbrechen*, Vol. 4, 437.
256. Rüter und Rüter, eds., *Justiz und NS-Verbrechen*, Vol. 4, 438.
257. Rüter and Rüter, eds., *Justiz und NS-Verbrechen*, Vol. 4, 438–439.
258. Rüter und Rüter, eds., *Justiz und NS-Verbrechen*, Vol. 4, 439–440.
259. Rüter und Rüter, eds., *Justiz und NS-Verbrechen*, Vol. 4, 440–441.
260. Rüter und Rüter, eds., *Justiz und NS-Verbrechen*, Vol. 4, 441.
261. Rüter und Rüter, eds., *Justiz und NS-Verbrechen*, Vol. 4, 441–442.
262. Rüter und Rüter, eds., *Justiz und NS-Verbrechen*, Vol. 4, 442.
263. Rüter und Rüter, eds., *Justiz und NS-Verbrechen*, Vol. 4, 442–443.
264. Rüter und Rüter, eds., *Justiz und NS-Verbrechen*, Vol. 4, 444.
265. Rüter und Rüter, eds., *Justiz und NS-Verbrechen*, Vol. 4, 444–445.
266. Rüter und Rüter, eds., *Justiz und NS-Verbrechen*, Vol. 4, 445.
267. Rüter und Rüter, eds., *Justiz und NS-Verbrechen*, Vol. 4, 445.
268. Rüter und Rüter, eds., *Justiz und NS-Verbrechen*, Vol. 4, 446–447.
269. Rüter und Rüter, eds., *Justiz und NS-Verbrechen*, Vol. 4, 721.
270. Rüter und Rüter, eds., *Justiz und NS-Verbrechen*, Vol. 4, 717.
271. Rüter und Rüter, eds., *Justiz und NS-Verbrechen*, Vol. 4, 752–753.
272. Rüter und Rüter, eds., *Justiz und NS-Verbrechen*, Vol. 4, 713, 722.
273. Rüter und Rüter, eds., *Justiz und NS-Verbrechen*, Vol. 4, 714.
274. Rüter und Rüter, eds., *Justiz und NS-Verbrechen*, Vol. 4, 760.
275. Rüter und Rüter, eds., *Justiz und NS-Verbrechen*, Vol. 4, 761.
276. Rüter und Rüter, eds., *Justiz und NS-Verbrechen*, Vol. 4, 753–754.
277. Rüter und Rüter, eds., *Justiz und NS-Verbrechen*, Vol. 4, 754–755.
278. Rüter und Rüter, eds., *Justiz und NS-Verbrechen*, Vol. 4, 755, 751–752.
279. Rüter und Rüter, eds., *Justiz und NS-Verbrechen*, Vol. 4, 755–756.
280. Rüter und Rüter, eds., *Justiz und NS-Verbrechen*, Vol. 4, 734–735.
281. Rüter und Rüter, eds., *Justiz und NS-Verbrechen*, Vol. 4, 764.
282. Rüter und Rüter, eds., *Justiz und NS-Verbrechen*, Vol. 4, 747.
283. Rüter und Rüter, eds., *Justiz und NS-Verbrechen*, Vol. 4, 747.
284. Rüter und Rüter, eds., *Justiz und NS-Verbrechen*, Vol. 4, 756.
285. Rüter und Rüter, eds., *Justiz und NS-Verbrechen*, Vol. 4, 756–757.
286. Rüter und Rüter, eds., *Justiz und NS-Verbrechen*, Vol. 4, 757.
287. Rüter und Rüter, eds., *Justiz und NS-Verbrechen*, Vol. 4, 747–748.
288. Rüter und Rüter, eds., *Justiz und NS-Verbrechen*, Vol. 4, 757.
289. Rüter und Rüter, eds., *Justiz und NS-Verbrechen*, Vol. 4, 757–758.
290. Rüter und Rüter, eds., *Justiz und NS-Verbrechen*, Vol. 4, 758.
291. Rüter und Rüter, eds., *Justiz und NS-Verbrechen*, Vol. 4, 715.
292. Rüter und Rüter, eds., *Justiz und NS-Verbrechen*, Vol. 4, 758–759.
293. Rüter und Rüter, eds., *Justiz und NS-Verbrechen*, Vol. 4, 759.
294. Rüter und Rüter, eds., *Justiz und NS-Verbrechen*, Vol. 4, 759.
295. Rüter und Rüter, eds., *Justiz und NS-Verbrechen*, Vol. 4, 760.
296. Rüter und Rüter, eds., *Justiz und NS-Verbrechen*, Vol. 4, 764.

297. Rüter und Rüter, eds., *Justiz und NS-Verbrechen*, Vol. 4, 764–765.
298. Rüter und Rüter, eds., *Justiz und NS-Verbrechen*, Vol. 4, 765.
299. Rüter und Rüter, eds., *Justiz und NS-Verbrechen*, Vol. 4, 717, 762.
300. Rüter und Rüter, eds., *Justiz und NS-Verbrechen*, Vol. 4, 762.
301. Rüter und Rüter, eds., *Justiz und NS-Verbrechen*, Vol. 4, 762–763.
302. Rüter und Rüter, eds., *Justiz und NS-Verbrechen*, Vol. 4, 763.
303. Rüter und Rüter, eds., *Justiz und NS-Verbrechen*, Vol. 4, 763–764.
304. Rüter und Rüter, eds., *Justiz und NS-Verbrechen*, Vol. 4, 770.
305. Rüter und Rüter, eds., *Justiz und NS-Verbrechen*, Vol. 4, 765–766.
306. Rüter und Rüter, eds., *Justiz und NS-Verbrechen*, Vol. 4, 766.
307. Rüter und Rüter, eds., *Justiz und NS-Verbrechen*, Vol. 4, 767.
308. Rüter und Rüter, eds., *Justiz und NS-Verbrechen*, Vol. 4, 767, 749.
309. Rüter und Rüter, eds., *Justiz und NS-Verbrechen*, Vol. 4, 767–768.
310. Rüter und Rüter, eds., *Justiz und NS-Verbrechen*, Vol. 4, 780–782.
311. Rüter und Rüter, eds., *Justiz und NS-Verbrechen*, Vol. 4, 782.
312. "OLG Hamm, 2. Strafsenat, Urteil vom 5. 8. 1948, 2. SS 370/48," *Monatsschrift für Deutsches Recht* 1949: 184-185.
313. Rüter und Rüter, eds., *Justiz und NS-Verbrechen*, Vol. 4, 783.
314. Rüter und Rüter, eds., *Justiz und NS-Verbrechen*, Vol. 4, 783–784.
315. Rüter und Rüter, eds., *Justiz und NS-Verbrechen*, Vol. 4, 782–783, 785.
316. Rüter und Rüter, eds., *Justiz und NS-Verbrechen*, Vol. 4, 792, 805.
317. Rüter und Rüter, eds., *Justiz und NS-Verbrechen*, Vol. 4, 793.
318. Rüter und Rüter, eds., *Justiz und NS-Verbrechen*, Vol. 4, 792.
319. Rüter und Rüter, eds., *Justiz und NS-Verbrechen*, Vol. 4, 786–787.
320. Rüter und Rüter, eds., *Justiz und NS-Verbrechen*, Vol. 4, 787.
321. Rüter und Rüter, eds., *Justiz und NS-Verbrechen*, Vol. 4, 792.
322. Rüter und Rüter, eds., *Justiz und NS-Verbrechen*, Vol. 4, 793.
323. Rüter und Rüter, eds., *Justiz und NS-Verbrechen*, Vol. 4, 785, 761.
324. Rüter und Rüter, eds., *Justiz und NS-Verbrechen*, Vol. 4, 792.
325. Rüter und Rüter, eds., *Justiz und NS-Verbrechen*, Vol. 4, 785, 761.
326. Rüter und Rüter, eds., *Justiz und NS-Verbrechen*, Vol. 4, 792.
327. Rüter und Rüter, eds., *Justiz und NS-Verbrechen*, Vol. 4, 787–788.
328. Rüter und Rüter, eds., *Justiz und NS-Verbrechen*, Vol. 4, 789–790.
329. Rüter und Rüter, eds., *Justiz und NS-Verbrechen*, Vol. 4, 788.
330. Rüter und Rüter, eds., *Justiz und NS-Verbrechen*, Vol. 4, 788–789.
331. Rüter und Rüter, eds., *Justiz und NS-Verbrechen*, Vol. 4, 789.
332. Rüter und Rüter, eds., *Justiz und NS-Verbrechen*, Vol. 4, 768.
333. Rüter und Rüter, eds., *Justiz und NS-Verbrechen*, Vol. 4, 794.
334. Rüter und Rüter, eds., *Justiz und NS-Verbrechen*, Vol. 4. 802–804.
335. Rüter und Rüter, eds., *Justiz und NS-Verbrechen*, Vol. 4, 798–800.
336. Rüter und Rüter, eds., *Justiz und NS-Verbrechen*, Vol. 4, 800–802.
337. Rüter und Rüter, eds., *Justiz und NS-Verbrechen*, Vol. 4, 805–806.
338. Rüter und Rüter, eds., *Justiz und NS-Verbrechen*, Vol. 5, 47.
339. Rüter und Rüter, eds., *Justiz und NS-Verbrechen*, Vol. 5, 47–48.

340. Rüter und Rüter, eds., *Justiz und NS-Verbrechen*, Vol. 5, 48.
341. Rüter und Rüter, eds., *Justiz und NS-Verbrechen*, Vol. 5, 48–49, 51.
342. Rüter und Rüter, eds., *Justiz und NS-Verbrechen*, Vol. 5, 49.
343. Rüter und Rüter, eds., *Justiz und NS-Verbrechen*, Vol. 5, 49–50.
344. Rüter und Rüter, eds., *Justiz und NS-Verbrechen*, Vol. 5, 50.
345. Rüter und Rüter, eds., *Justiz und NS-Verbrechen*, Vol. 5, 51.
346. Rüter und Rüter, eds., *Justiz und NS-Verbrechen*, Vol. 5, 51–52.
347. Rüter und Rüter, eds., *Justiz und NS-Verbrechen*, Vol. 5, 52.
348. Rüter und Rüter, eds., *Justiz und NS-Verbrechen*, Vol. 5, 53.
349. Rüter und Rüter, eds., *Justiz und NS-Verbrechen*, Vol. 5, 303–304.
350. Rüter und Rüter, eds., *Justiz und NS-Verbrechen*, Vol. 5, 304.
351. Rüter und Rüter, eds., *Justiz und NS-Verbrechen*, Vol. 5, 304–305.
352. Rüter und Rüter, eds., *Justiz und NS-Verbrechen*, Vol. 5, 305.
353. Rüter und Rüter, eds., *Justiz und NS-Verbrechen*, Vol. 5, 304.
354. Rüter und Rüter, eds., *Justiz und NS-Verbrechen*, Vol. 5, 305–306.
355. Rüter und Rüter, eds., *Justiz und NS-Verbrechen*, Vol. 5, 306.
356. Rüter und Rüter, eds., *Justiz und NS-Verbrechen*, Vol. 5, 306–307.
357. Rüter und Rüter, eds., *Justiz und NS-Verbrechen*, Vol. 5, 307.
358. Rüter und Rüter, eds., *Justiz und NS-Verbrechen*, Vol. 5, 307.
359. Rüter und Rüter, eds., *Justiz und NS-Verbrechen*, Vol. 5, 307.
360. Rüter und Rüter, eds., *Justiz und NS-Verbrechen*, Vol. 5, 308.
361. Rüter und Rüter, eds., *Justiz und NS-Verbrechen*, Vol. 5, 308–309.
362. Rüter und Rüter, eds., *Justiz und NS-Verbrechen*, Vol. 5, 309.
363. Rüter und Rüter, eds., *Justiz und NS-Verbrechen*, Vol. 5, 309.
364. Rüter und Rüter, eds., *Justiz und NS-Verbrechen*, Vol. 5, 309–310.
365. Rüter und Rüter, eds., *Justiz und NS-Verbrechen*, Vol. 5, 310.
366. Rüter und Rüter, eds., *Justiz und NS-Verbrechen*, Vol. 5, 310–311.
367. Rüter und Rüter, eds., *Justiz und NS-Verbrechen*, Vol. 5, 311–312.
368. Rüter und Rüter, eds., *Justiz und NS-Verbrechen*, Vol. 5, 312.
369. Rüter und Rüter, eds., *Justiz und NS-Verbrechen*, Vol. 5, 312–313.
370. Rüter und Rüter, eds., *Justiz und NS-Verbrechen*, Vol. 5, 313.
371. Rüter und Rüter, eds., *Justiz und NS-Verbrechen*, Vol. 5, 313–314.
372. Rüter und Rüter, eds., *Justiz und NS-Verbrechen*, Vol. 5, 314–315.
373. Rüter und Rüter, eds., *Justiz und NS-Verbrechen*, Vol. 5, 315.
374. Rüter und Rüter, eds., *Justiz und NS-Verbrechen*, Vol. 5, 315–316.
375. Rüter und Rüter, eds., *Justiz und NS-Verbrechen*, Vol. 5, 317–318.
376. Rüter und Rüter, eds., *Justiz und NS-Verbrechen*, Vol. 5, 318.
377. Rüter und Rüter, eds., *Justiz und NS-Verbrechen*, Vol. 5, 318.
378. Diewald-Kerkmann, *Politische Denunziation im NS-Regime*, 161.
379. Diewald-Kerkmann, *Politische Denunziation im NS-Regime*, 168.
380. Bundesarchiv. Koblenz. Z21/1359. Anlage "A" zum Schreiben Legal/MOJ/52308/4. 2. März 1949. Bericht des German Courts Inspectorate über die Inspektionsreise nach Düsseldorf und Wuppertal vom 17. bis 22. Feb.

CHAPTER 5

1. "Law No. 13: Judicial Powers in the Reserved Fields," *Official Gazette of the Allied High Commission for Germany* No. 6, 9 December 1949: 54–58; Elmer Plischke, *The West German Federal Government* (Bad Godesberg-Mehlem: Historical Division, Office of the High Commission for Germany, 1952): 127; Elmer Plischke, *The Allied High Commission for Germany*. Bad Godesberg-Mehlem: Historical Division, Office of the US High Commissioner for Germany, 1953: 72.

2. Jakobczyk, "Das Verfahren ist einzustellen," 251.

3. Claudia Bade, "Die Strafrechtliche Verfolgung von Denunziation aus dem Nationalsozialismus nach 1945 in den Westzonen und in der frühen BRD." Historical Social Research, Vol. 26 2001 No.2/3: "'Das Verfahren wird eingestellt'," 74

4. "Arrêté No 171: Abrogeant Certaines Dispositions de l'Arrêté No 154 en Date du 1er Juin 1950". *Official Gazette of the Allied High Commission for Germany* No. 65, 19 September 1951: 1137.

5. Archives de L'Occupation Française en Allemagne et en Autriche. Colmar. AJ 3655/p.326/12053. Haute Commission de la Republique en Allemagne. Le Conseiller pour les Affaires Judiciaires. Chef des Service de la Justice. Baden-Baden. 1 Octobre 1951. Object: Retrait, aux Tribunaux Allemands, de l'obligation d'applique la Loi No. 10 du Conseil de Contrôle dans les jugements de crimes contre l'humanité.

6. Freudiger, *Die juristische Aufarbeitung von NS-Verfahren*, 317.

7. "Ordinance No. 234: Repeal of Military Government Ordinance No. 47". *Official Gazette of the Allied High Commission for Germany* No. 65, 19 September 1951: 1138.

8. Bernhard Diestelkamp and Susanne Jung, "Die Justiz in den Westzonen und der frühen Bundesrepublik," *Aus Politik und Zeitgeschichte* 13 (24 March 1989): 25.

9. Claus Seibert, "Abschied vom KRG 10", *Neue Juristische Wochenschrift* 1952: 251–252.

10. Jakobczyk, "Das Verfahren ist einzustellen," 277, 281.

11. Diewald-Kerkmann, *Politische Denunziation im NS-Regime*, 164.

12. Jakobczyk, "Das Verfahren ist einzustellen," 277, 281.

13. Diewald-Kerkmann, *Politische Denunziation im NS-Regime*, 162.

14. Bundesarchiv. Koblenz. Z21/268. Legal/MOJ/52316. Zonal Office of the Legal Adviser. 21 October 1948. Subject: Renazification of the German judiciary and Legal Civil Service.

15. Archives de L'Occupation Française en Allemagne et en Autriche. Colmar. 3680/25/4. Gouvernement Militaire de la Zône Française d'Occupation. Délégation supérieure pour le Gouvernement Militaire de Hesse-Palatinat. Contrôle de la Justice Allemande. Rapport Mensuel sur la période du 1e Novembre 1949 au 30 Novembre 1949. Activité du service de la Justice Allemande.

16. Diewald-Kerkmann, *Politische Denunziation im NS-Regime*, 164; Martin Broszat, "Siegerjustiz oder strafrechtlicher 'selbtsreinigung'?,"518.

17. Jakobczyk, "Das Verfahren is einzustellen," 276–277.

18. Bade, "'Das Verfahren wird eingestellt'," 74.

19. Bade, "'Das Verfahren wird eingestellt'," 75
20. Diewald-Kerkmann, *Politische Denunziation im NS-Regime*, 164.
21. Bundesarchiv. Koblenz. Z38/132. Sts 88/49. Beglaubigte Abschrift. Verkündet am 5. Dezember 1949: 1–2.
22. Bundesarchiv. Koblenz. Z38/132. Sts 88/49. Beglaubigte Abschrift. Verkündet am 5. Dezember 1949: 2–4.
23. Bundesarchiv. Koblenz. Z38/132. Sts 88/49. Beglaubigte Abschrift. Verkündet am 5. Dezember 1949: 8–13.
24. Bundesarchiv. Koblenz. Z38/132. Sts 88/49. Beglaubigte Abschrift. Verkündet am 5. Dezember 1949: 13–16.
25. Adelheid L. Rüter und C.F. Rüter, eds., *Justiz und NS-Verbrechen: Sammlung deutscher Strafurteile wegen nationalsozialistischer Tötungsverbrechen 1945–1966*, Vol. 9 (Amsterdam: University Press Amsterdam, 1972): 169.
26. Bade, "'Das Verfahren wird eingestellt'," 74–75.
27. Diewald-Kerkmann, *Politische Denunziation im NS-Regime*, 166.
28. Diewald-Kerkmann, *Politische Denunziation im NS-Regime*, 241 fn. 136.
29. Diewald-Kerkmann, *Politische Denunziation im NS-Regime*, 167–168.
30. Diewald-Kerkmann, *Politische Denunziation im NS-Regime*, 168–169.
31. Article 1, Article 2(1), "Gesetz über die Gewährung von Straffreiheit. Vom 31. Dezember 1949," *Bundesgesetzblatt* 1949/1950 No. 9 (1949): 37.
32. Bundesarchiv. Koblenz. B136/3189. Rechtsanwalt Dr. jur. R. G. Zugelassen beim Landgericht München I und II. 28/10/50.
33. Bundesarchiv. Koblenz. B136/553. Begründung eines Gesetzes über die Gewährung von Straffreiheit. n/d.
34. Norbert Frei, *Adenauer's Germany and the Nazi Past: The Politics of Amnesty and Integration* trans. Joel Golb. (New York: Columbia University Press, 2002): 19.
35. Frei, *Adenauer's Germany and the Nazi Past*, 67.
36. Inge, Mar□olek. Die Denunziantin: Die Geschichte der Helene Schwärzel, 1944–1947 (Bremen: Edition Temmen, 1993): 102.
37. Diewald-Kerkmann, Politische Denunziation im NS-Regime, 169.
38. Richard Lange, "Kontrollratsgesezt Nr. 10 und deutsches Recht: Das Kontrollratsgesetz in Theorie und Praxis II", *Deutsche Rechts-Zeitschrift* 1948 3 (6): 188.
39. Diewald-Kerkmann, *Politische Denunziation im NS-Regime*, 171.
40. Diewald-Kerkmann, *Politische Denunziation im NS-Regime*, 171.
41. Diewald-Kerkmann, *Politische Denunziation im NS-Regime*, 172.
42. Jakobczyk, "Das Verfahren ist einzustellen," 258, 260, 277.
43. Jakobczyk, "Das Verfahren ist einzustellen," 264, 265.
44. Jakobczyk, "Das Verfahren ist einzustellen," 279
45. Jakobczyk, "Das Verfahren ist einzustellen," 278.
46. Jakobczyk, "Das Verfahren ist einzustellen," 264.
47. Jakobczyk, "Das Verfahren ist einzustellen," 270–272, 278.
48. Jakobczyk, "Das Verfahren ist einzustellen," 283.
49. Jakobczyk, "Das Verfahren ist einzustellen," 264.
50. Claudia Bade, "Das Verfahren wird eingestellt," 80.

51. Jakobczyk, "Das Verfahren ist einzustellen," *Demokratische Geschichte* 15 (2003): 273, 278, 279.

52. Bade, "Das Verfahren wird eingestellt," 76.

53. Bade, "Das Verfahren wird eingestellt." 78–79.

54. Diewald-Kerkmann, *Politische Denunziation im NS-Regime*, 166.

55. Diewald-Kerkmann, *Politische Denunziation im NS-Regime*, 159–160.

56. Adelheid L. Rüter und C.F. Rüter, eds., *Justiz und NS-Verbrechen: Sammlung deutscher Strafurteile wegen nationalsozialistischer Tötungsverbrechen 1945–1966*, Vol. 7 (Amsterdam: University Press Amsterdam, 1971): 293.

57. Rüter und Rüter, eds., *Justiz und NS-Verbrechen*, Vol. 7, 301.

58. Rüter und Rüter, eds., *Justiz und NS-Verbrechen*, Vol. 7, 295.

59. Rüter und Rüter, eds., *Justiz und NS-Verbrechen*, Vol. 7, 298.

60. Rüter und Rüter, eds., *Justiz und NS-Verbrechen*, Vol. 7, 304.

61. Rüter und Rüter, eds., *Justiz und NS-Verbrechen*, Vol. 7, 304–305.

62. Rüter und Rüter, eds., *Justiz und NS-Verbrechen*, Vol. 7, 305.

63. Rüter und Rüter, eds., *Justiz und NS-Verbrechen*, Vol. 7, 306.

64. Rüter und Rüter, eds., *Justiz und NS-Verbrechen*, Vol. 7, 306–307.

65. Rüter und Rüter, eds., *Justiz und NS-Verbrechen*, Vol. 7, 307.

66. Rüter und Rüter, eds., *Justiz und NS-Verbrechen*, Vol. 7, 307.

67. Rüter und Rüter, eds., *Justiz und NS-Verbrechen*, Vol. 7, 307–308.

68. Rüter und Rüter, eds., *Justiz und NS-Verbrechen*, Vol. 7, 308.

69. Rüter und Rüter, eds., *Justiz und NS-Verbrechen*, Vol. 7, 308–309.

70. Rüter und Rüter, eds., *Justiz und NS-Verbrechen*, Vol. 7, 309.

71. Rüter und Rüter, eds., *Justiz und NS-Verbrechen*, Vol. 7, 310.

72. Rüter und Rüter, eds., *Justiz und NS-Verbrechen*, Vol. 7, 310–311.

73. Rüter und Rüter, eds., *Justiz und NS-Verbrechen*, Vol. 7, 311–312.

74. Rüter und Rüter, eds., *Justiz und NS-Verbrechen*, Vol. 7, 312.

75. Rüter und Rüter, eds., *Justiz und NS-Verbrechen*, Vol. 7, 312–313.

76. Rüter und Rüter, eds., *Justiz und NS-Verbrechen*, Vol. 7, 313–314.

77. Rüter und Rüter, eds., *Justiz und NS-Verbrechen*, Vol. 7, 318–321.

78. Rüter und Rüter, eds., *Justiz und NS-Verbrechen*, Vol. 7, 321.

79. Rüter und Rüter, eds., *Justiz und NS-Verbrechen*, Vol. 7, 323.

80. Rüter und Rüter, eds., *Justiz und NS-Verbrechen*, Vol. 7, 323–324.

81. Rüter und Rüter, eds., *Justiz und NS-Verbrechen*, Vol. 7, 324–326.

82. Rüter und Rüter, eds., *Justiz und NS-Verbrechen*, Vol. 7, 332–334.

83. Rüter und Rüter, eds., *Justiz und NS-Verbrechen*, Vol. 7, 342–343.

84. Rüter und Rüter, eds., *Justiz und NS-Verbrechen*, Vol. 7, 343–346.

85. Rüter und Rüter, eds., *Justiz und NS-Verbrechen*, Vol. 7, 347.

86. Rüter und Rüter, eds., *Justiz und NS-Verbrechen*, Vol. 7, 344–345.

87. Rüter und Rüter, eds., *Justiz und NS-Verbrechen*, Vol. 7, 353–354.

88. Rüter und Rüter, eds., *Justiz und NS-Verbrechen*, Vol. 7, 314.

89. Rüter und Rüter, eds., *Justiz und NS-Verbrechen*, Vol. 7, 315.

90. Rüter und Rüter, eds., *Justiz und NS-Verbrechen*, Vol. 7, 315.

91. Rüter und Rüter, eds., *Justiz und NS-Verbrechen*, Vol. 7, 315–316.

92. Rüter und Rüter, eds., *Justiz und NS-Verbrechen*, Vol. 7, 316.
93. Rüter und Rüter, eds., *Justiz und NS-Verbrechen*, Vol. 7, 316–317.
94. Rüter und Rüter, eds., *Justiz und NS-Verbrechen*, Vol. 7, 334–335.
95. Rüter und Rüter, eds., *Justiz und NS-Verbrechen*, Vol. 7, 339–340.
96. Rüter und Rüter, eds., *Justiz und NS-Verbrechen*, Vol. 7, 357–359.
97. Rüter und Rüter, eds., *Justiz und NS-Verbrechen*, Vol. 7, 362–364.
98. Adelheid L. Rüter and C.F. Rüter, eds., *Justiz und NS-Verbrechen: Sammlung deutscher Strafurteile wegen nationalsozialistischer Tötungsverbrechen 1945-1966*, Vol. 10 (Amsterdam: University Press Amsterdam, 1973): 738-740.
99. Rüter und Rüter, eds., *Justiz und NS-Verbrechen*, Vol. 10, 740–741.
100. Rüter und Rüter, eds., *Justiz und NS-Verbrechen*, Vol. 10, 741–742.
101. Rüter und Rüter, eds., *Justiz und NS-Verbrechen*, Vol. 10, 715.
102. Rüter und Rüter, eds., *Justiz und NS-Verbrechen*, Vol. 10, 723–724.
103. Rüter und Rüter, eds., *Justiz und NS-Verbrechen*, Vol. 10, 724.
104. Rüter und Rüter, eds., *Justiz und NS-Verbrechen*, Vol. 10, 724–725, 727.
105. Rüter und Rüter, eds., *Justiz und NS-Verbrechen*, Vol. 10, 727–729.
106. Rüter und Rüter, eds., *Justiz und NS-Verbrechen*, Vol. 10, 730–732.
107. Rüter und Rüter, eds., *Justiz und NS-Verbrechen*, Vol. 10, 732.
108. Rüter und Rüter, eds., *Justiz und NS-Verbrechen*, Vol. 10, 734–735.
109. Rüter und Rüter, eds., *Justiz und NS-Verbrechen*, Vol. 10, 735–736.
110. Rüter und Rüter, eds., *Justiz und NS-Verbrechen*, Vol. 10, 736.
111. Adelheid L. Rüter and C.F. Rüter, eds., *Justiz und NS-Verbrechen: Sammlung deutscher Strafurteile wegen nationalsozialistischer Tötungsverbrechen 1945–1966*, Vol. 12 (Amsterdam: University Press Amsterdam, 1974): 63.
112. Freudiger, *Die juristische Aufarbeitung von NS-Verfahren*, 318.
113. Rüter und Rüter, eds., *Justiz und NS-Verbrechen*, Vol. 12, 63–64.
114. Rüter und Rüter, eds., *Justiz und NS-Verbrechen*, Vol. 12, 64.
115. Rüter und Rüter, eds., *Justiz und NS-Verbrechen*, Vol. 12, 64.
116. Rüter und Rüter, eds., *Justiz und NS-Verbrechen*, Vol. 12, 64–65.
117. Rüter und Rüter, eds., *Justiz und NS-Verbrechen*, Vol. 12, 64–66.
118. Rüter und Rüter, eds., *Justiz und NS-Verbrechen*, Vol. 12, 65–66.
119. Rüter und Rüter, eds., *Justiz und NS-Verbrechen*, Vol. 12, 66–67.
120. Rüter und Rüter, eds., *Justiz und NS-Verbrechen*, Vol. 12, 66–67, 76.
121. Rüter und Rüter, eds., *Justiz und NS-Verbrechen*, Vol. 12, 77–78.
122. Rüter und Rüter, eds., *Justiz und NS-Verbrechen*, Vol. 12, 66.
123. Rüter und Rüter, eds., *Justiz und NS-Verbrechen*, Vol. 12, 70.
124. *Entscheidungen des Bundesgerichtshofes in Strafsachen*, Vol. 3 (Berlin/Köln: Carl Heymanns Verlag, 1953): 110–111.
125. Rüter und Rüter, eds., *Justiz und NS-Verbrechen*, Vol. 12, 81–82.
126. Rüter und Rüter, eds., *Justiz und NS-Verbrechen*, Vol. 12, 83–85.
127. Rüter und Rüter, eds., *Justiz und NS-Verbrechen*, Vol. 12, 85–88.
128. Rüter und Rüter, eds., *Justiz und NS-Verbrechen*, Vol. 12, 67.
129. Rüter und Rüter, eds., *Justiz und NS-Verbrechen*, Vol. 12, 69, 71.
130. Rüter und Rüter, eds., *Justiz und NS-Verbrechen*, Vol. 12, 71–72.

131. Rüter und Rüter, eds., *Justiz und NS-Verbrechen*, Vol. 12, 74–75.
132. "StGB §§ 211 ff., 239," *Neue Juristische Wochenschrift* 1952: 1024–1026.
133. Diewald-Kerkmann, *Politische Denunziation im NS-Regime*, 165.
134. Adelheid L. Rüter and C.F. Rüter, eds., *Justiz und NS-Verbrechen: Sammlung deutscher Strafurteile wegen nationalsozialistischer Tötungsverbrechen 1945–1966*, Vol. 11 (Amsterdam: University Press Amsterdam, 1974): 382, 392–393; "BGH, Urt. V. 6.11.1952 – 3 StR 59/50 (Schwg Duisburg)," *Neue Juristische Wochenschrift* 1953: 793.
135. Rüter und Rüter, eds., *Justiz und NS-Verbrechen*, Vol. 11, 392–393.
136. Rüter und Rüter, eds., *Justiz und NS-Verbrechen*, Vol. 11, 392.
137. Rüter und Rüter, eds., *Justiz und NS-Verbrechen*, Vol. 11, 394.
138. Rüter und Rüter, eds., *Justiz und NS-Verbrechen*, Vol. 11, 394.
139. Rüter und Rüter, eds., *Justiz und NS-Verbrechen*, Vol. 11, 394–395.
140. Rüter und Rüter, eds., *Justiz und NS-Verbrechen*, Vol. 11, 381.
141. Rüter und Rüter, eds., *Justiz und NS-Verbrechen*, Vol. 11, 385.
142. Rüter und Rüter, eds., *Justiz und NS-Verbrechen*, Vol. 11, 385.
143. Rüter und Rüter, eds., *Justiz und NS-Verbrechen*, Vol. 11, 387–388.
144. Rüter und Rüter, eds., *Justiz und NS-Verbrechen*, Vol. 11, 388.
145. Rüter und Rüter, eds., *Justiz und NS-Verbrechen*, Vol. 11, 385–387.
146. Rüter und Rüter, eds., *Justiz und NS-Verbrechen*, Vol. 11, 387.
147. Rüter und Rüter, eds., *Justiz und NS-Verbrechen*, Vol. 11, 388–389.
148. Rüter und Rüter, eds., *Justiz und NS-Verbrechen*, Vol. 11, 389–390.
149. Rüter und Rüter, eds., *Justiz und NS-Verbrechen*, Vol. 11, 390–391.
150. Adelheid L. Rüter and C.F. Rüter, eds., *Justiz und NS-Verbrechen: Sammlung deutscher Strafurteile wegen nationalsozialistischer Tötungsverbrechen 1945–1966*, Vol. 6 (Amsterdam: University Press Amsterdam, 1971): 605–606.
151. Rüter und Rüter, eds., *Justiz und NS-Verbrechen*, Vol. 6, 606.
152. Rüter und Rüter, eds., *Justiz und NS-Verbrechen*, Vol. 6, 607.
153. Rüter und Rüter, eds., *Justiz und NS-Verbrechen*, Vol. 6, 607–608.
154. Rüter und Rüter, eds., *Justiz und NS-Verbrechen*, Vol. 6, 608.
155. Rüter und Rüter, eds., *Justiz und NS-Verbrechen*, Vol. 6, 608–609.
156. Rüter und Rüter, eds., *Justiz und NS-Verbrechen*, Vol. 6, 606–607.
157. Rüter und Rüter, eds., *Justiz und NS-Verbrechen*, Vol. 6, 607.
158. Rüter und Rüter, eds., *Justiz und NS-Verbrechen*, Vol. 6, 609–610.
159. Rüter und Rüter, eds., *Justiz und NS-Verbrechen*, Vol. 6, 610–611.
160. Rüter und Rüter, eds., *Justiz und NS-Verbrechen*, Vol. 11, 403.
161. Rüter und Rüter, eds., *Justiz und NS-Verbrechen*, Vol. 6, 611.
162. Rüter und Rüter, eds., *Justiz und NS-Verbrechen*, Vol. 6, 611–612.
163. Rüter und Rüter, eds., *Justiz und NS-Verbrechen*, Vol. 6, 612–613.
164. Rüter und Rüter, eds., *Justiz und NS-Verbrechen*, Vol. 11, 403–404.
165. Rüter und Rüter, eds., *Justiz und NS-Verbrechen*, Vol. 11, 404.
166. Rüter und Rüter, eds., *Justiz und NS-Verbrechen*, Vol. 11, 399.
167. Rüter und Rüter, eds., *Justiz und NS-Verbrechen*, Vol. 11, 400.
168. Rüter und Rüter, eds., *Justiz und NS-Verbrechen*, Vol. 11, 400.

169. Rüter und Rüter, eds., *Justiz und NS-Verbrechen*, Vol. 11, 401.
170. Rüter und Rüter, eds., *Justiz und NS-Verbrechen*, Vol. 11, 401–402.
171. Rüter und Rüter, eds., *Justiz und NS-Verbrechen*, Vol. 11, 402.
172. Rüter und Rüter, eds., *Justiz und NS-Verbrechen*, Vol. 6, 645.
173. Rüter und Rüter, eds., *Justiz und NS-Verbrechen*, Vol. 6, 645–646.
174. Rüter und Rüter, eds., *Justiz und NS-Verbrechen*, Vol. 6, 646.
175. Rüter und Rüter, eds., *Justiz und NS-Verbrechen*, Vol. 6, 647.
176. Rüter und Rüter, eds., *Justiz und NS-Verbrechen*, Vol. 6, 647–648.
177. Rüter und Rüter, eds., *Justiz und NS-Verbrechen*, Vol. 6, 648.
178. Rüter und Rüter, eds., *Justiz und NS-Verbrechen*, Vol. 6, 648–649.
179. Rüter und Rüter, eds., *Justiz und NS-Verbrechen*, Vol. 6, 649.
180. Rüter und Rüter, eds., *Justiz und NS-Verbrechen*, Vol. 6, 631.
181. Rüter und Rüter, eds., *Justiz und NS-Verbrechen*, Vol. 6, 632–633.
182. Rüter und Rüter, eds., *Justiz und NS-Verbrechen*, Vol. 6, 633.
183. Rüter und Rüter, eds., *Justiz und NS-Verbrechen*, Vol. 6, 633–634.
184. Rüter und Rüter, eds., *Justiz und NS-Verbrechen*, Vol. 6, 634.
185. Rüter und Rüter, eds., *Justiz und NS-Verbrechen*, Vol. 6, 634–636.
186. Rüter und Rüter, eds., *Justiz und NS-Verbrechen*, Vol. 6, 636.
187. Rüter und Rüter, eds., *Justiz und NS-Verbrechen*, Vol. 6, 637.
188. Rüter und Rüter, eds., *Justiz und NS-Verbrechen*, Vol. 6, 637.
189. Rüter und Rüter, eds., *Justiz und NS-Verbrechen*, Vol. 6, 638.
190. Rüter und Rüter, eds., *Justiz und NS-Verbrechen*, Vol. 6, 639.
191. Rüter und Rüter, eds., *Justiz und NS-Verbrechen*, Vol. 6, 639–640.
192. Rüter und Rüter, eds., *Justiz und NS-Verbrechen*, Vol. 6, 640–641.
193. Rüter und Rüter, eds., *Justiz und NS-Verbrechen*, Vol. 6, 641.
194. Rüter und Rüter, eds., *Justiz und NS-Verbrechen*, Vol. 6, 641–642.
195. Rüter und Rüter, eds., *Justiz und NS-Verbrechen*, Vol. 6, 642.
196. Rüter und Rüter, eds., *Justiz und NS-Verbrechen*, Vol. 6, 642–643.
197. Rüter und Rüter, eds., *Justiz und NS-Verbrechen*, Vol. 6, 643.
198. Rüter und Rüter, eds., *Justiz und NS-Verbrechen*, Vol. 6, 643–644.
199. Adelheid L. Rüter und C.F. Rüter, eds., *Justiz und NS-Verbrechen: Sammlung deutscher Strafurteile wegen nationalsozialistischer Tötungsverbrechen 1945–1966*, Vol. 7 (Amsterdam: University Press Amsterdam, 1971): 697–698.
200. Rüter und Rüter, eds., *Justiz und NS-Verbrechen*, Vol. 7, 698.
201. Rüter und Rüter, eds., *Justiz und NS-Verbrechen*, Vol. 7, 698–699.
202. Rüter und Rüter, eds., *Justiz und NS-Verbrechen*, Vol. 7, 699.
203. Rüter und Rüter, eds., *Justiz und NS-Verbrechen*, Vol. 7, 699.
204. Rüter und Rüter, eds., *Justiz und NS-Verbrechen*, Vol. 7, 700.
205. Rüter und Rüter, eds., *Justiz und NS-Verbrechen*, Vol. 7, 700.
206. Rüter und Rüter, eds., *Justiz und NS-Verbrechen*, Vol. 7, 700–701.
207. Rüter und Rüter, eds., *Justiz und NS-Verbrechen*, Vol. 7, 701.
208. Adelheid L. Rüter und C.F. Rüter, eds., *Justiz und NS-Verbrechen: Sammlung deutscher Strafurteile wegen nationalsozialistischer Tötungsverbrechen 1945–1966*, Vol. 8 (Amsterdam: University Press Amsterdam, 1972): 307–308.

209. Rüter und Rüter, eds., *Justiz und NS-Verbrechen*, Vol. 8, 308.
210. Rüter und Rüter, eds., *Justiz und NS-Verbrechen*, Vol. 8, 309.
211. Rüter und Rüter, eds., *Justiz und NS-Verbrechen*, Vol. 8, 309–310, 312.
212. Rüter und Rüter, eds., *Justiz und NS-Verbrechen*, Vol. 8, 312–313.
213. Adelheid L. Rüter und C.F. Rüter, eds., *Justiz und NS-Verbrechen: Sammlung deutscher Strafurteile wegen nationalsozialistischer Tötungsverbrechen 1945–1966*, Vol. 10 (Amsterdam: University Press Amsterdam, 1973): 166–167.
214. Rüter und Rüter, eds., *Justiz und NS-Verbrechen*, Vol. 10, 153.
215. Rüter und Rüter, eds., *Justiz und NS-Verbrechen*, Vol. 10, 154–155.
216. Rüter und Rüter, eds., *Justiz und NS-Verbrechen*, Vol. 10, 155.
217. Rüter und Rüter, eds., *Justiz und NS-Verbrechen*, Vol. 10, 166.
218. Rüter und Rüter, eds., *Justiz und NS-Verbrechen*, Vol. 10, 155–156.
219. Rüter und Rüter, eds., *Justiz und NS-Verbrechen*, Vol. 10, 156.
220. Rüter und Rüter, eds., *Justiz und NS-Verbrechen*, Vol. 10, 154.
221. Rüter und Rüter, eds., *Justiz und NS-Verbrechen*, Vol. 10, 157.
222. Rüter und Rüter, eds., *Justiz und NS-Verbrechen*, Vol. 10, 166.
223. Rüter und Rüter, eds., *Justiz und NS-Verbrechen*, Vol. 10, 167–168.
224. Rüter und Rüter, eds., *Justiz und NS-Verbrechen*, Vol. 10, 168–169.
225. Rüter und Rüter, eds., *Justiz und NS-Verbrechen*, Vol. 10, 153.
226. Rüter und Rüter, eds., *Justiz und NS-Verbrechen*, Vol. 10, 160–161.
227. Rüter und Rüter, eds., *Justiz und NS-Verbrechen*, Vol. 10, 161.
228. Rüter und Rüter, eds., *Justiz und NS-Verbrechen*, Vol. 10, 161–162.
229. Rüter und Rüter, eds., *Justiz und NS-Verbrechen*, Vol. 10, 162–163.
230. Rüter und Rüter, eds., *Justiz und NS-Verbrechen*, Vol. 10, 163–164.
231. Rüter und Rüter, eds., *Justiz und NS-Verbrechen*, Vol. 10, 164.
232. Rüter und Rüter, eds., *Justiz und NS-Verbrechen*, Vol. 10, 597–598.
232. Rüter und Rüter, eds., *Justiz und NS-Verbrechen*, Vol. 10, 597.
233. Rüter und Rüter, eds., *Justiz und NS-Verbrechen*, Vol. 10, 598.
234. Rüter und Rüter, eds., *Justiz und NS-Verbrechen*, Vol. 10, 598–600.
235. Rüter und Rüter, eds., *Justiz und NS-Verbrechen*, Vol. 10, 600–601.
236. Rüter und Rüter, eds., *Justiz und NS-Verbrechen*, Vol. 10, 589.
237. Rüter und Rüter, eds., *Justiz und NS-Verbrechen*, Vol. 10, 590–592.
238. Rüter und Rüter, eds., *Justiz und NS-Verbrechen*, Vol. 10, 592.
239. Rüter und Rüter, eds., *Justiz und NS-Verbrechen*, Vol. 10, 592–593.
240. Rüter und Rüter, eds., *Justiz und NS-Verbrechen*, Vol. 10, 593–594.
241. Rüter und Rüter, eds., *Justiz und NS-Verbrechen*, Vol. 10, 594.
242. Rüter und Rüter, eds., *Justiz und NS-Verbrechen*, Vol. 10, 594–596.
243. Adelheid L. Rüter und C.F. Rüter, eds., *Justiz und NS-Verbrechen: Sammlung deutscher Strafurteile wegen nationalsozialistischer Tötungsverbrechen 1945–1966*, Vol. 12 (Amsterdam: University Press Amsterdam, 1974): 747–748, 757.
244. Rüter und Rüter, eds., *Justiz und NS-Verbrechen*, Vol. 12, 747–748, 751.
245. Rüter und Rüter, eds., *Justiz und NS-Verbrechen*, Vol. 12, 844.
246. Rüter und Rüter, eds., *Justiz und NS-Verbrechen*, Vol. 12, 843–844.
247. Rüter und Rüter, eds., *Justiz und NS-Verbrechen*, Vol. 12, 844–846.

248. Rüter und Rüter, eds., *Justiz und NS-Verbrechen*, Vol. 12, 846.
249. Rüter und Rüter, eds., *Justiz und NS-Verbrechen*, Vol. 12, 751.
250. Rüter und Rüter, eds., *Justiz und NS-Verbrechen*, Vol. 12, 752–754, 749.
251. Rüter und Rüter, eds., *Justiz und NS-Verbrechen*, Vol. 12, 754–755.
252. Rüter und Rüter, eds., *Justiz und NS-Verbrechen*, Vol. 12, 755–757.
253. Rüter und Rüter, eds., *Justiz und NS-Verbrechen*, Vol. 12, 757–758.
254. Rüter und Rüter, eds., *Justiz und NS-Verbrechen*, Vol. 12, 759–760.
255. Rüter und Rüter, eds., *Justiz und NS-Verbrechen*, Vol. 12, 761.
256. Rüter und Rüter, eds., *Justiz und NS-Verbrechen*, Vol. 12, 762.
257. Rüter und Rüter, eds., *Justiz und NS-Verbrechen*, Vol. 12, 762–763.
258. Rüter und Rüter, eds., *Justiz und NS-Verbrechen*, Vol. 12, 763–764.
259. Rüter und Rüter, eds., *Justiz und NS-Verbrechen*, Vol. 12, 764–765.
260. Rüter und Rüter, eds., *Justiz und NS-Verbrechen*, Vol. 12, 765–766.
261. Rüter und Rüter, eds., *Justiz und NS-Verbrechen*, Vol. 12, 767–770.
262. Rüter und Rüter, eds., *Justiz und NS-Verbrechen*, Vol. 12, 770–772.
263. Rüter und Rüter, eds., *Justiz und NS-Verbrechen*, Vol. 12, 772–773.
264. Rüter und Rüter, eds., *Justiz und NS-Verbrechen*, Vol. 12, 773.
265. Rüter und Rüter, eds., *Justiz und NS-Verbrechen*, Vol. 12, 774.
266. Rüter und Rüter, eds., *Justiz und NS-Verbrechen*, Vol. 12, 775–776.
267. Rüter und Rüter, eds., *Justiz und NS-Verbrechen*, Vol. 12, 777–779.
268. Rüter und Rüter, eds., *Justiz und NS-Verbrechen*, Vol. 12, 779.
269. Rüter und Rüter, eds., *Justiz und NS-Verbrechen*, Vol. 12, 782–783, 812–813.
270. Rüter und Rüter, eds., *Justiz und NS-Verbrechen*, Vol. 12, 813–814.
271. Rüter und Rüter, eds., *Justiz und NS-Verbrechen*, Vol. 12, 815.
272. Rüter und Rüter, eds., *Justiz und NS-Verbrechen*, Vol. 12, 822–823.
273. Rüter und Rüter, eds., *Justiz und NS-Verbrechen*, Vol. 12, 815–816.
274. Rüter und Rüter, eds., *Justiz und NS-Verbrechen*, Vol. 12, 817–818.
275. Rüter und Rüter, eds., *Justiz und NS-Verbrechen*, Vol. 12, 818–821, 824.
276. Rüter und Rüter, eds., *Justiz und NS-Verbrechen*, Vol. 12, 840–841, 747.
277. Rüter und Rüter, eds., *Justiz und NS-Verbrechen*, Vol. 12, 825, 829, 839.
278. Rüter und Rüter, eds., *Justiz und NS-Verbrechen*, Vol. 12, 848.
279. Rüter und Rüter, eds., *Justiz und NS-Verbrechen*, Vol. 12, 852–853.
280. Rüter und Rüter, eds., *Justiz und NS-Verbrechen*, Vol. 12, 854–855.
281. Rüter und Rüter, eds., *Justiz und NS-Verbrechen*, Vol. 12, 855–856.
282. Rüter und Rüter, eds., *Justiz und NS-Verbrechen*, Vol. 12, 856–857.
283. Rüter und Rüter, eds., *Justiz und NS-Verbrechen*, Vol. 12, 857.
284. Adelheid L. Rüter und C.F. Rüter, eds., *Justiz und NS-Verbrechen: Sammlung deutscher Strafurteile wegen nationalsozialistischer Tötungsverbrechen 1945-1966*, Vol. 14 (Amsterdam: University Press Amsterdam, 1976): 443–444.
285. Rüter und Rüter, eds., *Justiz und NS-Verbrechen*, Vol. 14, 444.
286. Rüter und Rüter, eds., *Justiz und NS-Verbrechen*, Vol. 14, 444–445.
287. Rüter und Rüter, eds., *Justiz und NS-Verbrechen*, Vol. 14, 445.
288. Rüter und Rüter, eds., *Justiz und NS-Verbrechen*, Vol. 14, 445–446.
289. Rüter und Rüter, eds., *Justiz und NS-Verbrechen*, Vol. 14, 446.

290. Rüter und Rüter, eds., *Justiz und NS-Verbrechen*, Vol. 14, 446–447.
291. Rüter undRüter, eds., *Justiz und NS-Verbrechen*, Vol. 14, 447–449.
292. Rüter und Rüter, eds., *Justiz und NS-Verbrechen*, Vol. 14, 449.
293. Rüter und Rüter, eds., *Justiz und NS-Verbrechen*, Vol. 14, 451–452.
294. Rüter und Rüter, eds., *Justiz und NS-Verbrechen*, Vol. 14, 452–453.
295. Rüter und Rüter, eds., *Justiz und NS-Verbrechen*, Vol. 14, 453–454
296. Rüter und Rüter, eds., *Justiz und NS-Verbrechen*, Vol. 14, 455.
297. Adelheid L. Rüter und C.F. Rüter, eds., *Justiz und NS-Verbrechen: Sammlung deutscher Strafurteile wegen nationalsozialistischer Tötungsverbrechen 1945–1966*, Vol. 20 (Amsterdam: University Press Amsterdam, 1979): 148–149.
298. Rüter und Rüter, eds., *Justiz und NS-Verbrechen*, Vol. 20, 149.
299. Rüter und Rüter, eds., *Justiz und NS-Verbrechen*, Vol. 20, 150.
300. Rüter und Rüter, eds., *Justiz und NS-Verbrechen*, Vol. 20, 150.
301. Rüter und Rüter, eds., *Justiz und NS-Verbrechen*, Vol. 20, 151.
302. Rüter und Rüter, eds., *Justiz und NS-Verbrechen*, Vol. 20, 151.
303. Rüter und Rüter, eds., *Justiz und NS-Verbrechen*, Vol. 20, 152–153.
304. Rüter und Rüter, eds., *Justiz und NS-Verbrechen*, Vol. 20, 148, 153.
305. Rüter und Rüter, eds., *Justiz und NS-Verbrechen*, Vol. 20, 154–155.
306. Rüter und Rüter, eds., *Justiz und NS-Verbrechen*, Vol. 20, 155.
307. Rüter und Rüter, eds., *Justiz und NS-Verbrechen*, Vol. 20, 158.
308. Rüter und Rüter, eds., *Justiz und NS-Verbrechen*, Vol. 20, 158–159.
309. Rüter und Rüter, eds., *Justiz und NS-Verbrechen*, Vol. 20, 159.
310. Rüter und Rüter, eds., *Justiz und NS-Verbrechen*, Vol. 20, 161–162.

CONCLUSION

1. Diewald-Kerkmann, *Politische Denunziation im NS-Regime*, 166.
2. Adolf Arndt, "Das Strafmaß," *Süddeutsche Juristenzeitung* (1946) 1: 30.
3. Diewald-Kerkmann, *Politische Denunziation im NS-Regime*, 173
4. Bundesarchiv. Koblenz. Z21/1334. 14 Js. 133/46. 11.6.48. Der Oberstaatsanwalt bei dem Landgericht Hamburg: 3.
5. Jakobczyk, "Das Verfahren ist einzustellen," *Demokratische Justiz* (2003) 15: 277.
6. *Verhandlung des Deutschen Bundestages. 4. Wahlperiode. Anlage zu den stenographischen Berichten.* Band 96. Drucksachen IV/3124. Bonn: Der Bundesminister der Justiz, 1965: 33.

Bibliography

ARCHIVE SOURCES

Archives de L'Occupation Française en Allemagne et en Autriche. Colmar.

AJ 806 p.616	3679/13/3
AJ 806/p.617	3679/13/4
AJ 806/p.618	3679/13/5
AJ 806 p.619	3679/15/2
AJ 3655/p.326/12053	3679/16/1
AJ 3674/17	3679/22/2
AJ 3679 p.20 d.2	3680/21/1
AJ3679/14/2a.	36780/21/2. 2 Kls. 59/47, p. 1
AJ c.372	36780/21/2. 2 Kls. 59/47, pp. 1–2
AJ c.372, p.16.	36780/21/2. 2 Kls. 59/47, pp. 1, 3
AJ c.3673/p.8.	36780/21/2. 2 Kls. 59/47, pp. 2–3
AJ c.3678, p. 8.	36780/21/2. 2 Kls. 118/47, p. 1
JA 3680/22/1	36780/21/2. 2 Kls. 118/47, p. 2.
C.3680/P.27/12	36780/21/2. 2 Kls. 118/47, pp. 1, 3–4
3674/17/2	36780/21/2. 2 Kls. 118/47, pp. 2–3.
3679/13/1	3680/25/4

Staatsarchiv. Darmstadt

Abt. H 13 DaNr. 889

Bundesarchiv. Koblenz

Z21/140	Z21/784	Z21/1334	Z21/1357
Z21/268	Z21/791	Z21/1352	Z21/1359
Z21/396	Z21/794	Z21/1354	Z21/2213
Z21/424	Z21/799	Z21/1355	Z38/132
Z21/776	Z21/1309	Z21/1356	Z38/653

Staatsarchiv. Darmstadt.
17/20–3/3 Legal Division, RG 260 OMGUS
17/201–3/2 Legal Division, RG 260 OMGUS
17/201–3/3 Legal Division, RG 260 OMGUS
17/262–2/15 Legal Division, RG 260 OMGUS
17/262–3/15 Legal Division, RG 260 OMGUS
71/201–3/2 Legal Division, RG 260 OMGUS
171/201–3/3 Legal Division, RG 260 OMGUS

Hessisches Hauptstaatsarchiv, Wiesbaden.
Abt. 463 Nr. 1191
Abt. 461 Nr. 30170
Abt. 461 Nr. 32004
Abt. 461 Nr. 30264
APO 633
APO 655
RG 260 OMGUS, 17/210–2/6

Landesarchiv Nordrhein-Westfalen. Detmold
D21 B 1908
D21 B 1920
D21 B 1964
D21 B 1967
D21 B 1968
D21 B 1969
D21 B 1970
D21 B 1974
D21 B 1976
D21 B 1982
D21 B 1983
D21 B 2554
D21 B 2564
D21 B 2565
D21 B 2593
D21 B 2596
D21 B 2599
D21 B 2601
D21 B 2602
D21 B 2607
D21 B 2608
D21 B 2610
D21 B 3286

GOVERNMENT DOCUMENTS

Journal Officiel du Commandement en Chef Français
Military Government Gazette. Germany. British Zone of Control
Military Governnment Gazette: British Zone of Control
Official Gazette of the Allied High Commission for Germany
Official Gazette of the Allied High Commission for Germany
Justizministerialblatt Zentraljustizamt für das Land Nordrhein-Westfalen
Verhandlungen des Deutschen Bundestages. 4. Wahlperiode. Anlage zu den stenographischen Berichten. Band 96. Drucksachen IV/3124. Bonn: Der Bundesminister der Justiz, 1965: 33
Zentraljustizverwaltungsblatt 1948
Zentraljustizverwaltungsblatt 1949

JOURNAL ARTICLES

"A. Anweisung des Zonal Office of the Legal Adviser. Verbrechen gegen die Menschlichkeit – Kontrollratsgesetz Nr. 10." *Zentraljustizverwaltungsblatt* 1948: 250–251.

"Anzeigeerstattung bei der Gestapo wegen antinazistischer Äußerrungen kann als Verbrechen gegen die Menschlichkeit bestraft werden." *Deutsche Rechts-Zeitschrift* 1946: 126

Arndt, Adolf. "Das Recht der politischen Säuberung." *Süddeutsche Juristenzeitung* (1948) 3: 110

——. "Das Strafmaß." *Süddeutsche Juristenzeitung* (1946) 1: 30–31

Arndt, H. "KRG 10. – Die wahre Anzeige für sich allein ist keine Verfolgung i.S. des KRG 10. OLG Kiel, StS Beschl. v. 16. 1. 1948 – Ws 8/48", *Neue Juristische Wochenschrift* 1948 1: 393

"Zur Auslegung des Kontrollratsgesetzes Nr. 10." *Deutsche Rechts-Zeitschrift* 1947 (8): 267–270.

Bade, Claudia. "'Das Verfahren wird eingestellt.' Die Strafrechtliche Verfolgung von Denunziation aus dem Nationalsozialismus nach 1945 in den Westzonen und in der frühen BRD." *Historical Social Research*, Vol. 26 2001 No.2/3: 70–85.

Bader, Karl S. "Umschau." *Deutscher Rechtszeitschrift* 1946: 140–142.

"Betr. Kontrollratsgesetz Nr. 10 – Verbrechen gegen die Menschlichkeit." *Niedersächsische Rechtspflege* 1948: 10.

Bettermann, Karl August. "Rechstaat ohne unabhängige Richter?" *Neue Juristische Wochenschrift* 1947/1948: 217–220.

"BGH, Urt. v. 6.11.1952 – 3 StR 59/50 (Schwg Duisburg)." *Neue Juristische Wochenschrift* 1953: 793–794.

"BGH, Urt. v. 28. 6. 1956 – 3 St R 366/55 (SchwurG Kassel)." *Neue Juristische Wochenschrift* 1956: 1485–1486.

Boberach, Heinz. "Die Verfolgung von Verbrechen gegen die Menschlichkeit durch deutsche Gerichte in Nordrhein-Westphalen: 1946–1949." Geschichte Westen 12 1997: 7–23.

Boesebeck, Ernst B. "Privatrechtliche Haftung des Denunzianten." *Neue Juristische Wochenschrift* 1947/1948 (1): 13–19.

Broszat, Martin. "Siegerjustiz oder strafrechtlicher 'selbtsreinigung'? Aspekete der Vergangenheitsbewältigung der deutschen Justiz während der Besatzungszeit 1945–1949." *Vierteljahrshefte für Zeitgeschichte* 1981(4): 518.

Citron, Curt. "Das Kontrollratsgesetz Nr. 10." *Die Gegenwart* April 1947: 23–24.

Coing, Helmut. "Zur Frage der strafrechtlichen Haltung der Richter für die Anwendung naturrechtswidriger Gesetze." *Süddeutsche Juristenzeitung* 1947: 61–64.

"Denunziation als Verbrechen gegen die Menschlichkeit. Stellungnahme zu der Rechtsprechung des Obersten Gerichtshof für die Britische Zone." *Niedersächsische Rechtspflege* 1947: 218–219.

"Die Denunziation ist nach dem Kontrollratsgesetz Nr. 10 nur strafbar, wenn sie eine unmenschliche Verfolgung aus politischen Gründen ist und der Täter sich dessen bei der Tat bewußt war." *Monatsschrift für deutsches Recht* 1947 1: 307.

"Denunziationsverbrechen und Zeugenpflicht, KRG 10. Urteil des OGH f. d.brit. Z. vom 6. 6. 50 – Ss 522/49." *Juristische Rundschau* 1950: 564–565.

Diestelkamp, Bernhard and Susanne Jung. "Die Justiz in den Westzonen und der frühen Bundesrepublik." *Aus Politik und Zeitgeschichte* 13 (24 March 1989): 19–29.

——. "Die strafrechtliche Ahndung von NS-Unrecht: ein Forschungsbericht." *Zeitschrift neuere Rechtsgeschichte* 21 1999: 417–435.

"Entscheidungen des Obersten Gerichtshofes für die Britische Zone." *Zentraljustizblatt* 1948: 160–168.

Erdsiek, "Das Zentral-Justizamt für die britische Zone." *Deutsche Rechtszeitschrift* 1946 (4): 121.

"Zur Frage der Strafbarkeit einer politischen Denunziation." *Monatsschrift für deutsches Recht* 1947 1: 305–306.

"Der Grundsatz „nullum crimen sine lege" wird durch das Kontrollratsgesetz Nr. No. 10 nicht verletzt. Zum Begriff der Verfolgung aus politischen Gründen i.S. des KRG Nr. 10." *Deutsche Rechts-Zeitschrift* 1947 (9): 308–310.

Güde, M. "Die Anwendung des Kontrollratsgesetzes Nr. 10 durch die deutschen Gerichte." *Deutsche Rechtszeitschrift* (1947) 4: 111–118.

Haensel, Carl . "Das Urteil im Nürnberger Prozeß." *Deutsche Rechts-Zeitschrift* 3 (2) 1948: 40–43.

Henneka, A. "OLG Dresden. Anmerkung." *Süddeutsche Juristenzeitung* 1947 (2): 522–527.

Hensle, Michael P. "Denunziantum und Diktatur als Mittel der Machtsausübung und Konfliktsaustragung im nationalsozialistischen Deutschland." *Zeitschrift für Geschichtswissenschaft* 2003 51(2): 144–161.

von Hodenberg, Hodo. "Zur Anwendung des Kontrollratsgesetzes Nr. 10 durch deutsche Gerichte." *Süddeutsche Juristenzeitung* March 1947: 113–124.

Jagusch, Heinrich. "Das Verbrechen gegen die Menschlichkeit in der Rechtsprechung des Obersten Gerichtshofs für die Britische Zone." *Süddeutsche Juristenzeitung* 1949: 620–624.

Jakobczyk, Mandy. "Das Verfahren ist einzustellen." *Demokratische Geschichte*, 15 2003: 239–290.

Johnson, Alvin [foreword]. "Denazification." *Social Research* 14 (1947): 59–74.

Katzenberger, K. "Das Recht der politischen Säuberung." *Süddeutsche Juristenzeitung* 3 1948: 41–49.

Kiesselbach, Wilhelm. "Zwei Probleme aus dem Gesetz Nr. 10 des Kontrollrats." *Monatsschrift für deutsche Recht* 1 1947: 2–6.

Klefisch, Theodor. "Die NS-Denunziation in der Rechtsprechung des Obersten Gerichtshofes für die Britische Zone." *Monatsschrift für Deutsches Recht* 1949 (3): 324–329.

Koehler, W. "Das Recht der politischen Säuberung: der Grundsatz der individuellen Verantwortlichkeit in Article2 Befreiungsgesetz." *Süddeutsche Juristenzeitung* 2 1947: 39–40.
Kogon, E., W. Lafontaine and W.E. Süskind. "Denunziation als Verbrechen." *Frankfurter Hefte* 3 1948: 292–300.
"Kontrollratsgesetz Nr. 10." *Justizministerialblatt für das Land Nordrhein-Westfalen* 1947 (1): 19–20.
"Kontrollratsgesetz Nr. 10." *Monatsschrift für deutsches Recht* 1947 1: 241–243.
"Zum Kontrollgesetz Nr. 10." *Neue Justiz* 1947: 137–139.
"Zum Kontrollgesetz Nr. 10." *Süddeutsche Juristenzeitung* 1 1946: 105–106.
"Zum Kontrollrats-Gesetz Nr. 10." *Juristische Rundschau* 1948: 53–56.
"KRG Nr. 10, StGB § 60." *Deutsche Rechts-Zeitschrift* 1948 (7): 259.
"KRG 10 II 1c, IIc; StGB §§ 239, 73; stop §§ 267 Abs. 1, 358 Abs. 2." *Deutsche Rechts-Zeitschrift* 4 1949: 21–22.
Laage, Clea. "Die Auseinandersetzung um den Begriff des gesetzlichen Unrechts nach 1945." *Kritische Justiz* 1989 (4): 408–432.
Lange, Richard. "Anmerkung." *Deutsche Rechts-Zeitschrift* 2 1947: 200–201.
——. "Zum Denunziantenproblem." *Süddeutsche Juristenzeitung* 3 1948: 302–311.
——."Kontrollratsgesezt Nr. 10 in Theorie und Praxis." *Deutsche Rechts-Zeitschrift* 1948 3 (6): 155–161.
——. "Kontrollratsgesezt Nr. 10 und deutsches Recht: Das Kontrollratsgesetz in Theorie und Praxis II." *Deutsche Rechts-Zeitschrift* 1948 3 (6): 185–193.
——. "Zu neuen Ufern im Strafrecht." *Neue Justiz* 1 1947: 7–13.
——. "Die Rechtsprechung des Obersten Gerichtshofs für die Britische Zone zum Verbrechen gegen die Menschlichkeit." *Süddeutsche Juristenzeitung* 3 1948: 655–660.
——. "Zur Strafrechtsreform". *Neue Juristische Wochenschrift* 2 1949: 695–698.
"LG Freiburg i. Br. V. 12. 9. 47 – 1B 254/46 [rechtskräftig]." *Deutsche Rechts-Zeitschrift* 1948: 145.
"LG Konstanz." *Süddeutsche Juristenzeitung* 1947 (2): 337.
Karl Loewenstein, "Justice," *Governing Postwar Germany* Edward H. Litchfield, ed. Ithaca: Cornell University Press, 1953: 236–262.
——. "Reconstruction of the Administration of Justice in American-Occupied Germany." *Harvard Law Review* 1947–1948 61: 419–467.
Meister, Hans-Georg. "Die Widerspruchlosigkeit der Rechtsordnung." *Monatsschrift für deutsches Recht* 2 1947: 47–49.
Meyer. "Das Kontrollratsgestz Nr. 10 in der Praxis der deutschen Strafgerichte." *Monatsschrift für deutsches Recht* 1947: 110–112.
Neidhard, Hans. "Die Rechtspflege in der Gesetzgebung der amerikanischen Zone II. Die gemeinsame Gesetzgebung der drei Länder Bayern, Württemberg-Baden und Großhessen." *Deutsche Rechtszeitschrift* 1946 4: 117–120.
"Oberster Gerichtshof. Köln." *Monatsschrift für deutsches Rechts* 1948: 303–304.
"OGH Köln." *Monatsschrift für deutsches Rechts* 1948: 425–427.

"OGH, Strafsenat, Urteil vom 19. 10. 1948 Sts 56/48." *Monatsschrift für deutsches Recht* 1949: 179–180.

"OLG Bamberg. § 239 StGB." *Süddeutsche Juristenzeitung* 1950: 207–210.

"OLG Bamberg, Beschluß vom 27. 7. 1949, Ws 152/49." *Deutsche Rechts-Zeitschrift* 1950: 302–304.

"OLG Bamberg, Beschluß vom 27. 7. 1949, Ws 152/49." *Monatsschrift für deutsches Recht* 4 1950: 55–56.

"OLG Düsseldorf. ArticleII 1c KRG 10. Denunziation als Teilnahme an der Verfolgung aus politischen Gründen, Bewußtsein, Vorraussetzungen des Vorsatzes, Vollendung und Versuch." *Süddeutsche Juristenzeitung* 1948: 328–332.

"OLG Hamburg." *Monatsschrift für deutsches Rechts* 1947: 241–243.

"OLG Hamm. ArticleII 1c KRG 10. "Denunziation als «Gewalttat» i.S. der ersten Gruppe der Verbrechen gegen die Menschlichkeit, Bedeutung der Tatfolgen." *Süddeutsche Juristenzeitung* 1948: 332–334.

"OLG Düsseldorf. ArticleII 1c KRG 10. Denunziation als Teilnahme an der Verfolgung aus politischen Gründen, Bewußtsein, Vorraussetzungen des Vorsatzes, Vollendung und Versuch." *Süddeutsche Juristenzeitung* 1948: 328–332.

"OLG Hamm, 2. Strafsenat, Urteil vom 5. 8. 1948, 2. SS 370/48." *Monatsschrift für Deutsches Recht* 1949: 184–185.

"OLG Saarbrücken, Beschluß v. 16. 1. 48 – Ws 2/48." *Deutsche Rechts-Zeitschrift* 3 1948: 219–221.

Ostler, Fritz. "Das Gesetz zur Befreiung von Nationalsozialismus und Militarismus vom 5. März und sein Vollzug." *Neue Juristische Wochenschrift* 1996 (13): 821–825.

Pauli, Gerhard. "Ein hohes Gericht – Der Oberste Gerichtshof für die Britische Zone und seine Rechtsprechung zu Straftaten im Dritten Reich." *50 Jahre Justiz in Nordrhein-Westfalen. Juristische Zeitgeschichte* Band 5, ed. Justizministerium des Landes NRW. Düsseldorf, 1996.

Radbruch, Gustav. "Anmerkung." *Süddeutsche Juristenzeitung* 2 1947: 343–344.

Radbruch, Gustav. "Zur Diskussion über die Verbrechen gegen die Menschlichkeit." *Süddeutsche Juristenzeitung* 2 (March) 1947: 131–136.

——. "Gesetzliches Unrecht und übergesetzliches Recht." *Süddeutsche Juristenzeitung* 2 1947: 105–108.

"Rechtsprechung." *Justizministerialblatt für das Land Nordrhein-Westfalen* 1947 (1): 111–116.

"Rechtsprechungsübersicht: B. Strafrecht und Strafverfahren. I Gesetze des Kontrollrats und der Militärregierungen." *Zentraljustizverwaltungsblatt* 1948: 13–14.

"Rechtsprechungsübersicht: B. Strafrecht und Strafverfahren. I Gesetze des Kontrollrats und der Militärregierungen." *Zentraljustizverwaltungsblatt* 1948: 210–211.

Sauer. "OLG Bamberg, Beschl. v. 27. 7. 1949, Ws. 152/49." *Neue Juristische Wochenschrift* 1950 (1): 35–36.

Schönke, Adolf. "Unrechtsbewußtsein, Vorsatz und Irrtum." *Deutsche Rechtszeitschrift* 1946 (4): 101–102.

Schulz, Georg. "OLG Braunschweig, Beschl. v. 25. 11. 1947 – Ws 30/47." *Neue Juristische Wochenschrift* 1947/1948: 309–311.

Schulz, Georg. "OLG Braunschweig, Urt. v. 28/29.11.1947." *Neue Juristische Wochenschrift* 9 (1947/48): 353–354.

Schultz, Günther. ""Rundschau. Blick in die Zeit." *Monatsschrift für deutsches Recht* 1951: 719–720.

Seibert, Claus. "Abschied vom KRG 10." *Neue Juristische Wochenschrift* 1952: 251–252.

"StGB §§ 211 ff., 239." *Neue Juristische Wochenschrift* 1952: 1024–1026.

"Die Strafbarkeit der Denunziation nach dem Kontrollratsgesetz Nr. 10." *Monatsschrift für deutsches Recht* 1948 2: 123–127.

Georg Strucksberg, "Zur Anwendung des Kontrollratsgesetzes Nr. 10." *Deutsche Rechts-Zeitschrift* 1947 2 (9): 277–280.

"Der subjektive Tatbestand des KG 10." *Monatsschrift für deutsches Recht* 1949 3: 59.

"Urteil des KG v. 13. 7. 49 – 1 Ss 156. 49." *Juristische Rundschau* 1949: 510–511.

"Die Voraussetzungen des objectiven und subjectiven Denunziations-Tatbestandes nach dem Kontrollratsgesetz Nr. 10." *Monatsschrift für Deutsches Recht* 1948 (2): 94.

"Zum Vorsatz gehört das Bewußtsein der Gesetzwidrigkeit oder sonstigen Unrechtsmäßigkeit." *Deutsche Rechts-Zeitschrift* 1946: 126.

Von Weber, Hellmuth. "Das Verbrechen gegen die Menschlichkeit in der Rechtsprechung." *Monatsschrift für Deutsches Recht* 1949 (3): 261–266.

Welzel, Hans. "Zur Kritik der subjektiven Teilnahmlehre." *Süddeutsche Juristenzeitung* 1947: 647–649.

Werner, WolfhArticle"Die ersten Entscheidungen des OGH zum Kontrollratsgesetz 10." *Neue Juristische Wochenschrift* 1949 (5): 170–174.

Wimmer, August. "Die Bestrafung von Humanitätsverbrechen under the Grundsatz '*nullum crimen sine lege*'." *Süddeutsche Juristenzeitung*, 2 (March) 1947: 123–132.

DISSERTATIONS

Eberhardt, Albert. "Die Denunziation im Spiegel des Kontrollratgesetzes Nr. 10 als Verbrechen gegen die Menschlichkeit." Munich: Ludwig-Maximilian Universität zu München, 1950.

Johannsen, Uwe. "Zum Problem der Strafbarkeit von Denunziationen nach dem Kontrollratsgesetz 10." Hamburg: Universität Hamburg, 1948.

Lachmann, Werner. "Die Denunziation unter besonderer Berücksichtigung des Kontrollratsgesetzes Nr. 10." Munich: Ludwig-Maximilian Universität zu München, 1951.

BOOKS

Barck, Heinz-Günther and Dieter Kerber, eds. *Beiträge zu 50 Jahre Geschichte des Landes Rheinland-Pfalz*. Koblenz: Verlag der Landesarchivverwaltung Rheinland-Pflaz, 1997.

Becker-Jákli, Barbara, Harald Buhlan and Horst Matzerath, eds. *Versteckte Vergangenjeit. Über den Umgang mit der NS-Zeit in Köln*. Köln: Emons Verlag, 1994.

Diestelkamp, Bernhard. "Die Justiz nach 1945 und ihr Umgang mit der eigenen Vergangenheit." *Justizalltag im Dritten Reich*, eds. Bernhard Diestelkamp und Michael Stolleis. Frankfurt-am-Main: Fischer, 1988: 131–149.

Diewald-Kerkmann, Gisela. *Politische Denunziation im NS-Regime oder kleine Macht der "Volksgenossen"*. Bonn: Dietz Nachfolger, 1995.

Entscheidungen des Bundesgerichtshofes in Strafsachen Vol. 3. Berlin/Köln: Carl Heymanns Verlag, 1953.

Entscheidungen des Obersten Gerichtshofes für die Britische Zone in Strafsachen Vol. 1. Berlin/Hamburg: Walter de Gruyter & Co, 1949.

Fischer, W. "Gerechtigkeit und Politik. Ein Beitrag zur Bestrafung und Ausschaltung der Nationalsozialisten in Hamburg." *Festschrift für Wilhelm Kiesselbach*. Hamburg: Gesetz und Recht Verlag, 1947.

Frei, Norbert. *Adenauer's Germany and the Nazi Past: The Politics of Amnesty and Integration* trans. Joel Golb. New York: Columbia University Press, 2002.

——. *Vergangenheitspolitik. Die Anfänge der Bundesrepublik und die NS-* See *Vergangenheit*. München: C.H. Beck: 1999.

Freudiger, Kerstin. *Die juristische Aufarbeitung von NS-Verbrechen: Beiträger zue Rechtsgeschichte des 20. Jahrhunderts 33* (Tübingen: Mohr Siebeck, 2002).

Friedrich, Jörg. *Die Kalte Amnestie: NS-Täter in der Bundesrepublik*. Fischer Taschenbuch Verlag, 1985.

——. *Freispruch für die Nazi-Justiz. Die Urteile gegen NS-Richter seit 1948*. Hamburg: Rowohlt, 1983.

Götz, Albrecht. *Bilanz der Verfolgung von NS-Straftaten* (Köln: Bundesanzeiger 1986.

Hammerschmidt, Helmut. ed. *Zwanzig Jahre Danach. Eine Deutsche Bilanz 1945–1965*. München: Kurt Desch, 1965.

Hoffmann, Friedrich. *Die Verfolgung der nationalsozialistischen Gewaltverbrechen in Hessen*. Baden-Baden: Nomos Verlagsgesellschaft, 2001.

Jerouschek, Günter, Inge Marßolek and Hedwig Röckerlein. *Denunziation: Historische, juristische und psychologische Aspekte*. Tübingen: Edition Diskord, 1997.

Killen, John. *The Luftwaffe: A History*. Barnsley: Pen & Sword Military Classics, 2003.

Meyer-Seitz, Christian. *Die Verfolgung von NS-Straftaten in der Sowjetischen Besatzungszone*. Berlin: Arno Spitz, 1998.

Marβolek, Inge. *Die Denunziantin: Die Geschichte der Helene Schwärzel, 1944–1947*. Bremen: Edition Temmen, 1993.

Noakes, Jeremy and Geoffrey Pridham, *Documents on Nazism*: 1919–1945. New York: Viking Press, 1974.

Rückerl, Adalbert. *NS Verbrechen vor Gericht. Versuch einer Vergangenheitsbewältigung*. Heidelberg: C.F. Müller Juristischer Verlag, 1984.

——. *Die Strafverfolgung von NS Verbrechen 1945–1978. Eine Dokumentation.* Heidelberg/Karlsruhe: 1979.

Reiter, Raimond. *30 Jahre Justiz und NS-Verbrechen: Die Aktualität einer Urteilssammlung*. Frankfurt-am-Main: Peter Lang, 1998.

Rüter, Adelheid L. and C.F. Rüter, eds. *Justiz und NS-Verbrechen: Sammlung deutscher Strafurteile wegen nationalsozialistischer Tötungsverbrechen 1945–1966*, Vol. 1. Amsterdam: University Press Amsterdam, 1968.

——. *Justiz und NS-Verbrechen: Sammlung deutscher Strafurteile wegen nationalsozialistischer Tötungsverbrechen 1945–1966*, Vol. 2. Amsterdam: University Press Amsterdam, 1969.

——. *Justiz und NS-Verbrechen: Sammlung deutscher Strafurteile wegen nationalsozialistischer Tötungsverbrechen 1945–1966*, Vol. 3. Amsterdam: University Press Amsterdam, 1969.

——. *Justiz und NS-Verbrechen: Sammlung deutscher Strafurteile wegen nationalsozialistischer Tötungsverbrechen 1945–1966*, Vol. 4. Amsterdam: University Press Amsterdam, 1970.

——. *Justiz und NS-Verbrechen: Sammlung deutscher Strafurteile wegen nationalsozialistischer Tötungsverbrechen 1945–1966*, Vol. 5. Amsterdam: University Press Amsterdam, 1970.

——. *Justiz und NS-Verbrechen: Sammlung deutscher Strafurteile wegen nationalsozialistischer Tötungsverbrechen 1945–1966*, Vol. 6. Amsterdam: University Press Amsterdam, 1971.

——. *Justiz und NS-Verbrechen: Sammlung deutscher Strafurteile wegen nationalsozialistischer Tötungsverbrechen 1945–1966*, Vol. 7. Amsterdam: University Press Amsterdam, 1971.

——. *Justiz und NS-Verbrechen: Sammlung deutscher Strafurteile wegen nationalsozialistischer Tötungsverbrechen 1945–1966*, Vol. 8. Amsterdam: University Press Amsterdam, 1972.

——. *Justiz und NS-Verbrechen: Sammlung deutscher Strafurteile wegen nationalsozialistischer Tötungsverbrechen 1945–1966*, Vol. 9. Amsterdam: University Press Amsterdam, 1972.

——. *Justiz und NS-Verbrechen: Sammlung deutscher Strafurteile wegen nationalsozialistischer Tötungsverbrechen 1945–1966*, Vol. 10. Amsterdam: University Press Amsterdam, 1973.

——. *Justiz und NS-Verbrechen: Sammlung deutscher Strafurteile wegen nationalsozialistischer Tötungsverbrechen 1945–1966*, Vol. 11. Amsterdam: University Press Amsterdam, 1974.

——. *Justiz und NS-Verbrechen: Sammlung deutscher Strafurteile wegen nationalsozialistischer Tötungsverbrechen 1945–1966*, Vol. 12. Amsterdam: University Press Amsterdam, 1974.

——. *Justiz und NS-Verbrechen: Sammlung deutscher Strafurteile wegen nationalsozialistischer Tötungsverbrechen 1945–1966*, Vol. 14. Amsterdam: University Press Amsterdam, 1976.

——. *Justiz und NS-Verbrechen: Sammlung deutscher Strafurteile wegen nationalsozialistischer Tötungsverbrechen 1945–1966*, Vol. 20. Amsterdam: University Press Amsterdam, 1979.

Rüter, C.F., ed. *Die westliche Strafverfahren wegen nationalsozialistischer Tötungsverfahren: 1945–1997*. Amsterdam: Univ. Press; München Saur, 1998.

Karl-Alfred Storz, *Die Rechtsprechung des Oberstern Gerichtshofes für die Britische Zone in Strafsachen*. Tübingen: J.C.B. Mohr, 1969.

Szanajda, Andrew. *The Restoration of Justice in Postwar Hesse, 1945–1949*. Lanham: Lexington Books, 2007.

Vereint Vergessen? Justiz und NS-Verbrechen in Deutschland. Düsseldorf: Landeszentrale für politische Bildung, 1993.

Wrobel, Hans. *Verurteilt zur Demokratie. Justiz und Justizpolitik in Deutschland 1945–1949*. Heidelberg: Decker & Müller 1989.

Index

About the Author

Andrew Szanajda is an associate professor at the Overseas Chinese University in Taichung, Taiwan, and has been the recipient of the Taiwanese National Science Council research grant. He is the author of *The Restoration of Justice in Postwar Hesse, 1945–1949* and *Making Sense in History: The Process of Research, Critical Reading, and Writing*.